Phenomenology and the Norms
of Perception

Phenomenology and the Norms of Perception

MAXIME DOYON

OXFORD
UNIVERSITY PRESS

Great Clarendon Street, Oxford, OX2 6DP,
United Kingdom

Oxford University Press is a department of the University of Oxford.
It furthers the University's objective of excellence in research, scholarship,
and education by publishing worldwide. Oxford is a registered trade mark of
Oxford University Press in the UK and in certain other countries

© Maxime Doyon 2024

The moral rights of the author have been asserted

All rights reserved. No part of this publication may be reproduced, stored in
a retrieval system, or transmitted, in any form or by any means, without the
prior permission in writing of Oxford University Press, or as expressly permitted
by law, by licence or under terms agreed with the appropriate reprographics
rights organization. Enquiries concerning reproduction outside the scope of the
above should be sent to the Rights Department, Oxford University Press, at the
address above

You must not circulate this work in any other form
and you must impose this same condition on any acquirer

Published in the United States of America by Oxford University Press
198 Madison Avenue, New York, NY 10016, United States of America

British Library Cataloguing in Publication Data

Data available

Library of Congress Control Number: 2024930841

ISBN 9780198884224

DOI: 10.1093/9780191993527.001.0001

Printed and bound in the UK by
Clays Ltd, Elcograf S.p.A.

Links to third party websites are provided by Oxford in good faith and
for information only. Oxford disclaims any responsibility for the materials
contained in any third party website referenced in this work.

À Nora et Liam

Contents

Acknowledgements ix
Introduction xiii

PART I WHAT ARE PERCEPTUAL NORMS? INSIGHTS FROM CLASSICAL PHENOMENOLOGY

1. Husserl's Normative Account of Perception 3
   1.1. Concordance as Law of Coherent Experiencing 8
   1.2. Perception as Geared toward Optimality 13
   1.3. Illusions and Hallucinations as Transgressive Phenomena 18
   1.4. Husserl's Idealism and Normativity 23
   1.5. Conclusion 26

2. Perceptual Normativity in Merleau-Ponty 29
   2.1. Concordance and Evidence 30
   2.2. Optimality and Maximal Grip 32
      2.2.1. Dreyfus on Absorbed Coping 34
      2.2.2. Kelly on Perceptual Horizons 42
   2.3. The Challenge of Illusions 47
   2.4. Hallucinations as Interruptions 52
   2.5. The World as the Bedrock of Experience 55
   2.6. Conclusion 60

PART II THE EMBODIMENT OF NORMS

3. Bodily Self-Awareness and Agency 67
   3.1. Spontaneity and Self-critical Control 70
   3.2. The Motivational Role of Kinaesthesis in Husserl 77
   3.3. Body-schematic Attunement in Merleau-Ponty 84
   3.4. Norms of Self-assessment in Perceptual Agency 88
   3.5. Conclusion 93

4. Multisensory Perception 96
   4.1. Husserl on Multisensory Awareness 102
   4.2. Merleau-Ponty on the Ontological Structure of Perception 108
      4.2.1. Sensory Communication 109
      4.2.2. Readiness to Act 113

Contents

- 4.3. The Normative Impact of Sensory Integration — 115
  - 4.3.1. Perceptual Increase and Epistemic Loss — 116
  - 4.3.2. Bodily Normality and Agency — 119
- 4.4. Conclusion — 123

5. **Perceptual Learning** — 128
   - 5.1. Cognitive-affective Plasticity — 131
     - 5.1.1. Husserl's Early Non-conceptualism — 132
     - 5.1.2. Husserl's Account of Typification — 134
     - 5.1.3. The Weight of Our Perceptual History I — 140
   - 5.2. Bodily Plasticity — 148
     - 5.2.1. The Habitual Style of the Perceiving Ego — 149
     - 5.2.2. The Plasticity of the Body Schema — 155
     - 5.2.3. The Weight of Our Perceptual History II — 164
   - 5.3. Conclusion — 167

PART III SOCIALITY AND NORMATIVITY

6. **Perceiving Others** — 173
   - 6.1. Bodily Norms in Basic Empathy — 178
     - 6.1.1. The Lived Body (*Leib*) as Originary Norm (*Urnorm*) — 178
     - 6.1.2. Harmony, Continuity, Unity — 180
   - 6.2. Norms of Validity in Higher Forms of Empathy — 183
     - 6.2.1. Stein's Three-step Process — 184
     - 6.2.2. Levels of Empathy in Husserl — 187
   - 6.3. Attunement and Responsiveness as Norms of Interpersonal Interaction — 189
   - 6.4. The Challenge of Critical Phenomenology — 194
     - 6.4.1. The Normal Body — 197
     - 6.4.2. Perceptual Biases — 203
   - 6.5. Conclusion — 206

7. **Perceiving Together** — 209
   - 7.1. Responding Together: Sharing Space and Agency — 215
     - 7.1.1. Intercorporeal Coordination in Joint Attention — 218
     - 7.1.2. Embodied Coordination and Norm-following in Athletic Performances — 226
   - 7.2. Interbodily Temporality — 230
   - 7.3. Conclusion — 238

References — 241
Index — 263

Acknowledgements

The first spark for this book goes back to 2012, when I was a postdoctoral researcher at McGill University in Montréal and co-organised with Thiemo Breyer a conference entitled *Normativity in Perception*. The success of the conference, and of the volume of collected papers that came out of it, motivated me to keep on exploring what was then a relatively new area of philosophical research. As time went by and publications on the topic started to accumulate, I have been more and more regularly asked by friends and colleagues *when I would write my monograph on normativity*. This is it. This book encapsulates much of what I have to say on this fascinating question. For their steady support and encouragement throughout the years, I would like to express my deepest gratitude to Steven Crowell and Sara Heinämaa. Thanks, too, to Bernardo Ainbinder and Maren Wehrle, who at times seemed more convinced than I was myself that my work was worth putting together in book format.

Most of the material gathered has been presented in one way or another at conferences across Europe and the Americas in recent years, including at the University of Copenhagen, University of Reykjavik, Universität zu Köln, Julius-Maximilians-Universität Würzburg, Friedrich-Schiller-Universität Jena, Università di Parma, Katholieke Universiteit Leuven, Charles University (Prague), University of Helsinki, Memorial University of Newfoundland (St. John's), Ruprecht-Karls-Universität Heidelberg, University of Lisbon, Universidad Nacional Autónoma de México, Universidad Alberto Hurtado (Santiago), Humboldt-Universität Berlin, University of Warsaw, Emory University (Atlanta), Université de Montréal, Loyola University (Chicago), Universität Wien, Simon Fraser University (Vancouver), and the annual meetings of the International Society for Phenomenological Studies. My thanks to the organizers and the participants of each of these meetings. I benefited immensely from the discussions that these presentations occasioned.

None of this would have been possible without the generous support of the four funding agencies that provided me with financial support at various stages of the project: the *Fonds de Recherche du Québec en Société et Culture* (FRQSC), the *Social Sciences and Humanities Research Council of*

Canada (SSHRC), the *Chaire Ésope de philosophie* at Université de Montréal, and the *Humboldt-Stiftung* (Germany). I would like to express my gratitude to my academic and non-academic hosts for the two long-term research stays that these grants made possible during the final writing period: my friends Thiemo Breyer (Cologne), Dan Zahavi (Copenhagen), and Sandra Ernst and Andreas Digel (Berlin).

Many thanks to my all readers, starting with the two anonymous referees at Oxford University Press. Both their incisive criticisms and deeply encouraging words were instrumental in the shaping of this book. Heartfelt thanks, too, to Sepehr Razavi and Emanuela Carta, who read an earlier version of the book from cover to cover and provided me with all kinds of advice as well as linguistic, logistical, and bibliographical assistance throughout the process. Thanks, too, to Félix Tremblay for finalizing the reference list and compiling the index. Every chapter has also benefited from the comments of careful readers, who generously accepted to read drafts of certain specific chapters: Peter Antich, Diego D'Angelo, Denis Dzanić, Katrin Felgenhauer, Shaun Gallagher, Sara Heinämaa, Tristan Hedges, James Jardine, Hayden Kee, Felipe León, Maren Wehrle, and Dan Zahavi. Thank you all very much for your valuable input. Finally, I would also like to thank my graduate students (Alejandro Macías Flores, Aida Rezaii, Angela Peraza, Pascal-Olivier Dumas-Dubreuil, Philippe Ouellet-Dumont, Laurent Lafrenière, Emmanuel Cuisinier, Hugo Garant, Nicolas Hamman-Legris, Rachelle Passuello-Dussault) for their enthusiastic participation in our reading group and their insightful remarks and questions on various aspects of the book.

Early versions of some of the material that made its way into the book have been previously published. Every single passage has been revised and partly rewritten, many sections of the original papers were cut off, others rearranged, expanded, translated, or otherwise improved. As a result, none of the chapters correspond one to one to any formerly published work, but there are some notable overlaps with the following articles: 'The Normative Turn of Intentionality and its Metaphysical Implications (or why Husserl was neither a disjunctivist nor a conjunctivist)', in *The Husserlian Mind*, ed. Hanne Jacobs (London: Routledge, 2022), 172–83; 'On the Phenomenology and Normativity of Multisensory Perception: Husserlian and Merleau-Pontian Analyses', in *Contemporary Phenomenologies of Normativity: Norms, Goals, and Values*, ed. Mirja Hartimo, Sara Heinämaa, and Ilpo Hirvonen (London: Routledge, 2022), 107–25; 'La Gestalt d'autrui. Note sur l'étendue de l'influence de la *Gestaltpsychologie* chez Merleau-Ponty', in *Phänomenologische Forschungen*, Special Thematic Issue on *The Given*, ed. Manca and De Santis (2021(2)), 159–78; 'Review of Corijn van Mazijk, *Perception and Reality in Kant, Husserl and McDowell*', in *Husserl Studies* 37/1 (2021), 93–101; 'Kant and Husserl on the (Alleged) Function of Imagination in Perception', in *The New Yearbook for Phenomenology and Phenomenological Philosophy* XVIII (2019), 180–203; 'Husserl on Perceptual Optimality', in *Husserl Studies* 34/2 (2018), 171–89; 'Quelle est la norme de la perception?', in *Philosophiques* 45/1 (2018), 271–8; 'The "As-Structure" of Experience in Husserl and Heidegger', in *Phenomenology of Thinking: Investigations into the Character of Cognitive Experiences*, ed. Thiemo Breyer and Christopher Gutland (London: Routledge, 2016), 116–33; 'Perception and Normative Self-Consciousness', in *Normativity in Perception*, ed. Maxime Doyon and Thiemo Breyer (London: Palgrave Macmillan, 2015), 38–55; and 'Husserl and McDowell on the Role of Concepts in Perception', in *The New Yearbook for Phenomenology and Phenomenological Philosophy* XI (2011), 43–76. Thanks to the publishers for their permission to reproduce this material.

Despite all its obvious downsides, the pandemic was in a way an occasion for me as it gave me the opportunity to carve out some time to develop more holistically the project I had been working on in the preceding years and to establish contact with Peter Momtchiloff, my editor at Oxford University Press. I would like to thank him for the chance he has taken on me and for his guidance throughout the writing process. Thank you, too, to Neil Morris for his precious assistance and impeccable copy-editorship.

Last but not least, I want to thank my family for their love and constant support: first, Julie, Nora, and Liam, but also Martin, Isabelle, Gilles, Claudette, and my parents Nicole and Gabriel.

Maxime Doyon
October 2023

Introduction

Human activity and rationality are governed by a variety of norms. Morality, public policies, legal organizations, political institutions, and economic governance illustrate how large swathes of society are organized around norms that determine what is just, good, legitimate, desirable, permitted, or expected in our communal lives. Normativity also pervades rationality, both theoretical and practical: beliefs, inferences, assertions, intentions, emotions, and actions are standardly understood as being governed by norms of truth, reliability, consistency, fittingness, or justification, which set the standard or measure for what should or ought to be done. For Kant, even the domain of aesthetics, or, more precisely, our experience of the beautiful, is governed by a norm, viz. 'a rule that we cannot state', and in recent years some philosophers invested the field of affects and developed normative accounts of feelings, well-being, and happiness. The immense variety of expressions of normativity in nearly every aspect of our lives attests to its philosophical significance, which has translated into a rapidly growing number of publications in recent years in all areas of philosophical thinking (for a partial survey, see Baker 2018; Finlay 2019).

Phenomenology, which investigates conscious experience from the first-person (singular and plural) point of view, is no exception to this trend. Since Crowell's (2013) now classic *Normativity and Phenomenology in Husserl and Heidegger*, phenomenologists of all allegiances have explored and sought to account for our *experiences of norms* by examining its relation to intentionality (Crowell 2013; Madary 2016), perception (Doyon and Breyer 2015; Wehrle 2017), ethics and morality (Crowell 2016; Drummond 2019; Römer 2019), agency (Doyon 2015; Burch 2019), knowledge (Cerbone 2019; Hopp 2019; Siewert 2019), metaphysics (Zahavi 2019c), essences (Carta 2021), imagination (Aldea 2022), and society (Taipale 2014; Salice 2022), to name but a few fields of inquiry. The extreme variety of areas and topics that involve normative phenomena hints at a vibrant, but also deeply eclectic and multifaceted, field of research, one in which multiple conflicting definitions of 'norm' have come to circulate. While Crowell (2013) suggested that 'a norm is anything that serves as a standard of success or failure of any kind' (2), several readers have either disputed the reach or validity of this definition, which might be too broad or too vague to capture anything significant in this or that area of phenomenology (see the essays compiled in Burch, Marsh, and McMullin 2019). Or else they have noted the striking 'ambiguity' (Heinämaa 2019, 9) of the use of the term 'norm' in phenomenological research and pleaded for the necessity of proceeding to an in-depth clarification of its meaning in each area.[1] This book takes up the challenge and provides the first book-length phenomenological investigation of the norms that govern our perceptual experience.

In the philosophical literature, it is customary to think of perception as being assessable with respect to *epistemic* norms. The whole discussion around disjunctivism (Hinton 1973; Snowdon 1981; McDowell 1998), which is now often considered to be the dominant, if not the default, position (Hinton 1973, 26f.; Martin 2002, 2004) in the philosophy of perception, is, by and large, framed and motivated by epistemological concerns about truth and falsity, which act as norms for distinguishing the cases under discussion. Very generally, 'the disjunctivist holds that veridical perceptions and hallucinations differ mentally in some significant respect—i.e., there are certain mental features that veridical perceptions have that hallucinations cannot have' (Soteriou 2020). There are a variety of disjunctivist theories, depending on how we understand the metaphysical implications of this claim, but most disjunctivists agree on at least one corollary epistemological point, namely that illusions and hallucinations are non-veridical experiences, perceptual errors in that sense. While illusions are standardly held to be false perceptions in the sense that they bear on real objects whose properties they fail to correctly grasp, hallucinations are usually conceived as perceptual-like experiences that involve a reference to something that is not present or non-existent. So conceived, both types of experiences are held to be false because they involve a certain gap with respect to the fabric of reality. They are, for this reason, commonly called 'the bad cases', whereas veridical perceptual experience represents 'the good case'. Following from the (apparent) indiscriminability of veridical and non-veridical experiences, the urge to account for the commonsensical distinction between the good and the bad case and thereby to guarantee judicative access to facts, which would correspondingly be true or false, is

---

[1] As this passage attests, Husserl himself at times seemed to work with a fairly permissive concept of norm: 'All the questions, evaluations and decisions directed at correctness or incorrectness, at value or disvalue, are called "normative".' (2005a, 6). To that extent, Crowell's definition is acceptable on Husserlian grounds.

symptomatic of most of twentieth-century analytic philosophy of perception, which has delved deep into epistemic waters (see Siegel 2017, xiii, who makes a convergent assessment).

This book argues that perception is normative in another, more fundamental, sense. Perception is governed by norms that I call *perceptual*, that is, immanent to its own structure. This does *not* mean that perceptual norms are 'intrinsically' perceptual in the sense of being cut off from contextual matters and external facts; rather, it means that they are constitutive moments of our experience of these facts. Perceptual norms are, in that sense, *constitutive* or *enabling* norms, for they establish what perception *is*. To articulate my view, I will draw on the repertoire of the phenomenological tradition, on the work of Edmund Husserl and Maurice Merleau-Ponty in particular. Like Kant, both phenomenologists were concerned with the question of the unity of experience and sought to identify the conditions of possibility for having a perception, which they conceive not as a mere sensible experience of the outer world but as a continuous and meaningful experience of reality. Unlike Kant, however, neither phenomenologist immediately identified these conditions with cognition or epistemic criteria.[2] For both phenomenologists, *perception has its own standards*, its own conditions of possibility. Fundamentally, perception obtains when it unfolds concordantly or coherently, two words that I will use as synonyms throughout. And when the perceptual progression corresponds to or is in harmony with one's goal or interest, perception can also be said to be optimal. From the phenomenological point of view, concordance (*Einstimmigkeit*) and optimality (*Optimalität*) are the two basic norms governing over perceptual experience, and much of the book is devoted to clarifying their meaning and to addressing the philosophical consequences that follow from this insight.

Coherence concerns, first, the *unity of the appearances* within the flow of my experiences (past, present, future), which must concord to yield a meaningful experience of reality. For Husserl, perceptual intentionality involves intending acts that will be either fulfilled or disappointed as

---

[2] Kant's notion of the unity of experience is indissociable from his theory of knowledge. In the *Critique of Pure Reason*, Kant argued that the mind's synthetic activity is what enables us to have knowledge of the external world. By the same token, it also sets limits on what can be known, for the unity of experience is thought as a necessary condition for the possibility of objective knowledge. Husserl does not necessarily disagree with there being a privileged connection between perception and knowledge, but he is adamant that the sets of conditions enabling both do not coincide. I will address aspects of this issue in Chapters 1, 3, and 5.

experience progresses, and, depending on the outcome, experience amounts to a perception or to something else, say, an illusion or a hallucination. Merleau-Ponty saw things similarly: for him, too, coherence acts as a transcendental condition of possibility of perception insofar as it assumes a constitutive function, instituting it as the type of experience that it is. In the language of contemporary philosophy, the phenomenological concept of coherence should thus be understood as a constitutive norm in roughly the same way that the rules of chess or basketball constitute the kind of activities that they are (Glüer and Pagin 1999; cf. Heinämaa 2019, 13; Carta 2021, 130).

Perception does not only unfold concordantly or coherently: it also has standards of correctness or adequacy, which can be seen in the fact that I can perceive correctly or incorrectly, better or worse, sometimes even optimally with respect to some goals or intentions. That's why it is normally possible to *improve* one's perception by making certain adjustments (turning up the volume, diming the light, moving closer to the source, etc.) in light of our pursued objectives. True, perceivers might not necessarily *try* to perceive well or even just correctly; but the fact is that, in perceiving, we *are* situated in a space where such normative distinctions typically make sense. Husserl made this question a central topic of his reflection on perception in *Thing and Space* (1997), in which he affirms that an experience is 'optimal' when the thing is perceived 'in the sense of the defining interest' and 'the interest is satisfied' (107). Insofar as it sets an ideal to attain or to strive for and thus requires some kind of evaluation or assessment with respect to it, it may be helpful to think of optimality as belonging to the class of *evaluative* norms in the same way that norms of correctness do (Mulligan 2004; Mulligan 2017; Carta 2021, 131); however, since anything is susceptible to becoming an object of interest at any time, one could also plausibly say that optimality *constitutively* belongs to every perceptual *horizon*.

From the phenomenological point of view, there are thus two main norms governing over perceptual experience, namely coherence and optimality, one being constitutive and the other evaluative or constitutive, depending on the point of view. There is at least one other essential difference between both worth mentioning here. On the one hand, concordance, which defines the relation between past, current, and future appearances, is a necessary condition for *every* perception, including self-, object, and background perceptions. As such, it must be regarded as a constitutive norm in the strictest sense: completely failing to meet it implies nothing less than a perceptual collapse.[3] On the other hand, optimality, which describes the correlation between perceivers and the intended object or environment with respect to some goals or others, *only concerns interested perceptions*. The reason for this is simple: since the norm (viz. what counts as optimal) comes from the interest and is therefore relative to the pursued goal, it follows that not all perceptions are susceptible to being optimized since not every perception is interested (e.g. background perceptions are not interested). Since Husserl typically discusses concordance and optimality in their relation to normality, of which they would be two moments, this difference does not come across very clearly in his own writings, but the chapters to come will show that and why the distinction matters.

The goal of the book is to analyse the phenomenology of perception as a norm-governed experience or practice in these two dominant senses, that is, to spell out how perception involves normative assessments with respect to coherence and optimality that are first-personally lived through by perceivers. It is organized around seven chapters. In the first two, which constitute together the first part, I lay out the conceptual and historical background for the view I'm defending by outlining Husserl's (Chapter 1) and Merleau-Ponty's (Chapter 2) account of perception, illusions, and hallucinations in view of the two basic perceptual norms introduced above. In my interpretation, perception is coherent and geared toward optimality, whereas illusions and hallucinations are understood as experiences of deviation from these norms. The following five chapters put this theory to the test in the broader philosophical landscape by engaging in five ongoing debates in the philosophy of mind and perception.

The three chapters constituting the second part stress in different and complementary ways the role of the body in perception. Together, they aim to show that the kind of perceptual norms that I have in view are not formal categories or empty principles but, rather, themselves embodied. In Chapter 3, which concerns the intrinsic connection between perception and bodily self-consciousness, I argue that perception displays its norm-sensitivity in the way it guides, elicits, or constraints action and behaviours. Chapter 4 looks at the philosophical and scientific literature on multisensory perception and provides a normative analysis of our experience of its functions

---

[3] From the phenomenological point of view, perception is not a mere sensible experience of the outer world (which may well be, in certain limit conditions, totally chaotic) but a *meaningful* experience of reality. For this reason, it requires a certain level of coherence. I will come back to this later, particularly in Chapters 1 and 2.

and mechanisms. While sense cooperation and interaction are known to influence and sometimes even enhance the reliability of our perceptual judgments, the argument I am defending highlights their role in agency and shows how they promote coherence and optimality. Finally, Chapter 5 examines the long-term transformations and alterations of our perceptual dispositions (both bodily and cognitive) via learning and analyses the nature of these changes in terms of their capacity to facilitate perceptual discrimination and enhance practical familiarity.

While questions relating to sociality and intersubjectivity were only implicitly informing my analyses until that point, both sets of issues take centre stage in the third part of the book. Chapter 6 aims to test the applicability of my account in the specific context of the perception of other people and argues that perceiving others, too, is guided by norms. Lastly, Chapter 7 provides an analysis of the phenomenon of shared perception by introducing the notion of 'shared perceptual responsiveness', which I take to be necessary for understanding the phenomenon. The argument suggests that it is in the way that individuals jointly respond to commonly perceived cues that shared perceptions are enacted. Again, I interpret this shared perceptual responsiveness in normative terms.

The notion of norm that I work with throughout the book may perhaps seem very thin, but it rests, as we are going to see, on all kinds of embodied and passive tendencies that led both Husserl and Merleau-Ponty to significantly enlarge their conceptions of intentionality, perception, and attention beyond the traditional understanding of these terms. Furthermore, coherence and optimality are not the only norms bearing on experience. All kinds of 'sociocultural' norms circulate in our lifeworld, and some of them do have an impact on perception, e.g. in the form of perceptual biases. Their top-down influence on perception, which will be discussed in the last two chapters, will be distinguished from the kind of bottom-up impact that coherence and optimality have on perception insofar as the latter are constituted through repeated action and habitualized behaviours. What makes things both complicated and interesting is that all these different types of norms coexist and are typically *intertwined* in experience. Top-down and bottom-up norms can even interfere with and mutually impact each other. Chapters 5–7 will address some questions raised by this complex situation.

Throughout the book, I draw freely on the phenomenological repertoire in order to articulate the thesis sketched out above. Although Husserl and Merleau-Ponty are my two main sources of inspiration, other phenomenologists—both classical and contemporary—have provided me with important productive cues. The thesis that I defend is my own—it is not proper to either Husserl or Merleau-Ponty—but I take it to be Husserlian and Merleau-Pontian in spirit. Since there is a rapidly growing body of literature on the topic of normativity both inside and outside phenomenological circles, I will, while formulating my view, provide a survey and a critical assessment of some of this literature at the same time. I will thus situate my own endeavour both vis-à-vis the work of my peer phenomenologists and within the broader context of contemporary philosophy of mind and perception, weighing the relative strengths and weaknesses of the account I defend by comparing it to other interpretations and other theories of perception, including neuroscientific enactivist theories. Throughout the book, I also provide some of the historical background for the claim I am defending by tracing its origins back to Brentano and Kant.

PART I
WHAT ARE PERCEPTUAL NORMS?
Insights From Classical Phenomenology

1
Husserl's Normative Account of Perception

Perhaps the most important, albeit often overlooked, feature of Husserl's critical appropriation of Brentano's concept of intentionality resides in the introduction of a normative motif at the heart of the intentional relation. Stated simply, Brentano's thesis stipulates that all conscious mental states are intentional states, which means that they are all characterized by their *direction* toward an object (*Richtung auf einen Gegenstand*) or their *relation* to a given content (*Beziehung auf einen Inhalt*).[1] Note that nothing in Brentano's definition of intentionality suggests that intentional objects have normative import or that they are experienced meaningfully. The notions of *direction* and *relation* are simply meant to convey the idea of *having an object* (in the sense of having it before the mind's eye), leaving aside the question of *how* any such thing is given within experience. This much and nothing more is common to all mental states.

Against the background of this minimal definition of mental states, Brentano then distinguishes between three fundamental kinds of intentional relations: one founding relation, and two founded ones. The paradigm case for all intentional attitudes is provided by presentations (*Vorstellungen,* sometimes also rendered as representations), since every intentional relation is either itself a presentation or based on a presentation. That is why presentations are said to *found* intentional relations. As for the founded ones, they are either judicative or affective. Cognitive judgments and phenomena of love and hate are derived intentional phenomena because they are based on presentational states, which provide them with

---

[1] In *Psychology from an Empirical Standpoint*, Brentano defines mental phenomena by their intrinsic intentional nature: 'Every mental phenomenon is characterized by what the Scholastics of the Middle Ages referred to as the intentional (or mental) inexistence of an object, and what we might call, though not wholly unambiguously, relation to a content (*Beziehung auf einen Inhalt*), direction upon an object (*Richtung auf einen Gegenstand*) .... Every mental phenomenon includes something as object within itself, although they do not all do so in the same way. In presentation something is presented, in judgments something is affirmed or denied, in love loved, in hate hated, in desire desired and so on' (1995, 68).

their objects in the first place. The kind of relation they instantiate is specific, however, since they both display a normative polarity. Whereas mental *presentations are normatively neutral* in the sense of being neither true nor false, neither correct nor incorrect, cognitive judgments and phenomena of love and hate are modifications of basic presentational states that introduce a normative dimension: in addition to being presented, the object is either affirmed or denied (in judgments), or it is loved or hated (in affective acts). Again, none of this is true of basic presentational states. To present an object consists in nothing more than having it present to mind.[2]

Brentano's tripartite classification of intentionality can be misleading, however, for the most important distinction that he makes actually divides up all intentional relations into *two* (not three) basic kinds: there is a founded, normative concept of intentionality on the one hand, and an original, non-normative concept on the other. In this picture, perceptions belong to the class of normative presentations. For Brentano, perception is indeed normative because it is realized in the form of an existential judgment: as it purports to present things as they are, perception thereby affirms their existence.

While Husserl agrees with Brentano that perception is a normative phenomenon, his reason for holding this view differs radically from his former mentor. Perception is normative for Husserl not because it is realized in the form of a judgment but because it *aims* at its object (Benoist 2008a, 2008b). In the *Logical Investigations*, Husserl asserts that perception belongs to the class of objectifying acts, which are the intentional experiences by which something experienced acquires an objective character. Characteristic of objectifying acts (judgments, perceptions, etc.) is their capacity to establish a reference and present the experienced thing as an object to consciousness. However—and this is key—perceptual consciousness can only fulfil this function insofar as it transcends what is sensibly intuited in the direction of *what it posits as an object*. What is aimed at in perception is the object itself, not the aspect or profile (*Abschattung*) that is sensibly intuited. (All things

---

[2] This view is expressed very clearly in Brentano's *The Origin of our Knowledge of Right and Wrong* (1889): 'Comparison of these three classes of phenomena reveals that the last two exhibit a certain analogy that is not shared by the first. The last two but not the first involve an opposition of intentional relation. In the case of judgment there is the opposition between affirmation or acceptance, on the one hand, and denial or rejection, on the other. In the case of the emotions there is the opposition between love and hate or, as we may also put it, the opposition between inclination and disinclination, between being pleased and being displeased. But in the case of mere presentation—in the mere having of an idea—there is no such opposition' (Brentano 2009, 10).

being equal, it is the house that I see, not the façade of the house.) Through this constitutive accomplishment (*Leistung*), perception has an intrinsic normative status in Husserl's phenomenology, for, unavoidably, it either succeeds or fails in grasping adequately the object that it posits; that is, it correctly or incorrectly posits the object as it really is.[3]

Thus, from Brentano to Husserl, a reversal surreptitiously takes place: for the latter, perception is a rule- or norm-governed activity not because the (neutrally) presented object is *then* affirmed as existing. For Husserl, there is just no 'neutral' givenness or pre-givenness of anything. In perception, the aiming act (*meinender Akt*) is *originally normative* because it is *originally positional* (Staiti 2022, 89).[4] Through the aiming act, perception posits its object as being thus and so, and in so doing, it brings into play conditions of correctness (*Richtigkeit*) in relation to which it can either be correct or incorrect, succeed or fail.

Another way of capturing the reversal of Brentano's thesis that Husserl operates consists in analysing the contrast between positionality and neutrality. Contrary to Brentano, neutrality is derivative in Husserl's framework; that is, it is a modification of positionality. In this regard, his conception of imagination (*Phantasie*), which he conceives in opposition to perception, is illuminating. In contrast to perception, recollection, and anticipation, which are positing acts that imply the *existence* of the targeted object, imagination (*Phantasie*) is a non-objectifying act; that is, it is an act of *modification* of the original positing presentation. For Husserl, imagination is a non-normative form of intentionality precisely because it is a neutrality-modification of the thetic character of the original presentation (usually a perception). In other words, *this neutralization*, which Husserl conceives as 'the counterpart in consciousness to all accomplishing' (*Gegenstück alles Leistens*) (2014, 213), *comes second*: it presupposes a prior thetic presentation of the object (see Huang 2023).

Now, to decide on the question of whether perception succeeds or fails— that is, whether it apprehends the object as it really is—it is necessary to

---

[3] While the specifically normative interpretation of this intending structure is only indirectly expressed in the *Logical Investigations*, in his 1908/9 *Vorlesungen über Grundprobleme der Ethik* Husserl has explicitly recourse to normative terms to describe all 'objectifying acts', which are, in virtue of this aiming tension, 'directed towards' their object 'in the teleological (normative) sense' (1988, 339f.; my translation).

[4] Again, Husserl expressed this very clearly in his lecture on ethics: 'Objectifying acts are not complications made up of a consciousness that make us aware of an objectivity and a position-taking toward this something we are objectively conscious of' (1988, 338).

deepen the analysis and consider another dimension of experience, namely perception's embeddedness in a temporal horizon. One of Husserl's most profound insights is that perception's tacit original belief in the object's existence as this or that will necessarily be confirmed or disconfirmed by the way the experienced object will be integrated or not into the larger temporal and thematic context. My belief in there being a loaf of bread in front of me will hold only as long as its appearances manifest themselves concordantly (*einstimmig*); that is, if my (visual, olfactive, gustatory, haptic) experiences of the bread continuously blend with one another in a coherent or harmonious fashion. If this condition is not met, a correction of belief typically ensues.[5] A fundamental aspect concerning Husserl's conception of perceptual normativity emerges here: perception (*Wahrnehmung*) is quite literally a *Für-wahr-nehmen*, that is, a *holding-to-be-true* that steadily awaits a confirmation by the further course of experience. As a result, the object's status of *existence* appears to be contingent on how experience progresses; that is, on whether experience ongoingly meets our expectations and maintains the object's identity.[6] Leaving the metaphysical implications of this claim aside for the moment (but see Section 1.4), the fact is that in this picture, coherence or concordance (*Einstimmigkeit*), which belongs originally to perceptual consciousness, exerts a constant normative constraint on perception. In Husserl's idiom, one could speak of a transcendental condition of possibility: coherence (or concordance) is a transcendental or constitutive condition of perception for it serves as the measure for what counts as a perception at all. Conversely, a totally incoherent experience coincides with the limit of what can be considered a perception. As a result, coherence should be conceived as a constitutive or enabling norm, for it carves out the contours of what perception amounts to. Interestingly—but we'll come back to this later (see Section 5.2.1)—one of the defining features of Husserl's transcendentalism with respect to perception is that these expectations are

---

[5] I say 'typically' because this is not the only option. As Wehrle (2018) points out, experiences of deviation or interruption of the concordant course of perception provoke irritation, discomfort, or surprise, in response to which perceivers are automatically prone to restore concordance by adopting different coping strategies, like 'ignoring inconsistent inputs' (53) or treating deviations as exceptions, for instance.

[6] Terminologically, Husserl makes a distinction between anticipatory intentions (*Intentionen*), which correspond to a formal and universal aspect of time-consciousness, and expectations (*Erwartungen*), which are specific types of intentions empirically determined by our perceptual history. What the mature Husserl calls 'expectation' is an interested intention, or a forward-looking intention determined by a specific interest. A detailed analysis of this point is provided in Section 5.2.1.

gradually established in intentional consciousness in a bottom-up fashion thanks to repeated patterns of perceptual experiencing. As a result, one sees that the kind of conditions of perceptual experiencing that Husserl has in view are not formal or empty conditions; they are, rather, embodied and instituted in and through experience.

Perception's temporal horizon not only enables us to decide upon its thetic character (whether its object exists or not) but also opens another dimension of the normative, namely optimality, which Husserl thematized throughout his career in tandem with concordance. Optimality is a kind of evaluative norm, for it concerns the possibility of improving or enhancing our perceptual point of view with respect to some goals, intentions, or values. The idea, *which concerns not all perceptions but only interested ones*, is that object-perceptions involve possibilities of increases or improvements that are determined by the perceiver's context-specific goals and purposes. Hence, when watching a movie at home at night, we adjust our position, the volume, and the lighting such as to promote clearness of images, richness of sound, and fullness of experience in ways that differ markedly from when we unattentively watch a tennis match in the afternoon daylight while cooking. Even if a significant aspect of our perceptual lives remains uninterested (e.g. the constantly perceived background noises), the fact is that perceptual consciousness *can* be triggered by anything at any time, prompting perceivers to make all kinds of psychophysical adjustments to align their perception with their (constantly shifting) interest. In this sense, *optimality*, which is the second perceptual norm that Husserl works with, *belongs to the horizon* of every perceptually lived experience, even if not every experience is either optimal or suboptimal.

The main objective of this chapter is to provide an in-depth analysis of these two perceptual norms, namely concordance and optimality, thereby laying down the historical and conceptual basis for the analyses to come in the remaining parts of the book. In the next chapter, I will complete this task and look at how some of the insights found in Husserl's phenomenology have been further developed and productively transformed in the work of Maurice Merleau-Ponty. The analyses offered in both chapters centre on perceptions, illusions, and hallucinations, and aim to demonstrate that perception is best understood as governed by *perceptual*, not epistemic, norms, whereas illusions and hallucinations are experiences of deviation therefrom.

1.1. Concordance as Law of Coherent Experiencing

From the phenomenological point of view, concordance is a necessary condition of all meaningful perceptual experience, be it of objects, events, or people. To perceive something (anything) as what it is (as opposed to having a mere aggregate of sensations), it is necessary that incoming perceptual contents be harmoniously integrated into the context of experience; that is, that they cohere or concord both with what was experienced before and what will be experienced in the future. Since perceptual experience fails to establish reference when this requirement is not met, concordance is a constitutive feature of what perceptual experiencing is, a norm or transcendental condition in that sense.

This Husserlian insight is a direct consequence of the intrinsically temporal nature of consciousness, for which the experience of a melody, described in terms of the relation of expectation and the fulfilment of such expectation, provides the canonical example (Husserl 1991). In his early works on consciousness, Husserl argued that the perception of a temporally extended object (like a melody) as well as the experience of change and succession would be downright impossible if perceivers were only aware of what takes place in the punctual now, i.e. the 'now' in the narrow (or Aristotelian) sense of the term. The reason is that merely experiencing a series of disconnected and momentary conscious states does not allow us to perceive or be aware of succession and duration (Gallagher and Zahavi 2021, 82–4). But since *we are* experiencing succession and duration, Husserl—in contrast to Brentano (Dastur 1995, 48–54)—thought that we must recognize that perceptual awareness *does* encompass more than what is given in the now-phase. This is basically how Husserl came to develop an enlarged conception of the present (i.e. the living present, *lebendige Gegenwart*), which includes a horizon of the before and after, what he calls retentions and protentions, respectively. Thanks to its horizonal structure, every incoming tone of the melody is thus integrated into a continuous whole of past and future tones: while the just perceived tones are retentionally retained in consciousness, which gradually lets them fade away, the new ones enter perceptual consciousness as belonging to a horizon of protentionally anticipated tones. This is how the listener can transcend the punctual now and experience something like a temporally extended object like a melody. In Husserl's words,

> When, e.g., a familiar melody begins, it stirs up definite intentions which find their fulfilment in the melody's gradual unfolding. The same is the

case when the melody is unfamiliar. The regularities governing the melody as such determine intentions, which may be lacking in complete definiteness, but which nonetheless find or can find their fulfilments. (2001b, 210)

The passage is immensely important because Husserl grants to this structure an unlimited reach. The auditory experience of a melody is for Husserl paradigmatic of every objectual (*gegenständlich*) consciousness: *every* experience has a horizon of more or less definite intentions that build a tripartite structure made of the primal impression, focused on the now-phase of experience, the retention, directed towards past moments, and the protention, oriented towards future phases. The presence of *any* object to consciousness involves such a temporal extent; the living present therefore counts as an intrinsic feature of consciousness.

Thanks to its temporal extendedness, perceptual consciousness *always* transcends the now-phase and intends more than what is sensibly given by the impressions. The importance of this 'intending more' (*Mehrmeinung*) (Husserl 1960, 46) should not be underestimated, as it shows that the extended temporal nature of consciousness directly affects the *content* of intentional experience, which is correspondingly enlarged beyond what is presented in the now. As Husserl repeatedly pointed out, perception is not limited to any particular aspect or moment. Perceivable objects are transcendent by their very essence or nature[7]—therein lies their objective character (cf. Section 2.5 below)—but this is not a problem at all for individual perceivers, because each experience has a certain stretch or extent build into it such that one is invariably also aware of other aspects of the object, which are not presented, but appresented, that is, concurrently re-presented or made present in an empty mode.[8] This horizonal, appresentational awareness, which is made possible by retention and protention, explains why it is *the thing itself* that I perceive, not the sensibly presented profile. The point is that the retentionally preserved and protentionally anticipated contents constitute object-perception just as much as the sensibly intuited ones. To go back to the previous example: the sides of the house that are not sensibly given are not presented, but appresented; still, even as emptily intended, they belong to the phenomenological structure of the house. The same

---

[7] In *Ideas 1*, Husserl expresses this idea in the strongest possible way by writing that even 'God—as the ideal representative of absolute knowledge' could only intuit 'a thing in space' through 'appearances in which it is and must be given "perspectively"' (2014, 302).

[8] On the evolution of Husserl's reflection on this particular question, see Doyon 2019.

insight holds *mutatis mutandis* in the auditory sphere: it's the melody that I hear, not a series of disconnected tones.

In this analysis, the importance of concordance comes to the fore, for full (i.e. presented) and emptily intended (i.e. appresented) contents can only be synthesized into a single experiential stream, and thus yield a single object, if these contents are concordant with one another; that is, if they 'match' and 'fit' with one another in the overall context. The tone that I now hear constitutes the melody (as opposed to background noise) only insofar as it matches the melodic direction provided by the previous tones and 'announces' (however indeterminately) the next ones. The intrinsic connection between perceptual intentionality and normativity already begins to shine through, because thanks to this 'intending-beyond-itself (*Über-sich-hinaus-meinen*)', which is 'implicit in every consciousness' (1960, 46), one sees that perception automatically anticipates intentional contents that will or will not be fulfilled by the further course of experience. Depending on whether these expectations are fulfilled or not, perception unfolds coherently or not. As such, it can be said to succeed or fail.

Another helpful way of capturing what Husserl is getting at is to recognize that the perceived object is not a bare 'given'. Without the synthetic work of consciousness, there would be no intentional unity and therefore no objectivity either.[9] Thanks to the 'hidden constitutive performance' (1960, 47) of the ego, the sensibly intuited content always appears in the light of an aiming intention, which sets the standard of success or failure of perceptual progression. In the intentional process of object formation, whose genesis and transformation over time was uncovered by Husserl in his genetic phenomenology (see Section 5.1), there is always a kind of 'predelineation' (*Vorzeichnung*) (1960, 45) of intentional content at work. The heart of Husserl's normative account of perception lies precisely in this tendency of consciousness to anticipate intentional content in a more or less determinate way, for it implies that any series of appearances is unavoidably caught up in normative dialectics: its unfolding either confirms or disconfirms what consciousness has anticipated in the sense of matching or failing

---

[9] In this sense, Benoist (2016) contends that normativity belongs to the 'internal structure' (121) of phenomenality as such. What Husserl calls a phenomenon is nothing but the 'appearing site (*lieu d'apparaître*)' (129) of the object, which means that it is only in the light of an aiming intention that an object can appear or be experienced. In this sense, and in an effort to remain faithful to Husserl, Benoist writes: 'To say that perception is "perception of an object" means to place the perceived under a norm: that of an identity attributed to it. No object without the possibility of recognition. This is not a property of the object. It is its definition' (2017, 271; cf. 2013, 53) More on Benoist's (critical) relation to phenomenology in Section 2.6.

to match it. In the lectures on *Passive Syntheses*, Husserl makes this point in plain normative terms when he asserts that perceiving acts involve 'a determining rule for the [further] course of perceptions' (2001c, 266). The institution of this 'rule of lived-experiencing' (266), which specifies the law for the interconnection of appearances (often in their correlation to bodily movements; see Sections 3.2 and 4.1), explains in turn why Husserl holds that 'there are norms of verification' involved in every perception, that is, 'originally prefigured ways of verification' that are 'intrinsic to' and hence constitutive of 'the sense of every objectivity being experienced.' (2001c, 266) In short, perception is intrinsically normative because the very notion of aiming (*meinen*) sets into play immanent 'rules' or standards of experiencing.[10] In so doing, it opens the possibility of its eventual fulfilment, in relation to which it can succeed or fail. For this reason, the phenomenological conception of the normative is tightly tied up with the structure of fulfilment.

While Husserl thought as early as the writing period of the *Logical Investigations* that a perceptual object is an identity presented in a manifold of experienced profiles (2001b, 283–6), in the genetic phenomenology of 1920s Husserl showed that the appearance of objects as having certain specific determinations and relations is a synthetic achievement that reaches down the level of passive consciousness. Precisely how this works will be explained later in Chapter 5, but the basic idea is that, initially, constitution does not require the active stand-taking or predicating on the part of the ego (2001c, 390). To get going, the process relies on passive association of the intentional content within the subject's own stream of consciousness (what Husserl calls the level of primary passivity). What matters for us now is to recognize that even this process is normative, for, thanks to the work of associations, perceptual consciousness tacitly anticipates that the present object will unfold concordantly, that is, coherently with past and current experiences of the same (type of) thing. And when it does, perception is successful and the object's identity remains stable; that is, it confirms itself as the experience unfolds (1973a, 364–6). Generally speaking, then, the norm is the perceived object as normal, that is, from the noematic (or objectual) point of view the norm is an identical object that confirms its

---

[10] This does not imply that the object does not exercise a *constraint* on experience. As mentioned above, the object's transcendence imposes itself and cannot be experienced from every perspective at once. For Husserl, phenomenology is a science of correlations, and perception is conceived as occurring where object and consciousness meet.

identity again and again through the unfolding of the experience. In a 1921 and still unpublished research manuscript on normality and abnormality, Husserl makes this point explicitly: 'The normal thing is the norm to which all deviant phenomena must refer' (MS D 13 I; my translation).[11]

This Husserlian insight is an eidetic or essential truth, for it purports to be universally valid: even vaporous ambiances and hazy atmospheres are expected to follow, if only vaguely, anticipated perceptual patterns. The background sounds that make up our auditory environment when walking in downtown Chicago, or the unfamiliar smell we may experience in a restaurant of a foreign culture, may well be nebulous and atrociously vague; the indistinctness that we experience in either case is still (implicitly) measured against standards of coherence and concordance such that a sudden, unexpected change (the sirens of an ambulance, the smell of rot, etc.) will be noticed and experienced as break in harmony. As we are going to see below in Section 1.3, such discontinuity in the flow of experience, which Husserl conceives as a consciousness of conflict (*Widerstreitsbewusstsein*), is fundamental to his phenomenological conception of illusions and hallucinations, which he defines (negatively) by their gap vis-à-vis normal (i.e. harmonious) experiencing.

One last point. Conflicts of appearances play out not only at the individual but also at the intersubjective level. What is concordant from a personal point of view might well be discordant from an intersubjective point of view (Heinämaa and Taipale 2019, 8). A blind person's visual experience is a case in point: while the current experience of the blind person might well cohere with her past and future experiences, it still 'deviates in a consistent way from the proven or true world of experiences of others' (Husserl 2008, 657). This mismatch between individual and intersubjective concordance hints at two different but interwoven problems: whereas (dis)concordance at an individual level concerns the phenomenology of (un)familiar experiences, concordance at the intersubjective level has a transcendental function in Husserl's framework as it enables the establishment of 'a common ground or "world" as the basis for all social interaction and communication' (Wehrle 2018, 51). Given the thematic orientation of this book, which is about the phenomenology of perceptual experiences, the specific question concerning the (transcendental) constitution of the objective world need not preoccupy us any further (but see Heinämaa 2013 and Taipale 2014, 121–46). However,

---

[11] The original reads as follows: '*Das normale Ding ist die Norm, auf die alle abweichenden Erscheinungen hinweisen müssen.*'

the first-person experience of a divergence between individual and intersubjective concordance (say, between the blind and the non-blind person's visual experience) *does* play an important functional role in the perspective that I want to develop in this book, for it can 'render the underlying operative norms thematic and can lead to a critical appreciation of them' (Wehrle 2022a, 202). We will come back to this point at various junctures.

1.2. Perception as Geared toward Optimality

In analysing concordance in the previous section, perceiving revealed itself to be an intentional act constituted of an array of retentional, impressional, and protentional intentions carrying the presented and appresented contents of experience. When intentional objects continuously match the act-intentions, that is, when there is unity within the flow of my past, present, and future experiences, perception unfolds normally, viz. coherently. However, coherence is not the only norm governing perception. Depending on the goal or interest in play, perception can also be deemed correct or incorrect, adequate or inadequate, good or mediocre, etc. with respect to this goal or interest. Herewith, a second norm of perceptual experience reveals itself: optimality.

Central to Husserl's analysis of optimality is the notion of 'self-givenness' (*Selbstgegebenheit*). For Husserl, an optimal perception is one in which the intended object is self-given, that is, fully matches the aiming intention. Perception is teleologically oriented towards this 'limit', which Husserl understands as the 'consciousness of the most proper givenness' (1997, 105) of its object. The optimum is in that sense 'the goal of the perceptual movement' (1997, 105), one in which the identity of the object is experienced such that 'no further fulfilment' (1997, 104) or no further improvement is possible. An experience of the optimum thus represents something like the end or goal (*Ziel*) of the perceptual process.

Already at this stage an important difference between the norms of concordance and optimality shines through: While concordance governs *every* type of perceptual experiencing, optimality only concerns interested perceptions.[12] This is because interested perceptions, contrary to background

---

[12] As far as I'm aware, Husserl does not explicitly distinguish the scope of concordance (*Einstimmigkeit*) and optimality (*Optimalität*) in the way I do. Rather, he typically analyses them together as constituting the realm of normality (cf., e.g., Steinbock 1995a, 1995b; Taipale 2014; Wehrle 2015a; Heinämaa and Taipale 2019). However, for reasons I explain here (and in Ch. 5), I don't think that both norms have the same reach.

noise or diffuse olfactory atmospheres, are carried by specific goals. They can thus be evaluated with respect to these goals. Husserl is clear on this: optima 'do not pertain' to the 'appearances as such but to the interest' (1997, 112) that motivates the perceptual process. Hence, what counts as a self-given presentation varies according to the dominating interest, which is in turn why the norm—what he calls *optimal givenness*—is 'not a fixed one' (1997, 106). Optimal givenness is rather contextual; that is, it is a norm which is relative to the purpose or goal that the perceiving agent is pursuing. Consequently, Husserl contends that each interest has its own optimum, in relation to which the systematic relations between the appearances are implicitly measured (cf. MS D13 IV, 66a). Seeing things optimally amounts to seeing them 'in the sense of the defining interest', and a 'consciousness of the attained goal' is one where 'the interest is satisfied' (1997, 107).

Husserl illustrates this idea by contrasting two different types of interest one might have with regard to the same object. Take, say, flowers: 'The natural interest in a flower is different than the botanist's interest, and thus in the two cases the best appearances are different' (1997, 107). If what counts as a flower's 'best appearance' for a botanist and a layman differs, it is simply because what is required for each one's 'interest [to be] satisfied is essentially different in each case' (1997, 107). Different interests yield different expectations, and this explains why the layman and the botanist have perceptual experiences with different optima.

In everyday experience, we don't need much detail to see things properly or optimally. Our expectations are usually relatively low, and our intentions rather easily fulfilled. To take another example, Husserl contends that in the eyes of 'a buyer or a seller', for instance, a house can be 'quickly given optimally' (2001c, 61). With some luck, it can even 'appear at best' 'at first glance' (2001c, 61), thereby fulfilling his intention as a buyer. When this happens, the thing is said to be self-given, and the interest is satisfied. Of course, 'matching the currently dominating interest and fully satisfying this interest...does not mean to bring the thing itself to *adequate* givenness' (1997, 112; my emphasis), for adequacy corresponds to an infinite idea that only an infinite series of appearances could fulfil.[13] But in a practical context

---

[13] Correspondingly, and in line with his conception of perception as an infinite, teleologically oriented, process of cognition, Husserl developed a second concept of optimality as an ideal of completeness, that is, as an ideal possibility of experience. From a teleological standpoint, perception is 'an infinite, never closed, never finished synthesis' of appearances (1997, 112), and as such it is oriented towards absolute or 'perfect givenness', which is an 'Idea (in the

our interest *can* be matched, and the conditions of an optimal perception *can* be met.

Precisely, Husserl holds that these possibilities of fulfilment can be actualized when the psychophysical 'conditions prove to be the "normal" ones' (1989, 64). In the case of vision, these include healthy organs,[14] average distance, and normal lighting conditions. Husserl glosses on the latter in the following way: 'seeing in sunlight, on a clear day, without the influence of other bodies which might affect the colour-appearance. The "optimum" that is thereby attained then counts as the colour itself, in opposition, for example, to the red light of the sunset, which "outshines" all proper colours' (1989, 64). As this passage clearly indicates, experiencing an optimal appearance does *not* require that *ideal* circumstances be in place. A thing's optimal givenness depends on the circumstantial conditions of experience, and, when these are normal, the optimum properties of perceptual objects can be experienced.

In fact, Husserl is aware that things are actually a little more complicated than this, since the psychophysical conditions of experiencing are continually fluctuating as the experience unfolds, and this explains the inescapability of

---

Kantian sense)' (2014, 342). Given the ideal nature of this 'endless process of continuous appearings', Husserl is well aware that no physical thing could ever match it 'in a closed consciousness' (2014, 342). In normal, everyday contexts, perceptual objects 'can only be apprehended by privileging some particular features' (MS A VII 13, 22b) that we may well take *as starting points* for our apprehension of this ideal. But since not all thingly features can experienced optimally in a single experience, 'the idea of this continuum' (2014, 342) remains an abstraction. For this reason, the correlated object of such synthesis—what Husserl calls '*das Ding als ein Integral von Optima*' (MS A VII 13)—is nothing but an *ideal unity*, the noematic correlate of this infinite synthetic process oriented toward the idea of perfection. Corresponding to this insight, only *an idealized set of norms* can account for perceptual optimality when, in the transcendental-phenomenological attitude, the object is disclosed by such an 'intellectual seeing' (MS A VII 13). More precisely, the ideal experience of such perfect givenness would correspond to an experience of an *infinite continuum of optimal appearances* harmoniously interconnected. From a noetic point of view, the idea of perfect givenness is described as one wherein all the 'paths' or 'courses' taken in perceiving the object would be, if they are taken, characterized by both constant concordance (*Einstimmigkeit*) and closer determination (*Näherbestimmung*) of the object. Given the orientation of this book, this second sense of optimality need not preoccupy us any further (for details, see Doyon 2018). Unless stated otherwise, optimality will be understood in the first sense, that is, as a context-sensitive or situation-dependent concept.

[14] In *Ideas II* and elsewhere, Husserl wrote extensively on the connection between healthy organs and optimality. Husserl's basic idea is that having an optimal experience of anything requires that we are disposed to do so, and this starts with our own *Leib*, which must be healthy. Hence, the following remark: '*Gesundheit [ist] sozusagen das Optimum*' (MS D13 I, 218a). See the following passage as well: '*Die normale Leiblichkeit bedeutet dann diejenige, die einen Kreis von Optima herstellt oder ermöglicht. Mit verbranntem Finger betaste ich schlecht, mit myoptischen Augen sehe ich in die Ferne schlecht usw.*' (MS D13 II 63a).

the phenomenon of perceptual constancy, and the variations in shapes, forms, and colours that we permanently experience with vision (cf. Section 2.2). Taking this into account does not significantly change Husserl's main point, however: the colour 'itself'—that is to say, the 'real' colour—can still be given and experienced as such (at least in principle) when the circumstances are normal: 'only if we ensure good lighting and the normal perceptual conditions, only then do we see how the thing properly is and grasp its true qualities' (1997, 97). Very succinctly, then, Husserl takes *the optimal property to be the normal property*. The colour 'red' appears optimally in 'clear daylight' (1989, 65; italics in original).

But, of course, what counts as 'normal' conditions in painting, sightseeing, or science may not be exactly the same. The usual lighting conditions (e.g. clear daylight) may not be optimal for a specific scientific endeavour, which might require special equipment and a particular setting. But then, relative to *this* purpose, these (otherwise special) conditions are normal, that is to say, adequate or appropriate to the task, and the corresponding experience can be said to be optimal. For Husserl, the relationship between normality and optimality is stable across contexts, which does not mean, however, that that optimality refers to a stable, cross-contextual property (an 'objective' property). Optimality is a function of the interest, which fixes the relevant norm. Consequently, self-givenness alone is not sufficient for optimality; normal conditions must also be secured. These, however, are a function of the interest. Normality and abnormality are categories that only make sense with relation to certain interests.

Interestingly, Husserl specifies that when our 'interest is in tune with [the] appearances' (1997, 112), the eventual increase of fulfilment becomes irrelevant. Beyond a certain threshold, improvement of the perceptual conditions becomes superfluous (or isn't experienced *as* improvement), because my perception already fulfils my intention, and my interest is already satisfied. To illustrate: 'If I have, in regard to the box, "good light", then it makes no matter whether the sun is higher or lower in the sky, whether it is covered by clouds or not' (1997, 106). When our interest changes, however, 'the difference in the appearances, which previously were irrelevant, may possibly now become relevant.' (106) If, to stick with Husserl's recurring house example, we are interested not in its architectural form but instead in its building materials, then satisfying our interest will command actions and information of a different scale, for the two sets of properties are not accessible in the same way. Hence, 'for the physicist and the chemist', for instance, the buyer's or seller's ways of experiencing the house 'would seem completely superficial and miles away from its true being' (2001c, 61). Given their scientific interest in the house's building characteristics, the goal of their perceptual activity is almost incommensurate with that of a buyer or a seller. In Husserl's eyes, the object of their respective inquiry and the corresponding realm of normalcy differ almost completely.

This difference is not absolute, however, since neither the physicist nor the chemist can present or even aim at presenting *adequately* the house's *entire* material properties in the mode of givenness in the flesh. '[B]ecause in principle there always exist the possibilities of presentations that are more precise, more complete, and richer in content' (1997, 112), absolute or adequate givenness is not attainable in any practice within the lifeworld, be it scientific or not. If not absolutely, the intended object of a scientific inquiry can still be self-given in the sense of the defining interest, however. And when this occurs, perception has attained its goal and can be said to be optimal in the relevant sense. 'The interest terminates in the optimal givenness' (MS D13 III 151b; my translation).

Hence, we see that diversity of norms does not necessarily imply rational diversity, for rational constraints can be the same despite contextual variations. In Husserl's eyes, it is the interest itself that assumes this role insofar as the optimum 'is the predominating focus of the "interest", what the *experience is tending toward, terminates in*, is fulfilled in; and other modes of givenness become intentionally related to this "optimal" one' (1989, 65; italics in original text). In brief, the interest fixes the set of conditions of what counts as an optimal experience, and it does so by prescribing a matching realm of normalcy and by generating goal-specific expectations (*Erwartungen*), which may be fulfilled or not.

Just as with concordance, it should be added at last that optimality, too, operates both at the individual and intersubjective level. To go back to the example discussed earlier: what counts as the optimal viewing image for the healthy perceiver and the colour-blind person may differ insofar as people suffering from colour blindness have a decreased capacity to see some specific shades. Depending on whether the pathology affects colour discrimination along the red–green axis, the blue–yellow axis, or both, colour blind persons will typically call some colours by untypical names. Since the colours that are confused are very consistent among people with the same type of colour blindness, their experiences largely cohere with one another; they may even, in some circumstances, agree on what counts as the optimal appearances. However, their colour experience still marks a discrepancy with respect to the healthy or 'normal' viewers, who are habitually capable of more fine-grained colour discrimination. All things being equal, non-colour-blind subjects see better and may thus serve, according to Husserl, as the reference in a given community (e.g. in a family). Husserl holds in this respect that an entirely colour-blind population that would meet a population of healthy (or normal) viewers would acknowledge that colour perception is superior, that is, more capable of fine-grained colour discrimination (MS D 13 XIV, 31; for a critical discussion, see Heinämaa 2013). Again, this is a transcendental claim that primarily concerns the constitution of the objective world, which Husserl sees as dependent on normal bodily constitution (Taipale 2014; Heinämaa 2022). Since it does not bear directly on the phenomenological aspect of the question pursued here, we can safely put it aside for the moment, keeping the discussion of bodily (ab)normality for later (cf. Sections 5.2 and 6.4 below).

In the next section, I will analyse further the two perceptual norms I have disclosed thus far—concordance and optimality—against the background of illusions and hallucinations, which appear in this light as phenomena of transgression.

1.3. Illusions and Hallucinations as Transgressive Phenomena

If perception's unfolding is a process of confirmation of the object's identity, illusions and hallucinations are, phenomenologically speaking, experiences of deformation, disintegration, or crossing out of this identity. The crossing out plays out on two different levels.

In his 1906 lecture course *Thing and Space* and then again in *Einführung in die Phänomenologie der Erkenntnis* from 1909, Husserl draws a distinction between *Leibhaftigkeit* (presence in the flesh) and *Glaubhaftigkeit* (*believability or credibility*), which are two interwoven dimensions of perceptual experience. *Leibhaftigkeit* concerns the phenomenal character of experience: when, in perception, the perceived thing is *leibhaftig da*, Husserl means that it is present in the flesh or in person; that is to say, it is intuitively given in perceptual consciousness as being there. The distinction between *Leibhaftigkeit* and *Glaubhaftigkeit* is straightforward, for the latter concerns not the phenomenal character of the perceived thing but its modality of being, that is, its existence or being-character.[15] Every 'normal perception' originally contains a 'perceptual belief' about its object, which it posits as

---

[15] Since this distinction only makes sense within the reduction, Husserl does not, however, make a commitment on the specific metaphysical status of that existence. The question concerning the metaphysical nature of the perceived object is bracketed.

being 'actual' (*wirklich*) (2014, 206). In Husserl's eyes, perception is intrinsically *glaubhaft*; that is to say, it is imbued with credence such that it entails the actuality of its object, which is taken to exist as such (viz. as it appears). When considering 'perception in the usual sense' (1997, 13; 2005c, 109), both dimensions of *Leibhaftigkeit* and *Glaubhaftigkeit* need to be taken into consideration, as they are normally 'fused' with one another (1997, 13). This does not prevent them from lending themselves to different analyses, however. When, by effecting the epoché, we bracket the question of existence and consider perception abstractly solely in its phenomenal dimension (its presence in the flesh), Husserl holds that, for clarity's sake, we ought to use the word *Perzeption* (1997, 13; 2005c, 111ff.), not *Wahrnehmung*, which, as the etymology suggests, includes a moment of position-taking. In the customary sense, to perceive is to *take* (*nehmen*) the perceived thing to be *true* (*wahr*).

The distinction between *Leibhaftigkeit* and *Glaubhaftigkeit* is fundamental to understanding Husserl's account of illusions and hallucinations, for whereas perception passively involves the belief that the targeted object is actual (*wirklich*) or truly existing (*wahrhaft-seiend*), illusions and hallucinations are experiences of modification of this position-taking. When one undergoes an illusory or a hallucinatory experience, what 'we had just taken as realities now become unreal' (2005c, 109). In other words, illusions and hallucinations are experiences in which 'the character of reality, of being truthful' of the targeted thing 'has changed into the character of nothingness' (2005c, 110). Importantly, the use of the predicates actual (*wirklich*) and non-actual (*unwirklich*), or truly existing (*wahrhaft-seiend*) and non-existing (*nicht-seiend*), supposes that, from the noematic point of view, it is the object as identical (viz. in its true being) that acts as the norm. To recall, for Husserl an 'object' (*Gegenstand*) is not, as the etymology suggests, a mere thing that stands over against a subject. For there to be an object at all, intentional consciousness must confer on that thing a stable, recognizable unity: objects 'are constituted as intentional unities, as identifiable unities of actual and possible perception' (2001c, 265; cf. 1997, 285). This is the function of recognition, whose constitutive force lies in the possibility of repetition. From the noetic standpoint, an object is something that I (and my fellow subjects) can recognize as such in an indefinite number of experiences. As such, repetition belongs *essentially* to the phenomenological concept of 'objecthood' (1970, 365ff.). The phenomenological object is 'a pole of identity' (1960, 45), or an infinite series of concordant profiles (cf. 2014, 86–104), which Husserl conceives, noetically, as a 'unity of synthesis' (1960, 41).

Depending on whether the object is given in a self-evident way or not, that is, as confirming its identity or not, perceived objects are taken to be actual or non-actual, existing or non-existing.[16] This division between kinds of perceptual experiencing complies with *norms of truth*, for to say of an object that it exists or that it is actual (*wirklich*) amounts to saying that the meaning-intention that aims at it is true (cf. 2014, 290f.). In other words, a perception whose object is actual or existing is one that reveals its true being. It is, in that sense, a true perception.

In this context, one important question to ask is *how*, as sometimes happens, we come to revise our 'original belief' (2014, 208)? How can the being actual of the targeted object, which initially passively informs every perception, be transformed into the non-actual, the doubtful, the questionable, or the merely probable? To take a familiar example for Husserl readers: how is it that I may come to think that this is not a woman but a mannequin (1970, 138)? One possibility is that I benefit from new external information. If someone tells me that this is a wax figure, and not the woman that I think it is, and if I trust this testimony, then I will presumably modify my belief. This might not necessarily affect how I see things instantly, however. New information might provoke a modification of my doxic position independently of the phenomenology of experience, which may remain stable or unchanged for a while. (Think about the Müller-Lyer illusion.) Something like this is apparently what Husserl has in view when he writes that 'with this modification of perception, the character of in the flesh does not suffer' any transformation (2005c, 110).[17]

Things are more complicated, however. For, typically, new information does not leave *lastingly* the phenomenology unaffected. When one knows that this is a wax figure and not a woman, sooner or later the phenomenology of experience changes accordingly. Some possibilities of actions and behaviours are foreclosed, while others become available. (I may not be able to go and talk to the mannequin, but I can scrutinize its fabric.) This hints at another possibility: in a situation where I approach the silhouette of what

---

[16] There are, however, intermediate or, more precisely, transitory cases where 'both belief and disbelief are lacking, and instead of them we have doubt and perhaps the suspension of every position-taking' (1997, 13). This need not concern us here.

[17] The original reads as follows: '*Bei dieser Wahrnehmungsmodifikation leidet nicht der Leibhaftigkeitscharakter*' (2005c, 110; cf. 2001b, 83). Romano (2012, 2015) draws therefrom the consequence that *Leibhaftigkeit* and *Glaubhaftigkeit* are separated or independent, which is why he, like Bower 2020, reads Husserl as a conjunctivist about perception. For a criticism of this position from the opposite disjunctivist point of view, see Overgaard 2018, and for a more neutral or non-committal interpretation of Husserl, see Cimino 2021 and Doyon 2022.

I took to be a woman, only to realize, after scrutinizing it, that it is actually made of wax, *it is a change in the phenomenology that prompted me to modify my belief in the character of being of the perceived object.*

This is, incidentally, how illusions and hallucinations are standardly discovered: hallucinatory and illusory experiences *reveal a breach in the lawful patterns of regular perceptual experiencing.* This breach can manifest itself in various ways. Sometimes, one sense can 'correct' another, as when one visually takes the stick to be bent until one manipulates it and realizes that it is, in fact, straight.[18] Sometimes, it is the intentional link between perception and action that comes undone.[19] Whereas perceived objects have a horizonal structure that opens onto almost infinite possibilities of exploration (1997, 112; 2014, 342), hallucinations (and most illusions) eventually fade away, like the rainbow that vanishes (1989, 39–44). This is due to the fact that illusory and hallucinatory things are not sensuous things but, rather, mere phantasms: they have no spatiality or materiality, no profile, and no depth either. As such, they prevent perceptual agents from exploring or manipulating them. With empty phantoms, no lasting action is possible; the motivating loop between perception and action is 'broken', so to speak. Sooner or later, the delusional or illusioned subject will thus find herself in a practical deficit: she will realize that she cannot skilfully (that is, normally) exercise her perceptual skills and act as she usually does on the basis of her perceptions. For this reason, Husserl considers illusions and hallucinations to be 'abnormal' phenomena. They are abnormal in that they are experiences of deception (*Enttäuschung*), for they *fail* to correspond to our expectations.

If *Leibhaftigkeit* and *Glaubhaftigkeit* can be analysed on their own, in normal perception, they are tightly intertwined, such that changes in the phenomenology of illusory and hallucinatory experiencing effect a change in the character of being of the object. In *Ideas I* Husserl holds that it is the progression of our perceptions and their intuitive fulfilment that is responsible for our endorsing one thetic position over another. Perceptual evidence is 'capable of increase and decrease' (2014, 276), which in turn

---

[18] Here's a revealing passage on this: 'The bent stick in water is a fiction, an illusion: for in deceptive perception the visual apprehension is supplemented by certain tactile apprehensions. Actual investigation by touching and grasping yields a "straight" stick, which, for its part, normally requires a different visual appearance' (2005d, 52).
[19] This is the main theme of the second part of the book (Chapters 3–5). At this occasion, the crucial importance of the body in Husserl's account of perception, which I have downplayed in this chapter, will come to the fore.

provides perceivers with reasons for either confirming or adjusting their original belief. In this continuum, the higher term is the optimum, which guarantees effectiveness. Whereas object-perception is generally a seamless and unproblematic experience teleologically aligned on this optimum, illusions and hallucinations challenge our implicit belief, which is thereby transformed into a new modality (2001c, 16–33). For Husserl, this doxic adjustment has far-reaching consequences, for not only does it indicate a change in the character of being of the object it is correlated with, but it also leads to a reorganization of the whole perceptual flow and a transformation of our horizon of expectations (1973c, 12f.), which sets its own new standards.

These analyses will be further developed in the subsequent chapters, but this should already suffice to convey the idea that Husserl conceived of perceptual phenomena in normative terms. As we have seen, *Leibhaftigkeit* and *Glaubhaftigkeit* concern two different dimensions of perceptual experience: while the second bears on the existence or the being character of the object, the first concerns the phenomenality and the progression of the experience. Nevertheless, *both are not on a par*: it is the way in which I (and the community of subjects to which I belong) experience an object that determines whether it has true being.[20] Existence, if it is to be experienced at all and not simply presupposed, *must be motivated*, and, according to Husserl, what motivates its corresponding belief is the experience of concordance. For Husserl, the point generalizes: the things' status of existence (whatever they may be) is determined by the laws of experience that they match of fail to match (perceptual laws, imaginative laws, ideal laws, etc.). The same holds even for the 'fact' of 'the existence of the world', whose 'facticity' resides only in its corresponding 'motivational nexus' (1997, 250). Hence, while it is no doubt true that Husserl's whole phenomenological project is geared towards epistemological concerns and that, in the realm of perception, optimality implies truth; the fact is, however, that optimality can only assume this epistemic role because it is first experienced as such in perceptual consciousness.[21]

---

[20] Illusions and hallucinations are equals with respect to this motivating function in that they both entail a belief-modalization. Since this is what Husserl seemed to be most concerned with when analysing illusions and hallucinations, he tends to treat them together, rarely insisting on their differences. On this score, Merleau-Ponty's analyses differ markedly from Husserl's (see Sections 2.3 and 2.4).

[21] The question concerning the relation between perceptual and epistemic norms takes center stage in Ch. 3 and is also addressed in the context of Husserl's genetic project in Section 5.1.

1.4. Husserl's Idealism and Normativity

To understand how Husserl came to defend this normative view on experience, it might be useful, methodologically, to distinguish the position he espouses in the *Logical Investigations* from the one he will defend after the so-called transcendental turn.

In the Fifth Investigation, Husserl asserts on a couple of occasions that the metaphysical questions concerning the existence and mind-independent reality of intentional objects lie outside the scope of phenomenological analysis. From the methodological point of view of the *Investigations*, 'it makes no essential difference to an object presented and given to consciousness whether it exists, or is fictitious, or is perhaps completely absurd' (2001b, 99).[22] This and related passages have been quite correctly interpreted—first by Jocelyn Benoist (1997) and most recently by Dan Zahavi (2017)—to imply a sort of agnosticism or neutrality with regard to the metaphysical question of whether or not the intentional object has any mind-independent reality. The point, it should be noted, is methodological: phenomenology, as a purely descriptive discipline, precedes any possible metaphysics. Since metaphysical questions can neither be proven nor refuted on purely descriptive grounds, phenomenology suspends their validity (which does *not* mean that metaphysics is incompatible with Husserl's project; see De Santis 2022). In this sense, Husserl contended that phenomenology has no straightforward metaphysical implications, which, Husserl's first enthusiastic students and readers notwithstanding, might not necessarily be a good thing, for it seems to imply that phenomenology deprives itself of the means of distinguishing hallucination from veridical perception (Zahavi 2017, 48).

With the so-called transcendental turn, marked by the discovery of the epoché and the reduction, Husserl notoriously changed his mind and began to see the questions concerning existence and non-existence and being and non-being of intentional objects as fully fledged topics of phenomenological research (1960, 56). After the effecting of the epoché, that is, the suspension of one's belief, characteristic of the natural attitude, in the existence of the world and its object as existing independently, the metaphysical problem of

---

[22] Or again: 'In real [*reell*] phenomenological treatment, objectivity counts as nothing: in general, it transcends the act. It makes no difference what sort of being we give our object, or with what sense or justification we do so, whether this being is real (*real*) or ideal, genuine, possible, or impossible, the act remains "directed upon" its object' (2001b, 427).

securing our access to this independent 'reality' is set aside, since it is a conception that belongs to a naive ontology. Through this methodological manoeuvre, our natural inclination towards realism and our corresponding belief in an 'independent' reality are both suspended or bracketed: in the reduction, *reality as phenomenon* becomes manifest. Now that 'the experienced world' is 'deprived of its naïve acceptance' (1960, 18), reality (*Wirklichkeit*) is phenomenologically grounded, and it is conceived as the correlate of a synthesis of verification (1960, 59). Objectivity is in that specific sense transcendentally structured reality, that is to say, the correlate of a process of validation. This is, in essence, the core thesis of Husserl's transcendental idealism.

Husserl's conception of objects undergoes a similar ontological change: as a phenomenon, the reality of the object does not fall outside the scope of intentional consciousness, with which it is essentially correlated. Rather, it coincides with the possibility of validation and verification. 'The "object" of consciousness, the object as having identity "with itself" during the flowing subjective process, does not come into the process from outside; on the contrary, it is included as a sense in the subjective process itself and thus as an "intentional effect" produced by the synthesis of consciousness' (1960, 42). Contrary to Kant, Husserl explicitly conceived this process as a collaborative or intersubjective achievement. Real existing objects must be accessible to others and lend themselves to intersubjective confirmation to count as 'real'. They are 'objective' precisely because they are intersubjectively constituted, that is to say, valid for everyone.[23]

As we have seen, this insight in turn rests on Husserl's conception of consciousness as temporal, or as possessing a temporal horizon. Thanks to the involvement of retentions and protentions in the constitution of consciousness, perception thus always includes a reference to other appearances of the object. In their succession, these appearances are expected to confirm the object's identity. From the transcendental standpoint, perceived objects only appear *as* real in a process of self-legitimization where their being is confirmed again and again in repeated acts of consciousness (2006, 178ff., 259ff.). Husserl's descriptions of illusions and hallucinations as 'crossed out' or 'corrected' perceptions illustrate this negatively: the experience of

---

[23] I come back to this question in Section 2.5, but one should bear in mind the difference that Husserl makes between weak transcendence, viz. the fact that perceived objects exceed our momentary perspectives, and strong transcendence, viz. the fact that they are given for a community of subjects and not only to me.

discordance (*Unstimmigkeit*) between the appearances leads to a conflict (*Widerstreit*) in consciousness, which reveals the illusory or hallucinatory character of experience.[24] Husserl's characterization of illusions and hallucinations as implying a belief modification aims precisely at highlighting the fact that both phenomena are constituted by a deficit of validity. Precisely for this reason, they exclude any possibility of optimization; that is, they can't be optimized without being turned into perceptions first. Crucially, these traits are not merely accidental; rather, they constitute what perceptions, illusions, and hallucinations are.

Here we have come full circle, for the analysis shows that the correlation that Husserl has in view when describing his transcendental-phenomenological idealism is itself a normative structure. Reality is objective only insofar as it is measured by a sense-bestowing consciousness, which provides it with its norm of objectivity. In essence, this is the meaning of the asymmetry between world and consciousness for which Husserl advocates. To hold, as Husserl famously does in *Ideas I*, that consciousness is capable of self-manifestation while being requires consciousness to appear amounts to saying that consciousness provides the standard by which the real can count *as* real. This statement should not come as a surprise insofar as it echoes Husserl's conception of the thing, which displays the very same normative structure, only at a more local scale. Hence, when Husserl calls for a return to the 'things themselves', he does not aim at the things as bare things, for there are no such things. The 'thing' is always the thing of a certain intention, the synthetic unity of a determinate intentional aiming. The 'thing itself' belongs to a fulfilling structure (or to a synthesis), and this in turn means that it is a thing to which a norm or a standard is applied. This, in essence, is why Husserl's understanding of intentionality yields a *transcendental* realism.

Finally, it should be noted—and this is important—that one does *not* have to take a position on Husserl's metaphysical stance to recognize the intimate connection that holds between intentionality and normativity. As a matter of fact, Husserl gave intentionality a normative bent long before he came to explicitly endorse idealism. As we saw, it is already powerfully at

---

[24] This does not mean, however, that illusory and hallucinatory experiences *only* appear as such after the fact, in retrospect. This view, which Staiti (2015) correctly attributes to Husserl, wrongly presupposes that the illusory or hallucinatory subject cannot be aware of the illusory or hallucinatory character of his experience *as he has it*. As Merleau-Ponty showed in the *Phenomenology of Perception*, this, however, does not correspond to the experience of delusional subjects that suffer from real hallucinations. I come back to this in the next Chapter.

work in the *Logical Investigations*, which was widely understood by his own Göttingen students as a realist work, but which in the more contemporary landscape has yielded both realist (Levinas 1995, 91; Smith 2013, 161) and metaphysically neutral (Benoist 1997) interpretations. To make matters worse, the transcendental turn Husserl came to espouse after 1906 also divides the community of interpreters. While some understand Husserl's transcendental idealism as implicating a form of ontological phenomenalism (Philipse 1995), other readers see therein a kind of experiential monism (Blouin 2023) almost diametrically opposed to the sort of correlationism that Sokolowski (1970) and more recently Zahavi (2003a, 2017) advocate. However, regardless of where one stands on this otherwise important question, the normative moment at the heart of intentionality, which comes about in fulfilment, is left intact. In the rest of this book, which is not a work of metaphysics, I will (with the exception of Section 2.6) leave the question of Husserl's transcendental idealism and its connection to realism behind and be solely concerned with perceptual intentionality to show how its inherent normativity plays itself out in various philosophical contexts.

1.5. Conclusion

In this chapter, I have provided an outline of Husserl's phenomenology of perception by highlighting the determining function of perceptual norms in his account of perceptual experience. First, I have shown the determining role of coherence or concordance and demonstrated that, for Husserl, perceptions, illusions, and hallucinations are distinct from one another in the way they follow or deviate from expected patterns of perceptual experiencing. When what perceptually comes in is concordant (*einstimmig*)—that is, coherent with current and other past experiences—we have a perception. The object lends itself to a continuous exploration of its qualities or features, its identity is confirmed, and its ontological status as real is fixed. When, on the contrary, experience diverges from what is (normally) expected or anticipated and thus interrupts the flow of normal experiencing, it is lived in perceptual consciousness as a discordant or incoherent experience that prohibits the object's identity (or some of its properties) from being recognized. This is precisely what happens in illusory and hallucinatory experiences, which are lived from the first-person perspective as experiences of (partial) non-fulfilment—failures in that sense. Building on Husserl's phenomenological model, I will show in the chapters to come how illusions and

CONCLUSION 27

hallucinations distinguish themselves both from perceptions and from one another in the specific ways our habitual patterns of (verbal, motor, etc.) interaction are frustrated.

If concordance operates as a specifically *perceptual* norm, it is because it concerns *regularities of the correlation* between the perceiving subject and the intended object. Concordance has, in that sense, a *constitutive* function in perception. It is also, and for the same reason, a transcendental condition of experience. But it is not the only one. Throughout the chapter I have identified a second perceptual norm, namely optimality, and demonstrated in which sense they differ in scope. From the phenomenological point of view, coherence is a necessary condition of *all* perceptual experiences. Coherence can be quite low—our fulfilled expectations can be largely underdetermined and the experience very surprising—but if we are to talk of a perception at all, the surprise can't be absolute.[25] Optimality, however, does not have the same reach. Since the optimum is determined by the goals and interests of the perceiving agents, optimality only concerns interested perceptions. Background perceptions (e.g. background noises, bodily sensations, etc.) are not optimizable until I turn them into objects. When they do—that is, when I turn my attention to them and draw them into the thematic focus—they detach themselves from the background and acquire a determinate figure. In this operation, they are elevated to the status of 'object'. As a result, it appears that the contrast between figure and background, or focal point and horizon, is essential to the process of optimization. This is why it makes no sense to speak of optimization in a monochromatic experience where the figure/background structure has completely dissolved.[26] This also applies to mindfulness experiences, the training of which consists precisely in suspending the subject–object distinction (Thompson 2015). When this state of mind is reached, the goal is attained, as it were, and perception is already optimal. However, since everything else that is inscribed in my perceptual horizon *could* be turned into an object of perception, optimality remains a permanent possibility.[27]

---

[25] We will return to this question in detail in Section 5.1 and develop an argument to that effect that revolves around the role Husserl ascribes to what he calls 'types', which are proto-conceptual categories that guarantee a minimal level of coherence in the fabric of our perceptual lives.

[26] Thanks to an anonymous reviewer for raising this point.

[27] On this score, perceptions and hallucinations are clearly opposed insofar as, in the case of hallucinations, possibility of improvements completely vanished. More on this in Section 2.3.

Much more needs to, and will, be said in the next chapters. For one thing, I will, in Chapter 5, explain the *genetic constitution* of these norms by analysing the contribution of passivity, which I have completely left out in this opening chapter.[28] The same holds for the determining role of the body (Chapters 3–4) and of others (Chapters 6–7) in the experience of these norms. For the most part, this book aims at refining the descriptions of concordance and optimality that I provided here, and at showing how they differ from other kinds of norms (e.g. sociocultural norms, norms of truth, etc.), which may well play a functional, but not a constitutive, role with respect to perception. Before getting there, let us turn our attention to Merleau-Ponty, whose work will provide a second major source of insights for the argument defended in this book.

Phenomenology and the Norms of Perception. Maxime Doyon, Oxford University Press. © Maxime Doyon 2024.
DOI: 10.1093/9780191993527.003.0001

---

[28] The genetic analysis of the *origin* of these norms differs to a significant extent from the kind of ontological analysis that Crowell (2013) develops in his reading of Heidegger. Here's an illustration of his account: 'the stream of *Erlebnisse* is not intrinsically intentional, but only insofar as it belongs to an entity which is intentional, namely Dasein' (263). Essentially, Crowell argues that if intentional experience is to be assessable in terms of success or failure, it can only be because the agent is fundamentally committed to 'being something' (28–9), e.g. a writer, a teacher, or a father. Only insofar as he is *trying to be* something can he understand himself as 'being up to something at which [he] might succeed or fail' (28–9). In the rest of the book, I will neither address this ontological interpretation directly nor discuss the question pertaining to the possibility of naturalizing normativity, viz. of explaining the origin and 'law-like character' of (perceptual and/or non-perceptual) norms in non-intentional or natural terms (in the language of biology, say). While philosophically interesting and certainly worthwhile, the question concerning the origin of norms is not my central concern.

2
Perceptual Normativity in Merleau-Ponty

Despite Merleau-Ponty's well-known reservations about some aspects of Husserlian phenomenology, the analyses of perceptual experiences carried out in the *Phenomenology of Perception* accord with Husserl's on a fundamental respect: there, too, perception, illusions, and hallucinations are conceived both in intentional and normative terms. The pages on optimality in 'The Thing' chapter are deservedly notorious in this respect, and they will be discussed at length in the following, but Merleau-Ponty's interest for questions of norms and normativity, and their relation to perceptual experiences, is much broader in scope. When Merleau-Ponty describes a successful perception as one where we 'experience the harmony between the given and the evoked' (2012, 23), or defines the perceived thing as 'a question to which [my senses] respond exactly' (2012, 331), it becomes plain that the motifs of *harmony* and *responsivity*, which assume a fundamental role in the dialectics of question and answer that Merleau-Ponty develops throughout the book, must be regarded as normative in the sense I have been developing thus far.

Arguing for this latter claim, I will, in what follows, deploy a strategy similar to that in the previous chapter and demonstrate, first, how Merleau-Ponty, too, came to regard concordance (Section 2.1) and optimality (Section 2.2) as norms of perceptual experiencing. Against this backdrop, which will provide me at the same time with the opportunity to critically engage with some of the literature on normativity in the Merleau-Pontian scholarship, I'll then provide a sketch of Merleau-Ponty's phenomenological conception of illusion (Section 2.3) and hallucination (Section 2.4) in turn, exposing how he defines both types of experiences in terms of the unique relations they bear with these norms. Throughout the chapter, but also in the rest of the book, I will be more concerned with the commonalities than the differences between Husserl's and Merleau-Ponty's accounts (Section 2.5), which does not mean, as we are going to see, that these differences do not exist or that they are not important. Given the systematic nature of the argument I wish to defend, what matters most, however, is that Merleau-Ponty, too, conceived of perceptual phenomena as governed by perceptual norms. On this score, the proximity with Husserl is striking.

2.1. Concordance and Evidence

In the previous chapter we saw that, for Husserl, reality manifests itself in consciousness through a sequence of horizonal profiles succeeding one another in an orderly and continuous fashion. Given our embodied nature, perception is essentially perspectival, that is, tied to a particular vantage point, but perceivers can transcend this seeming limitation and grasp the thing themselves. Thanks to the unity provided by the temporality of consciousness (the interplay of impressions, retentions, and protentions), perceived and apperceived profiles build together a system of concordant appearances that Husserl identifies with the thing itself. Since concordance is a necessary condition for having a thing-consciousness, it enjoys, in the Husserlian account of perception, a transcendental status.

In Merleau-Ponty's work, concordance plays a more discreet role. It is an operative, that is non-thematic, concept, but it still punctuates his reflections on perception throughout the *Phenomenology*, and its weight in the overall economy of the argument is decisive all the same. Like Husserl, Merleau-Ponty did not conceive of concordance as a thought or an abstract principle; it is, rather, a *phenomenological* concept by means of which he describes our *experience* of things as fundamentally tied to a particular embodied perspective. Here's an illustration of how Merleau-Ponty mobilizes the concept:

> My point of view is for me much less a limitation on my experience than a way of inserting myself into the world in its entirety. When I gaze upon the horizon, it does not cause me, *to think* of that other landscape that I would see if I were there, nor does that one cause me to think of a third, and so on; I do not *imagine* anything, but all of the landscapes are already there in the concordant series and open infinity of their perspectives. (2012, 345; emphasis in original)

According to Merleau-Ponty, perceptual landscapes are always given in profiles in virtue of the portion of the world that we, as embodied beings, occupy at any given moment. This perspective, which is not a restriction on my perception but an occasion to anchor my position in the world, is transcended in perceptual experience thanks to the harmonious integration of past, current, and anticipated appearances that constitutes the horizon. When the current appearances align with both our past and future experiences, there is a sense of concordance or coherence. More explicitly so than in Husserl's view, for Merleau-Ponty this is achieved first and foremost at the level of bodily consciousness. There is concordance when our perceptions are supported by our *bodily* anticipations, that is, when our encounters with the surrounding world are facilitated by a range of anticipated movements, actions, and behaviours. We will come back to this specific point in the three upcoming chapters, which emphasize different aspects of bodily consciousness and its relation to agency.

At this stage, I wish to highlight the metaphysical function concordance assumes in Merleau-Ponty's framework. The experience of the concordance of any given thing's appearances, that is, of their progressive and orderly interlocking, opens onto a metaphysical truth in that it provides phenomenological evidence that there is something at all rather than nothing. This is because Merleau-Ponty thinks, as any good phenomenologist does, that one just cannot reach the 'being' of anything without *going through* the phenomenon. Of course, this is paradigmatically true of perceptual phenomena, be they veridical or not. Perceptions, for instance, can only appear as such as long as they conform to the law for the interconnection of appearances. The following passage provides support:

> There is sense, or something rather than nothing; there is an indefinite interlocking of concordant experiences, testified to by this ashtray that is before me in its permanence, and the truth that I perceived yesterday and to which I believe I can return today. This evidentness of the phenomenon, or again of the 'world,' is…misunderstood when the attempt is made to reach being without passing through the phenomenon…. (2012, 417f.; emphasis in original)

Since the phenomenological evidence that there is being, viz. that there is 'something rather than nothing', is provided (be it only in part) by the interlocking of successive experiences, it appears that, from the phenomenological standpoint, concordance is something like a test for the success or failure of having a perception at all. And this is precisely Merleau-Ponty's view: for him too, concordance is a transcendental condition of possibility of perception.[1]

As we are going to see later in the chapter and throughout the rest of the book, concordance is a general law or principle that can be broken down and analysed in several interrelated ways, depending on the specific type of object and the kind of experience that are concerned. Perceived material objects, for instance, have their own style, viz. their own way of revealing themselves and motivating specific exploratory movements (2012, 191). As such, they have nothing to do with illusions (Section 2.3) and hallucinations (Section 2.4), which distinguish themselves both from perceptions and from one another precisely in the way they interrupt the laws regulating concordant perception. Later in the book, it will be argued that even the experience of other people is norm-regulated and implies concordance (Chapter 6). The same holds for collective actions, chiefly shared perceptions, which require that the interlocking of the intentions of co-intenders follows concordant patters (Chapter 7). All in all, it thus seems that, for Merleau-Ponty, concordance is an essential structure or moment of all perceptions, and on this point his position does not significantly depart from Husserl's.

2.2. Optimality and Maximal Grip

More so than concordance, which all in all remains a subtle theme in the *Phenomenology*, the motif of optimality operates as a guiding thread throughout the book, provoking countless commentaries in the reception of Merleau-Ponty's work. Optimality is most expressly presented in the context of a phenomenological description of a visual encounter with a painting 'in an art gallery', where 'there is an optimal distance from which it asks to be seen' (2012, 315f.). In the phenomenological descriptions that follow this passage, we are told that perceptual optima are like demands to which perceivers are habitually inclined to respond by moving their body around

---

[1] Romano (2015) has suggested that the relation of dependence between the thing (the ashtray) and concordance (the harmonious experience of its successive appearances) runs in the opposite direction, which brought him to read Merleau-Ponty as holding a strong (i.e. naive) realist position. We will see in Sections 2.3 and 2.4 that Merleau-Ponty's conception of illusions and hallucinations is, broadly speaking, transcendental, for which reason I will argue in Section 2.5 that the opposition between Husserl and Merleau-Ponty that Romano insists upon is, in the end, too crude.

and adjusting their postures and behaviours. As it makes itself felt in experience, optimality has a motivating force: it triggers a process of self-assessment and self-adjustment oriented toward reaching a point of view where things reveal themselves most fully or fittingly. This is an important insight in the overall economy of the *Phenomenology*, one that we ourselves are going to go back to throughout this book.

While the passage about the art gallery might suggest that optimality is experienced only occasionally or in exceptional circumstances, this is not Merleau-Ponty's position. On the contrary, whenever perception aims at an object, optimality comes into play and governs over experience. The following passage is eloquent in this respect: 'When I simply glance at the surface that I am about to recognize as the surface of the table, it already invites me to a particular focus and calls forth the focusing movement that will give it the surface's "true" appearance' (2012, 331f.). The mention of 'truth' can be misleading for readers unfamiliar with Merleau-Ponty, since it concerns the appearance of the table, not our judgment about it. The true appearance of the table is one which can be experienced *before* it lends itself to reflection and judicative consciousness. The table's 'invitation' is, in that specific sense, a *pre*-reflective form of experiencing. As Merleau-Ponty writes, 'to perceive in the full sense of the word (as the antithesis of imagining) is not to judge, but rather to grasp, prior to all judgment, a sense immanent in the sensible. The phenomenon of true perception thus offers a signification that is inherent in the signs and of which the judgment is but the optional expression' (2012, 36). Very coarsely put, Merleau-Ponty's idea is that before and independent from our capacity to reflectively assess how things are, it is possible to experience a 'sense immanent in the sensible', something 'true' of the things themselves that could eventually be expressed (or not) in assertoric judgment, but which does not in any way depend upon it. By distinguishing these two levels of conscious activity and arguing for the priority of pre-reflective (or 'spontaneous') consciousness over reflective consciousness, Merleau-Ponty takes his distance from Kant (and neo-Kantians) and sides with phenomenologists like Husserl and Heidegger. In the next chapter, I will develop this point further and contrast the phenomenological point of view with the one defended by McDowell, which will serve here as paradigm of a certain neo-Kantian approach to perception and its relation to judgment.

For the time being, our attention should remain on the motivating function of optimality, which is a recurring theme in Merleau-Ponty's analyses. In his eyes, *every* object-perception involves something like a 'privileged perception' (2012, 315) which makes itself felt by exerting a normative pull on us. *Each* object-perception contains an implicit reference to this point of 'equilibrium' (2012, 316), which is where perceptual optimality can be experienced. In the visual sphere, this point of view corresponds to a situation where the thing offers a 'maximum of visibility' (2012, 332). Merleau-Ponty asserts that 'I will not name a phenomenon a "visible thing" if it fails to offer some maximum of visibility across the various experiences that I have of it (such as coloured areas), nor something that is far off and tiny on the horizon, that is vaguely located and diffuse at the zenith, that allows itself to be contaminated by the structures nearest to it and that does not oppose to them any configuration of its own (such as the sky)' (2012, 332). Although Merleau-Ponty does not specify it expressly, I take this view to be context-sensitive and to admit some degrees, viz. to contain some leeway. Even given the same interest, it is certainly possible that there are multiple optimal points of view, that is, a range of perspectives that are optimal with no one being better than the others. Granting this point still does not change much of the basic message: Merleau-Ponty thinks that our experience of objects in general contains an implicit reference to a maximum of visibility. This is one of its essential moments, as it were. But what does this mean exactly?

2.2.1. Dreyfus on Absorbed Coping

Merleau-Ponty's thesis has drawn, over the last two decades, a certain number of commentaries and interpretations, especially within the English-speaking world. Hubert Dreyfus might have been the first influential scholar to draw our attention to this specific issue. In a seminal paper of 1999 that explores the limitations of logical analysis from the phenomenological point of view, Dreyfus distinguishes between success conditions and conditions of improvement. Conditions of success, the primary focus of traditional logical analysis, refer to the specific criteria or conditions that must be met for a particular endeavour or activity to be considered successful. Conditions of improvement on their part stand for the ongoing development and refinement of skills, understanding, and expertise in a given domain. Dreyfus's main argument is that while conditions of success involve meeting predefined logical criteria and following formal rules, conditions of improvement cannot be adequately captured by logical analysis alone. Instead, Dreyfus suggests that a phenomenological approach is necessary to account for the intuitive, context-sensitive, and embodied aspects of skill acquisition and expertise, which are vital for continuous improvement and mastery. Specifically, Dreyfus argues that our context-dependent sensitivity to conditions of improvement enables us to constantly, but non-representationally, discriminate between better or worse ways to see things 'without the agent needing in any way to anticipate what would count as success' (1999, 6). In this setting, optimality is conceived in broadly Merleau-Pontian terms as an ongoing process of attunement and responsiveness to the specific demands of a situation, rather than rigid adherence to predetermined rules or goals. The point is illustrated by the following example: 'Without trying, one experiences one's arm shooting out and its being drawn to the optimal position, the racket forming the optimal angle with the court—an angle one need not even be aware of—all this, so as to complete the gestalt made up of the court, one's running opponent, and the incoming ball' (1999, 5). The phenomenology of our embodied skills, which are crucial for effective human engagement and expertise but are not adequately captured by notions of optimality in traditional logical analysis, bears the weight of the argument, and gave the paper its title ('The Primacy of Phenomenology over Logical Analysis').

In subsequent years, Dreyfus developed this line of interpretation further by elaborating on the notion of 'optimal' or 'maximal grip' in tandem with what he has come to call 'skilful' or 'absorbed coping'. In 'Intelligence without representation—Merleau-Ponty's critique of mental representation', Dreyfus has presented a significantly more intricate narrative of our evolving embodied skills, describing a progression from a novice to an early learner, then to a person who attains competence, proficiency, and eventually expertise. This final stage is commonly linked with athletes and individuals involved in sports in general. While the level of expertise reached by athletes is certainly rare and special, it has a heuristic function in Dreyfus's argument as it allows him to illustrate a universal dimension of agency. He writes: 'According to Merleau-Ponty, higher animals and human beings are always tending towards getting a *maximal grip* on their situation' (2002, 378, emphasis in original; cf. 2004, 137). The crucial point for Dreyfus is that this maximal or optimal grip need not be self-consciously represented to exert its pull on us:

> Merleau-Ponty is clear that for this movement toward maximal grip to take place, one does not need a representation of a goal. Rather, acting is experienced as a steady flow of skilful activity in response to one's sense of

the situation. Part of that experience is a sense of whether or not coping is going well. When one senses a deviation from the optimal body–environment gestalt, one's activity tends to take one closer to an optimal body–environment relationship that relieves the "tension." As Merleau-Ponty puts it, "our body is not an object for an 'I think,' it is a grouping of lived-through meanings that moves toward its equilibrium". (Dreyfus 2004, 137f.; cf. 2002, 378)

The take-home message here is this: when we engage in absorbed and skilful actions, we don't require a mental representation of our goal. Instead, our actions unfold as a continuous, skilful response to our practical understanding of the situation. This experience encompasses a sense that when our bodily relationship with the environment deviates from an optimal state, our actions naturally guide us back towards that equilibrium, alleviating the tension of the deviation. The specifics of this optimum state often remain implicit and unspoken; our body, attuned to the situation, simply strives to harmonize with it. This is apparently what Merleau-Ponty (1963, 153) wants to say by stating that our body, whether a system of motor or perceptual faculties, isn't an object for 'I think' but, rather, a collection of experienced meanings that moves toward its state of balance.

This powerful interpretation of Merleau-Ponty has had a tremendous impact not only in the phenomenological community but also in the philosophy of mind and perception more generally thanks to the sprawling debate it has provoked with John McDowell (see the 2007 special issue of the journal *Inquiry* and Schear 2013). The dispute, which revolves around the role of concepts in perception as well as the relationship between self-consciousness and agency, was rather frontal. While Dreyfus argues, as we've just seen, that our perceptual experiences are deeply rooted in our bodily engagement with the world and that we do not need to possess pre-existing goals or representations to non-conceptually make sense of our surroundings, McDowell contends that our perceptual experiences are permeated by concepts that shape our understanding of the world, including our practical ways of interacting with it.

In his response, Dreyfus brought in resources he found in Heidegger, and elaborated a reading largely converging with the Merleau-Ponty interpretation sketched out above. This time, the question concerning the putative role of representations is confronted by examining Heidegger's conception of the phenomenological 'as-structure' in the analyses carried out in the works of the 1920s. According to Dreyfus (2013), one reason to reject

McDowell's claim about the pervasiveness of concepts in experience is that everyday experience does *not* involve any 'as-structure': things do not show up *as* this or that in our 'everyday background coping practices' (2013, 19) such as sitting at our desk or picking up our morning mug. In skilful, absorbed coping, the objects simply 'withdraw' (2013, 19) from our contemplative gaze, for which reason he concludes that perceptual experience must be non-conceptual.[2]

In this passage, Dreyfus borrows the term 'withdrawal' from Heidegger, who explains in *Being and Time* that the objects making up our familiar environment (*Umwelt*) solicit our action without appearing thematically as what they are. In circumspection (*Umsicht*)—which is Heidegger's concept for the mode of awareness of our everyday preoccupation—things register in consciousness 'without our apprehending them in thought' (Dreyfus 2013, 18). However, as Dreyfus himself seems to recognize, this 'unthought' has a clear meaning for Heidegger: '"Unthought" means that it is not thematically apprehended for deliberate thinking about things' (1982, 163). For Heidegger, that objects 'withdraw' or go unnoticed in the kind of activity that characterizes the sphere of absorbed coping means that they do not appear thematically as such *in judgmental* or *deliberative consciousness*. But this is not exactly how Dreyfus reads that passage, whether here or elsewhere. Dreyfus's interpretation is much more radical, for he holds that familiar objects do not appear *at all* in everyday absorbed background coping. In his own words:

> To be true to the phenomenon we should add that when we are ready to leave a familiar room we not only do not need to *think that* the door affords going out. We need not even respond to the door *as* affording going out. Indeed, we needn't apprehend the door at all. From the perspective of the skilled coper absorbed in the solicitation of a familiar affordance, the affording object, as Heidegger puts it, simply 'withdraws'. We need not even be aware of the solicitations to go out *as* solicitations. (Dreyfus 2013, 18; cf. 2013, 34)

Inasmuch as objects solicit the absorbed coper in the usual, familiar way, he is directly drawn to act upon it in an unmediated, unthought, and

---

[2] In this contribution, Dreyfus glosses on the sentence 'absorbed coping' by gesturing at Heidegger's characterization of Dasein in the *History of the Concept of Time* as 'concerned absorption in the world' (Heidegger 1985, 197).

unthematized manner. For Dreyfus, this implies not only that perception must be non-conceptual but also that *such objects do not appear as such at all* in perceptual consciousness. It is *only* 'in the face of a disturbance' (2013, 19) or some kind of malfunctioning that everyday background objects reveal themselves as such. Dreyfus turns again to Heidegger's classical example of the hammer to make his point:

> In *Being and Time* Heidegger describes a case of hammering where the hammer does not withdraw, but where the hammer shows up *as* too heavy.... In the face of a disturbance, a distance opens up between the coper and what he is acting on which is bridged by a situation-specific concept. The coper can make the judgment that the hammer is too heavy. (Dreyfus 2013, 13)

However groundbreaking this interpretation might have been in some circles, it is both philosophically and philologically wrong.

First, Dreyfus's reading misses the target on philological grounds. Not only does Heidegger recognize that the phenomenological 'as-structure' is pervasive in experience, but the point of this analysis is precisely to argue that we need not wait that judgment or concept kick in to appreciate its crucial contribution. Thinking, deliberating, and judging only make *more* explicit what was *already* present *as such* in perceptual consciousness. This comes across very clearly both in his Marburg lectures of the mid-1920s and in *Being and Time* (1927). There it is argued that the objects of our surrounding world are typically experienced in a totality of involvements (*Bewandtnisganzheit*), where they appear in their usefulness or practical utility. Seeing something amounts to grasping how this thing functions in what Heidegger (1962, 167) calls a 'referential context of significance' (*Verweisungszusammenhang der Bedeutsamkeit*), where it reveals itself *as that which it is for*. Contrary to the standard empiricist picture, seeing something does *not* amount to seeing its physical or material properties; the analysis of Dasein's being-in-the-world shows, rather, that the objects of our perceptual world reveal themselves first and foremost in a meaningful network of relations in the form of *serviceability*, where they appear as that which they are *for*. The classic example here is that of the hammer, which Dreyfus gestures at and which manifests itself *as* practically available *for something*—for building a house, for instance; but, for Heidegger, even natural objects such as 'the sun' (1962, 103) or 'the south wind' (1962, 111) are ready-to-hand (*zuhanden*), inasmuch as they are first perceived in their function or relative utility.

In distinguishing the ready-to-hand (*Zuhandensein*) from the present-at-hand (*Vorhandensein*), and arguing for the derivative character of the latter, Heidegger wishes to demonstrate that we normally encounter things in a horizon of familiarity. This is well known. But there's another point to distil from these descriptions. Contrary to what Dreyfus suggests, our capacity to *perceive as* is *not* tied to representations and concept possession. The phenomenological as-structure does *not* only come about in our judicative or assertoric claims about the world. On the contrary, the whole point of Heidegger's analysis is to show that the phenomenological as-structure is *already* operative in prepredicative experience, structuring Dasein's pre-ontological understanding of its own being-in-the-world *before* Dasein makes any thematic statement about anything. The tools that are ready-to-hand (*zuhanden*) and make up our environment are *already* intentionally experienced as such; that is, they already have 'the structure *something as something* (*Etwas als Etwas*)' (1962, 189).[3] Still, the intentional structure of our prepredicative experience of worldly objects does *not* for that matter significantly differ from how the content of that experience is thought or expressed in predicative judgments (when it is). There is a structural similarity between the two. In Heidegger's view, there is a grounding–grounded relation at work here: it is precisely *because* 'the schema "something as something" has *already* been sketched out *beforehand* in the structure of one's prepredicative understanding' (1982, 411; my emphasis) that the content of my experience can *then* be expressed predicatively as such and such. In *Being and Time*, Heidegger makes this point in a remarkably clear fashion:

That which is understood gets articulated when the entity to be understood is brought close interpretatively by taking as our clue the 'something as something'; and this articulation [i.e. the as-structure] lies *before* [*liegt*

---

[3] Here's another passage from *Sein und Zeit* that supports this point: 'That which is disclosed in understanding—that which is understood—is already accessible in such a way that its "as which" can be made to stand out explicitly. The "as" makes up the structure of the explicitness of something that is understood. It constitutes the interpretation. In dealing with what is environmentally ready-to-hand by interpreting it circumspectively, we "see" it *as* a table, a door, a carriage, or a bridge; but what we have thus interpreted [*Ausgelegte*] need not necessarily be also taken apart [*auseinander zu legen*] by making an assertion which definitely characterizes it. Any mere prepredicative seeing of the ready-to-hand is, in itself, something which already understands and interprets' (Heidegger 1962, 189). See also Heidegger 1982, 71.

vor] our making any thematic assertion about it. In such an assertion the 'as' does not turn up for the first time; it just gets expressed for the first time, and this is possible only in that it lies before us as something expressible. The fact that when we look at something, the explicitness of the assertion can be absent, does not justify our denying that there is any articulative interpretation in such mere seeing, and hence that there is any as-structure in it. (1962, 190; emphasis in original)

Judgment, which is the dominant form of conceptual thinking, if not of philosophical thinking *tout court*, is in Heidegger's view a derivative mode of experience precisely because its possibility is grounded in our original intercourse or acquaintance with things.[4] Hence, while non-representational and non-conceptual in character, our interaction with our surrounding environment is still pervaded by self-conscious activity thanks to which things appears meaningfully, that is, as such. For Heidegger, the structural similarity between the predicative and prepredicative layers of intentional experience is ultimately explained by Dasein's self-understanding capacities: if the mere seeing of something already implies that it will appear *as* something or other, it is because that seeing already understands and interprets. (Of course, what holds for seeing holds *mutatis mutandis* for the other modes of experiencing.) Understanding for Heidegger is not just a mental or representational activity but, rather, a pervasive dimension of our being-in-the-world, and that's why he regards the phenomenological 'as-such' as the meaningful structure of Dasein's *whole* experiential life.[5] So much for the philological point.

Second, and more importantly still, Dreyfus's thesis is philosophically unjustifiable. For, manifestly, the kind of withdrawal Dreyfus has in mind here cannot be total. Whatever withdraws cannot be absent *tout court*;

---

[4] Further support for this foundational model can also be found in his 1928 lecture course on *The Metaphysical Foundation of Logic*, where Heidegger writes the following: 'Making statements about objective things [*Vorhandenes*] discovers them in a mode peculiar to it, namely, as a determining of something as something. This is the real sense of synthesis (*symploké, connectio*). "Something as something" is of itself irreducible but nevertheless founded. It is only possible on the basis of the disclosing that is already to be found in our having to do with things [*Umgang mit*]. This discovering performed in the proposition is always in reference to something; it is nurtured by the primordial discovering that there is our intercourse with things' (127f.)

[5] For a structurally analogous argument concerning the ubiquity of the phenomenological as-structure in Husserl, see Section 5.1.

otherwise, it would not solicit us at all.[6] Indeed, if the objects of my everyday life elicit my action and draw me to optimize my perspective or grip on them, they need to appear in some way or other, otherwise I would not even notice them, and this would render totally incomprehensible why I was drawn to act upon them in the first place.

As I see it, the root of the problem with Dreyfus's gloss on this issue is that he opposes presence and absence too crudely. As Heidegger shows in *Being and Time*, it is precisely *as absent* that daily objects manifest their *presence*. The hammer is not absent *simpliciter*; it manifests its presence by referring in a pragmatic or practical way to that which it is *for*. This is what he calls serviceability. So, it is true that the hammer withdraws from our contemplative gaze; but it does not withdraw completely. If it did, it would not be ready-to-hand, i.e. practically available for something. In distinguishing between *Zuhandensein* and *Vorhandensein*, Heidegger is *not* naively opposing presence and absence; he is, rather, distinguishing between two different modes of the presence of objects, both of which sharing a similar 'as-structure' of significance.

In *Being and Time*, Heidegger makes explicit the transition between these two modes of manifestation. As Dreyfus rightfully recognizes, it is only when it stops fulfilling its task properly that the hammer becomes an object for thought, that is to say, an object offered to a certain (theoretical) look. However, Heidegger does not think—as Dreyfus wants us to believe—that it is only *then* that it appears *as such*. It already did. The point is, rather, that the theoretical mode of encounter is not primordial. When the hammer is not where it is supposed to be, or when it breaks, our engaged attitude of absorbed coping suffers a certain modification. Things show up *differently*: we look at them *differently*. The passage from *Zuhandensein* to *Vorhandensein* therefore marks a change in the object's mode of presence, not a passage from absence to presence. For related reasons, the 'as-structure' undergoes a similar change: it does not enter on the scene; it just becomes more explicit.

---

[6] This is something Alva Noë (2012, 9) discusses as well in the first chapter of *Varieties of Presence*: 'even if they are withdrawn into the background', worldly objects 'are *there*, after all, for the agent; they are within reach; they are taken for granted, relied on. The baseball glove, and the hammer, like the view out the window, are always available.' This is why Noë insists that whatever recedes into the background is not simply absent; it is *present as absent*, or, better still, it is *present in and through absence*. Obviously, this view is fully compatible with the phenomenological analyses of Heidegger, from which, strangely enough, Noë distances himself for having missed that basic phenomenological truth (see 2012, 8–12).

Of course, the same must be true about perceptual optima: if they are to guide our actions at all, they must register as such in perceptual consciousness in some way or other. And while I agree with Dreyfus that they need not be represented as such in *reflective* consciousness, this does not in any way imply that they can bypass consciousness *tout court*. The weak spot of Dreyfus's interpretation lies in his homogeneous treatment of self-consciousness, which, *pace* Dreyfus, admits diverse modes. As we are going to see in the next chapter, skilful agents and perceivers rely heavily on *bodily* self-consciousness, which is recessive, implicit, and pre-reflective, but very much 'aware' all the same. As will be argued, only as such can it play the kind of normative role Dreyfus wants it to play.

2.2.2. Kelly on Perceptual Horizons

Sean Kelly, a former student of Dreyfus, developed another, related account of optimality that insists, besides our unreflective bodily engagement, on the notion of perceptual horizon. Kelly (2004) moves to thematic focus the problem of property constancy, that is, the problem of explaining our capacity to perceive a property as the same despite the variations across its appearances, and he suggests that Merleau-Ponty's analysis of object-perception in the *Phenomenology* provides a convincing solution. Kelly's interpretation revolves around the crucial importance of 'the indeterminacy of the visual background', which plays according to him 'a normative rather than a descriptive role in visual experience' (2004, 82). Specifically, Kelly argues that the indeterminacy of the visual background assumes a positive function in perception insofar as it provides perceptual experience with a norm. Take lighting. Kelly suggests that I experience the current lighting condition as deviating from a norm that forms the implicit background of my perception. This norm—optimal lighting condition—is one where the light is constant, that is, normally or uniformly distributed on the surface of things. Even if I now only indirectly experience it, my current experience of this optimum is such that it renders perceptually salient the ways in which I could reach 'a maximum grip' (90) on what I am currently looking at. The same point can be made with respect to colour: the 'real colour, implicitly referred to in every experience, is the constant colour I see the object *to be*. Yet it is experienced not as a determinate shade but, rather, as the background to the particular experience I'm having now. It is, in other words, like the normal context that reveals it, indeterminately present in every particular experience' (86). In short, the real colour is the constant colour, say 'red', not the specific shade of red that I am experiencing in the suboptimal context of my current perceptual state.

Central to Kelly's conception of property constancy is that their norms—optimal lighting, optimal colour, or optimal size, etc.—can't be experienced. These optima, which correspond to the object's 'real' or constant properties, rather form a normative horizon 'from which every perspective is felt to deviate' (95), but they themselves are not experienced in perceptual consciousness. '[T]he real colour is *never* determinately seen' (87; emphasis in original). This is because real properties are correlated to an ideal point of view, viz. a point of view that I, as an embodied being, cannot possibly adopt. Kelly calls it 'the view from everywhere' (92). As curious as it may sound, the view from everywhere is the vantage point constituted by the totality of all the *objects* surrounding the focal object as if *they* were looking at it. The totality of perspectives forming this horizon is, of course, unreachable all at once, but, according to Kelly, it still represents the ideal context that would give us a maximal grip on the scene. In short, it is 'the optimum perspective' (91), and, in Kelly's eyes, perception involves a form of 'normative self-referentiality' (2010, 150) such that 'I always experience myself to be drawn toward' this perspective where I would have 'a maximal grip on an object' (2010, 152). As a result, Kelly claims that 'experiencing the object itself involves optimizing the perceptual take that I have on it' (2010, 152).

This thought-provoking interpretation surely is inspired and attractive in many ways, but in the end it is not entirely persuasive either. It faces at least three sets of problems. The first—which has been raised by Matherne (2017)—is that if, as Kelly himself recognizes, 'the view from everywhere is not a view that *I* can have' (2004, 91), then it is not an experienceable point of view. As such, it could hardly correspond to Merleau-Ponty's *phenomenological* account; and it does not either. The view from everywhere rather belongs to what Merleau-Ponty calls Objective Thought, which he compares with 'the death of consciousness, since it congeals all of experience' (2012, 74). In positing its objects absolutely, that is, as existing in themselves or independently of observation, the objectivist fails to recognize that 'the origin of the object [lies] at the very core of our experience' (2012, 74). For this reason, Merleau-Ponty—who here adopts a transcendental perspective on things—thinks that our contribution to experience just cannot be bypassed. It should thus come as no surprise that this position isn't Merleau-Ponty's but, rather, serves him as a foil to present his own, which Samantha

Matherne meticulously reconstructs in her essay by drawing on various sources of the same period (2017, 695–705).[7]

The second problem with Kelly's interpretation is that he wrongly identifies the norm of perception with a particular point of view (be it the view from everywhere). As such, the norm appears to be disconnected from its context of emergence, and this does not correspond to how Merleau-Ponty saw things either. On the contrary, Merleau-Ponty holds that it belongs to the very 'nature of the perceived' to 'tolerate ambiguity, a certain "shifting" or "haziness" [*bougé*], and to allow itself to be shaped by the context' (2012, 11). And if the context is 'always noted in my perception' (2012, 314), then no perspective can be said to be optimal in itself, as Noë (2012, 52ff.) aptly remarks. The point is simple: if perception is necessarily contextual, then the norm of perception must be contextual too. We have seen earlier how this works with Husserl (cf. Section 1.2): perceptual norms vary according to the projects and activities *in the service of which* we put our perceptions into play. I can be looking for something (my wallet) or at something (a painting), and it is this interest that determines the norm of each perception, which may very well have different standards. (I don't need to have an *excellent* or *maximal* perspective on my wallet to fulfil my goal when I'm merely trying to retrieve it.) The point here is that the set of real properties Kelly has in view only serves as a norm in *certain specific* contexts—for instance, in a scientific or epistemological context where the goal of perception is to know the object in the totality of its determinations. In most everyday situations, however, something less than ideal perceptual conditions in this sense obtains. Merleau-Ponty has something analogous in view when he stresses the importance of distinguishing between a 'spatiality of situation' and a 'spatiality of position' (2012, 102). While our position in space is determined by a set of measurable objective coordinates, the spatiality of the perceiver is by and large defined by her intentional projects, practical interests, physical and bodily imperatives, acquired, ingrained

---

[7] This passage from *The Primacy of Perception* provides the strongest support for her interpretation: 'The perceived thing is not an ideal unity... it is rather a totality open to a horizon of an indefinite number of perspectival views which blend with one another according to a given style, which defines the object in question' (Merleau-Ponty 1964a, 16). Matherne's commentary opens onto a presentation of her own 'style-based' alternative reading of these issues, in which she argues that 'Merleau-Ponty is able to account for the normativity of perception by appealing to the object's style and our motor intentions that are sensitive to this style' (2017, 724). In what comes next, I won't discuss her account directly, but the argument that I develop throughout the book, which aims to show that perceptual norms emerge from the feedback/feedforward loop that ties together action and perception, understood here as a motor practice, largely concurs with Matherne's view. I will return to the specific question of style in Section 5.2.

habits, emotional connections, and the like. Consequently, her body becomes inherently aligned with these objectives, effectively coiling upon itself in pursuit of its objectives (cf. 2012, 103). Through various forms of 'bodily recognition' (2012, 81), we align ourselves with the 'practical meanings' made accessible by our circumstances and incorporate their significance into our own experience.

So, although Merleau-Ponty defines the optimum as a perceptual situation where a 'maximum of visibility' (2012, 316) can be experienced, it must be emphasized that this is a contextual, not an absolute, claim. More information is beneficial only to a certain point. Beyond a certain threshold, more details and differentiations make perception poorer, because things no longer appear as they should or as we expect them to be. The point is phenomenological: when things are saturated by perceptual details, they lose their meaning and become unrecognizable. We just can't see them for what they are. Even something as familiar as a living body can look so strange that its perceptual meaning remains concealed. Here's the relevant passage:

> Hence, we tend toward the maximum of visibility and we seek, just as when using a microscope, a better focus point, which is obtained through a certain equilibrium between the interior and the exterior horizons. A living body seen from too close, and lacking any background against which it could stand out, is no longer a living body, but rather a material mass as strange as the lunar landscape, as can be observed by looking at a segment of skin with a magnifying glass; and, seen from too far away, the living body again loses its living value, and is no longer anything but a puppet or an automaton. The living body itself appears when its microstructure is visible neither too much, nor too little, and this moment also determines its real form and size. The distance between me and the object is not a size that increases or decreases, but rather a tension that oscillates around a norm. (2012, 316)

The general principle of Merleau-Ponty's solution, which is inspired both by Husserl and gestalt psychology, is that perceptual experience is optimal when it achieves the appropriate balance between background and foreground, interior and exterior horizons, detail, and distance, etc., within a given contextual framework. However, given the number of our perceptual practices and the complex nature of our steadily changing contextual background, which often is also affectively charged (see Section 6.4), what optimality and optimal grip amount may vary substantially. Unsurprisingly, it has thus been analysed in vastly different fields and contexts—e.g. architecture (Rietveld and Brouwers 2017), disability studies (Salamon 2012), sports (Dreyfus 2002; Fuchs 2017b). In the chapters to come, our own interpretation will be spelled out in various philosophical contexts with respect to problems concerning agency (Chapter 3), empathy (Chapter 6), and collective intentionality (Chapter 7), to name but a few.

The third problem with Kelly's interpretation is the neglect of the question of time. The horizontality of perception is not just spatial; it is also temporal. The bodily tension that Kelly describes in terms of a normative deviation from the optimum is fundamentally temporal. The interplay of absence and presence, or determination and indeterminacy, that he describes only makes sense if it is embedded in a temporal horizon in which this unfolding takes place. This is something that Rietveld (2008) saw acutely. Leaning on Gibson's (1979) phenomenology of affordances[8] and Wittgenstein's (1967) notion of 'directed discontent' to describe the way in which skilled (or expert) individuals dynamically respond to the solicitations offered by their field of experience, Rietveld notes that 'being moved to improve is a transient state' (2008, 986), where perceivers *gradually* alter their grip on their environment to optimally fulfil their intentions. Even if they seem to occur almost immediately, the kind of adjustments that perceivers steadily make to improve their situations are not immediate but in fact reflect a temporal normative sensitivity that may reach the far experiential past. Rietveld (2008) illustrates this point by explaining how, over time, professional architects pick up and develop the aesthetic sensibility required by the performance of their duties from the professional community to which they belong. By integrating certain typical ways of acting and perceiving in their own practice, they acquire what is sometimes called a *second nature*: 'It has become a practice or custom due to this training and to a continuously refined history of lived experience. Due to all this largely unobtrusive and unnoticed disciplining of the body the architect has learned to see what is right and what is not' (Rietveld 2008, 989). For each experience, a temporal horizon thus lines the background of our

---

[8] James J. Gibson, a prominent figure in the field of ecological psychology, introduced the concept of 'affordances' to describe the relationship between an organism and its environment. According to Gibson (1979), affordances are possibilities or opportunities for action that the environment offers to an organism. Crucially, these possibilities for action are objective, but relational; that is, they are dependent not solely on the physical properties of objects but also on the capabilities and intentions of the agent or organism. See Section 5.2.2 for more details.

perceptions and recedes to make possible the continuous flow of our experiences and their appearance of immediacy. If this is correct, then it seems that the perceptual horizon that Kelly has in view is temporal just as much as it is spatial.

More on the questions of bodily self-consciousness, contextuality, and time will be said in the upcoming chapters, where my interpretation of Merleau-Ponty will be refined and my own account of perceptual optimality and experience will be further developed. For the time being, let us note that, given the importance that Husserl gave to the same three aspects of the question (see Chapter 1), there are, it seems, no fundamental disagreements between Husserl's and Merleau-Ponty's conception of optimality either. Minimally, let us say that their commonalities far exceed—both in numbers and importance—their discrepancies. In the next two sections, dedicated to Merleau-Ponty's account of illusions (Section 2.3) and hallucinations (Section 2.4), respectively, more important differences will begin to emerge. For while Husserl has the tendency to run the analysis of illusions and hallucinations together as entailing a retrospective correction of beliefs, Merleau-Ponty, who does not share Husserl's epistemic ambitions, submits them both to independent analyses.

2.3. The Challenge of Illusions

Of all the things to retain from Merleau-Ponty's analyses of illusions, the first and perhaps most fundamental one is his implicit reminder that a certain caution is called for when it comes to analysing 'illusions'. The word is an etiquette that, in the history of philosophy, refers to an assorted class of phenomena that just cannot all be lumped together. Like Austin (1962), who likely read the *Phenomenology* at least in part (Leeten 2021), Merleau-Ponty does not, for instance, treat perceptual constancies as illusory experiences. *Pace* Russell (1912) and Ayer (1940), these are perfectly normal perceptual phenomena, not perceptual errors without qualification. The kind of illusions that in the *Phenomenology* Merleau-Ponty deems worthy of their name can be split into two groups: while his attention is at times drawn to perceptual phenomena that are artificially 'constructed' (2012, 37) and specifically designed to trick us, like Zöllner's or Müller-Lyer's optical illusions, at other times he is concerned with phenomena that induce a momentary 'disequilibrium' (2012, 316) in the perceptual field without, however, having been voluntarily brought about by anyone, as for instance when I take a walk and 'see a large flat stone, which is in reality a patch of sunlight' (2012, 310). Whereas Merleau-Ponty agrees with Husserl that each class of phenomena is defined by a certain gap with respect to what I have thus far called 'perceptual norms', Merleau-Ponty, and this time in contradistinction to Husserl's largely undifferentiated treatment of illusions, is adamant that these two sorts of illusions call for different analyses.

When I perceptually take a patch of sunlight for a flat stone, I wrongly identify what I perceive. As a result, I can surely distinguish the two scenarios with respect to the epistemic norms of truth and falsity: when a new perception takes over, it makes sense to say that my initial perception was false, whereas the one that I now hold is true (at least until further notice). However, the distinction between both situations does not only, or even primarily, play out in judicative consciousness. More fundamentally, both experiences can be distinguished with respect to perceptual norms. From the phenomenological point of view, it is precisely *because* illusions transgress the norms governing normal perceptual experiencing that they motivate a belief-modification at the level of judgment. Given the experiential character of these norms, which are no accidents but constitutive of what illusions are, Merleau-Ponty asserts that 'the truth of perception and the falsity of illusion must each be marked by some intrinsic characteristic, for otherwise we would never have a consciousness of a perception or an illusion as such' (2012, 308). In identifying the patch of sunlight as a flat stone, it thus seems that I do not chiefly make an error of judgment. The mistaken identification is, rather, the *consequence* of a misperception of certain characteristics or features constitutive of regular perceptions.

But what are these characteristics exactly? Merleau-Ponty's analyses provide a two-part answer. First, illusions break with the *temporal laws* regulating normal (i.e. successful) experience. The patch of sunlight that I mistakenly take for a flat stone does not modify its appearance in progressive and expected ways when I move around it, or when the lighting conditions change. Its appearances do not cohere with one another; they are volatile, unstable, and to a certain degree unpredictable. Since they lack concordance, illusions 'never offer…the firm and definitive appearance that the thing, in the end, assumes' (2012, 22). Illusions are ephemeral or evanescent, for which reason they cannot secure or confirm the thing's identity. They are passing or transitory phenomena: with time, illusions vanish or dissolve themselves, and turn into new perceptions. As Merleau-Ponty writes, the illusion 'only disappears in order to leave a place for another perception that corrects it' (2012, 359f.).

Second, the fleeting temporality of illusions greatly impacts *agency*. While perceived objects admit all kinds of enduring bodily engagements (manipulation, handling, manoeuvring, etc.), illusions prevent these. True, I can 'see the illusory stone in the sense that my entire perceptual and motor field gives to the light patch the sense of a "stone on the lane." And I already prepare to sense this smooth and solid surface beneath my foot' (2012, 310). But this anticipation will soon be disappointed if acted upon. Rapidly, I realize that 'my body is not geared into it, and I cannot spread it out before myself through some exploratory movements' (2012, 310). What Merleau-Ponty is hinting at here is that illusory phenomena disrupt perception's intimate connection to action (see Chapter 3) because they do not accord with my habitual style of interaction with that kind of object (see Chapter 5). Illusions are marked by an 'I cannot': whereas typical experiences with stones imply a certain style of behaviour (I can hold them, throw them, scrutinize them, etc.), the experience of an illusory stone disrupts habitual bodily actions and unravels the natural fit between my embodied skills and the environment. For this reason, the illusion soon dissolves itself and the object acquires a new identity. Often, this change does not only impact my relation to that specific object but, rather, provokes a transformation of the whole perceptual situation, which exercises a different pull on me. New possibilities of action are now opened, while others are blocked or have become irrelevant: I stop walking in the direction of the stone and consider new paths or perhaps even a wholly new course of action. In sum, 'the illusory thing and the real thing do not have the same structure' (2012, 360). Since it lacks concordance, it unsettles the intentional loop between perception and action, thus explaining why illusions can't be acted upon in controlled ways. Consequently, illusory experiences can't be optimized without turning into perceptions either.

Artificial illusions like Zöllner's call for a wholly different type of analysis, however, for these are *lasting phenomena*. When you look at Zöllner's lines, it is difficult not to see them as converging even though they are parallel. The same holds for the Müller-Lyer's lines: the 'exceptional arrangement' (2012, 8) of the lines is such that the illusion of their being unequal typically persists even when perceivers know that they are equal. Phenomenologically, this type of illusion differs from the above-discussed examples, for they pose an entirely new challenge. The Müller-Lyer illusion works in the way it does not because it breaks with the norms of regular experiencing (it doesn't—more on this below) but, rather, because the apposition of these two figures provokes *a tension between two sets of norms*: objective norms of measurement, by means of which we know that the lines are equal, and norms of perception, which induce perceivers to treat them as unequal (see Benoist 2011, 115–17; 2013, 38–40, 89–95; 2021, 70–5, for a detailed defence of this point). The illusion, which resides in the conflict between these two sets of norms—one inherent to perception, one extrinsic to it—works the way it does because it partly relies 'on perspectives unavailable within illusory experience' (Morris 2015, 75).

The context of the experiential setting is of massive importance here, because we do not normally *see* things as being equal or unequal. When confronted with the experiment, we may well recognize that the lines are equal even though this equality can hardly be viewed. But norms of measurements are exogenous to experience. They may be applied to it from without, but they do not belong to the experience itself. Phenomenologically speaking, then, Merleau-Ponty correctly holds that 'the two straight lines...are neither equal nor unequal' (2012, 6). If we consider the lines from the phenomenological standpoint as the perceptual gestalts that they are, 'they cease to be equal without thereby becoming unequal—they become "different"' (2012, 11). In other words, if we shovel aside the objective set of norms of measurement unnaturally induced by the experiential setting, the question of the lines being equal or unequal is irrelevant, that is, foreign to the experience.

Phenomenologically, there is another point worth raising. If we bracket these norms of measurement, it is not at all clear that the Müller-Lyer illusion really is an illusion, for it is precisely *as uneven* that the lines *do* look and indeed *should* look to anyone in normal psychophysical conditions in the Western world.[9] The victim of a Müller-Lyer type of illusion still exercises her perceptual skills normally and competently; she sees what she is supposed to see. In that sense, the 'illusion' is in fact 'only a particular kind of perception' (Benoist 2021, 75). What happens is simply that, with the addition of the arrows at the end of both lines, the gestalt possesses a new *objective* feature or property, which induces every 'normal' perceiver to judge that the lines are unequal. Precisely for this reason, their look is

---

[9] I add 'in the Western world' because the Müller-Lyer illusion appears not to be equally effective across cultures. Around the turn of the twentieth century, W. H. R. Rivers (1901) noted that indigenous people of Australia's Murray Island were less susceptible to the illusion than were city-dwelling Europeans. Rivers suggested that this difference may be because Europeans live in urban environments, which are more rectilinear. For a more detailed explanation, see Gregory 1966.

something that can be communicated and intersubjectively validated, just like any perception.

Various other 'illusions' call for the same kind of explanation. Take the so-called ventriloquism effect, in which the perceived location of a sound source is misattributed to the location of a visual stimulus (Howard and Templeton 1966). While one may very well describe the phenomenon as a crossmodal illusion in the sense that there really is a mislocation of the apparent sound source, there is a sense in which it is not an illusion at all. In a cinema, it is not only perfectly *normal*, that is *expected*, to experience the voice of the actors as coming from their mouth instead of from the speakers around me; it also clearly benefits my overall experience of the movie that I do so (O'Callaghan 2012). Insofar as the effect is anticipated by the perceiver and contributes to enhancing the coherence of her experience of the movie, we cannot without further ado describe this experience as illusory. Noë raises a similar point about the rubber hand illusion (Botvinick and Cohen 1998), a phenomenon where a person experiences a sense of ownership and embodiment over a rubber hand that is visually and tactically stimulated in synchrony with their own hidden hand, and which leads to the sensation that the rubber hand is part of their own body. As Noë aptly remarks, in a way 'there's no illusion' here either, 'or rather, the mechanisms at work in this illusion, if we want to call it that, are those of normal, successful perception' (Noë 2009, 74; I return to this issue below in Section 4.3).

The lesson to draw from all this is that *what is deemed illusory and what isn't very much depends on the norms we use,* that is, on the relevant *concept* of perception we have in view. Whereas mundane or everyday illusions (like the patch of sunlight that I misidentify as a stone) disrupt the laws of perceptual experiencing (concordance and optimality), artificially constructed illusions (like Müller-Lyer) result from a tension between normative perceptual patterns, which can be intact, and norms of measurements, with which they are hardly compatible. In all this, illusion comes out as a parasitic concept: it only makes sense against the background of a specific set of norms, which specifies the concept of perception at play.[10] Whence, again, the importance of the context and the interest (see Sections 1.2 and 2.2).

---

[10] In Section 2.5 it will be shown that illusions are parasitic in another, more fundamental sense, for they presuppose perception.

2.4. Hallucinations as Interruptions

The main reason for treating illusions and hallucinations separately is that the kinds of hallucinations that interest Merleau-Ponty are *pathological*. Whereas some contemporary philosophers of perception like to analyse the *concept* of hallucinations, sometimes even entertaining the possibility of 'perfect hallucinations' (Martin 2004; for a criticism of this perspective, see Farkas 2013 and Benoist 2017) as kinds of experiences that are subjectively indistinguishable from perceptions, Merleau-Ponty is primarily interested in real, clinical cases. He draws our attention to four such cases (2012, 349f.). First, Merleau-Ponty discusses schizophrenics who suffer tactile hallucinations of injections or electric currents and mention their awareness that the shocks were, in fact, induced by their own doctor. Second, there is the mention of another schizophrenic patient who reports seeing a man standing in his garden beneath his window and is astonished when a man wearing the same clothes and adopting the same posture is actually standing at the exact same spot in the garden. Thirdly, Merleau-Ponty speaks of a woman suffering from auditory hallucinations and who reports hearing inner voices; she is then played similar voices on a recording, and immediately notices the difference. Finally, he analyses an alcoholic patient who takes his doctor's hand for a guinea pig and instantly reacts when a real guinea pig has been placed in the doctor's hand.

The first thing Merleau-Ponty notices in all four cases is that the hallucinating subjects *can* actually distinguish their hallucinations from their perceptions (2012, 349). Delusional patients have deceiving experiences and receive medical treatment precisely *because* they are aware that the experiences that they have respect neither the norms of governing normal perception nor the intersubjective norms of truth or correctness. This ambiguity, which Merleau-Ponty deems constitutive of hallucinatory phenomena, brings him to reject both the empiricist's interpretation of hallucinations, which attempts to explain its causal origin from sensation, and the opposing intellectualist's interpretation, which reduces it to a false belief or a mistaken judgment. As Merleau-Ponty observes, 'although the hallucination is not sensory, it is even less a judgment' (2012, 357). Both views, which together form what Merleau-Ponty calls Objective Thought, are untrue to the lived experience of the hallucinatory subject since both fail to capture the inherent conflict which she is steadily confronted with.

If we pay attention to the phenomenology, Merleau-Ponty characterizes this conflict in very general terms first by describing the tension towards the world that inhabits the hallucinatory subject. Hallucinations appear to 'play out on a different stage than that of the perceived world; it is as if they are superimposed' (2012, 355). The hallucinated world seems to be 'superimposed' upon the real one because hallucinations are characterized by a phenomenology that marks a gap with respect to the norms of regular perceptual experiencing. This gap manifests itself in at least five ways.

1. Since perception possesses a horizon, it generates expectations, which are either fulfilled or not by the future course of experience. Hallucinations, however, are *discordant experiences*: they disrupt the horizon of the perceptual world and interrupt the experiential flow. Since the hallucination phenomenon 'is not part of the world, that is, it is not *accessible*, there is no definite road that leads from this phenomenon to all the other experiences of the hallucinating subject' (2012, 354; emphasis in original). And this is precisely how the hallucination presents itself. *The hallucination interrupts the cohesiveness of the perceptual world and disturbs its meaningful fabric* because it 'lacks the plenitude and the internal articulation' (2012, 355) of the perceived thing.
2. Secondly and relatedly, hallucinatory phenomena have no profiles: 'hallucinations are not things with many facets, but rather ephemeral phenomena, injections, shocks, explosions, drafts, hot or cold flashes, sparks, points of light, glimmers, or silhouettes' (2012, 356). Whereas perceptual and illusory things have concordant profiles in virtue of which they are constitutively open to being explored by perceptual agents, *hallucinations lack 'depth'* (2012, 338; my emphasis).
3. This deficit of depth or thickness manifests itself—thirdly—in their temporal character. Contrary to perceived objects, which have a structure with an open-ended horizon, *hallucinations are experienced as temporary lapses in perceptual consciousness*. Much like illusions, the 'hallucinatory thing is not, like the real thing, a deep being that contracts a thickness of duration in itself; the hallucination is not, like perception, my concrete hold upon time within a living present' (2012, 355). Since it lacks concordance, 'the hallucination slides across time, just as it slides across the world' (2012, 355).
4. Fourthly, this lack of temporal thickness in turn explains why the hallucinatory thing, too, prevents its being probed and manipulated lastingly by the experiencing subject. *No lasting action with respect to the hallucinatory thing is possible*. Hallucinatory phenomena can very

well motivate or provoke certain actions and behaviours, such as when, in the woods, I hallucinate a wolf and run away. However, sooner or later, this impression will disappear, and the hallucination will dissolve itself. In brief, in hallucinatory experiences, the motivating loop between action and perception is disrupted.[11] Since hallucinatory subjects lost their grip on the perceptual world, they can neither optimize nor self-correct their experience.

5. Finally, the relationship to others, who in normal perceptual experiencing can corroborate and validate the objective character of perception, is strongly impaired for delusive patients. The 'hallucinating subject makes use of being in the world in order to carve out a private world within the common world' (2012, 358). But since her experience is private, or at least not easily 'accessible' to 'healthy subjects' (2012, 354f.), *the delusional subject cannot successfully engage in shared practices or collaborative efforts* (be they linguistic, perceptual, or whatever). As a result, delusional subjects often make eccentric assumptions about the world and are commonly immune to revision by contrary evidence. Their perspective on things is inflexible, or self-enclosed, and the expertise of the psychotherapist is usually needed for it to be disentangled.[12]

More will be said on illusions and hallucinations in the upcoming chapters, but these analyses should suffice to make compelling the view that, from the phenomenological perspective, there are important differences between the experiential style of perception, illusions, and hallucinations. Very

---

[11] This is what Romdenh-Romluc (2009) is getting at when she writes that 'the power of summoning...functions normally or properly when it is exercised' by normal perceptual agents 'in response to the prompting of the world. For Merleau-Ponty, hallucinations result from the "running wild" of this power' (80). For the hallucinatory subject, 'appearances are summoned in the absence of appropriate worldly cues' (80), thereby explaining their incapacity to respond adequately to worldly solicitations.

[12] Shared delusions are possible, but rare. As Ritunnano and Bortolotti (2022) assert, the content of delusions is normally idiosyncratic, that is, unique to the person reporting it and unlikely to be shared by the other members of the person's social groups. Although people in the same religious community may share an overarching belief (say, in an all-powerful God), the person with religious delusions will have specific beliefs that other people from the same community reject, such as the belief that God assigned to her a special mission. Sometimes, two persons may have largely converging delusional experiences, but it is rare, and the convergence is never total, which is why delusional subjects cannot *fully* engage in shared practices or collaborative efforts. In this case, hallucinations seem to have an 'in-between' status: they are neither strictly private nor strongly objective.

generally, my contention is that *these phenomena mainly differ from one another in the ways in which they either meet or fail to meet the norms governing the perceptual world.* For Merleau-Ponty, the key lies in his characterization of intentional experience in terms of questions and answers, or solicitations and responses. Perceptual experience is normative precisely because it is a response to a worldly solicitation (2012, 70, 140, 222, 323). The world of perception solicits us, and it is through the ways we enact our response (or fail to do so) that experience displays its normative character. Crudely speaking, victims of illusions and hallucinations fail to act or speak suitably with respect to perceived things and events; that is, their motor or verbal behaviour marks a certain *écart* with respect to the kind of actions and interactions prompted by normal perceptions. This gap, which I have briefly sketched out in five different ways above, is not merely contingent; it is, rather, constitutive of the hallucinatory phenomenon itself.

2.5. The World as the Bedrock of Experience

Together with Chapter 1, the preceding four sections intimate that Husserl's and Merleau-Ponty's conceptions of perceptual intentionality converge insofar as they both see it as being inherently normative. This is not to say that there are no differences between their analyses, or that these differences are not significant. Still, there are methodological reasons that explain why they came to endorse a relatively close view on perception, and this is what I would like to discuss in this and the following section.

To begin with, it appears that the normative account of perception analysed thus far can only be disclosed within the transcendental reduction (see Sections 1.4 and 6.4), which both thinkers used, albeit in different ways and for different purposes (see Heinämaa 2002; Smith 2005). This comes as no surprise. For even if Merleau-Ponty is at times critical of Husserl, especially of the evolution of his thinking during the transcendental period, it remains that he himself took up—albeit always in a modified way—many of the latter's core transcendental claims and motives, including not only the reduction (Kee 2020) but also the constitution (Zahavi 2002), the operative intentionality (Landes 2018), and the transcendental ego (which, *pace* Inkpin 2017, is not incompatible with Merleau-Ponty's conception of embodied subjectivity). In this context, it's no wonder that Merleau-Ponty himself came to espouse a transcendental conception of perception

(Gardner 2013, 2015; Matherne 2014, 2016; Mooney 2023). While this label certainly needs qualification, many things speak in favour of it. As we've seen earlier, Merleau-Ponty criticizes Objective Thought precisely for failing to recognize that 'the origin of the object [lies] at the very core of our experience' (2012, 74). Since perception is not 'one of the facts that happens in the world' (2012, 215), it needs the contribution of the subject, which is a recurring theme in the *Phenomenology*.[13] While certainly more discreet, this position was nonetheless firmly in place as soon as in *The Structure of Behaviour*, where Merleau-Ponty held—despite the broadly naturalistic outlook of the book—that 'Perception is not an event of nature' (1963, 145). As a result, the whole programme of the early 1940s, which revolved around the question of the primacy of perception, was transcendental (for a defence of this kind of reading, see Romdenh-Romluc 2018; Berendzen 2023).

As transcendental, the real (thing) is essentially intertwined with the embodied ego. While Husserl conceives of being and consciousness as forming an *irreducible structure*, he also (in)famously stressed the asymmetry between both terms of the correlation in *Ideas I*, thereby provoking all kinds of interpretations and misunderstandings on the nature of his transcendental-phenomenological idealism (for an overview of the alternative readings, see Zahavi 2017). Merleau-Ponty was certainly more prudent in that respect. If anything, Merleau-Ponty may at times be guilty of the reverse claim, as he increasingly emphasized the ontological weight of the *world* in his phenomenology, especially in later texts like *Visible and Invisible* or *Eye and Mind*, but we can set this question aside here. In the *Phenomenology of Perception*, the correlational structure, that is, the body–world intertwinement, is firmly in place, and what Merleau-Ponty calls 'perception' describes a relation to the world beyond which no experience is at all possible since it 'is our existence' (Landes 2018, 371).

The implication for the question we are pursuing in this chapter is straightforward: *all* perceptual phenomena—be they illusory, hallucinatory, or not—presuppose a relation to the world, which is the bedrock of all experience. On this score, Husserl and Merleau-Ponty are again, by and

---

[13] Here are a couple of other passages supporting a transcendental reading of the *Phenomenology*: 'External perception and the perception of one's own body vary together because they are two sides of a single act' (2012, 211); 'The thing can never be separated from someone who perceives it; nor can it ever actually be in itself because its articulations are the very ones of our existence, and because it is posited at the end of a gaze or at the conclusion of a sensory exploration that invests it with humanity' (2012, 334). One last: 'Thus, the thing is the correlate of my body and, more generally, of my existence of which my body is merely the stabilized structure' (2012, 334).

large, in agreement. This, however, is not how everyone sees things. In the context of a discussion about the conjunctive or disjunctive nature of experience, Claude Romano (2015) accuses Husserl of falling prey to the threat of scepticism insofar as, within the framework of transcendental phenomenology, 'the possibility of an isolated doubt entails the possibility of universal doubt' (288). This, of course, is an unhappy outcome for any theory of perception, and he argues on that basis for the superiority of Merleau-Ponty's model, whose realist phenomenology would be better suited than Husserl's to avoid the kind of sceptical problems that this kind of position leads to.[14]

Staiti (2015) concisely and by and large correctly already responded to this criticism: for Husserl, illusions and hallucinations are 'unmasked (*entlarvte*) phenomena' (2015, 137f.); that is, they are the conscious outcome of a correction of conflicting beliefs.[15] This correction of beliefs, which is rooted in experience and concerns the ontological status of the thing, does not imply anything about the existence of the world. This is because, from the phenomenological standpoint, the possibility of global illusions and/or hallucinations is a non-starter. For Husserl, the existence of the world just can't be doubted. It is a fact; it may very well be 'an irrational fact' (Husserl 1997, 289), but it is still a fact. In Husserl's eyes, perceptions, illusions, and hallucinations alike thus presuppose a reference to an indefeasible *Urglaube* concerning the existence of a world. Whether veridical, fictive, imaginary, oneiric, illusory, or hallucinatory, 'experience' in the broadest sense 'is the force which guarantees the existence of the world' (1997, 290). For Husserl, then, the kind of 'anomalous appearances' that constitute illusions and hallucinations only make sense against the 'background of continuously valid and believed realities' (1997, 288) that make up our world. In the very last section of *Thing and Space*, Husserl sums up his thought on this by asserting that the 'non-being' of the hallucinatory thing 'takes its measure from Being', and only makes sense as a 'conflict against pre-given Being' (1997, 249).

---

[14] Ultimately, Romano (2015) shows himself to be dissatisfied with Merleau-Ponty too and argues for a broadly Heideggerian approach to perception (chs 16–18) that I won't discuss any further.

[15] Zahavi (2017) points out the limit of this paradigm and contends, quite justly I think, that 'it is not obvious that hallucinations are only recognized as such after the fact, at least not if we are talking about real hallucinations' (88 n. 5). In all fairness, one must recognize that Husserl is not Merleau-Ponty, and that real (or clinical) hallucinations were not Husserl's main concern. In that sense, Zahavi's critique does not necessarily alleviate the validity of Staiti's interpretation, which was primarily driven by exegetical concerns. It does, however, point to the limit of Husserl's analyses on this specific aspect of the question.

For this reason, and regardless of how we may conceive of them, experiences of illusions and hallucinations cannot possibly entail the inexistence of the world. On the contrary, they are, to varying degrees and diverse ways, world-involving (Hopp 2011, 152–60; Drummond 2012, 115–33; Zahavi 2017, 88–90; Benoist 2013, 75–81, 2017, 223ff.). They are events *of* this world, both in the trivial sense that they appear *in* this world and in the less trivial sense that they tell us something about how we *conceive* of our 'world', which is a *normally regulated* lifeworld.[16] Our experience and knowledge of the world, including our knowledge of and experience with others, rest on the conviction that the world is continually there for us. Husserl's response to the sceptics lies precisely therein: experience and knowledge would not be possible at all if we did not presuppose a 'world that is already valid for me' (Husserl 1975, 135f.). That's why the world itself, or, rather, our irrepressible faith in it, has normative import in Husserl. This is something that Merleau-Ponty (1968) picked up: 'When Husserl speaks of a "norm," ... [o]ne sees then that the norm ... derives from a total phenomenon which is finally the "world"' (196). Although this indefeasible trust in the existence of the world is not a sufficient condition for having worldly knowledge, for there are the structures of the lifeworld that need to be in place for securing knowledge (Hartimo 2018), Husserl, like Merleau-Ponty, regarded it as a necessary condition (see Dastur 1994; Hopp 2018). *Pace* Romano (2015), then, and regardless of the other disparities we may identify between both thinkers, there is no reason to *oppose* Husserl and Merleau-Ponty in the way they deal with the sceptical menace. On the contrary, the notion of perceptual faith which Merleau-Ponty develops *in extenso* in the first part of *The Visible and the Invisible*, but which is already massively at work in *Phenomenology of Perception*, aims to convey the idea that the existence of the world is a certitude, a thesis that, as we've just seen, is also explicitly endorsed by Husserl (and Wittgenstein[17]).

---

[16] This is, incidentally, precisely what the famous thought experiment of *Ideas I* is supposed to show in a negative way by showing the consequence of a non-regulated world-consciousness. On the possibility of a worldless consciousness, see Jacobs (2018) and Crowell (2013, 72–6).

[17] In Wittgenstein's so-called 'hinge epistemology' (e.g. as displayed in *On Certainty* (1972)), engaging in a meaningful process of seeking knowledge inherently involves assuming certain things as true. Wittgenstein contends that if we were to constantly question every foundational belief, we would undermine the possibility of acquiring any knowledge whatsoever. These two passages are very explicit on this point: 'If you are not certain of any fact, you cannot be certain of the meaning of your words either... If you tried to doubt everything you would not get as far as doubting anything. The game of doubting itself presupposes certainty' (§§114–15); 'That is to say, the *questions* that we raise and our *doubts* depend on the fact that some propositions are exempt from doubt, are as it were like hinges on which those turn... But it isn't that the

Moreover, the claim that *the world itself is the absolute bedrock of experience* does not only concern the possibility of perceptual knowledge. Like Husserl, Merleau-Ponty holds, rather, that the existence of the world must be presupposed by *all forms* of experience, *including deceptive experiences like illusions and hallucinations*, which can only be evidenced as false by reiterating their irreducible connection to the world. This passage is eloquent in this respect:

> Each perception, although always potentially 'crossed out' and pushed over to the realm of illusions, only disappears in order to leave a place for another perception that corrects it. Of course, each thing can, *après coup*, appear uncertain, but at least it is certain for us that there are things, that is, that there is a world. To wonder if the world is real is to fail to understand what one is saying, since the world is not a sum of things that one could always cast into doubt, but precisely the inexhaustible reservoir from which things are drawn. The perceived, taken in its entirety, along with the worldly horizon *that simultaneously announces its possible disjunction and its eventual replacement by another perception*, does not fully trick us. There could be no error where there is still no truth, but rather reality, and where there is still no necessity, but rather facticity. (Merleau-Ponty 2012, 359–60; emphasis in original)

Merleau-Ponty thus agrees with Husserl that not only perceptions but illusions and hallucinations, too, are world-revealing or world-involving. They are perhaps false, epistemically speaking, but they are still revelatory of the world in that they both confirm (in different ways) its existence. This is what Merleau-Ponty means when he affirms that perception and hallucination are 'modalities of a single primordial function' (2012, 358). Evidently, the same point can be made with regard to illusions:

---

situation is like this: We just *can't* investigate everything, and for that reason we are forced to rest content with assumption. If I want the door to turn, the hinges must stay put' (§§341–3). According to this point of view, the regression of reasons and the production of justifications have an end. When we reach this level, we find—and I quote again here—'something that lies beyond being justified or unjustified; as it were, as something animal' (§359) or 'primitive' (§475). Since it was first published only in 1969 (although written in 1950/1), Merleau-Ponty could hardly have read Wittgenstein's *On Certainty*, but the very first footnote of *The Visible and Invisible*, which bears on the notion of perceptual faith, has a strikingly similar tone: 'Notion of faith to be specified. It is not faith in the sense of decision but in the sense of what is before any position, animal and [?] faith' (1968, 3 n. 1).

For if we speak of illusion, this is because we have previously recognized illusions, and we could only do so in the name of some perception that, at that very moment, vouched for itself as true, such that doubt, or the fear of being mistaken, simultaneously affirms our power of unmasking error and could thus not uproot us from the truth. We are in the truth, and evidentness is 'the experience of truth.' (2012, lxxx)

The kind of 'truth' Merleau-Ponty talks about in this passage is not the epistemic notion of truth, which is always about some particular being or other, but the truth of the perceptual world that the notion of perceptual faith hints at and reveals. In this context, Antich (2021, 123–46) justly argues that perceptual faith is not an epistemic notion (for it can't be justified) but an *ontological* one. It is, one could also say, an *existential* one, for it concerns the relation between perception and the world, viz. the structure of existence within which there can be particular ontic experiences and epistemic truths. That's why Merleau-Ponty can write without contradiction that 'There is an absolute certainty of the world in general, but not of any particular thing' (2012, 311).

The similarities between Husserl's and Merleau-Ponty's normative conception of the perceptual realm appear to go far: not only have they developed detailed phenomenological analyses of perceptual phenomena in terms of conforming or diverging from perceptual norms, but the phenomenological method they both had recourse to led them to espouse a strikingly similar metaphysical picture (from which, it is true, Merleau-Ponty will more and more take his distance). As we are going to see in the concluding section, the real opposition is not between Husserl and Merleau-Ponty but between the intentional and the new realist points of view.

2.6. Conclusion

In the perspective of the realist, the problem of phenomenology is clear enough: since phenomenology studies the (immanent) laws for the interconnection of lived experiences, it is not concerned with the world itself but solely with our *experience* of the world. In the idiom deployed in this chapter, that our experience of the world is regulated according to normative laws has no bearing whatsoever on being itself. This, it would seem, is the problem of all philosophy of correlation (Meillassoux 2006), phenomenology being here only a case in point. Of course, the critics insist that *there is* a difference between reality and intentionality, and protest that phenomenologists are committed to flatten, if not erase, it purely and simply.

This objection came from different directions. It was first formulated very early on *within* the confines of the phenomenological tradition with Husserl's own students, Reinach (1989) in particular. As we discussed above (cf. Section 2.5), the same critique surfaced again more recently from the pen of Claude Romano (2015). Outside phenomenological circles, the most virulent version of this criticism to surface in recent years came from Jocelyn Benoist, a former phenomenologist. Most if not all of Benoist's recent works articulate in one way or another the distinction between reality and intentionality, which is for Benoist absolute or categorical.[18] Naturally, Benoist insists on the precedence of the former over the latter: 'The grammar of representation presupposes that of reality, not the other way around' (2017, 279f.). Faced with this observation, there is, according to Benoist, no way out; we must leave phenomenology behind and embrace realism, viz. contextual realism, which is exactly what he did (2022, chs 1–3; 2021, ch. 5; 2017, chs 7–8; 2013, ch. 3).

As I see it, all phenomenologists are sensitive to the difference between reality and intentionality, even if they don't necessarily agree on how to conceive either term. But since Benoist's objection targets what he considers to be *the* defining feature of intentionality, and therefore of phenomenology, giving voice to his criticism will still be helpful both for defining my own endeavour and for clarifying further the relation that holds between reality and normativity. What is this feature? The intrinsic connection between intentionality and normativity. Beyond the specific ways in which they deploy the phenomenological method, we have seen that both Husserl and Merleau-Ponty espouse a form of intentionalism and are, *for that very reason*, committed to the normative point of view sketched out this far. On this view, the real, conceived as the correlate of consciousness, is always already experienced as meaningful, and therefore as norm-governed. This means that there is no description, or in general no grasp on the real, that does not presuppose a form of normative commitment (but this does not, just as such, contradict realism, of course).

---

[18] Here's a revealing passage: 'Philosophically, we must clearly distinguish between what belongs to representation and what belongs to the thing, between intentionality and reality. This is the fundamental difference, in the precise sense of a difference between being and logos, between what is and how we determine it by speaking and thinking about it' (2017, 280; throughout, the translations of Benoist are my own).

One way to get at this is to consider the diversity of ways of orienting oneself in the world, including the ways of determining the 'reality' of this or that thing as such or such. The real is what it is, certainly; it is what I see as soon as I open my eyes. But when reality perceptually manifests itself as such to consciousness, it is, so to speak, elevated to the rank of object: it is identified as this being and not that other. The sensible plays a central role in this work of objectification. Not only do we perceive the real by becoming familiar with some of its sensible aspects, but these aspects are also constitutive of the identity of the perceived.[19] Not that such aspects are enough to give it its identity, of course; for there to be an object, these aspects will also have to be experienced in a diversity of acts. The normativity inherent in the concept of object presupposes a gap with the factual that consciousness can fill. By repeatedly experiencing some of these aspects, the real is instituted as a 'pole of identity'. As argued for in Chapter 1, the phenomenological object is 'a pole of identity' (Husserl 1960, 45), or an infinite series of concordant profiles (Husserl 2014, 71–85), which Husserl conceives as a 'unity of synthesis' (1960, 41). An object is nothing other than the concept of such an identity, to which Benoist correctly attaches the possibility of being named as such in statements: 'It is a part, or a face of the concept of perception that it can be expressed in such statements' (2017, 271).[20]

But it is not the only one. Phenomenology has not limited itself to displaying this so-called 'cognitive' aspect of perception (which does not mean that it has never done so). It is even one of the defining features of phenomenology to attempt to transform, reform, or at least broaden this concept of object, which phenomenologists across generations have deemed

---

[19] In Husserlian phenomenology, the synthesis of identity operates at the sensible level through the perceived appearances. While this insight was already at work in the *Logical Investigations* (2001b, 283–6), in his genetic phenomenology of the 1920s Husserl follows the synthetic process back to its origins in the lowest level of temporal organization. This is the central topic of Section 5.1.

[20] The idea is not new. Benoist already argued in *Le bruit du sensible* that the identification of the perceived as such '1) is always linked to the context in which it makes sense to say that such and such a thing is perceived, 2) precisely expressed by the way in which it would be appropriate to say what is perceived, in this case' (2013, 62). The thesis, which is taken up and extended in *L'adresse du réel*, leads Benoist to argue that 'to attribute to perception a real object means precisely to take a step into the "conceptual" space' (2017, 273). This idea, which represents an important (but not substantial) aspect of John McDowell's thesis (Benoist 2017, 265–71), would also be true for 'phenomenology' insofar as it would operate with a similar concept of perception: by saying that 'perception is always perception of something', phenomenology would only 'unfold the properly conceptual nature of what is called "perception"' (2017, 272), i.e. it would do nothing else than reiterate the idea that the object of perception is normed insofar as it is reiterable as such in the logos.

irreducible to an object of mental attitudes. On the contrary, phenomenology was quick to recognize the 'practical identity' of perceived objects, even affirming on occasion the priority of this form of identity over the classical cognitivist one. If this notion of practical identity is certainly less obvious to spot in the early Husserl, it is powerfully at work from *Thing and Space* (1907) onward as well as in Heidegger, Merleau-Ponty, and most enactivists and American pragmatists, among others.

This is because our forms of engagement with the real are multiple, and in most contexts the question of the logos of the thing simply does not arise. The object of perception is not only the object that I talk about (although I can do that too); the object of perception is just as much the one with which I interact or 'transact', to use Dewey's expression. Often, the identity of the object is played out at this level. This means that the identity of the thing can also be crystallized through the indefinite (but not infinite) quantity of possibilities of interaction that it allows or makes possible. Consider this chair on which I am currently sitting. It is only insofar as it provides me with the opportunity to sit each time that it has the identity that it has (for me). It is not as a being endowed with speech and language that I give it its identity as a chair each time; in the context in which it most often appears, this chair is first and foremost what offers me the possibility of sitting each time. It is insofar as it performs this (practical) function that it is this thing and not that other thing. Note, however, that this does not stand in contradiction with realism. The claim is not that the chair exists *because* it affords sitting. Of course, the chair can only afford sitting because it exists. But the chair owes its practical identity to its users: it exists *as a chair*, that is, *as a practical object that affords sitting* only in relation to our capacities. This comes across very clearly in Gibson, whose realism about affordances is coupled with their being relational: affordances are not simply objective; they are also self-referential properties. This means that those objective features of the environment that are perceived as affordance are grasped in conjunction with the perceptual agent's skills and abilities. That's how they elicit different responses from the agent based on their situation and their abilities. In this setting, the distinction between reality and intentionality is *not* blurred.

We find similar ideas in Husserl, Heidegger, and Merleau-Ponty. Indeed, one of the important legacies of post-Husserlian phenomenology lies precisely in this powerful attempt to think coherently about the question of the identity of the object of perception in its constitutive relations to notions like embodied consciousness or motor intentionality, which are found in germ in *Thing and Space* before being developed more systematically in *Phenomenology of Perception* (see Sections 3.3 and 5.2.2). One of the lessons to be drawn from these analyses is to recognize that the traditional characterization of object as a reiterable identity in logos does not exhaust the notion of object. Just as it is true that this or that sensible aspect opens up the possibility of the object being described in a certain way, it is also true that this same aspect may also allow, on other occasions, certain possibilities of actions or interactions through which its identity as an object will be revealed or confirmed. In certain contexts, the priority of this 'practical dimension' seems difficult to contest, as is the case, for example, for the jazz improviser who hears this or that segment as being conducive to his intervention, or as a sign that marks the resumption of the theme or melody. But we can leave jazz aside; the general lesson here is this: perception not only opens the possibility of thematizing being as such or such but also opens a field of possible actions that provide the yardstick for determining the thing's identity and meaning. The chapters of Part II will deal with this issue in diverse ways, but, again, none of this is a priori incompatible with realism.

More importantly for the economy of this book, we can see that if the concept of practical identity is acceptable, then the concept of 'norm of perception' would have to be expanded accordingly beyond the standard epistemic norms of truth and falsity. So even if we were to agree with Benoist that 'language is the paradigm of all norms' (2017, 120), it appears that we can still make room in our analyses for another form of normativity. This is, essentially, what this and the previous chapter have argued for. In the next five chapters, some of the consequences of this paradigm will be assessed in the context of contemporary philosophy of mind and perception, beginning with Chapter 3, in which I will tackle head-on the question of the relationship between perceptual and epistemic norms.

Phenomenology and the Norms of Perception. Maxime Doyon, Oxford University Press. © Maxime Doyon 2024.
DOI: 10.1093/9780191993527.003.0002

PART II
THE EMBODIMENT OF NORMS

3
Bodily Self-Awareness and Agency

The idea that our perceptual openness to the world is normative can mean different things. In the Kantian tradition of Strawson, Sellars, and McDowell, this openness is essentially tied to *epistemic justification*, that is to say, to our readiness to provide *reasons* for our actions and our beliefs about how things are. In the phenomenological tradition inaugurated by Husserl, and especially in the work of Merleau-Ponty, the notion of norm-responsiveness that is relevant to perceptual experience has less to do with epistemic justification than with perception's capacity to *guide action* or elicit certain behaviours. Despite this divergence, philosophers of both Kantian and Husserlian inspiration agree by and large that being answerable to the world presupposes that we are, as rational beings, in a position to attend to and assess our perceptual situation. They all recognize, in other words, a necessary connection between perceptual consciousness and self-consciousness, or between outer and inner (or self-) experience; it is on the nature of this link that disagreements arise.

Perceptual awareness of the normative kind essentially depends, according to McDowell, on our capacity to rationally self-ascribe experiences. This is a central element of the connection he sees holding between action and perception. In McDowell's view, there is an abyss between the kind of causal responsiveness typical of reflexive action and the kind of rational world openness regulating genuine perception. By McDowell's lights, the difference between human and animal experience lies precisely therein: our capacity is normatively world-disclosing, whereas that of animals isn't, because ours involves what he calls 'self-critical control' (1996, 49). Self-critical rationality entails a disposition to provide reasons that justify what one perceptually takes in and how one acts on that basis. Given the discriminatory nature of this exercise, McDowell thinks that our perceptual openness to the world is normative precisely because it relies on our conceptual powers.

While McDowell insists on the necessity of ascribing a self-reference by drawing on the spontaneity of the mind, phenomenologists typically place the emphasis on the experiential dimension of self-awareness. As I experience worldly objects, there is a simultaneous, but implicit, self-consciousness of my own ongoing experience. Specifically, for Husserl and Merleau-Ponty, it is thanks to this pre-reflective form of bodily consciousness that I am originally self-aware. My aim in this chapter is to show *that and how this pre-reflective bodily activity has normative import,* even if it is not linguistically or conceptually structured.[1] Contrary to the analytical readings of Kant alluded to above, self-consciousness is norm-responsive below the threshold of linguistic and conceptual formation, and thus independently of their eventual contribution. Support for this view can be found in Husserl's and Merleau-Ponty's investigations of the motivational structure of perception.

From the 1907 lecture course *Thing and Space* on, Husserl claims that perception includes a self-reference that contains kinaesthetic information about my bodily situation that registers self-consciously in the form of the 'I can'. Husserl's fundamental insight is that the implicit self-awareness of the actual and possible movement of my body contributes to shaping perceptual experience by generating expectations, which will then be fulfilled or unfulfilled within experience. It is in this horizonal structure that perception acquires its normative character, for it is only against the background of these fulfilled or unfulfilled expectations that perceptual content can be said to be accurate or inaccurate, correct or incorrect, better or worse, just fine or optimal, etc.

In *Phenomenology of Perception*, Merleau-Ponty takes up and elaborates on this set of ideas as he explains that most of our everyday actions and behaviours are not the outcome of cognitive activity but, rather, are engendered by perceived opportunities to act in certain ways. The experiencing subject perceives its environment as eliciting certain (types of) activities, or demanding certain (kinds of) behaviours, and when one has the required skill, this experience motivates their performance. Crucially, the capacity to respond to one's own perceived surroundings by engaging in the right kind of behaviour does not usually require that one deliberate about the course of action prior to its enactment. It is, rather, triggered pre-reflectively in intentional consciousness. Even as such, my perceptual behaviour *does* have a normative aim or orientation, because the kind of pragmatic understanding involved in perceptual experience is coupled with a pre-reflective form of bodily self-knowledge or self-relating, thanks to which the experiencing subject can take measure of her surrounding and adjust her behaviour

---

[1] I develop a structurally analogous argument in the context of shared perceptions in Chapter 7.

accordingly. The kind of support Merleau-Ponty provides for this claim is phenomenological: if the perceived environment elicits certain kinds of actions and behaviours, it is not because they are reflexively or causally related; it is, rather, because action and perception are *intentionally* integrated into pre-reflective consciousness at the level of the body schema, which embodies the norm. This is particularly evident in sports, where certain configurations *motivate* certain kinds of actions, like, say, when an opening on the tennis court calls forth a certain type of shot, but the idea is valid for perceptions in general.

In sum, and regardless of the specific differences in their respective accounts of the motivational structure of perception, both Husserl and Merleau-Ponty believe—rightly, I think—that the intentionality that characterizes our normative grasp of the content of experience needs the 'guiding lights' of the various bodily forms of self-referential intentionality. From this angle, the difference between McDowell and the phenomenologists could hardly be clearer: if they all agree (with Kant) on the necessary connection between perceptual consciousness and self-consciousness, and on the necessity to appeal to some form of self-conscious activity to account for the normative character of our actions and perceptions, there is a fundamental disagreement about the nature of this relation. At stake here are two different conceptions of intentionality: while the first is essentially understood as a mental or cognitive disposition that concerns our rational capacity *to represent what there is*, the second is bodily informed and includes the set of motor activities relevant for *orienting and guiding perception*. Since most of our daily perceptual activities are not epistemic but pragmatic in nature, the chapter argues that the phenomenological model provides the best alternative to account for the normative character of perception.[2]

With this aim in view, I will now sketch, in very broad strokes, the role of self-consciousness in Kant's and McDowell's analyses of perceptual experience (Section 3.1), in view of the argument that the minimal form of bodily self-awareness we see at play in the thought of Husserl (Section 3.2) and Merleau-Ponty (Section 3.3) is more apt to seize the normative character of perception. In Sections 3.4 and 3.5, I compare the two views by looking more specifically at the question of perceptual agency and its connection to norms of rationality.

---

[2] In Section 5.1 I develop another argument in favour of the phenomenological over the epistemological model of perceptual intentionality by explaining how the former grounds and justifies the latter.

3.1. Spontaneity and Self-critical Control

The central argument of Kant's *Critique of Pure Reason* is contained in the Transcendental Deduction, in which Kant attempts to deduce the objective reality of the pure concepts of the understanding. In the Deduction, Kant makes a number of connected claims about what a subject of experience must be or do in order to have experiences with objective purport. There are three such claims that seem to be particularly crucial for the question pondered here, and they concern identity, unity, and self-consciousness (Pippin 1989, 16ff.). Given the argument I defend, I will rapidly pass over the first two claims and deliberately spend more time on the third.

First, for a subject to have objective experiences, Kant thinks it must be *an identical subject through time*, and this means that the said experiences must belong to that subject, i.e. to that apperceptive 'I', otherwise no synthesis would ever take place. Second, Kant argues that the synthetic unification of these representational states can only occur in one identical subject if *the work of unification is performed by that very subject*. Otherwise put, for the relevant unity of representations to take place in a single subject, that subject must itself spontaneously—that is, actively—accomplish their unity. Finally, and most importantly for our purpose, Kant also contends that such elements could not be unified if such a subject 'could not become conscious of the identity function whereby it synthetically combines [the manifold] in one knowledge' (2007, A108). For Kant, this last claim entails that *self-consciousness is a condition of possibility of experience*. If I could not become conscious of the set of rules or laws that I was spontaneously applying in unifying my representations, Kant contends that I could not possibly distinguish between merely associatively produced subjective states and representations with objective purport. And since the overall aim of the Transcendental Deduction is to prove that our experiences *are* objective, Kant maintains that self-consciousness *is* a condition of experience in general.

Kant's insistence on the necessary role of self-conscious activity in perception is something virtually all phenomenologists agree with (Zahavi 2005). And the phenomenologists also agree with McDowell's (2009) Kant interpretation that we should not understand the truth of Kant's apperceptive claim as implying an explicit or reflective form of self-monitoring. Kant was not the forerunner of the *higher-order* theories of consciousness (Carruthers 2000; Lycan 1996; Rosenthal 2005); he is merely contending that perceiving implies a minimal self-ascription of experiences such that 'I' am rationally responsible for what I take to be the case. Very simply put, the act of perceiving does not require two acts; it is rather a double act, as it were, where perception includes a self-conscious reference. This means, for Kant, that my implicitly taking myself to perceive is an inseparable feature of what it is to perceive. On this score, too, there is, by and large, an agreement between philosophers of the phenomenological tradition (and Brentano (1995, 97–9, 119f.) for that matter).

One of the greatest insights provided by Sellars's and McDowell's readings of Kant—and this is where the difference with phenomenologists becomes apparent—is to have shown that it is by virtue of this self-relating experience that perceptual consciousness figures in the normative space (the 'space of reasons', as Sellars (1997) puts it). To recall, Sellars's position is articulated around his critique of what he calls the Myth of the Given, which targets a certain understanding of the traditional foundationalist position, namely empiricism. The definition of the Myth, which has directly or indirectly generated so many debates in contemporary epistemology, is the following:

> One of the forms taken by the Myth of the Given is the idea that there is, indeed must be, a structure of particular matter of fact such that (a) each fact can not only be non-inferentially known to be the case, but presupposes no other knowledge either of particular matter of fact, or of general truths; and (b) such that the non-inferential knowledge of facts belonging to this structure constitutes the ultimate court of appeals for all factual claims-particular and general about the world. (1997, 68f.)

The mythical apprehension of the 'Given' denounced by Sellars is described both notionally as a non-inferential, immediate, non-discursive, and non-conceptual experience (say, having a visual sensation of red in the presence of a red apple) *and* functionally as grounding empirical knowledge (in this case about the colour of the apple). According to Sellars, whatever is given in experience cannot enjoy such a dual function. The problem with the empiricist position is to believe that the space of reasons and justifications extends below or beyond the space of concepts, and that there can therefore be experiences (say, perceptions) that are primitive and non-conceptual, but which could nevertheless rationally ground and justify knowledge. In Sellars's view, these two ideas are mutually incompatible. The epistemic space of knowledge is an intersubjective space governed by the 'game of giving and asking for reasons', to cite Brandom's (1994) much celebrated phrase. This means that knowledge can only exist in the light of rational and socially accepted reasons. To be effective, the subject must appropriate these norms, that is, recognize them as such, and use them to critically evaluate what is perceptually given. Whatever comes in perceptual experience is therefore never self-justifying; it is, rather, the perceivers themselves that can confer or refuse it the status of knowledge. This, to put it briefly, is the mainspring of Sellars's resolutely internalist conception of knowledge. In Sellars's own words: 'The essential point is that in characterizing an episode or a state as that of knowledge, we are not giving an empirical description of that episode or state; we are placing it in the logical space of reasons, of justifying and being able to justify what one says' (1997, 76).

Here's another way of articulating the same idea: beliefs derive their epistemic efficacy not from the fact that they are self-justifying experiences, but insofar as they are terms of justificatory relations. It is true that the visual sensation of red that I am experiencing has indeed been caused by the presence of this or that red object; but this experience is not sufficient to justify my claim to know anything, including knowledge of the colour of the thing that is there in front of me. That is because having a (say, visual) sensation is not in itself an epistemic state in the same way as holding a belief or formulating a judgment. The problem, which is strictly logical, is that the object of sensation is a particular (an instance of red), whereas the object of belief, knowledge, or judgment is always a fact or rather a proposition ('the object is red'). There is therefore a gap to be bridged between the content of the sensation—which is supposed to be epistemically independent and autonomous—and the epistemic efficacy of the proposition, which authorizes us to justify a certain number of things (a certain number of other propositions). According to Sellars, here we must choose; we can't have it both ways. The given cannot be required to be both autonomous (as the foundationalist wants) and epistemically effective (as knowledge requires). Either it preserves its autonomy but does not count as knowledge, or whatever is given is an instance of knowledge, but it is not autonomous (i.e. self-justifying). The return to Kant, who undercut this difficulty when arguing that 'intuitions without concepts are blind' (2007, A51/B75), finds just therein its justification.

In his first *Woodbridge Lectures*, McDowell affirms that he 'shares this belief with Sellars that there is no better way...to approach an understanding of intentionality than by working towards an understanding of Kant'

(2009, 3).³ The interpretation he developed in *Mind and World* (1994) is that experience would not even be conceivable if the conceptual content of our discursive activity were to be understood as derived from or radically independent of the sensory manifold. The very idea of the possible availability of sensory content that would not be conceptually informed is just impossible, because it leads to the Myth.

Following in Kant's footsteps, McDowell argues in *Mind and World* against any kind of strict separability between the deliverances of sensibility and the discursive activity of the understanding. A passage from *The Clue to the Discovery of all Pure Concepts of the Understanding* put him on this path. Kant writes: 'The same function which gives unity to the various representations *in a judgment* also gives unity to the mere synthesis of various representations *in an intuition*' (2007, A79/B104-5; the emphasis is mine). McDowell's reformulation of this insight reads as follows: 'There is only one unity, common to the Aesthetic and the Analytic; not two separate and independent unities' (2009, 74 n.). In his interpretation, McDowell clearly takes a stand against a certain interpretation of the Deduction according to which the reception of sensory data *precedes* and *causes* the subsequent application of concepts on the data (itself understood as being nonconceptual). As a very careful reader of Kant, McDowell is well aware that some isolated passages of the first *Critique* legitimize such a reading;[4] but there are, he insists, other passages that speak resolutely against this two-step

---

[3] On this issue, see also the following passage from the first lecture: 'I do not think it is far-fetched to attribute to Sellars a belief on the following lines: no one has come closer than Kant to showing us how to find intentionality unproblematic, and there is no better way for us to find intentionality unproblematic than by seeing what Kant was driving at. That means rethinking his thought for ourselves and, if necessary, correcting him at points where we think we see more clearly than he did what he should have been doing. Sellars does not hesitate to claim, on some points, to have a better understanding of the requirements of Kantian thinking than Kant himself achieved' (McDowell 2009, 3).

[4] Here are two examples of such passages. Take, for instance, the one at B1: 'There can be no doubt that all our knowledge begins with experience. For how should our faculty of knowledge be awakened into action did not objects affecting our senses partly of themselves produce representations, partly arouse the activity of our understanding to compare these representations, and, by combining or separating them, work up the raw material of sensible impressions into that knowledge of objects which is entitled experience? In the order of time, therefore, we have no knowledge antecedent to experience, and with experience all our knowledge begins.' See this passage from B129-30 as well: 'The combination of a manifold in general can never come to us through the senses in general, and cannot, therefore, be already contained in the pure form of sensible intuition. For it is an act of spontaneity of the faculty of representation; and since this spontaneity, to distinguish it from sensibility, must be entitled understanding, all combination—be we conscious of it or not, be it a combination of the manifold of intuition, empirical or non-empirical, or of various concepts—is an act of the understanding. To this act

view, and these passages not only seem to him to be more in line with Kant's own intuitions[5] but also have the great merit of bypassing the difficulties entailed by the Myth.

In *Mind and World*, McDowell draws the consequence that if there is no strict separability between the contribution of the understanding and sensibility, then the content of experience must itself be propositional, i.e. the structure of experience must itself be judgmental. In response to the some of the epistemological problems that his critics have raised (notably Travis 2004), McDowell eventually made some adjustments to his approach by drawing a distinction between empirical experience (conceived as the conceptual activity relevant to judgment) and empirical judgment (i.e. the fully fledged assertoric content itself). In the essay 'Avoiding the Myth of the Given' (2009), McDowell argues that the *form* of empirical experience is transferable into judgment, but it is not itself a judgment. In a view that slightly differs from the one advanced in *Mind and World*, McDowell now believes that perception does *not* have propositional content as such, but the content of perception can always be actualized in a judgment of that form. There is, in other words, a strict parallelism between the deliverances of sensibility and potential future judgments of experience.

What informs this new interpretation is a more cautious reading of the passage from the *Clue* discussed above. When Kant writes that it is 'the same function which gives unity to the various representations *in a judgment*' and 'to the mere synthesis of various representations *in an intuition*,' he does not affirm—as McDowell suggested in *Mind and World*—that the roles of sensibility and understanding are indistinguishable.[6] His contention is, rather, that their functions are not strictly separable. As Kant puts it, the

---

the general title "synthesis" may be assigned.' For McDowell's gloss on these passages, see 2009, 70–1.

[5] In this respect, the footnote at B160 is one to which McDowell frequently returns: 'Space, represented as object (as we are required to do in geometry) contains more than mere form of intuition; it also contains combination of the manifold, given according to the form of sensibility, in an intuitive representation, so that the form of intuition gives only a manifold, the formal intuition gives unity of representation. In the Aesthetic I have treated this unity as belonging merely to sensibility, simply in order to emphasize that it precedes any concept, although as a matter of fact it presupposes a synthesis which does not belong to the senses but through which all concepts of space and time first become possible' (2009, 71–2).

[6] As I see it, it is exactly to forestall that kind of misunderstanding that Kant wrote a couple of pages earlier in the *Critique* that 'these two powers or capacities cannot exchange their functions. The understanding can intuit nothing, the senses can think nothing. Only through their union can knowledge arise. But that is no reason for confounding the contribution of either with that of the other; rather is it a strong reason for carefully separating and distinguishing the one from the other' (2007, A51/B75).

unity of that which is given in sensible intuition 'is no other than that which the category... prescribes' (2007, B144–5). So instead of identifying perceptual and propositional contents, the later McDowell introduces a new subtlety and distinguishes between different modalities of the apperceptive function. We are now told that our conceptual capacities are *passively* drawn into play in empirical experience, whereas they are *actively* exercised in judgments.

Here is not the place to judge the merits of such an undertaking and to see whether the latter position really improves on the former. What I rather wish to insist upon is the crucial role of self-consciousness in Sellars's and McDowell's respective accounts of experience. For Sellars, self-conscious activity, which involves our ability to reflect upon and make explicit our conceptual commitments, enables us to assess and revise our beliefs in light of new evidence, to make judgments, and, more generally, to engage in rational discourse. In this picture, knowledge appears as the self-conscious product of an ongoing process of conceptualizing, interpreting, and critically reflecting upon our experiences. For McDowell, the key is to understand that the language of different modes of actualization introduced in 2009 serves one main purpose, namely to guarantee *judgmental accessibility*. Perceptual experience raises the question of whether things are as our experiences present them as being. That is, to have a perceptual experience is to be confronted with a possible way the world is. According to McDowell, this normative dimension of experience is constitutive of every perception. Even if it is true that McDowell came to recognize that what is disclosed in perceptual experience is not itself a fact or a judgment—judgments and experiences can diverge and even contradict each other—he still believes that if perceptual content can really capture how things are or be wrong about it, then its content must at least be able to figure in a judgment. And this means that perceptual content must be of such a form that it is always accessible to thought, a function guaranteed by self-consciousness, which for Kant is inseparable from the mind's spontaneous power. Normativity and self-consciousness are thus intrinsically connected, for it is just insofar as I am self-aware as I perceive that I can be justified to take things as right or wrong when I experience them.

We can shed further light on this issue by considering more closely the notion of self-correction to which McDowell sometimes appeals. Our normative sensibility about how things are can be seen in our tendency to correct ourselves when things do not happen the way they should or when evidence counts against our initial judgment. I can correct my belief about how things are when new facts contradict my original view. As we have seen earlier, apperception is not a sufficient condition for perception, *a fortiori* for self-correction; but it is necessary, for without such a self-referential capacity we wouldn't even realize that experience is always putative, and so no rational adjustment of our beliefs and behaviours would ever be possible. Very basically, then, the idea is that some form of critical assessment of our situation is necessary for our perception to have objective purport. And McDowell's point, borrowed from Kant, is that this self-critical assessment is *constantly* achieved because *I apperceive what I perceive*.

Here we come full circle since this capacity for self-correction essentially depends, for McDowell, on the pervasive role of concepts in perception. Normative comportment is not just a regular response pattern; rationality must be involved in the form of concept possession. It is because perceiving is conceptual that it can be weighed in the light of rational norms. Only then can one be mistaken about what one takes in. This conceptual capacity translates linguistically. In perception, McDowell holds that we are rationally responsible for what we do or what we take to be the case, and the proof is that our justification for acting in certain ways *could* be verbally expressed if the situation demanded it (say, if someone asks me why I do what I do). Even if it is true that perception is most often achieved without verbalizing anything, the mere possibility of verbally justifying our beliefs is a constant feature of all perception. According to McDowell—and this is what comes out of his exchange with Dreyfus (2007a, 2007b)—the same basic structure holds for when it comes to explaining agency. For McDowell, it is this intrinsic feature that is responsible for the normative character of our perceptual actions and behaviours, even those we perform 'absent-mindedly' in what Dreyfus calls 'absorbed coping', like catching a Frisbee (McDowell 2007b, 369; 2013, 48f.).

But is this the best way to capture the phenomenology of our normative experiences? For if our capacity for self-correction is, as I take it, indeed a reliable indicator that we find ourselves in a normative space, this capacity can take different forms; and if they are all forms of self-assessment, they need not be realized in concepts and through language, not even in the minimal sense that McDowell conceives of them. By interpreting Kant's basic apperceptive claim about the pervasiveness of self-consciousness in experience in terms of concept possession, McDowell is perhaps well equipped to explain how perceptual experience can warrant or justify our epistemic judgments (which is his main goal), but I do not think that he can explain agency or the connection between perception and action just as well. For if it is true, as McDowell rightly contends, that the body cannot *itself* engage in a self-critical activity of a justificatory kind (2007a, 350; 2007b, 369), this does not entail that we, as embodied beings, cannot be normatively attuned to our environment and adapt our perceptual behaviour when it is required by the situation. Actually, this happens all the time: by moving our bodies around, we *constantly* adjust to the situations we are in, and we do so in a way that cannot be reduced to either a mere reflex or the outcome of prior conceptual operations. To be sure, this bodily capacity requires a tacit recognition of the norm governing the situation, that is to say, an understanding or sensitivity to how our bodies ought to act in this or that context. However, and contrary to what McDowell claims, the kind of practical understanding required here is normally realized pre-reflectively, so prior to and independently of our conceptual or linguistic engagement. As we shall see, this is what phenomenologists have convincingly argued for.

3.2. The Motivational Role of Kinaesthesis in Husserl

Apart from Hubert Dreyfus, who, strangely enough, denies that self-consciousness plays any role in everyday perceptual experience (see Section 2.2.1), phenomenologists agree that some sort of self-conscious activity pervades intentionality (Zahavi 2020). Husserl formulated this idea explicitly for the first time in his 1904/5 *Lectures on Internal Time-Consciousness* by asserting that 'every act is consciousness of something, but there is also consciousness of every act' (1991, 130). Contrary to Kant, who conceives of this principle in a priori terms, or philosophers of the analytic tradition like Sellars or McDowell, who think that this self-relating must be conceptually or linguistically mediated, Husserl's justification is phenomenologically, viz. experientially, grounded. The claim that self-consciousness and intentionality are interdependent features of experience specifically concerns the *pre-reflective* dimension of consciousness: *prior to* any subsequent reflective self-apprehension, intentional consciousness includes a form of self-reference, thanks to which it acquires its experiential and first-person character.[7]

---

[7] This Husserlian insight has been taken over and developed by a majority of phenomenologists, most notably by Jean-Paul Sartre (1936, 1943), Michel Henry (1963, 1965), and more recently Dorothée Legrand (2007, 2012) and Dan Zahavi (2020), who have made it a central theme of their research.

In the period between the *Logical Investigations* (1900/1) and *Ideas I* (1913), Husserl started to flesh out this insight in bodily terms. Self-consciousness (or self-awareness) is primarily experienced as a form of *bodily* self-reference. The phenomenological account of self-reference is not conceived as a purely formal condition of experience (as the Kantian 'I think') or merely induced as inherent within every form of object-intentionality. The idea instead is that in all forms of experience the body experiences itself, or rather manifests itself to itself, although not in an object-like (or intentional) way but, rather, as the *subject* of that experience. In the realm of perception, this means that it is not only the touched or perceived body (body as object) that is given to us; the claim—which is transcendental—is that we also have experiential access, however limited or unspecified, to the seeing, touching, or moving body (body as subject).

This insight led Husserl to distinguish conceptually between *Körper* and *Leib*, which correspond to two distinct point of views on my body (*Leibkörper*). My body is originally given and lived through as a phenomenally unified whole, but I can, thanks to a shift in attention, draw a distinction between the functioning, subjectively lived body (*Leib*) and the thematized, objective body (*Körper*). While I am permanently pre-reflectively self-aware of my lived body (*Leib*) as a sensing organism, this same body can also be sensed and localized in certain specific body parts.[8] In this regard, Husserl differentiates between a naturalistic and a personal attitude, by which he means that one can perceive the body both from a personal (or first-person) perspective, i.e. as the subject of perception (*Leib*), or else from a naturalistic (or third-person) perspective, i.e. as a physical thing (*Körper*). But there's a strict hierarchy here: the naturalistic attitude, which presents the body as physical *Körper, presupposes* the personal attitude or mode of apprehension. The reasoning is the following: if I apprehend the objective characteristics of my left hand, I have to *abstract* from the sensational qualities that enable its givenness as an object in the first place. The personal mode of apprehension

---

[8] The experience of reversibility of the sensing and sensed body shows that the body is the object of a double constitution, which Husserl analyses in *Ideas II* through the so-called experience of double-sensation (1989, §§36–7). In the experience of two hands that touch one another, the living body appears as both the object and subject of experience. This is due to a remarkable feature of all tactile sensations, which can alternatively be apprehended both objectively as sensed (*Empfindung*) and subjectively as sensing (*Empfindnis*). Since none of the other bodily sensations (be they auditory, visual, olfactive, or gustatory) display the reflexive specificity of tactile sensations, Husserl holds that the body constitutes itself originally through the sense of touch, which is thereby granted an ontological privilege over the other senses. For an overview of the reception of this claim in Merleau-Ponty and more generally French phenomenology, see Wehrle and Doyon 2022.

is thus primary and enjoys a transcendental status, while the naturalistic apprehension is secondary or derivative (Husserl 1989, 152ff.). In the same way that the naturalistic apprehension presupposes the personal, the experienced *Leibkörper* presupposes a primary experiencing *Leib* (see Doyon and Wehrle 2020).

In Husserl's eyes, it is precisely there, viz. at the pre-reflective level of bodily self-experience (*Leib*), that the normative character of perception gets its foothold. As the indexical 'here' of all directions and orientations (Husserl 1989, 166), the body is not only the egocentric centre around which perceptual space unfolds but also the disclosing principle of all intentional objects. While objects are only always perceived under a certain aspect or profile (2001b, 220),[9] 'consciousness reaches out beyond what it actually experiences. It can so to say mean beyond itself' (2001b, 211) and grasp the object itself by co-intending the presently unseen profiles. While in the *Logical Investigations* the phenomenological analysis of the body is at best indirectly implied in this co-intending structure (more on this point in Section 5.2.1), Husserl will soon come to fully recognize the fundamental role that the body must assume therein. First in *Thing and Space* (1907) and then again in the lectures of the 1920s on *Active and Passive Syntheses*, Husserl argues that this co-intending takes its initial cues from kinaesthetic sensations. The 'appearances are kinaesthetically motivated' (2001c, 52) in the sense that it is the *sensations* of one's own bodily *movement* that are responsible for ordering the flow of appearances in a coherent or meaningful way. My horizontal awareness of the absent facets of worldly objects is intentionally correlated to my kinaesthetic system, i.e. to the system of movements I can do. My relation to the non-visible sides is experienced in an intentional if–then relation: I am kinaesthetically aware that *if* I move in this way, *then* this or that profile will become visually accessible. There is, otherwise put, a bilateral relation that holds between the sensations by which one is aware of the movements of one's own body, and the appearances of the object. My sensations vary as the appearances vary, and the recognizable patterns of this covariation allow the experiencing subject to anticipate that things will follow a certain pattern or order as I move with

---

[9] This generates what is today called the problem of perceptual presence (cf. Noë 2004), which is brought about by the constitutive discrepancy between what is meaningfully intended (the object) in experience and what is sensibly given (the profile or adumbration, *Abschattung* in Husserl's vocabulary).

respect to it. Husserl's most explicit passage on this can be found in *Active and Passive Synthesis*:

> By viewing an object, I am conscious of the position of my eyes and at the same time—in the form of a novel systematic empty horizon—I am conscious of the entire system of possible eye positions that rest at my disposal. And now, what is seen in the given eye position is so enmeshed with the entire system that I can say with certainty that if I were to move my eyes in this direction or in that, specific visual appearances would accordingly run their course in a determinate order. If I were to let the eye movements run this way or that in another direction, different series of appearances would accordingly run their course as expected. This holds likewise for head movements in the system of these possibilities of movement, and again for the movement of walking, etc., that I might bring into play. (2001c, 51; cf. 1997, §55; 1970, §47)

In Husserl's account of perception, it is therefore the law of motivation—the if–then connection—that is responsible for the synthetic unification of intentional contents, and which thereby provides for the kind of unity that allows for objective reference.[10]

If our kinaesthetic system plays such a decisive role in perception, it is because the perceptual field is primarily experienced as a field of practical possibilities that I may actualize by moving in suitable ways. This is not without consequence for the question of normativity, for not only does our experience of objects acquire therein depth and coherence (which presuppose movement) but, thanks to this motivational structure, any (object-) experience is susceptible to being optimized at any time. Indeed, the optimum is a permanent possibility of perception (Ms. D 13 III 151a). Husserl's basic insight is that the systematic interconnection between appearances is kinaesthetically lived through (*erlebt*) as forming a motivational context in which things exercise a normative pull on us. In a famous passage from *Active and Passive Syntheses*, Husserl explains that 'it is almost as if the thing were calling out to us "there is still more to see here, turn me so you can see all my sides, let your gaze run through me, draw closer to me, open me up,

---

[10] In fact, Husserl goes even further than this. It is not just my anticipation of what is to come that is dependent on the flow of kinaesthetic sensations, but even my belief that there is something at all presupposes the felt experience of the object. 'The straightforward belief that a thing is there has to be built on the felt, incarnate experiences of some of its material determinations' (1975, 299ff.).

divide me up; keep on looking me over again and again, turning me to see all sides. You will get to see me like this, all that I am, all my surface qualities, all my inner sensible qualities, etc"' (2001c, 41). In this (otherwise slightly strange) passage, perception appears as 'normative' in the sense that it triggers a kinaesthetic response on our side: seeing things as thus and so is accompanied by an awareness of (more or less specific) movements I could produce with regard to the object in order to optimize my perspective. Our kinaesthetic 'freedom' (2001c, 52) is not total liberty, however, for of all the things I can do, only some appear appropriately suited for the realization of our current intentional project or the attainment of our perceptual goal (Ms. D13 I, 61a, 63a), which provides us with the norm (see Section 1.2). Husserl speaks in this sense of a 'tendency towards the optimum as a selection principle of practical possibilities' (Ms. D13 III, 151a).[11]

Needless to say, this view has serious shortcomings. As Drummond (1983) and Crowell (2013) rightly demonstrated, kinaesthetic sensations cannot *on their own* motivate a system of appearances. However one conceives of it, a kinaesthetic system just cannot be *determinate enough* to command or prefigure perceptual content.[12] And yet, I think that Husserl was fundamentally right about a crucial point. For Husserl, kinaesthetic sensations are relevant in a normative context not only because they generate expectations but also because they have a key role to play in the constitution of our perceptual space (Mattens 2018), and therefore for the assessment of our perceptual situation. True, kinaesthetic sensations *alone* cannot do this either, but once integrated into the proprioceptive system, their importance in this regard cannot be denied.

To see better through this, the distinction between kinaesthesis and proprioception needs to be introduced: whereas Husserl uses the term 'kinaesthesis' to refer exclusively to the *sensations* of one's own bodily *movement* (direction, speed, rhythm, etc.), proprioception registers our own self-movement by collecting 'information from kinetic, muscular, articular, and cutaneous sources' and the contributions of our 'vestibular and equilibrial functions' (Gallagher 2005, 45). Our proprioceptive system thus *includes*

---

[11] In the original, Husserl speaks of a '*Tendenz auf das Optimum als Auswahlprinzip der praktischen Möglichkeiten*'.
[12] According to Crowell, it is *the movement itself* that produces change in the appearance of the object, not the mere accompanying sensations. For this reason, Crowell locates the normative in perception in the bodily skill itself, and the goal for which the practice of this skill strives (cf. 2013, 143). This is the basic line of his criticism of Dan Dahlstrom (2007).

kinaesthetic sensations but is not limited to them.[13] In this context, one may wonder what the best way is to understand bodily self-awareness and how exactly it works, or, more precisely, how much work it does. When I am reaching for my glass of water, I am apparently neither conscious of the position of my eyes, nor of the shape of my grasp or the angle of my arm. I may be conscious *that* I am reaching, and *that* the thing I'm seeing and trying to grasp is off to the side—but reaching for my glass of water does not require a detailed awareness of the precise movements of my body. To make things clearer, Gallagher (2005) suggests that we distinguish between proprioceptive information (PI) and proprioceptive awareness (PA):

> [P]roprioception can be understood as having a twofold function. First, it consists of non-conscious, physiological *information* that updates the motor system with respect to the body's posture and movement. Proprioceptive information (PI) is processed on the subpersonal, non-conscious physiological level that subtends and operates as the basis for proprioceptive *awareness* (PA), a self-referential, but normally pre-reflective, awareness of one's own body. PI...contributes to the body-schematic control of posture and movement, and plays an essential role in the operations of body schemas. [But] the physiological processing of PI always involves more than PA. If I jump to catch a ball, I am not aware of the 'calibrations' that register in and between proprioceptors and neural structures and that allow me to maintain balance among a number of muscle groups; nor am I necessarily aware of the actual muscle adjustments. The calibrations and adjustments are carried out without the mediation of PA. Postural control and movement are normally governed by the more automatic processes of the body schema, and the majority of normal adult movements do not require anything like an explicit monitoring, although PA may be used to monitor and assist motor activity in certain instances. (73f.)

If action and perception are always accompanied by pre-reflective bodily self-awareness, Gallagher believes that not every relevant mechanism enters phenomenal consciousness (even marginally). I don't have to be aware of

---

[13] Sheets-Johnstone (2011) makes the same distinction: 'Proprioception refers generally to a sense of movement and position. It thus includes an awareness of movement and position through tactility as well as kinaesthesia, that is, through surface as well as internal events, including also a sense of gravitational orientation through vestibular sensory organs. Kinaesthesia refers specifically to a sense of movement through muscular effort' (73).

myself as a zero point for my body to function as a zero point; I don't have to be conscious of my bodily posture or condition or skill level for such things to modulate my perception of the world. Although rich in terms of the processes it includes, much of proprioceptive activity stays non-conscious (or, as Gallagher (2005) likes to say, 'prenoetic'). This is true. However, this does not in any way imply that the processing of PI has no impact on perceptual consciousness (which, for the record, is not what Gallagher is saying either). While we are not consciously aware of the bodily processes themselves, we are conscious—in a pre-reflective and very much an implicit, or recessive, way—of our perceptual situation, viz. of our relation to our perceptual milieu. We have, very basically, an awareness of our location vis-à-vis the perceived object that includes aspects of the 'I can', that is, a pragmatic sense of how I can move to accomplish something, and *this* is given (in part) through all that PI affords.[14] Cues about my bodily position and posture provided by our kinaesthetic and proprioceptive systems are absolutely crucial in perception, for in order to act and modulate the quality of my perception, I need to know how things stand in relation to me. I know, because I am bodily self-aware of my perceptual situation, that I am currently not having an optimal perspective on my monitor because I am aware (now in a more explicit way) of its relative position to my eyes. That's why I know, by the same token, what I need to do (at least approximately) to optimize my experience (e.g. drawing it a few centimetres closer). This does not mean that, without proprioceptive awareness, one could not perceive anything at all. The point here is, rather, that without bodily forms of self-relating provided by our proprioceptive systems one could still move one's bodily organs, but not 'intelligently', and without this skill our perception would not have the kind of normatively rich content it has.[15]

In short, my idea, which derives from Husserl's insight, is that bodily self-awareness *allows me to be sensitive to my own perceptual situation*. Although it is not presented as such, this is an essential ingredient of a phenomenological account like Husserl's, for our perceptions are not accurate, deficient, optimal, or suboptimal from a third-eye view; they can only be said to be better or worse in relation to a certain goal or aim, whose fulfilment

---

[14] As we will see in Chapters 5 and 6, the scope and specificities of the 'I can' are also partly determined by affective factors, i.e. whether I am motivated to do something (whether I feel like it, whether I'm in pain, etc.).

[15] Further evidence for this will be provided in the next chapter (Section 4.3.2) through a detailed analysis of the case of Ian Waterman, who lost his proprioceptive sense but developed compensatory strategies.

supposes that we have the capacity to cast our own performances in evaluative terms. As should be clear, this is not something very particular; it is something we continuously do pre-reflectively thanks to the pervasive self-referential sensitivity that structures our being-in-the-world. Bodily self-awareness thus contributes importantly to establish the normative character of perception, for it allows the practice to be goal- or norm-sensitive, and to correct itself when it's not 'on track'. In a word, the point is that if I am not sensitive to what I'm doing as I do it, I can't be sensitive to the relative merits of my performance either; and this can only mean losing grip on the normative.

3.3. Body-schematic Attunement in Merleau-Ponty

The phenomenological analysis sketched out in the previous section took a more elaborate turn in Merleau-Ponty's *Phenomenology of Perception*. Whereas Husserl was especially concerned with kinaesthetic sensations and their motivational role in the unfolding of perception, Merleau-Ponty enlarged the scope of the analysis and investigated what he calls the body schema, which is typically understood in the contemporary philosophical landscape as comprising the set of motor skills and control mechanisms enabling posture and movement.[16] In the work of Merleau-Ponty, the expression 'body schema' is used somewhat more loosely to refer to the performing body in its dynamical relation to its milieu (2012, 103). Habit is central to this endeavour. The schema functions as a set of active motor patterns that primarily belong to the domain of habitual behaviour rather than conscious decision-making (2012, 143). Again, this does not mean that the schema itself is completely non-conscious. For Merleau-Ponty at least, 'the body schema is also a certain structure of the perceived world' (2021, 104), which means that even if the body schema remains in the background, it still furnishes us with an 'implicit notion of the relation between our body

---

[16] Gallagher (2005) defines the body schema as 'the system of sensory-motor capacities that function without awareness or the necessity of perceptual monitoring' and which comprises 'certain motor capacities, abilities, and habits that both enable and constrain movement and the maintenance of posture' (24). For a historical overview of the development of this concept, see Mooney 2023, ch. 5.2. The specific question of the *acquisition* of motor skills and habits, and their transformative impact on perception, will be the focus of Section 5.2. In this chapter, I am solely interested in the body schema's impact on agency.

and things' (1964b, 5).[17] Hence, even if we are not aware of it as such, the body schema is not absent from consciousness *tout court* since it is integrated in intentional experience; that's incidentally how it can support intentional activity (including perception). Thanks to the way the body schema structures our practical relation to the world, we have a constant pre-reflective and operative form of awareness of ourselves as perceptually engaged bodies (Heinämaa 2015).

In the 1953 lecture course *Le monde sensible et le monde de l'expression* (2021), Merleau-Ponty sought to clarify some of these ideas and explicitly came to describe the relation between the body schema and its surrounding environment through the prism of *Gestaltpsychologie*. As Halák (2021, 36) points out, for Merleau-Ponty, 'our motor projects, and the perceived objects targeted by them, stand out as explicit figures against this implicit background (2021, 90; cf. 2012, 105).' In this setting, Merleau-Ponty conceives of the body schema 'as norm, as zero point of divergence, as privileged level or attitude' (2021, 90), in relation to which only specific objects and particular motor projects can consciously appear. As figures, they manifest themselves as 'divergence' (2021, 103) from the norm incarnated by the body schema.

Conceiving of the body schema as having normative import is an old idea. Already in 1911, Head and Holmes were arguing that the body schema, understood as the set of pre-conscious physiological functions that process sensory information, compares past and present postures in order to make the necessary postural changes. It is, in that sense, the norm, or the reference point of these changes (cf. Head and Holmes 1911, 12; Gallagher 2005, 19; 2023, 138f.). Merleau-Ponty's idea is similar in some respect, but the scope of his claim is much wider. Not only is the body schema the standard for prospective postural adjustments, but Merleau-Ponty also contends that the body schema takes its surroundings' measure in a normative way by registering our attitudes towards it as right or wrong, correct or incorrect, in view of our intentional activity (Carman 2008, 110). This is not something ad hoc or temporary but, rather, an ongoing process. Thanks to the set of bodily capacities and function that constitute our body schema, we are intentionally connected to our surroundings: 'I experience my body as the power for certain behaviours and for a certain world, and I am only given to myself as a certain hold upon the world' (Merleau-Ponty 2012,

---

[17] Thanks to J. Halák, who alerted me about the existence of these passages. The quotes from Merleau-Ponty in this sentence and in the next paragraph were all found in Halák 2021.

370). As perception unfolds, bodily postures and positions are in a constant process of regulation and adjustment, and their integration allows for the perceptual agent to respond adequately to the affordances of its surrounding world. This ability manifests itself just as much in routine daily actions, like when one readjusts one's position during sleep to promote comfort, for instance, or when one goes to a concert with no seating and continually tries to improve one's view of the stage by moving one's head around and craning one's neck.[18] In these and like situations, one feels the 'tension' (2012, 316) toward the norm or the optimum that Merleau-Ponty has in view (cf. Section 2.3); one literally feels it in one's body.

Part of what explains this natural 'attunement' to the affordances of the situation is our body's facticity: the upright posture, the fact that we have two forward-facing eyes, etc. But there's also an essentially phenomenological (or intentional) dimension here: being attuned to the perceived world means to be sensitive to its demands, and to respond to it in meaningful ways. Something like a bodily form of intelligence is required here: this intelligence manifests itself in our ability to unreflectively act in appropriate or suitable ways, even in the most banal of situations, like when I automatically adopt the appropriate hand posture to open the door. In this and similar situations, our embodied nature seems to fit in with the world around us.[19]

For Merleau-Ponty, such action can be performed without prior deliberation because perceptual experience is imbued with (intentional) meaning from the start. One perceives his surrounding world as something that has practical valence or significance, and in terms of its capacity to navigate through it. Of course, the ability to see opportunities for action, and hence to respond to them by acting in appropriate ways, depends on the possession of the right set of motor skills, which are physical abilities to perform certain actions. Such skills range from very basic capacities, such as the ability to turn one's head to avoid a blow, to more complex ones, such as the ability to play tennis or dance. One of Merleau-Ponty's most important insights is that, to exercise any motor skill, one must be in the appropriate

---

[18] I prefer this latter example to Merleau-Ponty's example of a painting in a gallery, because when you go to a concert with general admission, you are in *constant* reevaluation of your posture and position. Throughout the evening, you adjust to the multiple comings and goings of the people standing in front of you to feel comfortable and have a *good* look at the stage.

[19] It should be noted that, for Merleau-Ponty, the answer to the solicitation is not just sensorimotor. There's an affective, and especially an *existential*, component too: it is the significance of the perceptual world that matters to me. I come back to this question in Sections 4.2 and 5.2, where I address Merleau-Ponty's ontology.

setting. One must have the perceptual ability to recognize the environment as being suitable for the enactment of the skill. Crucially, recognizing an opportunity to engage in some activity is not a matter of judging that one may do so. Instead, the subject immediately perceives the environment as offering an opportunity to exercise its skills because *Leib* and world are so intimately intertwined in the body schema. Once integrated, however, and when one is in the right kind of environment, these skills operate pre-reflectively (see Romdenh-Romluc 2011).

Merleau-Ponty's fundamental insight is that we are bodily attuned to our environment in virtue of the meaningful relationships that the self sustains with the world, which are themselves inscribed in the system of sensori-motor capacities, abilities, and habits that constitute our body schema. So even if 'the body schema is not itself a form of consciousness' (Gallagher 2005, 26), we must still acknowledge that it is not totally unconscious either.[20] Since the body schema serves as the medium through which the world becomes available for us, perceptual experience is best understood as a two-way relation: the various functions of the body schema shape my perceptual experience; but, in turn, the environment contributes to form these functions by providing certain intersubjectively shaped affordances.[21] The body schema proves to be responsive (in a normative way) to these affordances, while these are in turn 'defined as such only on the possibilities projected by body schemas' (Gallagher 2005, 141). In short, the kind of meaning that consciousness receives is the result of the interaction of the body and its surroundings.

My contention is that it is precisely this meaning that contains the success conditions of one's perceptual experience. What Merleau-Ponty calls a 'privileged perception' (2012, 315) or the 'point of maturity of perception'

---

[20] As Gallagher (2005) rightly points out, Merleau-Ponty recognized that 'the schema works along with a marginal awareness of the body', but he 'left the relation between the schema and the marginal awareness unexplained' (20). While this is probably true of the *Phenomenology of Perception*, it was partly corrected in the 1953 lecture *The Sensible World and the World of Expression* (which came out in 2011 in French and 2021 in English translation). By stressing the normative role of different bodily forms of self-relating in their dynamic functioning, the account I am developing in this book attempts to fill in the blind spot left in the 1945 opus and is in line with Merleau-Ponty's 1953 effort.

[21] Since any action takes place in a shared world, the role of others can no longer be kept quiet. Others both shape the demands and my response to these demands. Needless to say, the question of the social context of perception, and of the role of others therein, is a serious deficiency in McDowell's and, more generally, in most contemporary theories of perception in the Anglo-American world. I am going to come back to this cluster of issues in Chapters 5–7, which are concerned with the social dimension of perceptual experience.

(2012, 316) is something we *experience bodily* (*éprouve*) when this perceptual meaning confirms what was expected or anticipated. Here's how Merleau-Ponty famously frames the point:

> My body is geared into the world when my perception provides me with the most varied and the most clearly articulated spectacle possible, and when my motor intentions, as they unfold, receive the responses they anticipate from the world. This maximum of clarity in perception and action specifies a perceptual ground, a background for my life, a general milieu for the coexistence of my body and the world. (2012, 261)

Thanks to our body schema and the habituated lifestyle it has incorporated, we have the ability to expect what the world has to offer; and our perception is deemed 'optimal' when our intentions receive from the world precisely what they had anticipated. In Merleau-Ponty's view, this experience translates into a feeling of appropriateness: just as we may feel the appropriateness of our point of view with regard to our goal or aim, we can feel the 'harmony' (2012, 167) of our action and behaviours in relation to the intentional project that motivates us (Siewert 2013, 217ff.). This does not mean that we can't experience anything 'new', viz. that there is no place for surprises. It suggests, however, that experiences of surprise are only possible against the background of such expectations, from which they diverge. And when this happens, a reconfiguration of our horizon of expectations is triggered.

3.4. Norms of Self-assessment in Perceptual Agency

The phenomenological analyses of kinaesthesis, proprioception, and the body schema surveyed in the previous two sections suggest that, in perception, the flow of incoming bodily signals allows agents to keep track of the relative success of their own experience. Fundamentally, the idea is that these bodily functions build a fundamental aspect of intentionality and are thus constitutive of both inner and outer perception. While Husserl, who saw in the law of motivation that ties together perceptual appearances and kinaesthetic sensations the matrix for the constitution of objectivity and the establishment of objective reference, might be one of the first to have articulated this idea, more recent work in neuroscience shows how perception unfolds by steadily updating incoming kinetic, postural, articular, vestibular, and equilibrial information. Since perception is standardly action-oriented, it is not decoupled from the movement and the proprioceptive/kinaesthetic feedback it generates. As I have argued so far, these channels have a normative function in perception for it is precisely through them that perceptual agents can keep track of objects and of their own actions. My aim in this section is to flesh out this claim by providing more phenomenological details. In so doing, I will come back to McDowell and use his position as a foil to sharpen my own, specifying the sense of my criticism along the way.

As we saw in the first section, the determinant feature of Kant's specifically *transcendental* approach to perception resides in the recognition that perceptual consciousness is not purely receptive; it is not just responding to sensory input. The whole point of Kant's apperceptive structure of consciousness (the 'I think') is to demonstrate that there is an active element in consciousness by virtue of which perceptual agents can justify their claim for objectivity. Specifically, consciousness has a constitutive, transcendental power only insofar as it can become self-conscious of the rules it applies in unifying our representations (Kant 2007, A108). In McDowell's reading, this means that perception has objective purport only to the extent that one has a 'self-conscious conception of how [one's] experience relates to the world' (McDowell 1996, 54, cf. 2007b, 368f.).

The specificity of McDowell's understanding of Kant lies in the way he ties the claim concerning the pervasiveness of self-consciousness in experience to rationality or conceptuality. Both are necessary features of experience. For our representations to have an objective purport, it is necessary, but not sufficient, to be self-aware of what one perceptually takes in; in addition, what comes into view for us in perception must also already be within the sphere of reason, already be within the ambit of our rational activity. In McDowell's picture, both claims converge and reinforce each other in the way that our rational power disposes us to verbally justify our actions and beliefs. Even if we usually don't need to, what we perceive and how we act on that basis *could* be verbally expressed, and therefore be rationally justified, if the situation demanded it. This is what the example of catching a Frisbee aims to show:

> The point of saying that the rational agent, unlike the dog, is realizing a concept in doing what she does is that what she is doing... comes within the scope of her practical rationality—even if only in that, if asked why she caught the frisbee, she would answer, 'No particular reason; I just felt like it.' (McDowell 2007b, 369)

As Siewert (2013) observes, the example, which exemplifies the intimate connection that holds between perception and action, is meant to illustrate 'our readiness to think of oneself as an agent, open in the light of norms of rationality' (196). The kind of pervasive readiness to rationalize what one is doing and thereby justify (even if only very roughly) what one does or perceives is fundamental to the question we are discussing here, for McDowell sees therein just the proof that we humans, as rational beings, stand in the realm of the normative, whereas dogs—which aren't prepared to give such rationalization—do not.

Given what has been argued thus far in this chapter, it should come as no surprise that I consider this view to be of limited relevance. Whereas I find myself in agreement with McDowell that human agency is normatively assessable only insofar as it engages in some sort of self-conscious activity, the normative character of this self-relation does not depend on its being understood as a rational disposition or in terms of concept possession. It is no doubt true that human agency *can* be and often *is* tied to the kind of norms of rationality that McDowell has in view; but it does not have to, and perception offers a powerful example of the kind of basic activity that can be achieved without mobilizing any such capacity. In the remaining space, I want to defend this claim, and provide further evidence that something less than self-critical rationality is required to account for the normative terms of our sense of agency (insofar as the latter is understood in its motivational connection to perception).

We, as perceivers, are agents. We do things: we peer and squint our eyes, we prick up our ears, we smell, taste, and manipulate things. Sometimes, we move our whole body around to modify our perspective on things, or to effect a change in the perceptual conditions (dimming the light, turning down the volume, etc.) Perception is not a passive intake of sensory information; it is a practice; it is naturally oriented toward action. While I, on top of all that, can think about and judge my perceptual take-in, these cognitive achievements are not perceptual per se. They are certainly *occasioned by* my perceptual practice in the sense of being enabled or motivated by it, but thinking and judging are not perceiving. This, however, does not in any way imply that perception is not beholden to norms. On the contrary, a closer phenomenological analysis shows that perception displays a form of norm-sensitivity whose contributories fall, at least in part, outside the scope of the conceptual.

When I perceive, I usually feel that I am the one who is perceiving. Even if not every aspect of my experience falls under my control, there is a sense in which I feel that I am, to a certain extent, in charge of what I perceptually take in. This manifests itself in all the ways I can enact certain perceptual possibilities and inhibit others: I can grasp *this* piece of cloth rather than *that* one, and I can haptically explore its texture by manipulating it in all kinds of ways. If necessary, I can also effectuate a few steps to the back or to the side to change my visual perspective on it. If I want to, I can stop all this and leave the room altogether, thereby removing it completely from my perceptual landscape. In the philosophical jargon, the kind of self-conscious experience that I enjoy when I control my own perceptual behaviour can be described in terms of agency: as a perceiver, I enjoy a sense of agency—a sense of perceptual agency, to be specific.

The phenomenology of perceptual agency is a complex affair, as its sources are varied. Some are reflectively conscious, some are pre-reflectively conscious, and some are even non-conscious. First, perception involves non-conscious motor-control processes that include *efferent processes*, which carry information away from the central nervous system to initiate action; *afferent processes*, which bring in exterior signals to the central nervous system; and *reafferent processes* (or sensory feedback), thanks to which I am bodily self-aware of the movements involved in perception. While strictly speaking non-conscious, these processes nonetheless contribute to generate a pre-reflective embodied awareness of our ongoing experience and, by the same token, to keep action on track (Pacherie 2007). As such, these processes, even as unconscious, assume an important normative function in our perceptual lives.

Of course, the whole story about the phenomenology of perceptual agency is not reducible to these non-conscious motor-control processes. A series of pre-reflectively *conscious* intentional processes are also involved in perception and enable us to self-monitor the unfolding of our experiences and evaluate the kind of effect our bodily movements have on the perceptual scene. As we have seen in our investigation of Husserl's and Merleau-Ponty's analyses of the motivational structure of perception in the previous two sections, these processes, which include visual and proprioceptive feedback, play an even more important normative role in perception by informing the agent both about the intentional trajectory and the current state of her experience. As such, these processes can motivate an optimization or self-correction response, depending on whether the experience's progression is aligned with our intentional goal or not.

The phenomenology of perceptual agency can, on top of all that, include reflectively conscious intentions and motivations as well, including those that McDowell has in view when invoking the notion of self-critical rationality. I can, for instance, consciously desire to adopt a very specific point of view on the painting that I am now contemplating—say, by standing very close to it—in order to appreciate certain specific details. I could, as McDowell rightly maintains, then justify this behaviour by invoking this explicitly (albeit perhaps silently) formulated aim. However, the fact is that the normative character of perception generally does not depend on these and like considerations. The reasons just referred to, or those McDowell appeals to in the Frisbee example, may certainly bind my action to some set of rational norms, but normativity plays out below the level of reflective consciousness and independently of the fact that I may (or may not) be able to reflectively realize and report why I acted the way I did. In other words, *the sense of agency McDowell sees at work in perception does not turn it into a normative practice, because it already is*. The upshot is this: whereas McDowell thinks that perception owes its normative character to the way it is tied to rational norms of justification, the analysis of the phenomenology of perceptual agency undertaken in this chapter demonstrates that perception involves lower-level *perceptual* norms.

As I see it, what McDowell calls 'self-critical control' seems to correspond not to our *experience* of the sense of agency but, rather, to a *retrospective attribution* of agency. In contradistinction to the idea that the sense of perceptual agency is pre-reflectively experienced and rooted in motor control and intentional processes, self-critical control requires higher-order processes of attribution by means of which one consciously and rationally self-ascribes a past experience. The kind of 'self-referential narratives' (Stephens and Graham 1995, 101) involved in retrospective attribution of agency is, as McDowell correctly points out, conceptually and linguistically mediated. This is because it is a form of judgment. But we need to distinguish between our *experience* and our *judgment* of agency. As Gallagher (2020) points out, 'the fact that I may fail to justify my actions...does not necessarily remove my pre-reflective sense of agency for the action' (50). This is not to say that such retrospective judgment runs parallel to our experience of agency and leaves it wholly unaffected. Retrospective attribution 'does have an effect' on agency by 'either strengthening or weakening' it, but—and this is the important point—it does not 'actually constitutes the sense of agency' (Gallagher 2020, 51). In short, it comes in too late, after the fact.

The same holds for the more specific question of the normative in perception. What matters most for normativity is the *prospective* aspect of experience. Perceptual consciousness is in perpetual flux and oriented towards the future. When you perceive something, you are already looking beyond, anticipating what comes next—or at least that something will come next. By drawing on past experiences and current state, perception continuously actualizes its own projected possibilities and establishes its own internal coherency by providing perceived items with a temporal context (Pennisi and Gallagher 2021, 7).

Crucial for our purposes is to recognize that this temporality, which Husserl called the 'living present' (see Section 1.1), translates at the level of the body.[22] This is perhaps nowhere as clear as in Merleau-Ponty's analysis of the body schema, which, he claims, incorporates traces of the past into the present: 'At each moment in a movement, the preceding instant is not forgotten, but rather somehow fit into the present, and, in short, the present perception consists in taking up the series of previous positions that envelop each other by relying upon the current position' (2012, 141). Simply put, perception is an embodied practice whose processes are organized in a temporal fashion. Since it has a practical orientation towards what is to come, perception is driven by anticipations whose eventual fulfilment (or lack thereof) will open some possibilities and foreclose others. If the bodily functions and processes that constitute the body schema play such an important normative role in perception, it is because they are themselves organized along the same temporal structure. The cues provided by efferent and afferent signals, as well as the sensory feedback processes enabled by proprioceptive and kinaesthetic information, have a flowing structure and a temporal direction that informs me about perception's ongoing progression, thus allowing me to measure it against its goal. By virtue of their temporal embeddedness, these bodily cues constitute a normative framework whereby my perception can be evaluated in light of anticipated meaning and intention. Perception is thus normative through and through, but these norms are neither epistemic nor rational without being irrational; rather, these norms constitutively belong to the perceptual process itself.

3.5. Conclusion

Elaborating on insights found in Husserl and Merleau-Ponty, I have argued in this chapter that bodily forms of self-experiences contribute to confer on

---

[22] In *Action and Interaction*, Gallagher explains how '[t]he general structure of this temporality...can also be applied to movement and to motor processes that are not conscious' (2020, 28). In fact, he goes even further and sees it as 'a rule' that even applies 'more generally on the level of neural systems' (27). Given the scope of this book, which bears on the *phenomenology* of perceptual experience, I will set this latter point aside.

experience its normative character. As it provides the experiencing subject with information about its own ongoing experience and situation, our proprioceptive system (which includes but isn't limited to bodily sensations) allows the experiencing agent to constantly *keep track of its performance*, and to *adjust* and *improve* his perception and the corresponding course of his action in light of the pursued goal.

I have contended that these phenomena do not fit in the model put forward by McDowell: these actions are neither mere reflexes (as they are adaptive and context-sensitive), nor conscious position-taking phenomena (as no prior deliberation is necessary). They are clearly rule- or norm-governed, but they don't imply any language or concept, not even implicitly. Since phenomenologists operate with a larger, embodied concept of intentionality, one that isn't tightly connected to judgment and epistemic justification but that still plays a normative function inasmuch as it guides action toward successful completion, I have argued that phenomenology is better equipped to accommodate cases like these.

In recent years, enactivists have radicalized the phenomenological point of view and adopted a strong anti-representational stance. From the enactive perspective, 'the problem of explaining our normative grip is no longer the problem of representation; it's rather the problem of explaining how we are dynamically coupled to the world' (Gallagher 2017, 105). This means that assessing whether or not experience is attuned to the environment will depend not on the organism's capacity to self-represent itself and its surroundings, but on the organism's capacity to adjust in suitable ways to the specificities of its situation. I conclude by briefly explaining the motivation behind this claim.

For Gallagher (2017), invoking representations—which, for him, are by definition decoupled from experience—is equivalent to going 'offline'. In the perspective that I have been developing here, this is problematic, for it amounts to losing touch (even if only momentarily) with one's own perceptual situation. To be clear, the problem is that if representations are in some ways 'decoupled' from the ongoing perceptual process, or if they come in succession, then the organism can't continuously cast its own actions in evaluative terms and make the required adjustments when they are needed, thereby making it impossible to perceptually track things. Gallagher makes a similar point when analysing action. In his eyes, the deepest problem of representationalism is that it is detached from the relevant state of affairs, which makes it hardly reconcilable with any normative constraint. In short, it seems that you can't have it both ways: you cannot both track your goal and be 'offline': 'But it is difficult to see how an aspect of motor control that is a constitutive part of the action can be considered decoupled from x, which it may be tracking, or, for that matter, from the context, or the action itself. Isn't this kind of anticipation fully situated in the action context?' (Gallagher 2017, 92). Insofar as motor control is part of the action, it *is* situated; but then it is not decoupled from the movement and the proprioceptive/kinaesthetic feedback it generates. It is online, and it is precisely for this reason that it can keep track of its object or of the action itself.

From the enactivist point of view, the predictive processing view (or at least some version of it) faces the same problem: 'To think that the anticipatory emulator involves a decoupled process is to think that such anticipations can be detached from perceptual and proprioceptive input, which they clearly cannot be. They are part of the online process of action; as such they register not simply some future state, but the trajectory of the action (from present to future)' (2017, 92). According to Gallagher, the perceptual and proprioceptive input is not only *de facto* part of the 'online' process of action but also *necessary* to meet the requirements of the normative constraint.

It's not clear to me why we should accept that representations are 'by definition' decoupled from experience and therefore that the above-mentioned argument is sound. Given the extraordinary lack of consensus on what representation actually means—even just within the enactivist camp!—I prefer to stay agnostic on this specific issue. To me, the important question is not whether or not we should retain something of representationalism—be it in its so-called 'weak' or minimal form (Alsmith and Vignemont 2012), or as body-formatted (viz. B-formatted) representations in the brain (Goldman 2014). What matters to me is to recognize that perception is normative not because it is conceptual (it isn't), but thanks to the functional role played by bodily self-awareness in perceptual experience.

Phenomenology and the Norms of Perception. Maxime Doyon, Oxford University Press. © Maxime Doyon 2024.
DOI: 10.1093/9780191993527.003.0003

4
Multisensory Perception

Perceptual experiences are standardly taken to involve the contribution of *some* of the five traditional senses (vision, audition, olfaction, smell, and touch). The senses may, to varying degrees, be combined or integrated to one another and yield different kinds of conscious experiences. In the contemporary scientific literature on multisensory perception, it is customary to distinguish between two kinds of multisensory achievements: *phenomenal unity* and *object unity*.

Right now, I hear music and other background noises coming from the street, I see the text I am writing on my computer screen, and I feel the weight of my body on the chair I'm sitting on. This first-person description captures an important aspect of the phenomenal unity of my present conscious life. While triggered by different objects and events, my experience is harmoniously lived through and has a unified phenomenal character. While some philosophers think that the unity of consciousness can sometimes break down (Nagel 1971), or even that consciousness is usually disunified (Dennett 1992), there is a large consensus in the contemporary philosophical and scientific communities around the idea that our conscious experiences are *always* unified in some way or other.[1]

Often, however, our senses not only are simultaneously exercised, and their corresponding contents unified in consciousness, but are, in addition, directed at the same worldly object or event, such as when you see your partner, hear her voice, and smell her perfume as you talk to her. This is a case of *object unity*, which characterizes perceptions in which various sensory cues are experienced as belonging to the same object or event.[2] One of

---

[1] In the philosophical canon, this view is attributed to Descartes, Kant, and Husserl. For a contemporary defence of this view, see Hurley 1998 and Deroy 2014.

[2] From a phenomenological perspective, things appear to be slightly more complicated, and not only because there are intermediate or blurred cases (Deroy 2014, 114ff.). The fact that perception has a spatial-temporal horizonal structure suggests that object unity is only ever lived through against a phenomenally unified horizonal background that constitutes the larger intentional context from which there can be discrete unities at all. As we have seen in the first two chapters, this gestaltist principle, which both Husserl and Merleau-Ponty have made their

the most intriguing topics in recent scholarship on perception concerns the proper way of characterizing the phenomenology of such multisensory experiences. Is the perceptual experience of your partner the harmonious outcome of multiple, aggregated sensory events, or are you, rather, perceptually aware, as you undergo the experience, of a seen body, a heard voice, and a smelled perfume as integrated parts of *one* perceptual event? Contemporary psychologist Charles Spence and philosopher Tim Bayne doubt that the second option is viable:

> it is debatable whether the 'unity of the event' really is internal to one's experience in these cases, or whether it involves a certain amount of post-perceptual processing (or inference). In other words, it seems to us to be an open question whether, in these situations, one's experience is of a MPO [that is, a multisensory perceptual object] or whether instead it is structured in terms of multiple instances of unimodal perceptual objects. (Spence and Bayne, 2015, 119)

According to Spence and Bayne (2015), it is doubtful that you *perceptually* experience the 'togetherness' of the seen body, the heard voice, and the smelled perfume as constituting a single perceptual event, that is, a multisensory perceptual object. A more plausible hypothesis is to conceive of the unified phenomenal character as resulting from post-perceptual processes and/or subconscious inferences being applied to a set of unimodal perceptual objects. Tim Bayne (2014) has dubbed this the 'decomposition thesis'. While we may easily grant that we are often concurrently conscious of various perceptual properties, Spence and Bayne (2015) contend that each property is instantiated by a specific sense modality: the seen body by vision, the heard voice by audition, the smelled perfume by olfaction, etc., which are *then* integrated in consciousness at a later stage. Since the senses run in parallel and yield their own representational content, our perception of our partner talking to us is therefore nothing beyond the (inferred) *sum of modality-specific contents*. Here's a passage that specifies that last point:

> When philosophers and psychologists suggest that consciousness is multisensory, what they typically appear to mean is that a subject's overall

---

own, has important metaphysical implications, for the horizonal character of perception assumes a necessary function in deciding upon their ontological status as objects. I will cast this metaphysical question aside here.

conscious state can, at a single point in time, include within itself experiences that can be fully identified with particular sensory modalities—i.e., that sense-specific experiences can be co-conscious. (Bayne and Spence 2015, 99)

This description, which is paradigmatic of the multisensory view that Spence and Bayne defend, entails what their opponents has called the thesis of Minimal Multimodality: 'The phenomenal character of each perceptual episode is *exhausted* by that which is associated with each individual modality, along with whatever accrues thanks to mere co-consciousness' (O'Callaghan 2015, 555; italics are mine).

The first objective of this chapter is to make a case for the opposing view and argue that the effect of multisensory integration is reflected *in experience* in a way that is *not* exhausted by (the sum of) modality-specific phenomenal features. This is an important step in the overall economy of the book, for one of the upshots of this claim is that it allows us to appreciate from a novel angle how the conscious experience of sense integration and cooperation impacts the normativity of perception. The second and main objective of the chapter is to defend this last claim. Since perception is, in a vast array of contexts, best understood as a form of practice or as action-oriented (see Chapters 3 and 5), my aim here will be to show how successful or failed operations of sense coordination can improve or impair what I will call *perceptual agency*, viz. our embodied capacity to respond in appropriate ways to the affordances of the perceived environment.[3] Before getting started, I'll specify these two objectives by considering Casey O'Callaghan's view, who developed a sequence of arguments that support both claims.[4]

In a series of recent papers, O'Callaghan has mounted an argument to the effect that not all perceptual experience is modality-specific: 'certain forms of multimodal perceptual experience are incompatible with the claim that each aspect of a perceptual experience is associated with some specific modality or another' (2015, 552). There seems to be little doubt that at least

---

[3] Given the phenomenological orientation of this book, I won't address directly the question of whether we need to postulate the existence of a subpersonal binding mechanism, or an associative learning process, in order to account for multisensory perceptions (Connolly 2019, 127ff.). What interests me is the *phenomenology* of multisensory experiences, that is, our perceptual awareness of, or experiential access to, such multisensory unities. I briefly come back to this question in Section 4.3.1.

[4] While I focus on Casey O'Callaghan's work in what follows, it should be noted that Mohan Matthen (2017, 129) also rejects the view about minimal multimodularity, which he labels 'empiricist atomism'.

some types of perceptual attributes that bind together discrete perceived objects *constitutively depend* on multisensory interaction. Here is a first series of examples:

> For instance, spatial, temporal, and causal attributes perceptibly hold between things perceived using different senses. Typical humans can multisensorily perceptually experience a causal relation's holding between something visible and something audible, a unified rhythm comprising audible sounds and felt taps, the pattern of motion between audible and visible happenings, or the identity of something seen with something felt. (2015, 552)

These descriptions, which are accurate, aim to suggest that there really is a phenomenology associated with multisensory interaction, and that what O'Callaghan calls 'intermodal feature binding awareness' (2014a, 73) is real. However, since such binding awareness could still be the outcome of postperceptual processes, these examples alone are not conclusive.

Further support in favour of the constitutive view can be found in the recognition that the perception of 'some novel types of features' (2015, 552) may sometimes *require* the interplay of more than one sense modality. To illustrate, O'Callaghan frequently has recourse to the phenomenon of flavour perception. 'Flavor experiences may have entirely novel phenomenal features of a type—even a qualitative type—that no unimodal experience could instantiate and that do not accrue thanks to simple co-consciousness' (2015, 567f.). The experience of flavours constitutively depends on multisensory interactions of touch, smell, and taste in the sense that flavours are irreducible to what these senses can provide individually. Mint provides a superb example: 'There is a distinctive, recognizable, and novel quality of mint…that is consciously perceptible only thanks to the joint work of several sensory systems' (2017, 174; cf. 2015, 552).

On the basis of this and like evidence,[5] O'Callaghan argues that the thesis put forward by Spence and Bayne (2015) cannot be generalized: 'not all ways of perceiving are modality specific' (2014a, 73). The phenomenal character of multisensory interaction does *not always* amount to the mere

---

[5] More examples can be found in O'Callaghan 2012. For a formalization of the argument, see O'Callaghan 2014a, and for an exposition of the philosophical importance of the thesis, see O'Callaghan 2019. Additional support for this view is provided by Briscoe (2019), who makes a similar point concerning haptic (viz. explorative or active) touch and egocentric space.

accumulation of unimodal experiences. Some experiences are, as he puts it, 'constitutively multisensory' (2015, 569).

The constitutive view that O'Callaghan defends entails a couple of interrelated, yet different, claims:[6]

- *Certain types of perceptual attributes could not be had without multimodal interaction*, e.g. spatial, temporal, and causal attributes (O'Callaghan 2015).
- *Multimodality introduces novel types of features to our experience that do not belong to any modality*, e.g. mint, which O'Callaghan (2017) presents as a qualitative feature that is irreducible to touch, taste, and smell.
- Finally, in other texts (e.g. 2012), O'Callaghan also points out, less controversially perhaps, that *some aspects of experience are not modality specific, i.e. can be presented to multiple modalities*, as, e.g., shapes, which can be presented visually or tactilely.

I think that O'Callaghan is right about all three claims, and the distinction he draws on that basis between the Minimal and the Constitutive Theses of multimodality is a welcomed one. While advancing my own reasons for rejecting the view held by Spence and Bayne, I will regularly refer to O'Callaghan's descriptions.

According to O'Callaghan, one of the upshots of the existence of intermodal feature binding awareness is that perception is thereby enriched or enhanced. The point is simple: since, e.g., the unique taste of mint simply isn't available without the coordinated effort of the sensory systems of touch, smell, and taste, perception is *richer* when resulting from sense coordination. This is the fourth claim entailed by the Constitutive Thesis:

- *Multimodality enriches our perception*, e.g. touch and smell enhance taste by allowing perceivers to have gustatory experiences I wouldn't otherwise have, thus making my perception richer (O'Callaghan 2017).

Although O'Callaghan hasn't thoroughly worked out the normative implications of multisensory perception, especially how they bear on agency (cf. Section 4.3), I agree with him on that point too; that is, I also believe

---

[6] Thanks to Peter Antich for proposing these formulations.

that sensory integration has a normative impact on experience in the sense of improving or optimizing it.

At a certain level, then, I consider O'Callaghan to be an ally as he shares my two ambitions, i.e. rejecting the thesis of Minimal Multimodality held by Spence and Bayne (2015), and arguing for the normative impact of sense integration on experience.

At the same time, O'Callaghan leans on the conception of phenomenality that Spence, Bayne, and most philosophers and scientist involved in this debate work with, and which appears to me to be overly narrow and ultimately unsatisfying. It is a definition that is aligned with what Anglo-American philosophers of mind, following Thomas Nagel (1974), typically call the qualitative features or the 'what it's likeness' of experience. In essence, the expression is meant to capture something like the 'raw feel' of sense experience—what it is like to have sensations of hearing, seeing, smelling, tasting, touching, or a combination of any of those sensory feels. Despite its widespread use in certain circles, this chapter provides reasons to think that the phenomenal character of multisensory experience cannot be adequately captured by what this locution is standardly taken to mean. By drawing conceptual resources in the classical phenomenological repertoire of Edmund Husserl (Section 4.1) and Maurice Merleau-Ponty (Section 4.2), the chapter looks at a blind spot in this discussion and argues that a vast array of bodily cues makes a fundamental, but still largely underestimated, contribution to the experiential make-up of our conscious lives. With respect to my first objective, it will be argued that the phenomenology of multisensory experience not only includes various forms of *bodily self-experiences* but often also contains *felt possibilities of actions and behaviours,* both being irreducible to any 'raw feels'. If successful, the argument concerning the widening of phenomenal consciousness will intimate that *all* forms of perceptual experiences constitutively depend on the interplay of two or more senses, thus providing a further, stronger reason to believe that Husserl and Merleau-Ponty would, too, reject the thesis of Minimal Multimodality and endorse the Constitutive Thesis that O'Callaghan (and Briscoe 2021) rightly defend(s).

Spelling out the details of these claims will put me on the road toward my second objective, which is to specify the intrinsic relation between normativity and perceptual experience (Section 4.3). In essence, I will argue not only that the mechanisms responsible for multimodality make an important phenomenological difference of which we are aware but also that this experience is evaluable in normative terms. Whereas the impact of sense cooperation on *perceptual judgments* is already well documented in psychology and briefly alluded to in O'Callaghan's work, the argument I am defending here concerns the impact of multisensory perception on *agency*. In this sense, the following analyses strengthen the argument developed in the previous chapter.

4.1. Husserl on Multisensory Awareness

Although multisensory perception was never, for Husserl, a central topic of phenomenological research, he did write on the topic on a few occasions. In *Ideas II*, we find some of Husserl's most sustained reflections on the senses and their central contribution to the constitution of the self and intentional life. Regarding perception, Husserl makes the seemingly trivial claim that perceptual objects (or some of their properties) are accessible through diverse sense modalities: the 'thing of perception has but one spatial corporeality' (1989, 42), but it can be apprehended in a manifold of ways, 'as a corporeality that is both seen and touched' (1989, 41), for instance. Perceptual objects have but one materiality or corporeality; they occupy one space because they are ontologically one. Nevertheless, this unity conceals a phenomenological complexity: these objects not only can be experienced from a variety of perspectives and by various egos but they are also structurally open for a variety of sense-experiences.

Phenomenologically, these experiences can be classified in a number of ways. With regard to the five traditional senses, it is possible to distinguish between their capacity to *individually* apprehend identical objective properties and their capacity to *jointly* perceive these properties. Upon perceiving a blanket in bright daylight, I could, say, haptically recognize that its texture, which I now experience as being smooth, is also responsible for its brightness. In this situation, Husserl contends that '[i]t is the same objective property which announces itself in the brightness and in the smoothness' (1989, 41). The fact that a single objective property can be perceived as identical through different sensory channels, as with textures, is important, for it suggests that it is in principle possible that it be multimodally perceived, that is, simultaneously perceived in the two or more modalities. For if I can identify the smoothness and the brightness of the blanket in a succession of unimodal experiences, then I can, presumably, haptically and visually experience the texture of the blanket *at the same time* as well.

The possibility of simultaneously exercising our sense modalities upon an object still does not exhaust the ways of cashing out the phenomenology of multisensory perception, however, for some perceptual events *depend* on the interplay of two or more senses. To recall, O'Callaghan (2015, 2017) sees this as evidence that the decomposition thesis held by Spence and Bayne cannot be generalized: the experience of, e.g., flavours, he suggests, shows that at least *some* perceptual events are *constitutively multimodal* in the sense that the joint exercise of taste, smell, and touch yields an experience that transcends their specific individual contribution. Even though Husserl never seemed to be particularly interested in this specific theoretical question, I think that he is committed to the Constitutive Thesis so understood.

Take vision. As Husserl describes it, visual perception is not limited to any given profile but integrates further possible perspectives. When seeing a cube, for instance, we do not just see its visible side but also co-perceive its currently non-visible backside, which we anticipate seeing by rotating the cube or effecting certain bodily movements. Husserl explains the integration of the cube's implicitly given content in perceptual consciousness by appealing to the so-called 'law of motivation', according to which visual appearances are dependent upon kinaesthesis (cf. Section 3.2). Simply put, Husserl's idea is that perceptual content is expected or anticipated in intentional consciousness thanks to the sensations that accompany bodily movements. In virtue of its motivational power, the flow of kinaesthetic sensations is deemed necessary for constituting temporally extended objects, and therefore for having perceptions at all. As a result, it seems that Husserl never conceived of visual perception in exclusively visual terms. The synthetic unification of intentional contents in visual consciousness is, rather, the outcome of the integration of visual inputs, horizonal contents, and kinaesthetic sensations; as such, it is indissociable from the consciousness of our embodied being.[7] It is true that the inclusion of bodily forms of self-experience does not make visual experience any less visual; but it shows that Husserl never regarded vision as a unisensory experience. Since Husserl believes that the perception of visual objects and their properties transcends what vision and kinaesthesis can individually provide, it follows that he is committed to at least this form of the Constitutive Thesis too.

---

[7] This idea was not only massively at work in Merleau-Ponty (see Sections 3.3 and 4.2), but it lies at the heart of sensorimotor enactivism as well: 'On the enactive view, one should expect that visual content requires integration with kinaesthesis and proprioception; after all, visual content depends on sensory effects of movement' (Noë 2004, 95).

But there is more. It is not only that kinaesthetic sensations generate expectations about how the phenomenology of *things* would change with respect to movement; Husserl also thought that perceptual features such as *distance, orientation,* and *direction,* too, are always experienced in relation to one's body, which serves as the reference point (cf. 1989, 158f.). Even if these spatial properties, too, are experienced as belonging to visual consciousness, their apprehension still relies on bodily self-awareness as well, for their perceptual meaning can only become manifest within an egocentric frame of reference. As argued in the previous chapter., this does mean that we are self-aware of all the relevant bodily functions and mechanisms themselves (e.g. I don't have to be aware of myself as a zero point for my body to function as a centre of orientation). Rather, it means that our proprioceptive and motor programmes support intentional activity in the way that they shape our perceptual and practical relation to the world, indexing it to our motor capacities (viz. the 'I can'). In that sense, they do enter perceptual consciousness, even if only indirectly and marginally. According to Husserl, the point holds for every phenomenally experienced spatial property (like distance, direction, and orientation): they all depend on an embodied frame of reference, which is the indexical 'here' relative to which they become manifest. As a result, with respect to those properties, Husserl unambiguously endorses the constitutive view: their perception *constitutively depends* on both proprioceptive and exteroceptive signals.[8]

Importantly, Husserl's point about vision can be generalized.[9] Not only things and spatial properties but *every* perception is multimodally constituted. The reason Husserl is committed to this claim is that, for him, perception cannot be reduced to outer perception. At least since *Ideas II*, Husserl contends that tactile, cutaneous, and kinaesthetic sensations are pervasive in *all* forms of intentional experiences. Every intentional experience includes an unthematic, pre-reflective form of bodily self-reference. Perception makes no exception. As we perceive outer objects, we feel the movements and the velocity of our body and body parts, and we are aware (in a very much marginal way) of our position and posture. Since proprioceptive experience is constitutive of how we perceive things, 'It makes no

---

[8] Considering spatial location, Briscoe (2021) recently developed a robust and empirically informed argument that leads to the same conclusion: 'Location in egocentric space is novel relative to the representational powers of *any* modality working by itself' (S3917).

[9] The claim that I am making here is not an eidetic, but a descriptive, one; that is, it does not belong to the essence of perception that it is multisensory. That's why there could be exceptions (in principle).

sense to assign to each sense its property-complexes as separate components of the thing.' On the contrary, 'The thing...is constituted in unitary apperception' (Husserl 1989, 75). In short, Husserl's idea is that bodily self-awareness and perceptual intentionality are interdependent features of consciousness (Husserl 1989, 57), for which reason it appears that *all* perceptual experiences are multimodal in that sense.[10]

Of course, recognizing that the multimodal character of *all* perceptual experiences on that basis requires that we accept counting proprioception as a sense, but this should not be too controversial. There is a rather large consensus in the scientific literature around the necessity of revisiting the traditional (viz. Aristotelian) list of the senses, and proprioception seems—and by far—to be the best candidate to join the group (which includes, among others, pain, time, and temperature awareness, as well as interoception).[11]

Even if we add proprioception, which constitutively belongs to the horizonal structure of perceptual consciousness, to the traditional list and recognize that it is always operative in perceptual experience, we might still want to resist ascribing to Husserl a view that moves beyond the standard (i.e. Anglo-American) conception of phenomenality that I see operative in O'Callaghan's account. For to hold that perception is never unilaterally directed at the world in the sense of involving a concomitant awareness of movement sensations and a marginal consciousness of the location of our body in space is compatible with the standard definition of phenomenality (viz. 'what it's likeness'), one might claim, insofar as it is in principle possible to conceive of proprioceptive and kinaesthetic sensations as yielding 'raw feels' in much the same way as the other senses do. But is this plausible?

---

[10] This does not imply that the constitution of the different *sensory fields* does not enjoy a certain independence. Elsewhere in *Ideas II*, Husserl writes, for instance, that 'The unity of the visual sense-thing does not necessarily require connection with the unity of the tactual sense-thing' (1989, 23). And in *Phenomenological Psychology* he contends that 'the data of different fields have no sensuous, therefore hyletic, unity with one another' (1977, 133). While the different sensory fields appear to enjoy a relative independence when described or analysed, their interplay in actual experience is beyond doubt. That's why Husserl adds, immediately after the previously quoted passage, 'But when the characters of apprehension are included, when therefore the concrete appearances are considered, the situation is different.' Since fully fledged perception obviously does involve the relevant 'characters of apprehension', these passages don't challenge the position here presented. For an in-depth analysis of the sensory fields and their interplay, see Taipale 2014, ch. 2.

[11] Arguments for the inclusion of proprioception can be found in Fridland 2011, Schwenkler 2013, and de Vignemont 2020. On the absence of widespread assent on this question, see Matthen 2017, Macpherson 2011b, and Durie 2005.

Let's backtrack. Very generally, Husserl contends that it is not possible to explain any type of perceptual experience without a reference to the background functioning of the body (cf. Section 3.2). He justifies this affirmation by insisting on the pervasive role of touch, which he considers to be *the* fundamental sense in virtue of its necessary role in the constitution of both self (1989) and perceptual objectivity (1997, 2001c). Now, since understanding the role of touch in perception hardly seems possible without a reference to the whole somatosensory system, and therefore to proprioception as well,[12] it is not clear to me that the notions of 'raw' or 'sensory feel' can adequately capture the complex phenomenal situation, even as combined.

This is admittedly not a conclusive argument, but it is not the only one either. Husserl also argued that even my perception of time and temporal objects depends on the body. The point is that both objective and subjective time would be impossible without experiencing a flow of changing appearances, which are themselves motivated by bodily intentionality. Since I need to experience change to experience time, and change depends on the motivational capacity of the body, it follows that even the perception of time constitutively depends on the body. If this argument is sound, then it seems that bodily self-awareness *does* make an impact on the overall phenomenology of experience that isn't reducible to any 'what it's likeness' talk, for *the sense of the object's temporal presence adds to the phenomenology of its perception without being itself sensorial*. I will leave it at that here, but in the next section I will consider another, better reason for moving beyond the traditional conception of phenomenality by considering Merleau-Ponty's conception of *felt possibilities* of action.

Before getting there, let's sum things up. I have suggested on various grounds that Husserl is committed to the constitutive view, which, to recall, entails the following claims:

- *There are certain types of perceptual attributes that could not be had without multimodal interaction*, e.g. spatial, temporal, and causal attributes. While Husserl discusses cases such as the perception of distance, direction, and orientation, I take him to be making essentially the same point as O'Callaghan insofar as his descriptions show that

---

[12] This is, incidentally, the reason why some philosophers and scientists treat touch and proprioception as constituting a single sense. See, for instance, Fulkerson 2014.

these perceptual attributes constitutively depend on both proprioceptive and exteroceptive signals.
- *Multimodality introduces novel types of features to our experience that do not belong to any modality*, e.g. mint, which O'Callaghan presents as a qualitative feature that is irreducible to touch, taste, and smell. Husserl is more radical here and argues that vision and proprioception are needed to yield *any* visual experience. This insight is the core of Husserl's law of motivation (cf. Section 3.2), which he first presented in 1907 in *Thing and Space* and still defended in the *Crisis* in 1937, which leaves little doubt about his commitment towards it.
- *Some aspects of experience are not modality specific, i.e. can be presented to multiple modalities*, as, e.g., shapes, which can be presented visually or tactilely. Husserl speaks more abstractly of spatio-temporal things, which can be perceived through various sensory channels, 'as a corporeality that is both seen and touched', for instance (1989, 41), but again, he seems to agree with O'Callaghan here too.

No doubt, then, Husserl would, like O'Callaghan, reject Bayne and Spence's thesis about consciousness being the mere sum of modality-specific features, but he disagrees with him on how to describe the relevant phenomenal features.

As we have seen earlier, for O'Callaghan the constitutive view not only is phenomenologically more accurate than the thesis of multimodality but also has a clear advantage over it: thanks to the coordinated effort of the sensory systems, perception is enriched or enhanced without any need to appeal to post-perceptual processes. This corresponds to the fourth claim entailed by the Constitutive Thesis:

- *Multimodality enriches or enhances our perception*, e.g. the contribution of touch, smell, and taste allow me to enjoy a richer gustatory experience than if they these senses wouldn't cooperate.

Husserl's conception of optimality confirms that he would accept this claim too. In the first chapter (Section 1.2), I have shown how our experience of things is teleologically oriented toward what Husserl calls the *ideal of perceptual givenness* (Husserl 1997, §§36–9; cf. Doyon 2018). In the D-manuscripts, there are some passages in which Husserl spells out his ideas on this in the context of analysis of multisensory perception, and we are told that this ideal of completeness corresponds to a *multisensory experience of the thing*, that is, one in which every sensory channel is systematically connected to the others such as to yield 'a *continuity of optima*' ('*eine Kontinuität von Optima*') (Ms. D 13 II 26a). Conceived as an infinite, teleologically oriented process, only such a multisensory experience of interconnected optimal points of view would bring the thing to this limit of ideal givenness, that is, to its maximum of clarity. In *Ideas II*, this led Husserl to draw the ontological conclusion that 'all senses must accord' for there to be an experience of 'what is Objective' (Husserl 1989, 73).

So, while it is no doubt true that the Constitutive Thesis entails various compatible, yet different, claims, Husserl seems to be endorsing them all directly or indirectly. Given the orientation of this book, I will come back, in the third section of this chapter, on the last of these claims and explain in more detail how the endorsement of the constitutive view impacts the phenomenological account of perceptual agency, which acquires its normative character precisely therein. Before getting there, however, let's take a close look at Merleau-Ponty's position on this cluster of issues.

4.2. Merleau-Ponty on the Ontological Structure of Perception

In *Phenomenology of Perception,* Merleau-Ponty espouses a number of theses that are very close to those put forward by Husserl in *Ideas II*, beginning with these two that play a pivotal role in his conception of multisensory perception. First, Merleau-Ponty agrees with Husserl that visual experience depends on some forms of bodily self-experience, or, as he puts it, that vision and touch 'communicate directly' (2012, 232) with one another in the normal adult. As a result, Merleau-Ponty's conception of motivation comes out as relatively close to Husserl's (see Sections 3.3 and 5.2). Second, Merleau-Ponty draws attention to the *permanence* of bodily self-awareness in *all* perceptual experience: 'My body is constantly perceived' (2012, 92) and 'remains on the margins of all my perceptions' (93). Merleau-Ponty specifies what this means by explaining the essential role of bodily awareness in the constitution of perceptual gestalts: 'one's own body is the always implied third term of the figure-background structure, and each figure appears perspectivally against the double horizon of external space and bodily space' (103). Given the central importance of the body for the emergence of perceptual gestalts, it is fair to say that Merleau-Ponty, again like Husserl, takes every perception to be constitutively multisensory. To recall, the point is not that we are merely co-conscious of our bodily selves as we perceive but, rather, that the body is something like the central organizing principle of the sensory field. The body is 'our means of communication' with the world, or 'the latent horizon of our experience' (95). In this sense, perception would not be possible at all if we were not also bodily self-conscious.

Beyond these two points of convergence, there are, however, a few notable differences between Husserl's and Merleau-Ponty's views on multisensory perception. Two seem particularly noteworthy. First, Merleau-Ponty has formulated clear arguments against the classical views (i.e. the intellectualist and the empiricist views) on multisensory perception. This double criticism opens onto a positive account of how the senses communicate in experience. In Section 4.2.1 I will briefly explain what the thesis concerning sensory communication amounts to and what it entails in the context of this chapter. In Section 4.2.2 I will lay emphasis on what separates Husserl from Merleau-Ponty's view on agency. In short and to anticipate what comes next: while Husserl thinks that bodily forms of self-relations have the singular capacity to generate *expectations* with regard to the ongoing flow of appearances, for Merleau-Ponty these expectations more explicitly take the practical form of *readiness to act* on the part of the subject. While there is no real opposition between the two views, I will show how the shift of emphasis effected by Merleau-Ponty led him to make the argument in favour of an enlarged conception of phenomenality even more plausible, thus lending further support to the constitutive view that he, too, defends.

4.2.1. Sensory Communication

In the *Sensing* chapter of the *Phenomenology*, Merleau-Ponty unequivocally rejects the traditional empiricist view on the separation of the senses, pointing out in passing its internal contradictions. Merleau-Ponty's phenomenological analysis aims to show that the pure sensible qualities that the empiricist attempts to find simply do not exist; from the standpoint of the intellectualist's rejection of empiricism, Merleau-Ponty holds that they are rather 'merged into a total experience in which they are ultimately indiscernible' (2012, 226). As is typically the case, this passage is shortly followed by Merleau-Ponty's rejection of opposing the intellectualist view on the grounds that the senses are not really indiscernible either, e.g. audition is not spatial in the same way that vision is (e.g. music reveals the space of the concert hall in a manner that vision does not).

As is often the case, Merleau-Ponty's position builds on insights found on both sides: while the senses present the world in importantly different ways, Merleau-Ponty holds that they 'communicate' (2012, 234) essentially with one another in the sense that they are moments of a comprehensive experience, or that they provide access to a style of being that is not reducible to any particular sense. Merleau-Ponty justifies this claim in three interrelated ways, stressing what he calls the *unity of the world*, the *unity of the lived body*, and the *unity of the things* themselves.

First, Merleau-Ponty repeatedly stresses throughout the *Phenomenology* the 'primordial unity' of the world, which he regards as 'the horizon of all horizons' (2012, 345) and 'the unique term of all of our projects' (493). The claim, which takes inspiration from Kant and Husserl, means that, ultimately, it is the world that ensures that my experiences have a meaningful unity. Merleau-Ponty's account of multisensory perception is the immediate consequence of this insight, for he considers the 'sensory spaces' or domains to be the 'concrete moments' of this 'overall configuration' (230). The critique of the empiricist position is thus clear: Merleau-Ponty thinks that investigating perception like the scientist or the empiricist does by claiming or simply assuming the separation of the senses and their corresponding regions of experience amounts to 'cutting oneself off' (230) from this primordial unity of the world. From a first-person or phenomenological point of view, however, it is precisely this *meaningful unity* of experience that needs to be retrieved and described. For this reason—and *pace* Spence and Bayne (2015)—the phenomenology of experience is not reducible to a mere assemblage of qualitative qualities (or qualia) produced by the senses. We perceptually encounter things in situations, and the significance and value of perceived objects depend not on an ensemble of sensory qualities but on the total context in which they are inscribed. The 'unity of the world' refers to this unsurpassable horizon of meaning that constitutes perceptual consciousness.[13]

Second, Merleau-Ponty's insistence on the crucial importance of the meaningful unity of the world has another consequence, for it goes hand in hand with the unity of the lived body. Essentially, the point is that the body, too, forms a unity and functions holistically. Contrary to the empiricist's belief, the 'body is not a sum of juxtaposed organs, but a synergetic system of which all of the functions are taken up and tied together in the general

---

[13] In the *Crisis*, Husserl finds himself in agreement with Merleau-Ponty as he contends that thing-consciousness and world-consciousness make up 'an inseparable unity' (1970, 131).

movement of being in the world' (2012, 243). Correspondingly, in action, 'the various parts of my body—its visual, tactile, and motor aspects—are not simply coordinated' (243); the body rather 'gathers itself together, and carries itself through all of its resources' (241) in order to 'perform a single gesture' (153), namely the action itself. If one may very well grant that our senses *appear* to be distinct from the perspective of the objective world, the phenomenological attitude does not admit this kind of separation: 'the experience of isolated "senses" takes place only within an abnormal attitude' (234), namely the naturalistic or empiricist attitude. But, as such, it 'cannot be useful for the analysis of direct consciousness' (234). From the first-personal or phenomenological point of view, the body functions as a unified whole, and the senses are in constant communication.

Specifying what the latter claim means necessitates, third, that we turn our attention to Merleau-Ponty's analysis of what he calls 'the inter-sensory unity of the thing' (2012, 248). His basic idea is nicely encapsulated in this beautiful, even if somewhat lengthy, passage:

> If a phenomenon—such as a reflection or a light breeze—only presents itself to one of my senses, then it is a phantom, and it will only approach real existence if, by luck, it becomes capable of speaking to my other senses, as when the wind, for example, is violent and makes itself visible in the disturbances of the landscape. Cézanne said that a painting contained, in itself, even the odor of the landscape. He meant that the arrangement of the color upon the thing (and in the work of art if it fully captures the thing) by itself signifies all of the responses that it would give to the interrogation of my other senses, that a thing would not have that color if it did not have this form, these tactile properties, that sonority, or that odor; and that the thing is the absolute plenitude that projects my undivided existence in front of itself. The unity of the thing, beyond all of its congealed properties, is not a substratum, an empty X, or a subject of inherence, but rather that unique accent that is found in each one, that unique manner of existing of which its properties are a secondary expression. For example, the fragility, rigidity, transparency, and crystalline sound of a glass expresses a single manner of being. (2012, 332)

Merleau-Ponty elaborates on this description by explaining how perceived things call for our engagement and interaction with them while speaking indifferently to *all* our senses. Therein lies their intersensory unity. In return, the senses communicate in their response to the perceptual scene, that is, in the way they jointly respond to the thing's solicitation. This is how Merleau-Ponty famously came to endorse the neighbouring claim about the synaesthetic character of *all* perceptions:

> Synesthetic perception is the rule and, if we do not notice it, this is because scientific knowledge displaces experience and we have unlearned seeing, hearing, and sensing in general in order to deduce what we ought to see, hear, or sense from our bodily organization and from the world as it is conceived by the physicist. (2012, 238)

The claim is strong: Merleau-Ponty holds that synaesthetic perception is not an exceptional state but, rather, the normal perceptual condition.[14] Taken literally, this is a shocking, if not downright false, assertion, for synaesthesia is standardly taken to be a rare and abnormal condition. It is abnormal since it results from an atypical and contingent sensory wiring, and it is rare since it occurs in only roughly 1 in 2,000 persons (O'Callaghan 2012; Bayne and Spence 2015). Merleau-Ponty thus seems to commit a category mistake when he extends the synaesthetic condition to everybody.

As Abath (2017) rightly pointed out, Merleau-Ponty's analyses are at times difficult to follow, since he quickly and seamlessly moves from proper cases of synaesthesia to related, but still qualitatively different, kinds of multisensory experiences (cf. Merleau-Ponty 2012, 238f.). Still, his descriptions are crucial with regard to his overall project, for they tell us something true of perception in general. The described experiences—which, to avoid any confusion, I prefer to qualify as *multisensory*[15]—show, namely, that perceptual experience involves what he calls 'an opening on to the ontological structure of the thing' (2012, 239). Thanks to its ontological depth or complexity, the perceptual thing solicits me across multiple sensory registers.[16]

---

[14] This is, in fact, a rather old idea. Already in 1935, Schilder held that 'synesthesia...is the normal situation' (1935, 38). In the *Visible and the Invisible*, Merleau-Ponty (1968) will develop this insight further and radicalize it by having recourse to the notion of 'reversibility', but this falls beyond the scope of this chapter. (See Dastur 2000, §III).

[15] I am aware that there is a cost to this terminological change, for it invites back in the 'separation' of the senses that Merleau-Ponty wanted to avoid. Still, I think that the conceptual distinction I make (and which reflects the current scientific consensus) between synaesthetic and multisensory experiences is necessary to appreciate the universality of the claim that Merleau-Ponty advances.

[16] Here's another example that illustrates Merleau-Ponty's point: 'it is impossible to describe fully the colour of a carpet without saying that it is a carpet, or a woollen carpet, and without implying in this colour a certain tactile value, a certain weight, and a certain resistance to sound' (2012, 337).

The 'communication thesis' refers to this basic experiential feature, which Merleau-Ponty thinks is constitutive of *all* perceptions.

In the next section, I will pursue my reflection on this and analyse in more detail how the perceiving agent *responds* to the thing's solicitation by analysing Merleau-Ponty's description of the dialectics between perceptual expectations and readiness to act. While sketching out his view on perceptual agency, the necessity of widening our analysis of multisensory experience beyond the standard 'what it's like' will become more apparent. This will have important implications for the argument defended in this book, for the normative motif at the heart of Merleau-Ponty's phenomenology of perception will also begin to shine through.

4.2.2. Readiness to Act

The key to understanding how Merleau-Ponty's claim about the universality of the synaesthetic condition impacts his view on agency lies in the normative dialectics of solicitations and responses at the heart of his theory of perception. As we saw in the previous chapter, the perceived world solicits me, and calls forth certain movements or actions, understood here as answers to worldly solicitations. However—and here's the new bit—the world does not speak to *one* sensory modality; it rather 'speaks directly to all of the senses' (2012, 238), as when one sees something one could also touch, smell, or taste (say, a fruit). One could even experience an objectual feature with a modality normally experienced by another, as when one sees the fluidity of water or the viscosity of syrup (cf. 2012, 238f.). These are, to be sure, properties normally revealed by touch, not by vision; but 'the senses communicate among themselves' (238), Merleau-Ponty contends, such that 'it becomes difficult to restrict my experience to a single sensory register: it spontaneously overflows toward all the others' (236). It is true that physical objects often catch our attention by affecting us through *one* specific modality. And yet, objects are 'poles of actions,' and, as such, they open up a field of possible interactions that is not limited to the potentialities of that specific modality. Since we are not mere spectators but, rather, existentially engaged in the perceptual field, the spectrum of possible actions and perceptions is open, as it were, and *these possibilities are felt or experienced as such*. This is why Merleau-Ponty holds that more than one sense is typically involved in experience, and that multisensory perception (or, as he prefers, synaesthesia) is the rule rather than the exception.

This argument rests on the idea that the phenomenology of multisensory interaction has a motivational or horizonal structure; that is, that it is not limited to *actual* manipulation and interaction but is also reflected in our *readiness to act* or explore things through various senses. In responding to the objects' demands, viz. in interacting with them in suitable or meaningful ways, our senses are intertwined and mutually dependent. They are, in this specific sense, *jointly responsible for the overall phenomenal character of experience*. This is what he explains when he stresses the fundamental role of movement or, rather, virtual movement: 'Movement, not understood as objective movement and shifting of locations in space, but rather as a movement project or as "virtual movement," is the foundation of the unity of the senses' (2012, 243). In perceiving things as offering certain opportunities for action, the body prepares itself to take up these opportunities, and this, in turn, triggers a virtual experience of the thing, one in which the thing's various objective properties are virtually experienced (Abath 2017). In Merleau-Ponty's eyes, this is by no means rare or exceptional; on the contrary, it is true of perception *in general*. On this score, Merleau-Ponty undoubtedly went further than Husserl, and provided at the same time more reasons to leave behind the traditional conception of phenomenality.

To be sure, Husserl clearly saw not only that we perceive actual content and properties (like colours, forms, and textures) but also that perception is always embedded in a horizon, conceived in terms of expectations, which are either fulfilled or disappointed. As we are going to see in great detail in Section 5.1, in *Experience and Judgment* and *Analyses Concerning Passive Synthesis* Husserl explains that these expectations derive from earlier experiences. What is sedimented and reactivated in perception is the result of our previous encounters with the same and/or similar objects. This intentional reference to past experiences is not limited to a single modality, however; it cuts across the sense-fields. Perceptual consciousness passively draws intentional resources in a reservoir of past experiences with a multimodal history, thereby accounting for the fact that our expectations are usually rich and not limited to any single modality. In Husserl's view, however, this passive reference to past experiences does *not* in and of itself suffice to make perception multisensorial in the relevant sense. While he demonstrated that perception generates expectations, which are experienced as possibilities of fulfilment, he never mentioned, whether directly or indirectly, that these possibilities are standardly experienced *as multisensory possibilities*. It is true that passive consciousness opens a field of potential actions and interactions that may be realized by multiple sense modalities, but this openness is not lived through (*erlebt*) *as* a multisensory openness in the sense discussed here. This, however, is a formulation that exactly corresponds to Merleau-Ponty's view, who thus gave himself the means to endorse much more explicitly than Husserl a further argument in favour of the constitutive view. Perception is multisensory not only because:

- *There are certain types of perceptual attributes that could not be had without multimodal interaction*; or because:
- *Multimodality introduces novel types of features to our experience that do not belong to any modality*; or because:
- *Some aspects of experience are not modality specific, i.e. can be presented to multiple modalities.*

Merleau-Ponty also thinks that perception is multisensory because:

- *Perception includes felt possibilities of action and behaviours that are not restricted to any single modality*; they rather engage my whole sensory-motor being.[17]

This last point lends further support to the claim that bodily self-awareness *does* make profound impact on the overall phenomenology of experience while being irreducible to any qualia or 'raw feel'. The sense of the object's perceptual presence as available to me for manipulation and interaction adds to the phenomenology of its perception without being itself sensorial (at least, not in the customary sense).

4.3. The Normative Impact of Sensory Integration

In the first two sections, I have argued for three main points, namely that both Husserl and Merleau-Ponty endorse the Constitutive Thesis on multisensory perception, that the thesis can be generalized, viz. applied to perception in general, and that both phenomenologists provide reasons to widen our conception of phenomenal consciousness beyond its standard

---

[17] The relationship between mother and newborn offers another illustration of this idea. Gallagher (2005, 1): 'More precisely and quite literally, we can see our own possibilities in the faces of others. The infant, minutes after birth, is capable of imitating the gesture that it sees on the face of another person. It is thus capable of a certain kind of movement that foreshadows intentional action, and that propels it into a human world.' I come back to this in Section 6.3.

definition by integrating temporal and agential phenomenal features. In this third section my goal is to explore further the normative impact of sense integration on perception and agency. In Section 4.3.1 I take a brief look at the neuroscientific literature and provide an overview of the kind of *epistemic effect* successful and failed processes of integration are standardly taken to have on perception and perceptual judgments. In Section 4.3.2 I then consider the enlarged conception of phenomenal consciousness I have been developing earlier and argue that the way bodily forms of self-relating are phenomenally manifest in experience contributes to sharpen our sense of *perceptual agency*. While the normative impact of enhanced sense integration on judicative experiences is—as we will see—already well documented, the analysis of its role in perceptual agency will yield novel results.

4.3.1. Perceptual Increase and Epistemic Loss

It is not difficult to see how processes of integration can be evaluated in normative terms: when information in one sense modality influences the information processing in another sense modality, the integration can succeed or fail. Usually, processes of integration occur successfully and yield rich conscious experiences of worldly objects and events. In contemporary neuroscience, the most important and universally recognized of these processes is called perceptual binding. When somebody speaks to you, your brain automatically binds together the perceived individual sounds into coherent and meaningful wholes that you experience as words and phrases. But there is more, for perceptual binding can also involve multiple senses. When you see and hear your partner talking to you, your brain binds together her mouth movements with the sounds that are coming out of it, and this yields a multimodal experience of your partner talking. There are exceptions, but, generally, perceptual binding is taken to be necessary for one to enjoy a unified experience of any given perceptual object or scene.[18]

Claims about multisensory interaction at the subpersonal level are generally not taken to straightforwardly entail anything about the phenomenology of

---

[18] Both multimodal and unimodal unity is standardly taken to involve binding, but not necessarily. When the senses interact, there can be binding, but there can also be interaction without binding—when a sense modality goes extinct, for instance. Conversely, there can be binding without interaction, for cognitive factors can also generate binding (Deroy 2014, 109f.). For an alternative model of integration based on learned associations, see Connolly 2019, 127ff.

multisensory experience (Deroy, Chen, and Spence 2014; Macpherson 2011a). But the fact that *there are certain types of perceptual attributes that could not be had without multimodal interaction*, or that *multimodality introduces novel types of features to our experience that do not belong to any modality* show that *at least some* of these processes of interaction make a phenomenal difference. This difference, which may be assessed in normative terms, is, for instance, experienced in the way that these processes *extend* or *enhance* our perceiving power (O'Callaghan 2015). The point is simple: since there are features and properties of the perceptual world that are just not perceivable without them (mint is a case in point), these processes *enrich* our perception. Given the first-person character of this perceived difference, there seems to be no reason to doubt that at least some processes of interaction make a notable difference in the phenomenology of our perceptual lives.

Furthermore, some recent empirical studies have shown that when there is greater integration, the *reliability* of perception is enhanced (de Vignemont 2014; O'Callaghan 2017). When various pieces of redundant information converge and are unified in a single experiential content, the overall trustworthiness of perception is improved. The point is rather intuitive: all things being equal, if you, say, see, smell, and drink the glass of wine in front of you, your perceptual judgment of it being a Pinot Noir is under normal circumstances *more certain or trustworthy* than if you are merely smelling it without seeing and tasting it as well. For the same reason, your corresponding perceptual judgment is also *more justified*. When you enjoy a multimodal experience of a thing or of a property, it is *as if* your senses were 'confirming' each other, very much like when witnesses corroborate each other's testimonies in a trial (Hohwy 2013).[19] Again, there seems to be little doubt that this enhanced perception is reflected in the phenomenology: when the senses are coordinated and jointly exercised, the experience not only is but also *seems* richer and more reliable, thereby generating enhanced epistemic confidence on top of that (Navajas et al. 2017).[20]

---

[19] For Hohwy (2013), however, this indicates that the different sense modalities are relatively modular, that is, *relatively* impenetrable to each other. On his view, the more the senses communicate, the more the reliability decreases. However, he thinks that the integration occurs higher up in the hierarchical arrangement.

[20] While Husserl never provided a detailed analysis of the relation between multisensory experience and the reliability of the corresponding perceptual judgment, these recent findings concord by and large with his normative conception of perception as a teleologically oriented epistemic process. I reconstruct the development of Husserl's conception of optimality in Doyon (2018).

Bayesian statistical calculations lend further support to this view. Since the initial estimates of sensory properties provided by the senses are standardly taken to be 'weighted' according to their relative reliability, the final perceptual appraisal of that property is the result of an 'optimizing multisensory integration' process (Briscoe 2021, 3913). The basic idea is that the brain weighs the relative contributions of each sensory modality based on their respective relative reliability for the overall experience, whose coherence the brain seeks to optimize in the sense of reducing the variance associated with the final multisensory percept. For this reason, this view is sometimes dubbed the Maximum Likelihood Estimation Approach.[21]

For various reasons, processes of integration sometimes fail or go astray. Psychologists and neuroscientists then talk of failed integration, or sometimes of illusory binding. In either case, it leads to incomplete and unreliable experiences, thus giving rise to a variety of crossmodal illusions. I'll mention three well-known examples very briefly. 1) The *McGurk effect* results in subjects reporting hearing /da/ when the phoneme /ba/ is dubbed onto the lips of a person uttering /ga/(McGurk and MacDonald 1976). Here, visual and auditory information are in conflict, and the experience can be interpreted as provoking some kind of epistemic loss in the sense that our perceptual judgment is inaccurate with regard to both the seen and the heard sources. 2) *Ventriloquism* is an illusory experience that cause listeners to incorrectly locate the sound source of what they hear. This misperception consists in a mistaken association between a heard sound and a visually observed object, such as a ventriloquist's dummy.[22] 3) Finally, in the classic set-up of the *rubber hand illusion*, participants report feeling as if they were touched on the rubber hand and as if the rubber hand were their own. In addition, the perceived location of one's own hand shifts towards the location of the rubber hand, an effect called proprioceptive drift. The illusion results from a three-way disturbed relation between vision, touch, and proprioception: visual information about the rubber hand being stroked is wrongly integrated with tactile and proprioceptive information. This yields a change of perceived location towards the rubber hand, which

---

[21] In contemporary philosophy of mind and perception, this paradigm is nowadays closely associated with the Predicting Processing view (Clark 2016). This view came to replace the Modality Appropriateness Hypothesis, which stipulates that when a conflict between two modalities arises, perceptual processes weigh the perceptual result in accordance with the more reliable modality (Welch and Warren 1980).

[22] Although the ventriloquist effect is commonly categorized as an 'illusion', O'Callaghan (2012) is right to insist that it need not be conceived in this way.

shows up in participants slightly mislocating their hand if asked to point at it. The problem, simply put, is that the integration should not occur, since the visual and the somatosensory information are not about the same object. The illusion is in any case robust and causes unreliable judgments about spatial awareness and a disturbed sense of ownership.

The lesson to draw from this series of examples is plain: all the above-mentioned scientific studies on perceptual increase, perceptual reliability, and crossmodal illusions support the normative interpretation of perception I have defended in the chapter thus far. Successful and failed multisensory integration are reflected in the phenomenology of epistemic experiences: perceptual judgment is enhanced through successful integration, and impaired when the integration fails (partially or completely).[23] If we leave the neuroscientific paradigm behind and adopt the phenomenological point of view, the thesis about the normative character of multisensory perception appears to play out in a different area. It is not only the case that each of the five traditional senses does better and yields more accurate perceptual *judgments* when they successfully mesh. If we consider the enlarged conception of phenomenal consciousness that I have argued for in this chapter, we can see that the integration of bodily forms of self-referential intentionality contributes to sharpening our *perceptual agency*, that is to say, our embodied capacity to act in meaningful ways on the basis of what we perceptually take in. This is the claim that I want to defend in the next section.

4.3.2. Bodily Normality and Agency

We already started to provide evidence in support of this claim in the previous chapter. Bodily self-awareness builds a fundamental aspect of intentionality and is thus a constitutive part of every perception. This is because

---

[23] There is, however, a notable asymmetry: while phenomena of perceptual increase and reliability are usually reflected in the phenomenology synchronically (notably by giving access to novel perceptual features), crossmodal illusions usually go unnoticed at least for a certain time or until the trick is revealed. It is true that I'm often not aware when integration is succeeding or failing, and so may experience enhanced confidence even in cases of illusion when integration is actually failing. And the apparent problem here is that this would seem to make the enhancement of perceptual judgment externalist in a way that our experienced confidence is not. However, we have seen that the phenomenological approach to perceptual judgment need not be externalist to resolve this tension, for sooner or later the illusion will reveal itself; that is, it will be experienced as illusory from a first-person perspective (see Sections 1.3, 2.3, and 2.4 for details).

perception, from the phenomenological perspective, is (at least in a vast array of circumstances) best understood as action oriented. As such, it is hardly dissociable from the movement and the proprioceptive/kinaesthetic feedback it produces. Even if some are non-conscious, bodily cues provided by incoming kinetic and proprioceptive signals still contribute in important ways to structure our perceptual space, thereby facilitating our capacity to skilfully navigate through it.

Fundamentally, our sense of perceptual agency—that is to say, our bodily disposition to respond in suitable ways to what we perceptually register—is pre-reflectively experienced and rooted in a series of body-schematic and intentional processes that are evaluable in normative terms. This shows up in the fact that these processes are incessantly self-regulating, viz. triggering motor control modifications and adjustments in light of the steadily evolving perceptual situation we are in. This is incidentally how perceptual agents can keep track of the relative success of their own practices without ever having recourse to reflective consciousness. It's late and I have just spilled my glass of IPA, but still I know, because I am proprioceptively self-aware, what to do to avoid further damage (say, quickly stepping back and rapidly picking up my book along the way). Thanks to this pervasive self-referential sensitivity that structures my perceptual space, I can adjust to the unfolding situation. Very generally, the point here is that the input of bodily awareness plays a fundamental role in perceptual consciousness for it allows perception to be goal- or norm-sensitive and, if needed, to initiate a process of optimization or self-correction, depending on whether the experience progresses in accordance with one's intentional goal or not.

The key here is to recognize how bodily forms of self-relating inform the phenomenological conception of the 'I can'. As the bearer of all intentional relations, the 'I can' is itself a product of multisensory integration: the loop of bodily sensations, perception, and movement that co-constitute the subjective space of the body is an intermodal achievement of intentional consciousness (Fuchs 2018, 20) that has, I contend, a powerful normative impact on our perceptual lives: together, they play nothing less than a *necessary function* for the satisfactory performance of any intentional action.

Further support for this view may be provided by considering the famous pathological case of Ian Waterman (Cole 2016). Due to a rare autoimmune disease (the acute sensory neuropathy syndrome), the sensory nerves underpinning his sense of touch and proprioception were permanently damaged from the neck down. Oddly enough, his movement nerves and the sensory nerves responsible for the sensations of pain and temperature were nevertheless left unaffected (Cole 2016; Gallagher and Cole 1995). The consequences were both massive and perplexing: Ian Waterman (from now on IW) could still experience cold and hot temperatures, as well as various sensations of pain; his vision was also intact, and yet he was unable to maintain posture and locate his own limbs without looking. The disruption of his proprioceptive sense, which no longer worked automatically and pre-reflectively, and the ensuing disturbance of normal sensory integration (touch/proprioception and vision in his case) had devastating effects: IW lost motor control. While IW could still initiate movements, he had no real mastery over the trajectory of his limbs and the end point of his movements. As a result, he not only would fail to maintain an optimal grip on his own perceptual situation but would also fail to accomplish the simplest day-to-day actions such as standing up, walking around, eating, or taking a glass of water.

After several years of self-training, during which IW developed a series of compensation strategies, he finally regained *some* control and competency over his movements and actions. With the help of his doctor, Jonathan Cole, IW addressed his motor difficulties on a behavioural level by relying on his body image, viz. the continuous monitoring of his bodily movements. Precisely put, IW 'learned to rely on a combination of visual kinaesthesia (i.e., visual feedback about one's own movement through the environment) and visual perception of limb movement; this enabled him to move around in a controlled way' (Gallagher and Zahavi 2021, 166; cf. Gallagher 2005, 47–50).

In the scholarship on bodily awareness, this extreme case has been used as a counterexample to show that O'Shaughnessy (1980) and Sheets-Johnstone (1998) weren't quite right to see in tactile and proprioceptive awareness a necessary condition for intentional action. While the control of motor action does depend on proprioception in the normal adult, IW found alternative ways to control his movement. In a way, he reinvented movement for himself. Since he never regained function of his body schema, or retrain proprioception, which was lost and stayed lost, it seems that the standard role attributed to proprioception in intentional action is not necessary, since it is not strictly universal (Gallagher 2005, 61, 175).

At the same time, this case study shows that for non-impaired perceptual agents (presumably you and me), proprioception *is* responsible for the norm-sensitivity of our intentional actions and behaviours. By paying sustained visual attention to every single aspect of his ongoing movements, IW did not learn to simply move his body around (he already could); rather, he learned to cope with the unbridgeable gap that now exists between his intentions and his embodied capacities. Since it integrates the relevant bodily and environmental cues, there is no such gap in a normally functioning organism. The healthy body *pre-reflectively* handles the situation it is immersed in, and it yields effortless and skilful movements, actions, and behaviours. In IW's case, however, his capacity for normally unattended movement is lost, and could only be partially compensated by incessant mental effort (concentration) and sustained visual vigilance (attention).

In the present context, the main lesson to draw from IW's case is that failed operation of sense integration can, at least in certain cases, seriously impact our sense of perceptual agency. With the loss of touch and of his proprioceptive sense, it is 'a capacity for specific kinds of intermodal communication' (Gallagher 2005, 51) that goes missing in IW's case, and this is precisely what disrupted his sense of agency. This is because perceptual agency relies, in every normally functioning organism, on a strong intermodal connection between proprioception and vision—a relation that Husserl and Merleau-Ponty already clearly identified, as we saw above.

Finally, IW's case also allows us to throw some light on the relation between normativity, optimality, and normality, for the compensation strategies he deployed *normalized* his experience in the sense of stabilizing the connection between action and perception, which generated until then unpredictable and undesirable behavioural results due to his illness. By developing new skills and dispositions—or, better, by recovering (some of) the skills and dispositions he had lost—IW could retrieve a sense of stability and steadiness in his day-to-day routine, thereby *optimizing* his experience of the world. The two senses of 'normality' Husserl worked with throughout his career are at work here: normality in the sense of coherence and in the sense of optimality (Heinämaa and Taipale 2019, 362ff.). While IW's pathological condition generated experiences that were *discordant* or not coherent with respect to both his own prior individual experiencing history and the larger community of experiencing subjects to which he belongs (Taipale 2014, 130ff.), his perceptual experiences were also *not optimal*: the correlation between movement and appearances was not fluid and yielded erratic outcomes. After years of treatment, however, IW learned to reorganize his perceptual field, which was now imbued with 'new' perceptual possibilities. Even if with some effort, he could finally go about his business and interact with people and objects in a more normal, viz. suitable and efficient, way. His movements were also more flowing, more graceful, more agile, and especially more responsive to what the surrounding world had to offer. Hence, even if IW's pathological condition gradually became the 'new normal' for him after some time, all the efforts he deployed over the years to improve his condition in fact amounted to a gradual *process of normalization of the body in the sense of optimality*, because a properly functioning body schema belongs to the constitution of the normal body. Admittedly, IW's body schema was forever totally lost; and that's why a process of normalization/optimization remained an open possibility. In his case, it required the establishment of a new mode of intermodal communication, an ersatz for the definitive loss of normal sensory integration. The combination of sustained visual attention and concentration was the answer.[24]

4.4. Conclusion

This chapter has aimed to show that both Husserl and Merleau-Ponty think of normal perception as being constitutively multisensory, that is, as always requiring the involvement of two or more senses. In presenting their view, I have shown how their respective account is, in significant respects, close to that of O'Callaghan, who also endorses the constitutive view. At the same time, I have offered a series of reasons as to why we ought to enlarge our conception of perceptual consciousness beyond the standard conception at work in the currently dominant positions on multisensory perception—those of Charles Spence, Tim Bayne, and Casey O'Callaghan himself—such as to include forms of bodily self-experiences and felt possibilities of action. Through my descriptions, I have suggested how these features inform perceptual agency in normatively assessable ways.

From the enactivist point of view, whose perspective on multisensory perception builds on and extends the phenomenological one, one reason to accept the constitutive view resides in what the enactivist perceives as a fundamental difficulty that plagues modularity. Thinking about the mind purely in terms of modular (or representational) processes is to miss something fundamental about it, namely that consciousness is primarily concerned with sense or meaning. To be sure, this is what Merleau-Ponty himself is arguing for when he pleads for reversal of the traditional

---

[24] The questions of normality and skill acquisition will be addressed in a more sustained manner in the next chapter.

empiricist perspective and stresses the unity of space, body, and things.[25] To cast aside the modular view of the mind and to insist, as Merleau-Ponty does, on the primordiality of meaning is to remind us that consciousness is intentional. While phenomenologists usually defend this claim on purely descriptive grounds and avoid any explicit recourse to representations in their descriptions, some enactivists have taken the argument one step further and argued for a strong anti-representationalist stance that extends to the subpersonal mechanisms of conscious experience (Gallagher 2017; Noë 2009; Fuchs 2018).[26] To close this section, I will sketch out in very rough strokes what the strategy amounts to.

From the enactive point of view, the discussion starts with the recognition that the relevant perceptual mechanisms are not inferential or representational but, rather, *embodied*. The brain–body–environment, which the enactivists regard as the most basic explanatory unity of the mind, is a *dynamical*, not a neural or inferential, process. As Gallagher explains, what is typically 'described as a Bayesian inferential process is in actuality a dynamical adjustment process in which the brain, as part of and along with the larger organism, settles into the right kind of attunement with the environment' (2017, 16). Simply put, the idea is that the organism is sensitive to certain environmental features and responds to them by adjusting in appropriate ways. This, of course, does not mean that the brain plays no role. There are neural processes involved in perception, even in the body-schematic processes themselves, but neural and bodily processes operate on the same dynamical model; that is to say, they participate in the same functional cycles. For this reason, the brain–body–environment dynamics is said to be irreducible.

Regarding the problem of multisensory integration, the difference between the representationalist and enactive paradigms can be illuminated by reflecting on two experiential features. First, enactivists point out the

---

[25] Merleau-Ponty's descriptions aim to show that the world, the lived body, and the things themselves are coextensive terms and thus also mutually dependent. He writes in this sense: 'We only grasp the unity of our body in the unity of the thing' (2012, 336), which in turn 'only stand out against the background of a common world', understood as this 'open and indefinite unity in which I am situated' (317f.).

[26] Recently, enactivists have tried to overcome what some consider to be the last remaining obstacle to a general anti-representationalist theory of intentionality by arguing that even sophisticated forms of cognition such as imagining, planning, reasoning, and thinking abstractly need not rely on (mental) representations. This has come to be known as the *scaling up problem* (cf. Clark and Toribio 1994; Shapiro 2014; see also Aizawa 2014). The challenge is to explain in non-representational terms cognitive activities that do not immediately (or constantly) depend on the interaction of the agent with its environment. For a response from the enactivist camp, see, among others, Gallagher 2017, 187ff.

massively overlooked importance of *time* in the representationalist account of multisensory phenomena. The neuroscientific view typically postulates an *automatic* binding process mechanism. While there are still numerous debates around the exact nature of this mechanism (see Connolly 2019, 133 n. 4), and on the conditions that must be met for it to be triggered, there is a large consensus in the neuroscientific community around the fact that perceptual binding operates over a very short period of time.[27] The coupling of spatially and temporally aligned stimuli might happen *just before* the experience, or perhaps even *during* the perception itself (Pourtois et al. 2000, 1329), but in either case it has a very limited time span, and it is temporally close to its outcome, that is, the percept or the representational image itself.

From the enactivist perspective, things are different, and it comes across very clearly in their conception of multisensory perception, which is taken to be geared toward an ideal of long-range synchrony between various brain regions. This is the fundamental insight of Thomas Fuchs's concept of *resonance*, which he sees as containing a key element of an 'enactive' answer to the problem of multisensory integration. Here are two quotes that illustrate his perspective on this:

> Thus mediated by the body, brain and environment mutually resonate with one another; they are linked by dynamic isomorphic patterns of oscillations. The justification for the notion of resonance, on the one hand, lies in its reference to these synchronous oscillations, which also represent a proposed solution to the problem of intermodal 'binding': Converging evidence suggests that the binding of sensory attributes as well as the overall integration of various dimensions of a cognitive act, including associative memory, emotional tone, and motor planning, are achieved through large-scale dynamical patterns of neural activity over multiple frequency bands.... Coherent perceptual and motor gestalts presuppose highly synchronous or resonant reverberations of the networks involved, in continuous alignment with the environmental stimulus configuration, that is, both internal and external resonance. (Fuchs 2018, 165)

> The most probable explanation [to the problem of integration] consists in long-range, phase locking neural synchrony between widely separated regions of the brain. (2018, 151)

---

[27] Connolly (2019), who argues that multisensory perception involves learned associative processes of unitization, is a notable exception.

If, to explain the possibility of multisensory perception, we need an account of how individual sensory elements are integrated into meaningful wholes, or transformed into perceptual gestalts, these passages suggest we need not think of these incoming signals in terms of representation or information. Rather, there are various patterns of neural excitation, which the brain seeks to synchronize with one another (internal resonance) and harmonize with external inputs (external resonance). Synchrony between brain regions and between the brain and the environment thus stand out as a core element of an enactive solution to the problem of intermodal binding. The concept of 'synchrony' means two different, but not incompatible, things here. The notion of 'synchrony between brain regions' refers to synchronized oscillations in the neural cortex, that is, when the participating networks oscillate in phase. Its boundaries are objectively measurable, and what is 'normal' and 'optimal' is statistically established by brain science. The notion of 'synchrony between brain, body, and environment' calls for another, more phenomenologically oriented, analysis, for being in 'synchrony' here amounts to something like being in a perceptual situation where the perceived objects fulfil or match our anticipations, that is to say, fit our expectations, thereby making it possible to 'be in the flow'.

In sum—and this is the first key here—it seems that the temporal extension of dynamical systems is hardly reconcilable with the standard notion of representation. To account for perception's normative character, enactivists think that we need a causal account that extends beyond the narrow time frame of the standard representationalist picture, and this is precisely what the enactivist account of body and brain plasticity offers.

Secondly, the dynamical system's *spatial* extension also puts pressure on standard representationalism. From the enactive point of view, the relevant mechanisms are not 'in the head' but distributed across brain–body–environment. This means that there is no 'centre' of integration either; integration is, rather, distributed across the system. Once again, Fuchs embodies this position well:

> There is agreement today that nowhere in the brain is there to be found a Cartesian 'center' of such integration, no brain region to which all other brain regions ultimately 'report' and in which the partial processes are conjoined into a 'perceptual image,' let alone into conscious perception. Much rather, the entire system constantly re-arranges itself according to the patterns with which it is in contact, until its self-oscillations resonate with these situational patterns and provide for fluid interaction of organism and environment. (2018, 155)

While the relevant mechanisms are connected with one another through interaction and coordination, what matters most in this context is that the connection is not 'centralized'. *And neither is its output.* For enactivists, there is no single percept or representation that gathers all the relevant bits of information together. The relevant perceptual intakes are, rather, functionally distributed in the dynamical set of brain–body–environment relations. This suggests that the spatial *extension* of motor and perceptual mechanisms cannot be squared with the standard notion of representation either, even the externalist conception. Indeed, even if we accept the externalist conception of the mind and assume that the world is a 'constituent' of mental states, what is here called a 'representation' is still based on a principled division between brain and environment, and it still has a specific, albeit extended, location. This is what the enactivist model rejects.

All of this shows that enactivists individuate perceptions in vastly different ways than the representationalists do, and this is the key element to think about multisensory integration in enactivist terms. From an enactivist point of view, perceptions appear not as individual mental states or episodes; they are (long-lasting) *experiences* inscribed in a network of other experiences (other perceptions, actions, etc.). Thanks to its open-ended horizonal structure, perception has no fixed or definitive boundaries. As a result, multisensory integration cannot simply amount to a combination of diverse sensory inputs processed by a centralized perceptual system. Multisensory integration is, rather, the ongoing experience of harmony between brain regions and between the organism and the environment. One of the interesting upshots of the enactive model is that it makes a strong case for thinking about the mechanism of integration as *perceptual*, but it comes with its own load of questions and problems, beginning with a clear and convincing explanation of the nature of relation that holds between the subpersonal and personal levels of explanation. Given the nature of this book, which is concerned with the phenomenology of perceptual experiencing, I will leave it at that and keep this otherwise fascinating question for another endeavour.

Phenomenology and the Norms of Perception. Maxime Doyon, Oxford University Press. © Maxime Doyon 2024.
DOI: 10.1093/9780191993527.003.0004

5
Perceptual Learning

Over the course of a lifetime, our perceptual capacities undergo all kinds of transformations and alterations. These long-term changes—which can be due to various factors, including genetics, growth, maturation, interpersonal relations, environmental transactions, intersensory interactions, sensory substitution, learning, ageing, etc.—impact our ability to recognize and process complex perceptual information. The result of this operation corresponds to what philosophers and scientists standardly refer to as 'perceptual plasticity', which is the ability of perceivers to adapt, modify, and reorganize one's sensory processing mechanisms and perceptual abilities in response to changes in sensory input, experiences, or dispositions. The kind of transformations responsible for perceptual plasticity can be grouped into three broad categories.

Perceptual experience can display some flexibility or malleability resulting from *cognitive or affective plasticity*, that is, changes at the level of the cognitive or affective accomplishments of the experiencing subject. Thanks, for example, to changes at the level of beliefs (Macpherson 2012) or emotions (Siegel 2017), which may interact with perceptual states, processes involved in how individuals perceive and interpret sensory information may themselves present some level of flexibility or adaptability. Perceptual plasticity may also result from *bodily plasticity*, that is, bodily transformations that may involve organic alterations (e.g. muscle growth, maturation) or changes at the level of the body's capacities or aptitudes (e.g. skills and habits). Both kind of changes may influence the phenomenal quality of perceptual experience, but they proceed in different ways: growth or maturation are causal processes essentially based on genetics, while phenomena such as skills acquisition and habit formation are motivational, that is, meaningful activities based on experience (Noë 2004; Gallagher 2017). Finally, perceptual plasticity may be based on bodily plasticity in a restricted sense. It can be the outcome of neurological alterations understood in terms of *neuroplasticity*, that is, the capacity of the brain to modify, transform, reconfigure, or reorganize its own internal structures, networks, and connections in response to changes in the environment or to sensory loss (Hurley and Noë 2003, Doidge 2007, Fuchs 2018).

Although phenomenologists have rarely tackled the question of perceptual plasticity per se, progress in our understanding of its first-personal manifestations can be made by drawing insights and conceptual tools from the phenomenological repertoire. This chapter makes this case by drawing attention to one specific class of phenomena, namely those involving what E. Gibson (1963) calls *perceptual learning*—that is, long-lasting perceptual change that results from practice or experience—and it shows how phenomenology can contribute in important ways to the ongoing discussion over both the nature and scope of perceptual learning. The analysis proceeds by examining both how the cognitive-affective (Section 5.1) and the bodily (Section 5.2) transformations of perceptual experiencing distinguished above may result from learning episodes. (I leave the question of neuroplasticity aside, as it falls outside the scope of the phenomenological account I develop here.)

The first section examines the first set of questions and argues that Husserl's account of type or typological recognition, which he developed during the so-called genetic phase of phenomenology (roughly from 1917 onward), is a clear instance of perceptual learning in the cognitive-affective sense. Briefly put, Husserl's idea is that our perceptual and recognitional dispositions *passively* evolve over time on the basis of our perceptual history. The process is rooted in associations of intentional content. Husserl holds that current experiences are vaguely associated with past experiences of similar objects, a process that leads to the formation of types, which act as filters on what perceptually comes in by generating more or less determinate expectations about what comes next. As a result, our lifeworld is 'experienced as a typified world' (Husserl 1975, 331), that is, the objects we encounter in our surrounding world are invariably perceived as belonging to certain types or general categories. 'Things are experienced as trees, bushes, animals, snakes, birds; specifically, as pine, linden, lilac, dog, viper, swallow, sparrow, and so on (1975, 331).'[1] Even new and totally unknown

---

[1] Not unlike Heidegger's mid-1920s descriptions, Husserl's analyses point to the network of practical intentions, from which perceived things gain their significance. This is not only true of natural things (like trees and birds) or ordinary objects (like hammers and radios). In the *Crisis* we are told that even scientific objectivities draw their significance from the practical context where they emerge (Husserl 1970, §34). In Section 6.4 I discuss the role of 'types' in the perception of others (Section 6.2), stressing along the way how past affective experiences may leave enduring traces in perception.

objects—objects that do not appear to have a particular typification—are apprehended as fitting certain vague or general categories and are integrated, for want of a better type, into the category 'object in general' (1975, 39). This is because the kind of unfamiliarity we may hereby experience is not absolute; '*unfamiliarity is at the same time a mode of familiarity*' (1975, 37f.; emphasis in original), by which Husserl means that 'what affects us' is always, in some sense, 'known in advance', even if only in the sense of being 'a something with determinations' (1975, 37f.). Since perception always unfolds against the background of previous experiences, the result is that there is no *radically* new experience of anything.

The second section of the chapter looks at perceptual learning from the phenomenological standpoint by examining the impact of bodily transformations on experience, or—but this is the same point—by studying the connections between the body, action, and perception. The idea is simple: if action and perception form a tight intentional, perhaps even an irreducible, explanatory unity, then the development of habits and the acquisition of motor skills must have a noticeable impact on perception. Thanks to these habits and skills, which develop through practice, the meaning of the perceptual world is established and facilitates a range of actions. From this embodied perspective, perceptual experience, which is inseparable from the perceiver's bodily powers, is plastic in the sense that it co-varies to a significant extent with our changing bodily skills.

Throughout the chapter I will pursue a second, related task and specify the kind of normativity involved in these learning processes. In the literature, learning is often understood as a success term. Goldstone (1998), for instance, writes that 'Perceptual learning involves relatively long-lasting changes to an organism's perceptual system that improve its ability to respond to its environment' (587). Others stress its role in "our epistemic evaluation" (Jenkin 2023a, 4) and contend e.g., that learning enhances our discriminatory and categorization power. Though he does not frame his account of perceptual learning explicitly in normative terms either, the view espoused by Connolly (2019) also lends itself to normative analysis, but at the cost of a certain detour. What he calls the 'Offloading View' of perceptual learning stipulates that 'in perceptual learning, tasks that were previously done in a controlled manner, get offloaded onto perception, thereby freeing up cognition to do other tasks.' (2019, 204) Perceptual learning assumes a normative function in Connolly's view in that the tasks that are transferred to the person's fast perceptual system allow that person to become more efficiently engaged 'in the process of discovery' (2019, 35) and learning, thus creating a 'positive feedback loop' in which 'improvements in information retrieval leads to even greater improvements in information retrieval' (2019, 120). In line with the argument developed in this book, I will argue that perceptual learning, from the phenomenological point of view, is a norm-guided process, albeit in a different sense than what Goldstone, Jenkin, or Connolly have in view. According to Husserl and Merleau-Ponty, perceptual learning is geared towards coherence and optimality, that is, it improves perception by enhancing concordance and promoting optimality.

Elaborating on these two points will enable me to specify an important idea for the overall economy of the book. While the norms of coherence and optimality were at times also described in the first four chapters as transcendental conditions of experience, in this and the following chapters it will become apparent that the phenomenological concept of the transcendental incorporates elements from the empirical world. Unlike Kant's, the phenomenological conception of the transcendental does not amount to a pure or formal category of the understanding but is inseparable from the contingencies of empirical experience. I'll make this point by demonstrating how the constitution of both types and perceptual skills follow bottom-up processes that start in lived experience. In this story it is the real, contingent history of the perceptual ego that lends types, skills, and habit their constitutive character. As a result, it will be shown how the transcendental features of experience are themselves plastic, that is, subject to transformations.[2]

5.1. Cognitive-affective Plasticity

All perceptual agents display some level of *cognitive-affective plasticity*. Thanks to their cognitive and affective history, the capacities and dispositions of perceivers change over time. Some of these changes may result from learning, that is, repeated exposure and engagement with the perceived environment, and lead to enduring modifications in the way the world is

---

[2] This does not imply that *every* aspect of perception is plastic or subject to change. There are invariant or 'essential' structures of perception (e.g. its perspectival character), and I will argue for this at length in Section 6.4.

experienced through perception. Although the expression 'perceptual learning' is not typically used by philosophers, the philosophical literature is filled with examples (for an overview, see Connolly 2019, 3–5 and Jenkin 2023a). The 'classical' strategy to prove their existence is to look at so-called 'phenomenal contrast' phenomena, such as 'the experience of a perceiver completely unfamiliar with Cyrillic script seeing a sentence in that script and the experience of one who understands a language written in that script' (Peacocke 1992, 89). While the change involved in phenomenal contrast cases is often understood as being brought about by top-down influences, e.g. through belief or concept possession,[3] some have argued that, in some cases at least, phenomenal contrast cases are better explained as resulting in bottom-up or data-driven effects that, through repeated exposure, induce changes in perception's own sensory mechanisms (Connolly 2019). Husserl explored both possibilities.

5.1.1. Husserl's Early Non-conceptualism

In the period surrounding the publication of the *Logical Investigations* in 1900/1, Husserl briefly considered the question of the eventual influence of beliefs and concept on perception and rejected it in favour of an account of perceptual experience that could be described, with respect to contemporary theories of perception, as non-conceptual. In various junctures of the text, Husserl emphatically urges his readers not to confuse the kind of intuitive process involved in perceptual experience with conceptual achievements like conceiving or naming an object. The outer perception of real, physical objects 'requires no articulation' whatsoever, 'no linkage' of any sorts. 'The act of perception' is 'a homogeneous unity, which gives the object "presence" in a simple, immediate way' (2001b, 284). Without being utterly

---

[3] Husserl was perhaps the first to have recourse to that kind of argument more than a hundred years ago when he claimed, in the *Logical Investigation*, that there is an experiential difference between hearing a string of sounds without really understanding what is meant by it and hearing it as a language that one understands. There is a 'surplus element' (Husserl 2001b, 398) that distinguishes the second from the first scenario. (See Zahavi 2003b for a detailed analysis.) More recently, Strawson and Siewert have argued along similar lines. They both defend the idea that there is an experiential difference between hearing a sentence that one understands and hearing that same sentence 'senselessly', as Siewert (1998, 275) puts it. There is a phenomenological *feel* associated with the experience of 'getting it', and, crucially, this difference is not a mere sensory difference but a cognitive one (Strawson, 2010, 5f.), for the sensory phenomenology (i.e. sound pattern) is the same in both instances.

superfluous, the discursive work of our thinking activity serves other purposes than providing the necessary form of our object-consciousness.[4]

The clearest texts on the question come from the working manuscripts that led to the first edition of the *Logical Investigations*, in which Husserl draws a clear difference between simple perceptual apprehension, on the one hand, and the kind of apprehension involved when I recognize (and thereby classify) objects *as such*, on the other (2005b, 331). The distinction between perceptual apprehending (*wahrnehmendes Auffassen*) and recognizing apprehension (*erkennendes Auffassen*, sometimes also *erkennende Auffassung*) aims at grasping a basic feature of the phenomenology of our perceptual lives, namely that most of our perceptual experiences do not involve any explicit thinking or conceptualizing. I can see a house simply and straightforwardly 'without the concurrence of words or concepts.' (2005b, 325) The specific non-conceptual nature of my experience is due to the '(purely) intuitive' character of the perceiving act (2005a, 127), which bears on its objects without any thinking or conceptual mediation whatsoever. In outer perception, our consciousness of objects is an intuitive presentation 'free of all conceptual thinking' (2005a, 127). Yes, it is even free of any sort of thinking *tout court* (2005a, 124).

According to Husserl, this is not only true of individual objects such as houses and trees; it is also valid for the perception of structured wholes as well. I can apprehend 'purely intuitively before any conceptual cognition' a structured unity such as the 'garden's fence' or 'the unified togetherness (*das einheitliche Zusammensein*) of trees and bushes in this garden' (2005b, 325f.). What I apprehend in such circumstances is a sensible arrangement or disposition (*Gliederung*), not a conceptual relation (*Beziehung*). As such, my perception falls within the realm of intuitive presentation (*anschauliche Vorstellung*), and it is devoid of all conceptual elements. In his 1904/5 lecture course on attention Husserl makes the further point that *most* of our daily perceptual experiences are of this kind, i.e. that *most* of our perceptions are non-conceptual in character. 'Perception is a homogeneous lived experience (*Erlebnis*) that can exist *and usually does exist independently*

---

[4] Even if there seem to be, on the whole, more indications that Husserl favoured the non-conceptualist interpretation sketched out above, there are some passages in the *Logical Investigations* that run against such a reading. Richard Cobb-Stevens (1990) put great emphasis on these passages and disputed the validity of the non-conceptualist interpretation of Husserl's early opus. In Doyon 2012 I expose my disagreements with Cobb-Stevens at length. Mulligan (1995), Hopp (2011), and van Mazijk (2020) have also put forward non-conceptualist readings of Husserl. Mooney (2010) provides a useful overview of the positions and the stakes of the debate.

of all conceptual thinking' (2005a, 125; italics are mine). While Husserl admits the existence of a class of cases where perception and cognition intermingle—e.g. when empty intentions are fulfilled and realized in knowledge—*the character of my perception is not thereby modified*. Since it involves two acts—an intuitive and a signitive one, the former fulfilling the latter—cognition does not affect the phenomenal character of experience, which may be described on its own terms.

5.1.2. Husserl's Account of Typification

Husserl's investigation of the second possibility—changes in perception's own structure that result from repeated exposures—is a major topic of his research of the 1920s, and he approached it by having recourse to the notion of type (*Typus*). In *Experience and Judgment*, a posthumously published lecture course that contains some of his most fertile genetic analyses, Husserl asserts that *every* perception involves a form of 'typical precognition' (1975, 31) in virtue of which it is imbued with some more or less vague meaning (1975, 37). Husserl's fundamental insight is that we passively grasp what we currently perceptually take in on the basis of what we have already experienced in the past. Fully understanding the ins and outs of this claim requires taking a step back and introducing the project of genetic phenomenology, which provided the conceptual framework for Husserl's account of passivity.

Husserl's great project of the 1920s was to account for the genetic constitution of intentional experiences by referring it back to the concrete associative process of sensory contents in consciousness.[5] While Husserl's early static analyses sought to identify the universal structures of consciousness by having recourse to the method of eidetic variation, genetic phenomenology deepened and extended the analysis to include 'the experiential history of our acts' (Lohmar 2012, 266). Genetic phenomenology not only is concerned with investigating the structural invariants of consciousness but also purports to explore the temporal dynamics that govern the unfolding of conscious life. Since time-consciousness is the original site (*Urstätte*) of all constitution, or the general form of any experience, Husserl hypothesizes

---

[5] On this point, Husserl part ways with Heidegger. Whereas Heidegger's hermeneutical phenomenology locates the origin of the so-called phenomenological 'as structure' in forms of self-understanding (see 2.2.1), Husserl's analysis remains within the confine of sensory phenomenology.

that the constitution of objects—any object—must start with an analysis of their genesis, or their coming to be for consciousness. The overt goal of Husserl's genetic investigations is to follow the synthetic process of object-constitution back to its origins in the lowest level of temporal organization.[6]

In *Experience and Judgment*, Husserl carries this project by pursuing a genetic investigation of the formal structures of logic and predication to demonstrate how they emerge from prepredicative experiences (1975, 11). Husserl's strategy, in sum, is to show that judgments of the form 'S is P' originate in basic, low-level perceptual syntheses that provide them with their experiential ground (1975, 112ff.). These perceptual syntheses are the prefiguring form (*Vorform*) of the fully fledged conceptual form (*Vollform*) carried by judicative expressions (Staiti 2018, 162f.). In much the same spirit, Husserl undertakes in that same work an investigation into the origin of concepts involved in universal judgments of the type 'dogs have four legs'. Again, the aim here is to show that the ideality of concepts finds its origin in prepredicative experience or, more precisely, in the 'associative synthesis' (Husserl 1975, 321ff.) of perceptual content.

The analysis of association undertaken in the 1920s is the extension of Husserl's earlier analysis of time-consciousness, but it marks a major step forward. While the temporal synthesis disclosed in the 1904/5 lecture on internal time-consciousness (viz. the interplay of retention, impressions, and protentions in the constitution of the living present sketched out in Section 1.1) is purely formal, association involves synthetically interconnected *contents* within the subject's own stream of consciousness (what Husserl calls the level of primary passivity). Based on an analogy between new and past experiences, consciousness passively establishes vague or rudimentary connections between incoming sensory data according to patterns of contrasts and similarities. Husserl's idea is that perceived sensory items are passively apprehended as being more or less alike other, previously experienced, similar items (1975, 331). Since these associative performances correspond to a *pre-egoical* organization of the manifold of appearances, Husserl refers to this level of constitution as a level of passive *pre-givenness*. At this level, the intended object has not yet been constituted;

---

[6] As D. Lohmar (2012) indicates, 'the first distinct indications of the genetic turn are already to be found in *Ideas II*. Here, the ego is first interpreted as a result of its formation in decisions and experiences, i.e., as an ego of habitualities' (268). For a detailed and more recent inquiry into this specific aspect of the problem, see Lohmar 2023.

we can't speak of full-blooded perceptual awareness just yet. But as it achieves the synthetic unification of intentional contents and weaves together sensory items, association, which is the law by which passive synthesis proceeds, provides for the kind of unity necessary for objective reference and recognition in later stages of constitution. Crucially, even though the object is only 'pre-given, pre-constituted', it is ready to be apprehended 'as this identical unity' (1975, 60) because it is already structured in intentional consciousness according to rule-like formations that Husserl calls 'types' (*Typen*).[7] Appearances that manifest a qualitative similarity with one another are retained in consciousness and exercise an affective force on the subject's present experience such that new appearances of the same or similar objects awaken old ones. As the perception unfolds, appearances are automatically grouped together, viz. assimilated as partaking in this or that type or category (1975, 321). For Husserl, the validity of this associative principle has no limit. Even those objects that we are confronted with for the first time are experienced as having at least some level of familiarity: 'Without doubt, it can happen that an affect lacks a particular typification, but at least it is still grasped as an object, and, if it is a sensible given, as a spatial object, and, as an object, as one within the absolutely necessary and most general form "object in general"' (1975, 39).

The consequences of this insight are massive. For it implies that appearing objects are *always* pre-given according to delineated patterns of sense. Based on our implicit awareness of our past perceptual and affective experiences, which have crystallized into types, our foregoing experiences are filled with expectations, which contribute to the subject's present grasp of what perceptually comes in (1975, 331). For instance, 'To the type "dog," e.g., belongs a stock of typical attributes with an open horizon of anticipation of further such attributes' (1975, 332). Based on the dogs I have experienced in the past, sensory contents associatively partaking to the type 'dog' generate expectations of what legitimately constitutes a dog (e.g. a

---

[7] It is true that a developed consciousness does not explicitly have worldly experiences that are even apparently like anything associative synthesis achieves. To the level of predicative experience corresponds the stratum of constitution where perceptual objects are not 'finished' yet, but only 'pre-given'. For there to be object-consciousness, there must be 'an active believing cognizance' (1975, 64), coupled with the pragmatic potentiality of moving one's own body appropriately (1997, 154–6; 2001, 10–15). However—and this is the whole point of the genetic project—Husserl holds that there couldn't be any kind of bodily or cognitive activity targeted at specific worldly items if consciousness wasn't intentionally related to these items in the first place. The very possibility of identifying objects presupposes the availability of these objects, and this is precisely what Husserl's theory of passive intentionality sought to account for.

four-legged hairy mammal with a muzzle and a tail). When I see a dog's head out of the window as I walk around the block, an open horizon of further typical features is anticipated: I expect it to have a tail, four legs, and to bark occasionally, all of which may elicit fear and discomfort, or enthusiasm and frenzy, depending on my previous interactions with dogs. In Husserl's own words, it is 'evident that further determinations are as a rule in regular connection with the determinations already apprehended or, what is the same thing, that in the course of experience they must be expected as copresent' (1975, 332) Of course, this singular dog may present new, unexpected attributes (1975, 331f.). Maybe it belongs to those breeds that have their tails cut off at birth. But types can accommodate such surprising phenomena, for types are not fixed categories but are continually revised and modified, integrating new attributes and discarding others as the stock of accumulated experiences grow:

> what is identified as a dog through the known attributes will also have, through empirical induction relative to dogs given and examined more closely, new attributes which are found in conformity with a rule, and so on and on. Thus, empirical concepts are changed by the continual admission of new attributes but according to an empirical idea of an open, ever-to-be-corrected concept which, at the same time, contains in itself the rule of empirical belief and is founded on the progress of actual experience. (1975, 333)

Types are flexible and adaptable. Since they are empirical structures, they can change and morph into new configurations. This is one of their essential features, which distinguish them from concepts: 'Unlike concepts, types do not have a definite intension and an indefinitely large extension' (Staiti 2018, 163). Contrary to concepts, which are essentially general, types are grounded on a *limited* set of objects and are context-relative, which confer on them their vague character. But this vagueness is not a weakness (Lohmar 2014). On the contrary, it is exactly this vagueness that allows typological recognition to remain active and responsive to the specificities of each perceptual situation.

As 'empirical generalities' (Husserl 1975, 321), types nonetheless function as 'a priori' (1975, 340) rules in the process of perceptual recognition.[8]

---

[8] Thanks to their rule-like character, D. Lohmar (2003, 2008) argued that types assume in Husserl's framework a function like Kant's schemata. For a critical discussion, see Doyon 2019.

Experienced objects are passively recognized as instances or expressions of such vague generalities. As soon as they are apprehended, a 'realm of possibilities' (*Spielraum*) (1975, 32) for their identification and further determinations opens. Since these possibilities both facilitate object identification and stay open to revision or modification, types assume a mediating function between the generality of concepts and the singularity of each experienced object. Types are the preform (*Vorform*) of concepts. They are pre-categorial rule-like formations that synthetically join different sensible properties, different profiles, and different modes of presentations of objects under a single experiential unit, but it bears within itself a part of indeterminacy. The result is a morphological or vague ideality: types are not exact idealities like numbers; but they are not the mere individual instances of a concept either.

Husserl's analyses of the experiential origins and genesis of empirical concepts, as well as of the capacity to recognize individual instances as expressions of such concepts, are of fundamental importance for his genetic project, for they show that it is the 'pre-affective lawful regularities' discovered in passivity that are ultimately responsible for 'the formation of unity' (1975, 202), and therefore for the experience of any kind of object (*Gegenstand*) at all. As a result, the capacity to be perceptually presented with particulars rests not on conceptual or judicative capacities but on perception's own synthetic work and affective-intentional laws. As Husserl observes, 'the thing presents itself persistently as something which is such-and-such, even if no concepts, no judgments in the predicative sense, are mediating' (1989, 22). This, however, does not mean that the passive world-disclosing activity of the ego is *discontinuous* with the conceptual realm. Constitution is a multilayered process of sense formation in which one layer sets the stage for the next. The structural joining together of the manifold of appearances at work at the level of association displays a rudimentary version of the kind of lawful regularity upon which empirical types and eventually fully fledged concepts are based. Husserl's foundational model is such that we find meaningful articulations of experiential sense in passivity (at the level of association), then some more in receptivity (perception), and still more in the spontaneity of the predicative act of judgment (thought). This is how Husserl came to see predicative forms of experience as grounded in perceptual and proto-perceptual experiences. This is in turn possible because *articulations of sense are present at every level of constitution*, not only at the level of higher-order achievements such as judgments and abstraction.[9] Judgments are the *expanded* or *refined* version of the kind of meanings we already find in the prepredicative experience of things, situations, and events. Given the similarity of structure between the layers of constitution, the transition from one to the next is simple. By a shift of focus from actual instances of dogs to the ideal 'something' that recurs as identical in all instances, we form concepts as new kinds of entities that, unlike types, allow us to judge in the mode of 'in general'. This is why Husserl conceives of predicative judgment as a judgment of higher degree. Since it enables the establishment of 'a store of knowledge that is communicable and usable in the future' (1975, 63), predication, unlike types, can yield lasting results (1975, 212). As van Mazijk (2020) explains, to achieve this, predicative judgments require that the ego 'repeat the passive process, but this time in a changed, active attitude. The extraction of the state of affairs is...a kind of doing over; it is an active repetition of what was, in a way, already accomplished in perception' (van Mazijk 2020, 105). In short, if Husserl posits an "explicative synthesis" (1975, 112) at the foundation of the predicative synthesis 'S is p', it is because perception and judgment already share the same basic intentional structure of significance.

Here's another way of putting things: Husserl's genetic analyses led him to the conclusion that there must be a form of passivity that precedes and triggers activity (be it perceptual, predicative, or otherwise), for to act upon something at all (say, bring it into focus or make a judgment about it), the targeted object must first be available to me. That's exactly how Husserl came to differentiate between active and passive forms of attention, or top-down and bottom-up attention. The point is that intentional relatedness presupposes a prior affection (*Affektion*) which passively triggers or initiates the attentional process. It is true that there could be no relation to the object without consciousness's receptivity, that is, without consciousness's responsive turning to (*Zuwendung*) the affecting item. Yet even this very basic form of attentional activity that Husserl calls 'receptivity' presupposes a

---

[9] Husserl expresses very clearly in the first lines of section 39 of *Cartesian Mediations* that intentionality goes all the way down and reaches the level of association: 'The universal principle of passive genesis, for the constitution of all objectivities given completely prior to the products of activity bears the title association. Association, it should be clearly noted, is a matter of intentionality descriptively demonstrable as that, in respect of its primal forms, and standing, in respect of its intentional performances, under eidetic laws. Owing to these, each and every passive constitution is to be made understandable—both the constitution of subjective processes, as objects in immanent time, and the constitution of all real natural objects belonging to the Objective spatio-temporal world' (1960, 80).

prior affection, which automatically sparks the associative process. Since associations are rudimentary forms of meaningful connections between sensory data, it appears that even the lowest forms of passive experiences are structured or articulated in intentional consciousness, however vaguely. With a little abuse of language, this had led Husserl to assert that perception, considered at the lowest level of experience, is itself already a form of judgment: 'Every apprehending turning-toward which arrests what is given in the flux of sensuous experience, i.e., turns toward it attentively and by way of contemplation searches into its properties, is already an achievement, a cognitive activity of the lowest level, with regard to which we can already speak of an act of judgment' (1975, 60). Otherwise put, 'with every prepredicative, objectifying turning-toward an existent, it is already necessary to speak of an act of judgment in the broader sense' (1975, 61), since these elementary associations are meaningful connections upon which explicit forms of judgments are based. From that angle, predicative experience really is a kind of reprise of what was already accomplished in prepredicative experience.

The conclusion to draw therefrom is clear: even before it finds expression in judgments, perception already has meaningful content. This is because intentional consciousness in every form implies associative connections that arise passively. This does not imply that thought and perception cannot be distinguished or, perhaps more subtly, that perception has propositional content; the point is, rather, that the content of perception can on occasion be lifted up into judgment *because* its content is structured analogously. In other words, there is some kind of parallelism between the deliverances of perceptual experience and potential future judgments of experience (what Husserl calls *Wahrnehmungsurteile*) because they are structured analogously.[10]

5.1.3. The Weight of Our Perceptual History I

In view of these analyses, there is no doubt that Husserl's account of typification *is* an instance of perceptual learning. Types fit the definition discussed in the introduction of this chapter: they induce long-term change in perception stemming from repeated practice or experience (Gibson 1963; Connolly 2019). Let us briefly look at all three features of this definition in turn.

---

[10] On this specific point, Heidegger defends an almost identical position; see Section 2.2.1.

Firstly, types cause *long-term* changes in perception. As I have shown, types are adaptable or flexible, not fixed sets. With the accumulation of experiences, both perceptual and affective, types morph and modify their own structures, integrating new attributes, discarding others along the way, thereby generating varying expectations. Given the indeterminate character of associations, the scope of types can be expanded or limited depending on whether experience fulfils or disappoints our expectations; in some cases, some types may even be completely abandoned, leading to the formation of new or more specific ones. However, despite the flexibility that both the type-formation process and the ensuing disposition for typological recognition display, types are not merely adaptive or short-term. Until new ones take over, their effect on perception is enduring.[11]

Secondly, the induced change in perception is intentional, not causal, and it results from repeated *practice or experience.* It is indeed the accumulation of encounters with particular objects and situations, and the interplay between variation and constancy in what we experience in different contexts, that allow for the formation of type and typological recognition. In that sense, typification is a process closely aligned on our individual perceptual and affective history, which themselves come about in a social or intersubjective context where others are always co-present. Types are therefore not solipsistic achievements of the individual egos even if they vary from individual to individual.

Thirdly, typification is a *perceptual* process that provokes a certain meaningful arrangement of perceptual content. As we have seen, the formation of type is a data-driven process. It is the external environment that, in affecting me, triggers the associative process in passivity. The same goes for the capacity of typological recognition at the heart of perception, which should not be understood as an inferential process. On the contrary, the reactivation of previous and familiar experience in typological recognition is an associative process, whereby presently affecting appearances are integrated in consciousness on the basis of their affinity with past appearances. During this practical accomplishment of the perceiving ego, similarities are noticed across variations and passively retained in consciousness, thus eliciting

---

[11] In some cases, the changes may even be permanent, or close to permanent. As a result of some traumatic events, it may be difficult—even with psychological treatments—to completely overcome some deeply entrenched associative schemes. When the affective charge is too important, the kind of changes induced in experience may be irreversible. Think, for instance, of somebody who has been severely attacked by a horse at a young age; for her, horses may always look fearful, no matter what she does. Of course, this does not imply that perception *itself* loses its plasticity, but only that one of its dimensions does.

more or less determinate expectations about how the experience will continue to unfold.

No doubt, Husserl's account meets the three conditions entailed by the definition of perceptual learning and stands in sharp opposition to philosophers like Dretske (1995) or Tye (2000), who reject the very possibility that learning could induce alterations in the way things phenomenally appear to us. (They both explain the changes in non-experiential terms by resorting to post-perceptual processes.) Now, even if we agree that perceptual learning is possible and that it can provoke phenomenal changes in experience, there are at least two ways of explaining how it can happen. Some hold that the relevant 'changes in the phenomenal character of perceptual experience' can, in some circumstances at least, be explained by the way one's perceptual system interacts with 'the states of one's cognitive system, for example, one's thoughts or beliefs' (Macpherson 2012, 24). In this story, the relevant changes in the phenomenal character of experience are the result of top-down influences of our cognitive system on our perceptual one, and may, if their effect on perception is long-term, be understood as a form of learning. But that's not the only option. Others think that the relevant changes can, in some cases at least, be entirely due to structural transformations of the perceptual *processes or mechanisms* (e.g. attention) themselves, which may improve through learning (Gibson 1963, 1969; Price 2009; Connolly 2019). According to this line of explanation, phenomenal changes are traced back to repeated patterns of exposure to the relevant sensory items, which exert a bottom-up influence on experience.

We could illustrate the difference between both types of explanation by dwelling on Siegel's (2010) argument concerning pine trees, where she contends that our capacity to identify pine trees, and to distinguish them from other kinds of trees, may improve over time due to learning. For Siegel, the change is sensory; that is, it occurs at the level of perceptual content: experienced perceivers acquire the capacity to *represent high-level-kind properties* in perception (e.g. being a pine tree) such that pine trees might look visually salient to them. It is not clear whether this acquired representational capacity, and the ensuing contentful transformation, rests on the possession of the relevant concept, but it is one possible and very intuitive way to understand her descriptions. For this reason, her account may be labelled as 'cognitivist'. Some philosophers (e.g. Macpherson 2012, 37; Arstila 2016; Connolly 2019, 65–99) reject that cognitivist interpretation and contest that Siegel's pine tree case is one of cognitive penetration. Instead, they suggest a bottom-up explanation of the case, that is, an explanation that relies on the intervention of specific perceptual, viz. attentional mechanisms. For Connolly (2019), for instance, the phenomenal difference between an unexperienced and an experienced perceiver of pine trees lies not in the high-level represented content that the latter but not the former can produce; the difference is, rather, entirely due to 'a shift in the weight of one's attention onto other low-level properties' (67), such as colours, shapes, size, and orientation, etc., which may, through practice, become more salient to the experienced perceiver. Let me call this second line of explanation the 'attentionalist' account.

My aim here is not to resolve the debate between the cognitivist and attentionalist interpretation of Siegel's pine tree example, which was brought up only to carve out the contours of the two dominant conceptions of perceptual learning in contemporary research. What interests me is where Husserl stands with respect to these two approaches. On the one hand, and despite his career-spanning investigation of attention,[12] Husserl unfortunately never directly explored the latter hypothesis; that is, he never entertained the possibility that perceptual and attentional skills and mechanisms themselves could improve over time thanks to learning. This is a shame, for there is evidence that perceptual and attentional skills *can* be trained, and perceivers *can* gain some control over the quality of their experiences through practice, instruction, and active guidance (see Jenkin 2023b for an argument to that effect in infants and nonhuman animals). In contemporary neuroscience, there is a vast and growing body of literature that looks at how certain (especially Eastern) traditions prioritize the cultivation of attentional stability and consider the training of active attention maintenance to be a defining aspect of focused attention meditation, which is said to provoke all kinds of phenomenal changes, notably the receding of the subject–object distinction (Thompson 2014). Nothing comparable can be

---

[12] For the most part, Husserl's long-standing interest in attention was due to its intrinsic connection to cognition. The early Husserl conceived of attention as a subjective act propelled by a desire for knowledge (*Begehren nach Erkenntnis*) (2005a, 118). In his 1904/5 lecture 'Wahrnehmung und Aufmerksamkeit', attention is defined as the 'motor of the cognitive process' (*das Motor des Erkenntnisprozesses*) of perception (Wehrle 2015b), for which reason he assigned it a central epistemological function in phenomenology (2005a, 112). Husserl's idea, in short, is that attention amounts to a progressive determination of the object (2005a, 30ff.): through focal attention, I throw into relief the perceived object or parts of it and elevate it to the status of cognition. In the later, genetic works, Husserl introduced a distinction between active and passive forms of attention, or top-down and bottom-up attention, where the latter is understood as a response to a prior affection. This receptive moment, in which consciousness responds to the affection by turning to it, is one in which the associative process is already underway, functioning along the lines analysed in this section.

found in Husserl or his immediate successors (such as Merleau-Ponty, Schütz, or even Gurwitsch). The topic greatly interested the experimental psychologists of his time, however, Stumpf (2020) and James (1908) in particular, and both thought that perception is plastic precisely because it can be trained through active attentional learning (see Depraz 2014, 205–86).

On the other hand, Husserl is not a clear cognitivist either: not only does he not affirm anywhere that our *occurrent* beliefs and concepts directly impact the very appearances of things,[13] but types should not straightforwardly be understood as *background* beliefs or dispositional concepts either, for they are empirical in nature. Types can even be *severed* from beliefs, that is, stand in contradiction with them (Berghofer and Wiltsche 2019, 309–13). I may know (and hence believe) that there are no more trains rolling down my village's track (say, because it has been recently rerouted), and still hear a specific sound as of a train when the wind blows. Since it impacts the phenomenology of things, viz. the way things are consciously experienced, we can't speak of cognitive penetration in the usual sense here. At the same time, the functional role of types in perception certainly brings them in the vicinity of background beliefs, since types do not concern the perceptual processes themselves but, rather, contribute to fix the *content* of perception by forming, expanding, and refining the horizonal contents of perception. They are thus assuming a role akin to Siegel's representations of high-level properties, which are also described as impacting perceptual content, but their contribution is at the same time different, since types do not directly concern the *sensory* phenomenology but, rather, bear on the perceptual *horizon* and the expectations that constitute it. Given this mixed result, Husserl could be seen, with respect to contemporary debates on perceptual learning, as endorsing a position between the straightforwardly cognitivist and the attentionalist approaches to perceptual learning, even if he, on the whole, seems to have more affinity with the former.

Concerning the normativity involved in perceptual learning, we have briefly considered three positions in the current literature: first Goldstone (1998), who claims that perceptual learning allows organisms to enhance their ability to respond to the environment; then Connolly (2019), who argues that perceptual learning frees up cognitive resources by transferring some tasks to the agent's fast perceptual system, thereby facilitating the

---

[13] Since cases involving *occurrent* beliefs are cases of cognitive penetration but not cases of perceptual learning anyway, they need not preoccupy us here.

executing of other tasks (be they perceptual or not); and finally Jenkin (2023a, 7), who argues that perceptual learning holds promise for enhancing perception in various epistemically relevant aspects, such as the beliefs perception supports, perception's responsiveness to reasons, and perception's role in justification. While there is no principled reason why Husserl would disagree with either of these three claims, his account of perceptual learning and type-formation is normative in a different sense, for it is best understood as following normative patterns of coherence and optimality.

Let's start with coherence. Thanks to types, perceived things are always given in a horizon of familiarity. The associative syntheses that constitute types facilitate the formation of coherent and meaningful perceptual wholes that will be experienced as more or less familiar, that is, concordant with our expectations. Even when the perceived object is new or has never been experienced before, perception has a permanent structure of acquaintance, or a sense of familiarity (Husserl 2008, 65).[14] We might, of course, be wrong in our typological apprehension. The expectations that are grounded thereon may be disappointed, thereby forcing a revision of our typological knowledge due to new acquisition. Yet, even in these cases, the process of typological recognition is not fully abolished; it is, rather, revised and corrected (in the good case at least—more on this below). It is improved such as to promote coherence both synchronically and diachronically, that is, both in actual experience and across time and events.[15] As a result, everything that perceptually comes in is measured according to this implicit standard: it is experienced as either normal or abnormal, that is, as fitting or not fitting with our typological expectations. Normality, experienced as concordance or practical familiarity, is therefore already well established at the level of passivity (Wehrle 2022).

The fact that types are continuously modified and refined as our stock of experiences grow enables them to fulfil another normative function in experience, for the new, more specific sets of expectations that this process

---

[14] Generalizing the scope of this insight, Husserl came to conceive of 'the world' itself, 'present to consciousness as horizon', as having 'the subjective general character of trustworthiness' (1975, 37).

[15] As surprising as it may be, one may recognize a certain affinity between Husserl's conception of typification and the so-called Predictive Processing View (e.g. Andy Clark 2015). Just as types are steadily updated in experience, thereby refining its expectations and facilitating typological recognition, the predictive processing model conceives of the brain as a predictive machine where priors are continuously updated within experience to minimize error and enhance the accuracy of our discriminative powers. Beyond this point of convergence, the two approaches remain largely different, but explaining this in detail would take me too far from my main objective.

opens onto facilitate perceptual distinctions and optimize perception. The point is simple: highly profiled types allow for more differentiations, and therefore for quicker and more accurate object recognition. To go back to Husserl's dog example, the more refined my typological knowledge of dogs is, the more specific my expectations of its appearances and behaviours are. This, in turn, facilitates his recognition and thus enriches my perception. Concretely: if my neighbour's dog gets lost in a pool of dogs, and I know that it's an Afghan hound, I may help him more easily to find his dog than if I don't know what breed it is. If I know that it's an Afghan hound and know what these dogs look like (roughly), it will stand out more clearly from the other dogs. This is the simple figure/background gestaltist principle that Husserl made his own despite his otherwise well-founded reservations regarding gestalt psychology.[16] Since it is subject to improvement and correction as experiences are accumulated, the process of type-formation is normative in the sense of optimality.

Before closing this section, I would like to address two sets of objections or worries that could be levelled against the kind of normative reading of Husserl's associative model just sketched out. First, one may think that types are not necessarily geared towards perceptual improvement but can also produce undesired results and *limit* an individual's ability to perceptually discern accurately. This can happen in various ways. Typological recognition can, for instance, lead to object misidentification. Most of us associate bananas with a specific colour, namely yellow. Nevertheless, numerous studies have shown that perceivers are prone to perceive a banana as being yellow even when it is not. This is called the *memory colour* effect (Hering 1964), which refers to the tendency of people to perceive the colour of an object as being biased or influenced by their prior knowledge or expectations about the typical colour of that object. The memory colour effect, also known as the Hering effect, may result in misidentification or mislabelling of objects or properties, which can be problematic in contexts where colour accuracy is critical, such as in medicine, for instance, where proper colour identification may be a matter of life and death. Memory colour can also limit an individual's ability to learn or make new associations in the same way that limited typological flexibility can impact an individual's

---

[16] For an overview of Husserl's and Merleau-Ponty's position vis-à-vis *Gestaltpsychologie*, see Heinämaa 2009, who argues that Merleau-Ponty sought to subject gestalt theory to a kind of phenomenological-transcendental reduction inspired by Husserl. In the end, Heinämaa justly suggests that Husserl's critique of gestalt theory is much closer to Merleau-Ponty's than it's standardly taken to be.

ability to adapt and display context-sensitivity. More generally, the worry is that the drive towards coherence might involve disregard for novelty and what would otherwise make a real difference. Are we not sometimes ignoring differences (say, in others) precisely *because* they don't cohere with our expectations, goals, and values? It seems undeniable, as Connolly aptly remarks in the conclusion of his book, that the kind of associative work involved in 'perceptual learning has the ability to cause social harm, particularly in cases in which people's perceptual systems are tuned to harmfully distort their perceptions of members of social groups' (Connolly 2019, 217).

This is an important point, and it hints at an inherent weakness in Husserl's model, which did not prioritize contrast over similarity but, rather, put them both on an equal footing in the associative process. This is problematic, as it can lead to the difficulties just alluded to, but I don't think that this is an insurmountable problem. McLaren and Mackintosh's associative learning model has been used to argue that contrast is actually more significant than similarity (see McLaren, Kaye, and Mackintosh 1989; McLaren and Mackintosh 2000). In a nutshell, their studies have shown that shared or similar features are, with time, less noticed by the perceivers, and therefore less likely to enter in associations. The opposite holds for nonshared features, whose novel character make them fit for associative learning. Connolly's Blind Flailing Model of perceptual learning, 'whereby we come to recognize new kinds by attending to them in all sorts of ways (that is, by flailing our attention) until our attention settles on the low-level properties that make that kind novel to us' (2019, 67; cf. 2019 76–88), works in much the same way. Considering these results, which seem to be on track, we could still justly complain that Husserl has misunderstood an important aspect of his own discovery, namely the priority of contrast or novelty over similarity or likeness, without, however, rejecting the model itself. What seems to be missing in Husserl is an explicit recognition of the virtues of novel information, alternative explanations, and unexpected observations. Developing a sensitivity to this kind of cues is crucial, for it can help both to mitigate confirmation bias, viz. the tendency to seek out and interpret information in a way that confirms one's pre-existing beliefs, and to facilitate more rapid and flexible learning. In other words, a genuine openness when performing perceptual learning tasks can lead to greater inclusivity and diversity, and thus contribute to avoid some of the above-mentioned difficulties. I will return to some of these worries in the next chapter in the context of the perception of other people.

A second, related problem is that the sheer accumulation of experiences—even novel ones—does not guarantee optimality (or secure truth, for that matter). What is required is the accumulation of 'good' experiences, as it were, otherwise perceivers simply reinforce their prejudicial views. But how does this work? There are different aspects to consider here. Firstly, it is important to point out that typological recognition is a habitualized routine that generally facilitates our perceptual response to the environment even if fails to do so occasionally. However, the fact that not every instance of typological recognition yields accurate results is not a reason to ignore its benefits when it works. Secondly, even if one grants, as one should, that prejudices are hardly totally overcome, and, worst still, that their impact may even largely remain unnoticed by the perceiver herself, at other times their undesirable effect *can* be revealed in experience, even if only by the detour of language or the mediation of others. Once this is realized, our prejudicial views can be abandoned or corrected (at least to a certain degree), and therewith possibilities of optimization open themselves up. All this to say that the possibility of self-correction is constitutive of learning even if there are obstacles to its realization. Finally, it is important to keep in mind that, for Husserl, optimality is a matter of goal and interest, both at the subjective and intersubjective level, and that they can clash with one another. What is not optimal from an intersubjective point of view may still have some value at a personal level. The question of the benefits attached to perceptual learning is thus a complex, multifaceted one that I have cnot exhausted here.

5.2. Bodily Plasticity

The previous section provided a phenomenological analysis of noetic plasticity by examining Husserl's account of typification. But perception is not exclusively a cognitive or mental affair; it is also an embodied practice. Typological recognition has a motivational function in perception and can elicit movements, understood as responses to perceived objects and situations. These movements in turn presuppose previously acquired skills and habits and motivate the development of new ones. This section investigates these motor aptitudes and their effects on experience. The presentation will unfold along the lines of the previous one: it will be argued, first (and this time against Connolly 2017; 2019, 16–17), that both skill acquisition and the formation of motor habit *are* instances of perceptual learning; and second, that these bodily transformations follow the same normative patterns of coherence and optimality. I am going to take my initial cues from Husserl's work and then move to Merleau-Ponty's.

5.2.1. The Habitual Style of the Perceiving Ego

One of the most well-known and neat introductions of the concept of the lived body can be found in *Ideas II*, in which Husserl distinguished two attitudes one can have with respect to the body, namely a naturalistic one, which corresponds to that of the natural sciences, and a personal one, which is characteristic of the so-called humanities. While the body appears from a personal perspective as a sensing body (*Leib*) or a 'motivational-expressive' whole (Heinämaa 2012, 230), it manifests itself from a naturalistic perspective as a sensed body or physical thing standing in causal relations (*Körper*).[17] This insight into the dual nature of the *Leibkörper* is fundamental, for the body can only assume its constitutive role in perception insofar as it figures in these two registers at once. As the centre or 'zero point' (Husserl 1989, 166) of orientation, the *Leib* is the egocentric centre around which the perceptual space unfolds.[18] Husserl considers the body as a transcendental condition of possibility of the perception of spatial objects insofar as the *Leib* acts as the 'central here' (1989, 166) in relation to which all other spatial objects are oriented. However, the body can only play this functional role and serve as a perspectival sensing organism because it itself has extension or materiality, that is, because it itself occupies a portion of space thanks to its embodied nature (Zahavi 2003a, 98ff.). I see things in profile *because* I occupy a definite position in space; and I occupy a definite position in space *because* I have a material or extended body (Husserl 1989, 36). As a result, it is only insofar as the body is both a *Leib* and a *Körper* that the constitution of space is possible.

One of the key Husserlian ideas on perception is to conceive of the perceptual horizon in terms of our sensed capacity for movement. The

---

[17] This double nature of human embodiment as *Leib* and *Körper* was famously disclosed in Husserl's description of the so-called 'double sensation' in *Ideas II* (1989, 152ff.). For a detailed analysis, see Heinämaa 2012, 2021 as well as Doyon and Wehrle 2020.
[18] This scheme can be further complicated by taking not the body itself but a part of it as a reference point. For example, the object could be said to be in the centre of the visual field or more towards the periphery, where the eye is now the centre of orientation. For a detailed and step-by-step reconstruction of Husserl's argument in *Thing and Space*, see Drummond 1983 and Mooney 2023, §4.3.

body-centred spatial framework characteristic of perceptual experience is also the space of agency. The perceptual space is one that 'I can' inhabit (Husserl 1989, 253; 2001, 51). For Husserl, the body is an organ of the will, the seat of free movements, thanks to which I can realize my kinaesthetic freedom (1975, 83f.). This capacity is not a mere practical possibility; it also has constitutive force. As we saw in the two preceding chapters (Sections 3.2. and 4.1), movement is a transcendental condition of object perception. Perceived objects are synthetic unities, that is, the outcome of a dynamic sequence of concordant appearances or coinciding profiles realized in a kinaesthetic experience. For Husserl, the constitution of space and the constitution of perceptual objects go hand in hand: while object-constitution requires the capacity to move and self-consciously feel one's relevant organs (eyes, head, etc., in vision), the exercise of my kinaesthetic freedom in turn depends on my capacity to orient myself in a spatial framework where objects are perceived in relation to me as the centre of the perceptual field.

Here, a difficulty lurks: since *Leib* and *Körper* constitutively belong together (Husserl 1973b, 454–8), pointing to the transcendental role of the lived body (*Leib*) and its mobility in experience is not enough. The realization of these constitutive functions requires an analysis that goes beyond embodiment and mobility 'in general'; it necessitates a thorough investigation into our personal bodily engagement in the process of perception (Wehrle 2021, 203). The *Leibkörper* Husserl has in view is not only a formal support of transcendental possibilities; it has a personal history. It is affective, emotional, and vulnerable. This is not a surprising outcome, since the transcendental ego is inseparable from the concrete person or empirical ego. What is new, however, or what Husserl more lucidly began to realize in *Ideas II* and in the manuscripts of the 1920s, is that the empirical features of our bodies are not *simply* empirical or contingent; they have a constitutive value. They are integral dimensions or moments of our sense-making abilities, whose course of action they enable, facilitate, prevent, or hinder (see Section 6.3). For this reason, Husserl became growingly attentive to the development or coming-to-be of our embodied sense-making skills, which are subject to constant change and transformation throughout our lifetime. In this respect, one of Husserl's key ideas—which Merleau-Ponty would refine and adapt (see Section 5.2.2)—is that the history of our concrete individual embodiment has a transcendental impact on perception. Through the accumulation of repeated perceptual experiences, we develop skills and habits that, in turn, are largely responsible for the meaning the perceptual world comes to have for us. This genetic take on perception is very explicitly linked to the questions of plasticity and learning, since our bodily skills, which are steadily shifting as our stock of experiences grow, do not leave unaltered the phenomenal character of experience. On the contrary—and this is what the rest of this section is about—the deployment of our perceptual skills governs, rather, the transformation of the phenomenal field itself.

Elucidating all this requires that we go back to the question of time, or rather of time-consciousness. The interplay of impressions, retentions, and protentions, which provides the formal structure of experience, implies a dynamic of empty intending and fulfilment whose accomplishment in perception calls for movement. This, however, was not always how Husserl saw things. In the *Logical Investigations*, the phenomenological analysis of the body is at best indirectly implied by the concept of fulfilment. Perception is described as a fulfilling experience that involves the consciousness of a coincidence between an emptily intended sense and its corresponding intuitive content. When the intuitively given object is consciously presented as it has been emptily intended, the empty intention is said to be 'satisfied' or 'fulfilled'. Given the irreducible one-sidedness of every particular perception—viz. the fact that objects are always perceived under a certain aspect (Husserl 2001b, 220)—perceptual fulfilment can only ever be partial or incomplete. This generates what is sometimes called the problem of perceptual presence (Noë 2004) today, which is brought about by the constitutive discrepancy between what is meaningfully intended (the object) in experience and what is sensibly given (the profile or silhouette). As we saw in the preceding chapters, this, for Husserl, is unproblematic, for we are directed through the profile toward the object. Perceptual consciousness is transcendent and intentionally integrates the co-intended profiles.

It is in the context of explaining the details of this intending operation that Husserl implicitly refers to the body in the *Logical Investigations*. He develops his thought on this by means of a phenomenological description of a perception of a piece of furniture covering up a carpet: 'If I see an incomplete pattern, e.g. in this carpet partially covered up over by furniture, the piece I see seems clothed with intentions pointing to further completions—we feel as if the lines and coloured shapes go on "in the sense" of what we see—but we expect nothing. It would be possible for us to expect something, if movement promised us further views' (2001b, 211). The thesis advanced here—which counts as the very first appeal to bodily movement in Husserl's published works—states that the object's seen profile intentionally refers to other profiles or aspects of the thing that could become visible via movement. But then Husserl adds that the kind of 'occasions for possible expectations' that movement can generate 'are not themselves expectations' (2001b, 211). What Husserl is hinting at here is that the visual experience of the carpet does not de facto imply any concrete expectations, and therefore does not command any concrete movements either, because that experience is not—or does not have to be—oriented toward its future realization. Such an experience does prescribe possibilities of fulfilment; but these possibilities are *mere logical possibilities*, as it were; they do not command anything concrete. This explains Husserl's early distinction between intention and expectancy: 'Intention is not expectancy' (2001b, 211), which means that all intentions do not necessarily require fulfilment. Intentions *open up* the possibility of fulfilment, but, strictly speaking, they do not command anything, since 'it is not of its essence to be directed to future appearances' (2001b, 211; Benoist 2016, 128ff.).

Husserl's view on this will refine in subsequent years. Husserl eventually came to realize that of all the possibilities of perception, some are real, motivated possibilities. If I have no specific intention with respect to the carpet, then there is no actual expectation of the future course of my experience. There is just a possible expectation, corresponding to various courses of action. If, however, I have the intention of, say, moving the couch to clean the carpet underneath, I will expect it to continue according to the same pattern thanks to the association of my present experience of the carpet's pattern with my habituated experience of carpet patterns continuing in a regular style (2001, 236). This means that, when motivated, the connection of actual and past experiences opens onto perceptual possibilities which are not just logical, but real (2002, 178ff.). It is this very idea that Husserl starts to develop in the 1907 lecture course *Thing and Space*, and which will be polished in the so-called 'genetic' phase of phenomenology in the early 1920s.

In this story, the most important function of movement is carried by the accompanying sensations, which motivate the flow of appearances (see Sections 3.2. and 4.1). They do so by generating a more or less definite set of expectations, which are themselves the results of associated perceptual data or content (see Section 5.1). However, to fully understand the nature of this associative-motivating process, a crucial piece needs to be added: perceptual consciousness is not only carried by movement and expectations; it is also driven by interests (1975, 80–6).[19] Perception is not reducible to an

---

[19] The notion of interest is actually quite old and was already systematically worked out in the 1904/5 lecture course 'Hauptstücke aus der Phänomenologie der Erkenntnis', which was posthumously published in the volume *Wahrnehmung und Aufmerksamkeit* in 2005. However, it is not until the 1920s that interests are fully integrated in Husserl's account of perception alongside kinaesthesis and typological recognition.

intending process. In *Experience and Judgment* (1975) and *Passive and Active Synthesis* (2001c), Husserl explains how interests are first awakened by affections before being translated into practical possibilities. As a result, perception is now understood as an affective and emotional activity that develops in a general perceptual drive or 'tendency of the ego' (1975, 81) to explore the world. This tendency, which follows interests and preferences, and which is informed by habitual patterns, finds expression in the realization of a determinate course of action and the enactment of specific bodily movements. In this process, possible objects of perception turn into concrete ones (Wehrle 2021, 202f.).

Interests are of fundamental importance in Husserl's conception of perceptual experience for another, related reason: *they also motivate the acquisition of new perceptual skills and habits*. While stirring the course of action and the flow of appearances, interest drives the ego to develop the necessary skills to sustain its own inclinations and to act on its preferring tendencies by enacting the right moves. Again, a feedback loop informs this motivating process: while interests incite the development of skills and the acquisition habits, the enactment of these skills and habits in turn open new perceptual possibilities, whose realization may require the acquisition of new skills etc. Herewith, Husserl's account of perceptual learning vividly comes to the fore: through repeated experiences, perceptual agents develop habits and acquire skills that they constantly transform and enrich through further encounters, experiences, and transactions with the environment (1989, 267). In doing so, a 'habitual style' (1989, 260 n. 1) of perception crystallizes (Wehrle 2017). Skills and habits inform my ways of navigating the world; they make it easier and faster to find my bearings and orient myself in the lifeworld, whose significance accrues when we possess the relevant skills.

Since the individual ego lives in a historical and intersubjective context, the realization of the ego's potentialities is motivated not only by his own past experiential life but also by the capacities and dispositions of the human genre and of the cultural group to which each individual ego belongs. Wehrle and Breyer (2016) have caught on to this and addressed the issue in the following terms:

> The way that a subject realizes these potentialities is dependent on and motivated by its whole experiential life in its genetic-historical depth: it includes general (human) dispositions as well as the passively or actively acquired and developed skills, habitualities, preferences, and interests. The horizon of perception thus not only consists of an objective or spatial context, but also of the subject's potentiality. The concrete potential of a

subject depends on her former experiences and actions. Husserl differentiates in this regard between a "primary horizon" of "pre-givenness" and familiarity, which is relative to the former experiences and habitualities of the subject, and a "secondary horizon", which is the open horizon that provides us with new possible styles of pre-givenness or is able to change already established familiarities (Husserl, 2008, pp. 53ff.). Although the structure of pre-givenness changes throughout an individual's lifetime (due to new experiences or changes in the environment), some aspects remain stable and characterize the way in which a specific subject or a group of subjects who share similar experiences typically perceive the world. This familiar style of perception delineates what affects us in a certain situation and how we actualize noematic horizons. The world we perceive and relate to is therefore always pre-known to some extent, i.e. a familiar world, or as Husserl would also term it, a lifeworld. (51)

Here, a dialectic of styles unfolds. It is true, as we have seen previously in our analysis of typification (Section 5.1), that the perceived objects are always already apprehended as typified, that is, as more or less familiar to us. Thanks to the work of associations, the lifeworld is invariably experienced as a space of relative familiarity. There is, however, a 'bodily counterpart' to this experienced familiarity: each (type of) object enables or commands certain possibilities of action or interaction, while foreclosing or preventing others (Husserl 1989, 61). In turn, these possibilities determine (in part) the set of skills and habits that we acquire, and which eventually develop into a style of perceiving (1975, 360f.). As a result, there are typical ways of perceiving—habitual ways of engaging with things and navigating the lifeworld—that both enable and constrain *what* can be expected and attended to by specific individuals or groups, and *how* these can respond to the solicitation. As always, for Husserl (and Merleau-Ponty), these two aspects are dialectically linked: the perceiving style of the ego and the style of objects are intentionally correlated and stand in a relation of mutual attunement.[20]

As already indicated, none of this is fixed. Just as types are constantly evolving as experiences are accumulated, so is the style of the perceiving ego, which is not permanently set either. In specific situations, a transient equilibrium is achieved, which explains the relative stability or constancy of

---

[20] While Husserl's descriptions of this dialectic remain very sketchy, Merleau-Ponty provides more detail and radicalizes Husserl's point of view (see Section 4.2).

our experiences. But if we consider what Merleau-Ponty calls the 'intentional arc' (2012, 137) of our perceptual lives—that is, the trajectory or directedness of the subject's past, present, and future experiences—the transformation of our perceptual skills is steady and serves normative purposes in the sense of both coherence and optimality. Skilled and habitual behaviour establishes a sense of practical familiarity, thanks to which we navigate the world with ease and keep perceptual content stable. To take an example, visual perception requires the subject to achieve stability in the visual field despite the steadily changing flow of incoming signals or information (stimuli). Perceivers achieve a transient or relative stability by continuously making motor tunings, from eye saccades to overall motor adjustments and bodily balance. Since action and perception are intentionally connected and possess a shared experiential history, the series of required adjustments are not reinvented or reimagined from the ground up in each situation. On the contrary, the body habitually incorporates practical meanings and consistently develops skilful patterns of action and interaction that can be re-enacted in future similar situations. In that sense, coherence of perceptual content—phenomenal stability, familiarity, and conformity to expectations, etc.—is facilitated and sustained by habitual or skilled behaviour. By the same token, perceptual skills and habits also enable perceivers to enhance the quality of experience and optimize their grip on the scene with respect to their pursued goals or purposes. This is because new possibilities of improvements become available when perceivers possess the required skills in their repertoire. In that sense, possessing the right set of skills also contribute to optimize experience.

5.2.2. The Plasticity of the Body Schema

We find converging ideas in the scientific, phenomenological, and enactivist analyses of the body schema, which refers to the set of motor skills, habits, and mechanisms governing posture and movement. While the historical development of this notion is notoriously convoluted,[21] it is now customary to oppose the *body schema*, which runs habitually, to the conscious system of perceptions, attitudes, and beliefs that perceivers have in relation to their own body, and which constitutes the *body image*. While treated mostly just

---

[21] For a detailed reconstruction of the development of these two notions, see Ataria, Tanaka, and Gallagher 2021, xiii–xxx.

implicitly in the *Phenomenology* (1945), Merleau-Ponty would regularly go back to the question of the body schema in subsequent years and even dedicate it five full lectures in his 1953 Collège de France course *The Sensible World and the World of Expression* (2020). In that work, Merleau-Ponty explains the connection between the body schema and its surrounding environment by drawing upon gestalt psychology. According to Merleau-Ponty, our motor projects, along with the objects they aim at, emerge as explicit forms set against an implicit backdrop that incarnates the body schema (2021, 90). Within this framework, Merleau-Ponty understands the body schema as a norm or foundational reference point, from which specific objects and particular motor projects can consciously come into view. These objects and projects, as forms, reveal themselves as deviations from the norm embodied by the body schema (2021, 103; cf. Section 3.3). In this setting, perception is conceived as expression, that is, as response to perceived tasks or items. Here's how Halák (2021) puts it: 'Between the body-schematic ground and the figures of the sensible world, there is therefore an "expressive relation"' (63), for the world '"indicates" what is required from our body in terms of our movement, posture, and attitude, while conversely the body opens a field for something to be perceived and "completes the given" by appropriately adapting itself to it' (80). Perception, Merleau-Ponty concludes on these grounds, "is already expression" (1970, p. 6; similarly, 2011, p. 176)' (37).

In the *Phenomenology*, Merleau-Ponty described this expressive relation by stressing the body schema's anonymous functioning. The body schema frees us from having to think or deliberate before acting because it supports perception thanks to the non-representational organization of one's postures and movements that it affords, and the practical possibilities that it projects. The experience of typing on a keyboard exemplifies this point vividly: 'When the typist executes the necessary movements on the keyboard, these movements are guided by an intention, but this intention does not posit the keys as objective locations. The subject who learns to type literally incorporates the space of the keyboard into his bodily space' (2012, 146). Merleau-Ponty's key insight is that the body schema, which habitually follows predelineated courses of action and behaviour, can realize this and similar type of motor action because it has integrated the 'motor signification' (2012, 113) of the gesture or action to perform. 'I have no need of directing it toward the goal of the movement, in a sense it touches the goal from the very beginning, and it throws itself toward it' (2012, 97). Since the body schema and the movements and actions that it realizes are motivationally linked to the way we perceive and interact with the world, it stands at the core of Merleau-Ponty's conception of 'motor intentionality' (2012, 113), a term he uses to refer to the specific form of intentional relatedness that is exemplified by purposive, skilful, and unreflective bodily actions. Like cognitive or more abstract forms of intentionality, motor intentionality can initiate and govern movement, but unlike these it can also function independently of our representational powers.

In *Phenomenology of Perception*, this point was famously illustrated *ex negativo* by Merleau-Ponty's interpretation of the case of Schneider, a German soldier who was wounded in the head by mine shrapnel during the First World War. He was treated in the Department of Neurology at the Frankfurt Military Hospital, from which he was discharged in 1918 with a disability pension for mental blindness and cerebellar disorders. Schneider was first diagnosed by psychologist Adhémar Gelb and neurologist Kurt Goldstein as suffering from visual agnosia (Goldstein and Gelb 1918, 137), which is an impairment of the visual system caused by a damaged primary visual cortex (see Farah 2004; Jensen 2009). Even though basic visual functions were relatively intact, Schneider was unable to process visual information normally, e.g. to visually recognize objects when they are detached from their habitual or motivational contexts. For instance, he couldn't effortlessly identify a fountain pen when presented with one in an unfamiliar setting (Merleau-Ponty 2012, 133), or recognize Goldstein's house when he had not the intention of visiting him (2012, 136).

In subsequent analyses, Gelb and Goldstein understood Schneider's impairment as a form of dissociation between an intact ability to perform 'concrete movements' (such as scratching himself precisely where it itches) and an impaired ability to perform 'abstract movements' (e.g. pointing to his nose on command without touching it) (Goldstein 1923, 158–9). In Merleau-Ponty's interpretation, the fact that Schneider can perform concrete routine tasks but fails to perform abstract ones points to the existence of distinct ways of understanding our way around in space (2012, 116–21). While pointing to one's nose on cue requires one to have the capacity to form a representation of the positions of one's nose and hand in objective space, scratching one's nose in everyday life when it itches involves a practical understanding of bodily space, where 'the patient is conscious of bodily space as the envelope of his habitual action, but not as an objective milieu' (2012, 106). In neurotypical or non-disabled people, action and perception are fully integrated and do not require any distancing or representational effort. All that is needed to perform concrete motor tasks is a practical understanding of how our body is oriented in space and in relation to the relevant objects of the environment. This is what the example of the organist is supposed to show (2012, 146). To play the organ, one needs to be proprioceptively aware of where one's fingers and feet are with respect to the keys and pedals, and to have the skills to operate them. Except for when they learn new techniques or new pieces, which require a great deal of mental effort and attentional focus, organ players need not objectify their movements in thought as they play. Their knowledge is fully embodied.

Since the body serves a function of projection of one's intentions into the world, the skilful and habitual movements of the organ player cannot be explained in purely causal or mechanical terms like reflexes. Unlike reflexes, skills and habits are intentional and can adapt to different contexts and situations if they share the same meaning. This is, incidentally, why an organist who has never played on a particular organ can nevertheless quickly get used to it if he recognizes in his old and new instruments not an identity but a community of sense (2012, 143). Given his special neurological condition, it is exactly this community of sense that Schneider can't recognize in abstract or context-free situations, and why he had to consciously think about each individual movement required to perform certain actions that are otherwise effortless or close to automatic. This last point is fundamental: Schneider was able to compensate for his loss of automaticity by using alternative gestures or movements to achieve the same goal, such as using a different finger or hand position to complete a gesture. As Mooney (2023) explains, he seems to 'follow an invariant formula. He must first locate the limb, then make rough movements to establish a seen or felt route for realising the request, and finally refine the movements until the figure is completed' (134). This compensatory routine allowed Schneider to perform at least some of the requested actions even though he had lost the automaticity that once made it effortless.

The necessity to develop new behavioural patterns to compensate for functions that were damaged or destroyed shows Schneider's astonishing lack of body-schematic flexibility. Schneider, who is incapable of imaginatively projecting himself when he is extracted from his practical milieu, suffers from a kind of motor rigidity. Mooney (2023) has again found the right words here:

> Unlike Schneider's phenomenal field, that of the ordinary person is plastic. It can be spontaneously organised into a new orientation by way of an imagined action that is an immediate possibility. Should the action be

embarked upon immediately, the field becomes the actual landscape in which it unfolds.... With all such imagined actions the pre-reflective awareness of available agency is sub-reflectively warranted by potential motor intentional prefigurations for their realisation. Without the latter our powers of projecting into and reckoning with the possible would congeal into laborious planning, and our milieus would correlatively congeal into obstinately familiar pathways. (140)

Schneider lacks the flexibility that characterize the experience of the neurotypical person. Deprived of the capacity to project oneself imaginatively in counterfactual situations, he has become 'motor-rigid', so to speak. This is exactly what Merleau-Ponty is hinting at when he holds that 'the normal person *reckons with* the possible' (2012, 112). Perceiving agents exercise their motor skills by reckoning with various perceived possibilities, and by actualizing one or some of them by enacting certain specific behaviours (and not others). This is, in essence, the dialectics of solicitation and response explored in Chapters 2–4. The key here is that the average individual possesses a range of motor skills beyond those required by their present circumstances or surroundings. They can tap into these skills to accomplish hypothetical tasks that may arise within their environment. The typical individual can easily identify Goldstein's house, even if they simply pass by it on their route to another destination (Romdenh-Romluc 2011, 95).

Schneider's incapacity to exercise his motor skills on cue or in unfamiliar settings, which amounts to an incapacity to perceive opportunities for action other than those that are immediately relevant to him, is a serious impediment, for the capacity to project oneself into future or possible situations is essential to perceptual learning. While by no means unique to athletic performances, this is particularly evident in sports: developing new tactics and strategy, or learning new moves and techniques, requires the capacity to imagine alternate scenarios and project oneself into counterfactual situations. The rigidity of Schneider's body-schematic response testifies to his incapacity to do the same. For the neurotypical or non-disabled person, however, learning is unproblematic because the body schema, which acts as the habitual layer of the acting or perceiving body, is not a fixed entity but is, rather, constantly actualized, updated, and transformed by the current actions of the perceiving body. This idea is not new. As Shontz (1969) noted more than half a century ago, 'body schemata themselves are not fixed photographs of bodily structure but are active, changing processes' (162),

Since the sensory feedback that agents receive from perceived changes typically opens a set of possible reactions, the response is rarely entirely automatic; rather, it displays adaptivity or context-sensitivity. Even if the process of reconfiguration of the body schema is itself not a conscious or deliberate one, but is implicit and largely automatic, the body schema remains a dynamic and flexible system that steadily adapts and reconfigures its repertoire in response to perceived changes in the environment because it is intertwined with perceptual intentionality. In Halák's words, 'the body schema must therefore be conceived of as a *unity of praxis dynamically adapting to its tasks*' (2021, 39; italics in original).

Gibson's (1979) concept of affordances, whose experience in intentional consciousness are, from the phenomenological point of view, inextricable from the possibilities projected by the body schema, makes this point plain. For Gibson, affordances are perceived possibilities of action. As such, they can take different forms—an affordance can be an object, a person, a behaviour, or even a situation—but in all cases the idea is that perceived items open possibilities for certain actions or behaviours on the part of the perceiving agent. In this story, the agent's abilities and skills play a discriminatory role. That is, the meaning of things in our environment is perceived in relation to our abilities: a mountain is perceived as an obstacle for someone in a wheelchair, but as an opportunity for the hiker (Gallagher 2017, 97). This is because affordance is a self-relational property; it includes a reference to the subject. Precisely, Gibson's idea is that some objective properties of the world are perceived in relation to the skills and abilities of the perceptual agent; viz. they are perceived as soliciting her differently according to her dispositions.

Since affordances are not only self-referential but also objective and public properties, they are also dependent on the social context. The chair I perceive is less of an affordance if someone is already sitting on it (Gallagher 2017, 57). This point leads me to clarify the difference between affordance and solicitation: we will say that an apple gives us the possibility to eat, viz. it gives us (affords) this possibility, because it is edible. This is one of its objective properties. But it will not solicit me if I am not hungry or if it is rotten. The reason for distinguishing affordance from solicitation is that a third condition must also be met in order to say that the apple solicits me; namely, I must also be 'motivated', that is, this perceived possibility must, in addition, fit into my intentional project. Therefore, strictly speaking, when we speak of affordances as 'action possibilities' that solicit me, we are not talking about just any possibility but only those that are relevant to the execution of my intentional project. In other words, if affordance is an objective property of the perceived that is revealed as such by my capabilities, then affordance can only be spoken of in terms of solicitations if the implementation of these capabilities is contextually motivated.[22]

The importance of the motivational context also plays a central role in Merleau-Ponty's analysis of the process of habit acquisition. Habits are neither acquired through a fixed series of repeated physical movements (a view that corresponds to the empiricist approach that he rejects) nor the product of a rational decision or of an intellectual grasp of the movement (which corresponds to the intellectualist explanation that he also discards). Habit development, rather, implies a form of understanding of the meaning or significance of the situation in which it is deployed. For example, if we have developed a habit of walking in a particular way, we should be able to adapt that habit to walking on different surfaces or in different environments. Similarly, if we have developed a habit of sitting in a particular way, we should be able to adapt that habit to different chairs or postures. The same point holds *mutatis mutandis* with respect to skills. Perceptual skills involve the ability to interpret and make sense of sensory information from the environment by enacting the right kind of response. For example, learning to play a musical instrument involves developing perceptual skills in order to coordinate the movements of the hands and fingers with the sounds produced by the instrument. Here again, flexibility and adaptability go hand in hand. Acquiring a skill involves comprehending the context's meaning or importance in which it is applied such that mastering the art of playing an instrument comes with the ability to flexibly apply this skill to diverse settings.

It should be noted that the plasticity of the body schema cannot be reduced to the inclusion of bodily skills and habits in this standard or customary sense; it also enables the incorporation of objects and artefacts. The classic example in the phenomenological literature is Merleau-Ponty's

---

[22] These analyses again suggest that it is difficult, and sometimes simply impossible, to v action and perception neatly. In Gibson's analysis, which on this score is very close to Merleau-Ponty's, the interaction between the agent and its environment must be understood as a dynamic looping process. Action and perception form a unity: by moving in its environment, the agent or organism generates information (ecological information), which it detects or perceives and on the basis of which the agent controls or coordinates its own actions, thereby generating new information which it can detect again, thus restarting the process. These steps form a meaningful intentional loop that connects bodily space and external or objective space. In Merleau-Ponty's words, 'bodily space and external space form a practical system, the former being the background against which the object can stand out or the void in front of which the object can *appear* as the goal of our action' (2012, 105).

analysis of 'the blind's man cane', which has become so familiar that it 'has ceased to be an object for him' (2012, 144).[23] For the blind man, the stick so intimately belongs to his bodily experience of the environment that it is an integral part of his perceiving body (cf. Descartes 1965, 68). As a result, 'the world of tactile objects expands, it no longer begins at the skin of the hand, but at the tip of the cane' (Merleau-Ponty 2012, 153). To him, the stick feels like the extension of his arm; he can feel the street *with* or *through* the stick directly or immediately. The expansion of the body schema through artefacts is not rare or uncommon. It has often been noted that the experience of driving exemplifies the same degree of integration between body and environment. For the experienced driver, the car's actions are controlled without much cognitive effort or attentional control. Driving is easy because the car feels like an extension of the driver's body (Katz 1925; Grünbaum 1930, 395; Gallagher 2005, 58; Clarke 2003; Fuchs 2018). The same holds for clothing. Neurologists Head and Holmes (1911, 188) report a woman who used to wear a large feather hat that she no longer notices; she sees immediately whether she fits through the doorway or not.

Merleau-Ponty draws an important lesson from these three cases: 'To habituate oneself to a hat, an automobile, or a cane is to take up residence in them, or inversely, to make them participate within the voluminosity of one's own body' (2012, 144). Acquiring a habit, or a skill, is not reducible to developing a new capacity to execute certain specific movements or perform particular actions; rather, it transforms our entire body schema, and thus also our relationship to space. 'Habit expresses the power we have of dilating our being in the world, or of altering our existence through incorporating new instruments' (2012, 145). Habits participate in the voluminosity of the body itself. They can expand or contract its limits and, as a result, alter peripersonal spatiality, which appears here as plastic (Sykes 2023).[24]

---

[23] For an overview of Husserl's position on the question of the lived body's expansion through incorporation, see the luminous analysis of Taipale 2014, 60–3.

[24] The plasticity of our openness to the world may also involve the use of technological devices. In recent years, virtual reality (VR) technology has been used to simulate real-life situations in order to train individuals' skills in a variety of domains including surgery, sports, and factory work. Wearable technology, such as smart watches and fitness trackers, can also provide real-time feedback on bodily movements and habits (De Boer 2020). This can help individuals develop better posture, improve their athletic performance, and even break bad habits like nail-biting. Similarly, brain–computer interfaces (BCIs)—technologies that allow individuals to control computers or other devices using their brainwaves—can be used to train individuals in skills such as playing a musical instrument or controlling a prosthetic limb. Finally, augmented reality (AR) technology overlays virtual objects onto the real world, creating an immersive training environment. This can be particularly useful for training in complex tasks such as aircraft maintenance or assembly line work. It thus seems that we are responsive not only to the actual world but sometimes also to virtual ones.

But there is more. For the body can also adopt certain postures or movements perceived in *other people*, which appear here to be embodied in my body schema. This is more than a metaphor. For the most part, my body schema is shaped by skills and habits that have been transmitted in intersubjective contexts and learned through shared practices. We speak the way our parents speak, with their accents and intonation. Until a reflective distance develops between us, we walk like them, sit like them, behave like them, for better or worse. What is true of our close relatives holds for the members of our larger community. Through culture, others bestow upon us their expectancies; they command certain kinds of behaviours while disallowing others. This facilitates interactions between us and the establishment of common projects. In certain situations, my fellow people not only contribute to constitute my habituated lifestyle but *inhabit* my body schema (Garavito 2019; Bredlau 2019, ch. 2). Infants' and elderly people's reliance on their caretakers, or that of people with health conditions or impairments on care workers, are concrete illustrations of this idea, which Merleau-Ponty elaborated under the term 'intercorporeality' in *Visible and Invisible*. I will return to this point later in the book (in Section 7.2.1) in the context of shared perceptual practices. For the time being, I merely wish to bring attention to the fact that I am not the only source of my body schema. What I have integrated in my body schema depends as much on others as on myself.

The insight has important consequences, for in Merleau-Ponty's eyes the body schema is that by which we have a world in general. As a result, renewing one's body schema through actions and interactions does not only affect one's body or one's perception; it is, rather, the corollary of acquiring a new world. Since 'the body schema is, in the end, a manner of expressing that my body is in and towards the world' (2012, 103), transforming one's body schema is to open oneself to a new world, or to alter one's style of being-in-the-world. This is concrete: to integrate a new habit modifies the range of possibilities of navigating the world, opening avenues that were once foreclosed, shutting down others. It is precisely this possession of a world that is illustrated negatively by Merleau-Ponty's analysis of the phantom limb (2012, 75–91), which occurs in people who lose the use of a limb (normally due to amputation) but continue to feel nociceptive and tactile sensations and to retain the ability to have proprioceptive experiences in the missing limb. While it might have been anticipated that the patients' visual and tactile recognition of the missing limb's absence would gradually dominate and readjust their proprioceptive sensations, this adjustment frequently does not take place as expected. The experience of the phantom limb is thus felt as a mismatch between the body's habitual tendencies, which live on despite the lost limb, and the subject's current competencies, which failed to recalibrate. Whereas my body schema has a history of previous interactions with its environment, which prompts it to enact certain kinds of responses in certain specific situations, the current inability of my body schema to respond in projected ways to the world's solicitations causes a bodily illusion which is lived as a failed motor response.

5.2.3. The Weight of Our Perceptual History II

The overview of the phenomenological and scientific literature on the body schema carried in the last section demonstrate that the ongoing processes of skill acquisition, habit formation, and calibration of our motor programs are flexible and rectifiable. According to Merleau-Ponty, acquiring new skills and forming new habits amount to nothing less than a 'reworking' or a 'renewal of the body schema' (2012, 143). This transformation, I contend, *is* an instance of perceptual learning in that it provokes long-term change in perception stemming from repeated practice or experience (Gibson 1963, Connolly 2019). The three conditions entailed by this definition are indeed met. First, body-schematic transformations are not merely short-term but, rather, induce *long-term* change in perception. True, acquired skills and habits are not permanently inscribed in my motor repertoire: I can lose a skill and, with more difficulty, a (bad) habit. But, once acquired, skills and habit don't come and go at will. They may certainly change—some skills may improve, others decline—but skills and habits are by nature not ephemeral. Second, the kind of bodily transformations involved in the process of skills and habit development result from *practice* or *experience*, understood not as a mere causal process but resulting from a motivational (or intentional) one. It is repetition in varying situations and contexts that enables the formation of perceptual skills, which are, thanks to the adaptivity that they display, not to be confused with reflexes. Third, the change is *perceptual*, not merely physiological or motoric. Since perception is—pace Connolly 2017, 2019—precisely not just a product of both the brain and the world but essentially involves the body, perceptual learning includes the acquisition of skills, which, in turn, enable and facilitate, or hinder and prevent, further learning.

Obviously, this does not mean that habits and skills cannot *also* be transformed through intentional and reflexive practices. By purposefully engaging in training practices, for instance, we do have the ability to alter and adjust our perceptual skills. Skilled agents (and paradigmatically athletes) are cognitively flexible; that is, they know how to embrace new opportunities and effectively respond to new challenges by switching between different courses of action and strategies as needed. When successful, this process results in an increased and refined perceptual awareness of the smallest details and intricacies of our surroundings, which can—but do not necessarily have to (Dreyfus 2007)—lead to an enhancement of their performances or undertakings. Conversely, a negative body image can have a devastating impact on how we inhabit our body, which can, in turn, also affect our undertakings, be they perceptual or not (Young 1980; Fanon 2008). Be that as it may, the point here is that body-schematic processes can, but do not necessarily require cognitive control, guidance, or reflective or reflexive forms of self-awareness to modify their structure and display plasticity (Gallagher 2005, 27; Halák 2021, 42–8; Mooney 2023, 155ff.). Given its intentional nature, the body's immediate connection to the environment is itself continuously adapting.

Since action and perception belong to a single intentional loop, skills and habit development influence the phenomenology of perceptual experience in normative ways, something that Husserl and Merleau-Ponty clearly saw. As we have seen, the body, whose mobility is essential for object-constitution, also provides a spatial frame of reference in relation to which perceived objects are situated. Thanks to the pre-reflective bodily awareness informing the structures of action and perception, body schemas allow us to navigate through space with ease, avoiding obstacles while walking or running, accurately locating targets, perceiving depth, distance, and direction. Remarkably, these functions—which provide perceivers with a sense of normalcy—occur independently of any conscious discrepancy between our perception of our own body size and the size estimation of other objects, as studies have shown (Shontz 1969). Our body awareness, or body image, does not typically interfere with the performance of our body schema (Gallagher 2005, 141). While operating, body schemas continually exercise a normative function in perceptual experience by constraining and enabling certain bodily moves and behaviours in response to perceived environmental possibilities and demands (Romdenh-Romluc 2011, 77, 94). These adjustments affect perceptual content in the sense of both coherence and optimality: thanks to the continuing function that the body ensures, body schemas allow perceptual consciousness to maintain *coherence* both in the present experience and over time and events;[25] and thanks to the flexibility and adaptability of our habits and skills, our ability to effectively navigate and aptly respond to the challenges and opportunities of our environment is enhanced.

Unfortunately, this goes in the opposite direction, too. As individuals age, face injuries, or contend with diseases, there can be a decline in certain skills or abilities. This can pertain to physical, cognitive, or perceptual skills. For instance, an athlete may lose their agility due to ageing, or someone might experience memory impairment due to a neurological condition. In the realm of perception, sensory degradation is common; for instance, age-related hearing loss can lead to difficulties in discriminating between certain sounds. The same holds with respect to habits. Environmental factors, social pressures, and cultural norms can lead to the formation of habits that might not be conducive to optimal functioning. The constant use of smartphones might, for example, lead to attention span issues. The point here is clear: when skills decline or bad habits are formed, our ability to perceive and engage with the world can become impoverished. This could manifest as an inability to discriminate between different sensory inputs or adopt certain specific points of view. For example, if someone's visual acuity diminishes due to age, they might struggle to distinguish between fine details in objects, leading to a perceptual impoverishment in their ability to fully perceive the richness of their visual environment.

Addressing these challenges involves a combination of efforts. For skill loss, rehabilitation and training programmes can help individuals regain or compensate for lost abilities. To counter the influence of the milieu, conscious efforts to diversify experiences and perspectives can prevent the development of one-sided habits. While important, this is not my immediate concern here. What interests me is the more general lesson to draw from it: it appears that body-schematic plasticity is not one-directional; it is, for the most part at least, a multidirectional phenomenon. True, some changes are irreversible (say, due to traumatic injuries or certain medical conditions), but most are reversible such that what is gained can also be lost, and vice versa.

---

[25] Inspired by Sartre's analysis in *Being and Nothingness*, Gallagher (2005) provides an interesting example: 'In the case of eyestrain, body schema adjustments may motivate the subject first to fix on the environment or the text as problematic; the lighting seems too dim; the book becomes difficult or boring. Postural adjustments may allow the subject to continue reading by keeping her attention directed away from her body' (140).

5.3. Conclusion

Our foray into Husserl's genetic phenomenology (Section 5.1) has shown how perceptions are informed by the weight of our experiential history. Prior experiences are never simply past and gone; rather, they leave a trace in consciousness and turn into expectations, thus influencing the course and content of future perceptions. Husserl makes this point by having recourse to the notion of types, which act as categorial filters in perceptual consciousness. As sediments of past experiences, types function as a priori rules in the process of perceptual recognition such that what perceptually comes in is automatically categorized as having meaning or signification in virtue of associative patterns of contrast and similarity with past experiences. It has been suggested that processes of type-formation and typological recognition result from what is commonly called 'perceptual learning' (Gibson 1963) in the contemporary neuroscientific research. As experiences are accumulated, types are continually revised and modified. They are flexible and adaptable, not fixed categories. In virtue of the robustness of Husserl's account of type, which bears on modes of perception and attention, and incorporates elements of sociality and affectivity, I have contended that Husserl has a lot to contribute to our understanding of the mechanisms involved in perceptual learning and, more pointedly, that processes of type-formation and typological recognition follow normative patterns of coherence and optimality.

In the second section of the chapter, I analysed the kind of body-schematic changes perceivers undergo when they develop perceptual skills and habits. Taking my cues in Husserl and Merleau-Ponty, I have argued that skilled behaviour is characterized by its ability to adapt and adjust to a range of different situations, challenges, and environmental conditions. This flexibility is achieved through both motor learning, which explains the capacity skilled agents have to learn and refine their motor skills and habits over time, allowing them to adapt to new challenges and conditions, and cognitive adaptivity, thanks to which skilled agents are able to flexibly switch between different goals, strategies, and action plans as needed, which enables them to adjust their behaviour in response to unexpected events or changes in the environment. Through their combination, skilled behaviour is achieved, enabling skilled agents to adjust and adapt to a range of different situations and challenges.

Against this background, I have pursued two objectives. Firstly, throughout the chapter I have demonstrated the continued relevance of classical phenomenological analyses in the context of ongoing neuroscientific research on perceptual learning. While in the literature perceptual learning is treated almost exclusively as a mental or cognitive phenomenon (Connolly 2019, Jenkin 2023a, 2023b), phenomenologists provide convincing reasons to conceive of perception not merely in psychological but also in embodied and affective terms, thereby providing us with the conceptual tools to better articulate the complexity of the mechanisms at stake. Secondly, I have contended that processes of skills acquisition and habit formation are norm-governed phenomena that provoke change in the experiential character of perception in the sense of both coherence and optimality. Based on the perceived affordances in the environment, body-schematic processes impose limitations and provide opportunities for specific bodily movements and behaviours that can improve or limit an individual's ability to perceptually discern.

On these last two points, the phenomenological analyses have, once again, been taken over and further developed by enactivists. From the enactivist point of view, sensorimotor processes are temporally structured and stand in an evolving dynamical relation to the environment that reaches into the historical past of the organism. As a result of repeated interactions with the environment, the body changes its dispositional structures and acquires new skills and knowledge in the form of perceptual, motor, and behavioural capacities that enable richer experiences and easier interactions. While phenomenologists limit the scope of their inquiry to the descriptive level, enactivists also have examined the relevant brain mechanisms and their impact on perceptual phenomenology. The brain, too, is highly adaptable; it might well be, in fact, 'the most adaptable organ' (Fuchs 2018, 139), and this is not without significance for experience. For Fuchs (2018), the brain functions 'as a flexible control unit' (134) that incorporates the learning history of the organism's interactions, constantly changing its own microstructures along the way to facilitate its transactions with the outer world. Much like phenomenologists describe it, these changes are analysed in terms of coherence and optimality. In its interaction with the environment, the brain–body system seeks to adapt or adjust its operational patterns in order to *optimize the fluidity* of the process or to *maximize the coherence* of the experience. 'The basic principle of plasticity is the adaption of the brain to the interaction with the environment in the sense of optimal coherence' (Fuchs 2018, 143). Of course, the coherence of experience does not *always* reach an optimal state; very often, it settles for a certain level of acceptability, like when I tolerate my habitual sitting posture until it gets too uncomfortable. Still, optimization provides directionality to the system; sensorimotor and neural structures tend to establish relations with the environment that are as immediate and free as possible.[26]

Multiple studies of adaptation and compensation provide evidence for this. Psychologists and philosophers overwhelmingly agree that adaptive and compensatory changes occurring in phenomena of neuroplasticity (e.g. congenitally blind Braille readers) or sense-plasticity (e.g. Bach-y-Rita and Kercel's (2003) substitution system) normally happen to improve or optimize cognitive and perceptual processing (Connolly 2019; Noë 2009; Doidge 2007; Goldstone and Schyns 2006). Very simply, the idea is that compensation and adaptation have a purpose or a telos; they occur in an organized manner (Bayne and Spence 2015, 606f.; Spence and Bayne 2015, 1) because they aim at optimizing experience in the sense of normalizing it (O'Callaghan 2012, 5f.). This, of course, does not rule out that compensation and adaptation sometimes fail, as patients with phantom limbs show (Gallagher 2005, 86–106). But failure in this sense is nothing but a contrasting experience, a deviation from the normal or ideal perceptual trajectory that these compensatory strategies seek to re-establish.

Phenomenology and the Norms of Perception. Maxime Doyon, Oxford University Press. © Maxime Doyon 2024.
DOI: 10.1093/9780191993527.003.0005

---

[26] Defenders of the predictive processing view have tried to mathematically formalize the principle of this discovery. According to the free energy principle (Friston 2010), systems strive to follow paths that offer the least amount of surprise. This means that they aim to minimize the disparity between predictions generated by their internal model of the world and their sensory input and perception. This disparity is measured by variational free energy and is reduced by continuously updating the system's world model or by aligning the world with the system's predictions. By actively modifying the world to bring it closer to the anticipated state, systems can also minimize the free energy of the overall system. Friston proposes that this principle underlies *all* biological reactions.

PART III
SOCIALITY AND NORMATIVITY

6
Perceiving Others

The specificity of the problem that the perception of others represents in the philosophical landscape is beyond doubt. While it is true (albeit unfortunate) that most philosophers of perception to this day seem to see no real interest in the question and often do not even broach it indirectly, those who investigate it generally recognize the subject's particular nature. For Husserl and Stein, the perception of others (*Fremdwahrnehmung* or *Fremderfahrung*), understood as empathy, commands a *sui generis* form of intentionality.

In her 1917 doctoral thesis *The Problem of Empathy*, Stein contends that empathy is a 'sui generis experiential act' (2008, 20) that aims at 'the experience of foreign consciousness' (24) and its lived experiences.[1] Stein justifies empathy's distinctive status by demarcating it from other intentional acts, beginning with outer or external perception (*äußere Wahrnehmung*), with which it nonetheless shares essential features (14f.). For Stein, empathy is a complex, multifaceted phenomenon, with perceptual, affective, intuitive, and intellectual aspects, but in its most basic form empathy can be conceived as a kind of outer perception. By this Stein means, first and foremost, that empathy is not a matter of having *knowledge* of somebody's mental contents; in empathy, these are, rather, themselves perceived, viz. appresented, in her bodily comportment. I can directly see that my friend is sad; I don't need to infer it or imagine it. At the same time, and despite its essential kingship with it, empathy cannot simply be identified with or reduced to outer perception either. The sadness of the other cannot be sensorily apprehended in the same way that discrete sensory attributes of a spatial object are, because, unlike the object's properties, the other's interiority is not originally accessible. An emotion like pain is something the empathizer notices or becomes aware of 'in the pained countenance' (14) of the other

---

[1] Given the poor quality of the available English translation, which also leaves out certain passages, all the quoted passages have been translated anew from the German edition of Stein's collected works, *Edith Stein Gesamtausgabe* (*ESGA*) (Stein 2000–20). The page number given in parentheses refers to Vol. 5 of this edition.

person, that is, in her bodily behaviour or expression, without being itself first-personally lived through (*erlebt*) by the empathizer. In Stein's technical vocabulary, in empathy the 'originarily given expression "appresents"' the 'psyche that, as co-given, stands there itself as a presently existing reality' (2008, 15). The crucial difference between outer perception and empathy in Stein's account hinges on the phenomenological distinction between original and non-original modes of manifestation: while ordinary objects are originally (*originär*) given to perceptual consciousness as in the flesh (*leibhaftig*), the pain of others can only be co-perceived (or appresented) with that which is originally perceived (or presented), namely the physiognomy, behaviour, gestures, and expressions of the other. Empathy is thus a *sui generis* intentional act in that it cuts across the functional distinction between presentational and representational acts: unlike other acts of consciousness such as thinking, imagining, and remembering, empathy does not represent, but presents its content directly; but in contrast to perception, its object is not primordially or originally given to perceptual consciousness. As Stein economically defines it, empathy is a 'non-originary experience which announces an originary one' (24f.). As general as it is, Husserl, who supervised Stein's doctoral thesis, appears to agree by and large with this account.

Now, if empathy (*Einfühlung*) is a *sui generis* form of perceptual intentionality, one may wonder whether its unfolding is, like external perception, governed by norms, and, if so, whether these norms have a *sui generis* character as well. Taking his cue from Husserl, Zahavi (2012) suggests just the following and asserts, quite correctly I think, that it 'would be a mistake to measure empathy against the standards of either self-perception or external object-perception. Empathy has its own kind of originality, its own kind of fulfillment and corroboration, and its own criteria of success and failure' (230). 'Empathic understanding', he adds, 'has its own distinct optimality' (233f.). These claims strike me as right and in line with the argument developed thus far in this book, but they stand in need of detailed treatment. This is exactly the task I set myself in the present chapter: what are the norms at play in our empathic understanding of others?

Depending on the account we are considering, the answer is not simple, for empathy is a generic term that refers to diverse and distinct intentional accomplishments. Even just within the confine of Husserl's corpus, several kinds and levels of empathic understanding can be distinguished at various junctures of his career. In its most basic form, empathy simply allows the empathizer to apprehend the perceived body as another lived body. Here, empathy is understood as an elementary associative process by virtue of which the perceived other is passively apprehended as a sensing body similar to mine (Husserl 1960, 112; 1973a, 66, 70, 435f.). But there are also more complex and not strictly perceptual forms of empathic accomplishments that aim at understanding the mental states (*Zustände*), opinions (*Stellungnahmen*), intentions (*Absichten*), or even the personal character (*Charakter*) that are conveyed *in* the perceived bodily expressions (*leiblicher Äußerungen*) of other people (1973a, 435). This distinction between passive and active forms, or lower and higher levels of empathy, still does not exhaust the phenomenon of social cognition, for at times Husserl also recognizes different kinds of empathic understanding depending on the degree of self-awareness of the parties involved: whereas empathy can be unilaterally directed at someone else, it may also involve some degree of reflexivity, such as when one is aware that one is being perceived. Sometimes, empathy can take an even more complex form and open onto a state of mutual awareness and reciprocity, where both egos are aware of the other's attention (Zahavi 2019b).[2] Although the demarcation lines do not always completely coincide, Stein's account largely converges with Husserl's in that she recognizes as well different levels of accomplishment (*Vollzugsstufen*) of empathy (2008, 19), ranging from the basic perceptual operations of sensual empathy (65), whereby I directly grasp the other as a living and sensitive body (*Leib*), to the more complex set of intentional acts running in personal empathy, thanks to which I bring this first, still largely unspecified, encounter to an explicative fulfilment (*erfüllende Explikation*) (Stein 2008, 19 and 33).[3]

While recognizing that empathy is multifarious and involves various embodied, affective, and cognitive processes that yield vastly different heights and kinds of understanding of others, I will, for clarity's sake, work with a three-level distinction throughout the chapter: after an analysis of

---

[2] While the distinction between basic and more complex forms of empathy is recurrent in Husserl's writings on the topic, Zahavi calls for caution and reminds us that 'In a manuscript from 1931–2, Husserl operates with even more levels. The first level of empathy is the appresentation of *the other lived body as sensing and perceiving*. The second level is the appresentation of the *other as physically acting*, say, moving, pushing, or carrying something. The third level goes beyond this and attends to *the purposefulness of the action* and grasps, say, the running of the other as flight (Husserl 1973c: 435). On a few occasions, Husserl goes even further and also speaks of the kind of empathy involved in *appropriating foreign traditions* (Husserl 1973c: 436; 2006: 372–3)' (2014, 138).

[3] On the rather complex question of levels of empathy in Husserl, Stein, and beyond, see Jardine 2023; Szanto 2020, §2.3; De Vecchi 2019, 230f.; Fuchs 2017a; Zahavi 2014, 137–41, 2012, 242–6.

the basic structure of basic or sensual empathy (Section 6.1), I will investigate higher-level forms of social understanding (Section 6.2) to the exclusion of the specific phenomenon of reciprocal empathy, which will be analysed independently (Section 6.3). Restricting my analysis to the accounts of personal encounter that can be found in the works of Husserl, Stein, and Merleau-Ponty, my aim in the present chapter is to evidence that *each of these three levels of accomplishment is guided by norms.*[4]

The first section takes Husserl as its starting point and argues that *the most basic norms* involved in the perception of others are themselves *embodied*, that is integrated, in and carried out by the living body. In basic empathy, the apprehension of the other *as* other is rooted in a process of pairing (*Paarung*) and analogizing apprehension (*Analogisierung*), in which the body of the perceiver provides the necessary background for the very manifestation of others as others (Section 6.1.1). In *Cartesian Meditations*, Husserl expresses this idea by claiming that the perceiver's own *Leib* acts as the 'primal norm' (*Urnorm*) of the encounter (1960, 126) in the sense that it provides the necessary experiential background or disposition for the encounter with the other. This, however, is only half the story, for even at this initial stage of the empathic relation others can only be perceived as expressive unities—and therefore as other people—if their bodily behaviours, gestures, and expressions *concord with* or *conform to* anticipated patterns of human comportments (which may overlap, to some extent, with animal comportment—more on this below). The argument I want to put forward is that these patterns—of harmony, continuity, and unity—are *standards* for conferring mindedness to others, and they must accordingly be seen as having a normative function in the empathic process (Section 6.1.2).

Since the mind of others is, like ours, intricate and therefore never given all at once, interpersonal understanding does not have to stop here. Through more active, but still perception-involving, forms of communication and

---

[4] There are systematic reasons for this choice: while Husserl and Merleau-Ponty have been constant references in every chapter of the book thus far, the proximity of Stein's account to that of Husserl spoke in favour of her inclusion. I am aware, however, that a different starting point would have yielded different results. For Levinas (1979), for instance, our encounter with the other is also characterized in normative terms in the sense that I *must respond* to the other. The norm is thus ethical. In commenting, Crowell (2015) explains that, for Levinas, the normativity of the face is the ground for the objectivity in the widest sense, for it is only because the other faces me and calls my experience into question that I encounter a 'sense of the normative, of standards against which the validity of my experiences can be judged' (574) at all.

interaction, empathy can target *higher and more complex forms* of cognitive or affective states (such as beliefs and opinions), and our understanding of others can increase correspondingly. These empathic relations unfold as an objectifying process of verification, confirmation, and optimization where our initial and largely indeterminate grasp of the other can be clarified, validated, modified, adjusted, or corrected in light of newly acquired information (say, about the motivations, context, and personality of the empathized subject). Given that they open both the possibility of validating and self-correcting our passively informed original assessment, which appears as more or less adequate to its target—that is, more or less correct with respect to the other's expressive behaviour or conduct—it will be argued in the second section that these active forms of social cognition rest on *norms of correctness*.

The third section then investigates the specific phenomenon of *reciprocal empathy* and aims to show how the various sets of embodied, affective, and cognitive processes that are constitutive of this phenomenon are teleologically oriented toward a situation where self and others are *attuned* to one another—a claim which, when correctly understood, leaves room both for more positive or harmonious and for negative or more adverse forms of empathic relations. Taking my cue this time from Merleau-Ponty, my aim here is to show that reciprocal empathy is typically geared toward such a state of mutual understanding.

The fourth and last section, which is mostly concerned with methodological matters, argues that the norms that I have just introduced— embodied norms in basic empathy (Section 6.1), norms of correctness in more complex forms of social cognition (Section 6.2), and attunement in reciprocal empathy (Section 6.3)—*constitutively* belong to empathic acts. They are, as I would like to contend, structural or eidetic features of the empathic experience in much the same way that coherence and optimality are structural or eidetic features of object perception. As such, these norms should not be confused with the kind of social, historical, political, and cultural norms that critical phenomenologists have in recent years rightly drawn our attention to. If both sets of norms do indeed assume a transcendental (or, as we sometimes read, quasi-transcendental) role in experience, both sets of norms have a different scope. I will make this point and reflect on the phenomenological method by engaging with the emerging subfield of critical phenomenology and plead for the complimentary of the 'classical' and 'critical' points of views.

6.1. Bodily Norms in Basic Empathy

One of the main characteristics of the phenomenological analysis of the self–other encounter resides in its acute attention to *embodiment*. Since a central component of the empathic encounter is perceptual, the empathizer's body plays a fundamental role in the self–other relation, for it is only thanks to his own embodied intentionality that the other can appear as an other. At the same time, phenomenologists typically argue that the inner life of others is manifested through their bodily behaviours and gestures. As I will argue in what follows, each of these two aspects of the empathetic relation suggests the presence of perceptual norms regulating the self–other relation, and that these norms are themselves embodied.

6.1.1. The Lived Body (*Leib*) as Originary Norm (*Urnorm*)

As it has been evidenced in Chapters 3–5, as I perceptually experience the world I am always implicitly self-aware of (some aspects of) my own ongoing bodily activity, which registers in the form of the 'I can'. The role of embodied self-consciousness in the more specific case of the perception of other people is not less crucial. According to Husserl, Stein, Merleau-Ponty, and contemporary phenomenologists like Gallagher (2005) and Zahavi (2020), the self-apprehension of our own embodied self is no less critical for perceiving the other *as* other. In the Fifth *Cartesian Meditation*, Husserl makes the point by explaining how the other's perceived body (*Körper*) is constituted as a living body (*Leib*) through a process of 'analogizing apprehension' (*Analogisierung*), through which the perceiving subject 'transfers' into the other's body the sense of a 'living body'. The solution proposed in that text, which is not the only one Husserl advanced (see 1973a–c) and perhaps not the more satisfactory one either (Theunissen 1965; Schutz 1966; Gurwitsch 1979), still provides a valuable entry point to Husserl's embodied approach to the problem of empathy. For Husserl, it is the embodied self-apprehension of the empathizer that gets the empathic relation going, for only a perceived similarity between my own living body and the body of the other can serve as the motivational basis for the analogizing apprehension (1989, 118). Husserl's reasoning here is that just as my body is experienced as both something that I have (*Körper*) and something that I am (*Leib*), perceiving the bodies of others (*Körper*) motivates me to ascribe them a similar double-sided nature (*Leib/Körper*). Thanks to the original givenness of my own living body as the bearer of bodily sensations and the centre of movement and spatial orientation, I perceive the other's body as a subjective living body with much of the same sensing capacities and expressive dispositions.

Since the self-experience of my own lived body initiates the constitution process whereby others acquire their subjectivity as perceiving egos, Husserl sometimes describes the living body as an *Urleib*, that is, a primordial or original living body (1973b, 57; 1973c, 572). Thanks to its constitutive function in the empathetic encounter, the living body is an *Urleib* in that it provides the original underpinning of every experience of others. For Husserl, then, the *Urleib incarnates the Urnorm of the encounter* insofar as *it sets the standard for what counts as a living body at all* (whether human or non-human). There is thus, for Husserl (1989, 1973 a–c), a mode of empathy that is generically and formally operative in the apprehension of human and non-human animals alike. This is what Husserl expresses—somewhat controversially—in the Fifth *Cartesian Meditation* when he writes, 'I myself [am] constitutionally the original norm (*Urnorm*) for all human beings' and 'constitutionally the primal monad' (1960, 126) of the whole animal kingdom. As shocking as it may seem, the claim is actually very simple: since the apperception of others as others presupposes 'my "internally experienced" living body', which I then transfer onto the other, my own *Leib* can be said to 'provide the necessary norm' of the empathic relation. 'Everything else is a modification of this norm' (1973b, 126).[5]

While the very idea of conceiving one's own living body as an *Urleib* that provides the *Urnorm* of every self–other relation has provoked an avalanche of texts and criticisms throughout the history of phenomenology up to this day, the basic thrust of Husserl's conviction has received since the 1960s significant support from developmental psychology, which has shown that the kind of intermodal transfer (or 'translation', as Merleau-Ponty (1964a, 116–18) prefers to say) that Husserl has in view is operational since the beginning in early infancy (Gallagher 2005, 69–84; León 2021, 567f.). We will return to this below in Section 6.3. For the time being, I want to insist on the formal, yet universal, character of Husserl's claim. In asserting that the living body provides the necessary background for our apprehension of

---

[5] For more detail on the specific context of this passage, which discusses questions of normality and abnormality, see Taipale (2014), who explains at length that for Husserl 'our own perceptual abilities have a certain initial constitutive priority' (130) over that of the others. I will come back to these and related issues in Section 6.4.

other living creatures, and that it transfers or projects its own structure onto the others while constituting them, Husserl is not concerned at all with specific intentional contents and contextual matters. The point is, rather, that we passively, yet non-inferentially, confer mindedness to others on the basis of the perception of their expressive body because this is how we ourselves are constituted. As we will see in the fourth and last section of the present chapter, this leaves room for all kinds of historically emergent and content-specific differences between self and others.

6.1.2. Harmony, Continuity, Unity

While the empathizer's body assumes a necessary function in the empathic encounter, the body of others is just as crucial, for it is through the perception of their bodies that their inner life is revealed (Husserl 1960, 108–28). The other presents itself as another living organism—in the case of humans, as an alter ego, that is, a subject of cognitive and affective states (thoughts, beliefs, emotions, etc.) comparable to mine—through his bodily behaviour. Precisely, in Husserl's eyes, 'what is most significant in apprehending the other's intention is the pre-reflective awareness of the other's body dynamics, how movements and expressions change in time and space' (Pokropski 2015, 904).

The temporal horizon, which bears anticipations of lived experiencing, provides perception with direction, context, and meaning. As such, it plays a fundamental role in the normative interpretation of Husserl's account of empathy that I am developing here, for the other's body dynamics can only appear as meaningful and thus indicative of a rich inner life insofar as it coheres (at least to a certain degree) with these anticipated contents.[6] Encountering others is an essentially 'progressive experience' (2010, 435), as Merleau-Ponty acutely points out, and this plays out even at the very basic level of perceived bodily movements, which can only make sense if we take them to have direction and transcend the immediacy of the present. In apprehending them, one must 'retain the other's already past expressions and movements as well as anticipate those which are yet to come' (Pokropski

---

[6] Taipale (2015a) has also insisted on this: since 'lived experiences are joint by motivation, and motivational connections are always co-announced—whether explicitly or implicitly—along with the prominent, current state', the other's mental states could not appear as meaningful at all, 'if taken in isolation' (464). On the fatal consequences of the absence of any serious consideration of time in current discussions on social cognition, see Taipale 2015a, 464ff.

2015, 901). This is because the movements and expressions of others are themselves motivated by some circumstances, which provide them with meaning and direction. On this score, perceiving other people does not differ from object perception: it, too, requires an enlarged conception of the present, one that outflanks the narrow limits of the now and includes the interplay of retentions and protentions to co-constitute what Husserl calls the living present (*lebendige Gegenwart*).

Specifically, what is anticipated in perceptual consciousness is *normal bodily behaviour*. This is species-specific, that is, a determination of the generic apprehension of another as 'animal'. For Husserl, others are perceived as ego-subjects, that is, as living organisms endowed with a rich spiritual life, if their behaviours *cohere* or *concord* with the general human way of behaving. Husserl spells out what he means in the human context by this by singling out three factors: normal human behaviour displays harmony, continuity, and unity.[7]

The requisite of *harmony* refers to the *behavioural style* of others in relation to their milieu, that is, to the way they are motivated by their situation and responsive to it in characteristically human ways. Although a style is always culturally informed and ultimately an individual or a personal way of relating to the world, 'a certain manner of handling situations' (2012, 342), as Merleau-Ponty describes it, a more general and anonymous, yet distinctively human, style of comportment already shines through at the level of basic empathy and triggers the analogizing transfer. When encountering other people (as opposed to, say, animals), we spontaneously recognize their bodies as exhibiting a peculiar style of human bodily movement, which motivates the associative pairing of our living bodies. Others are apprehended as others thanks to the way in which they harmoniously move

---

[7] The design of robots has so rapidly evolved in recent years that, on certain occasions, it may be difficult, if not impossible, to differentiate their behavioural style from ours on the basis of these three criteria alone. To pin down our human specificity, other criteria may thus be necessary. In the phenomenological tradition after Husserl, some other distinctively human features have been discussed. For example, in *Lachen und Weinen* (*Laughter and Crying*), Plessner (1961) contends that laughter and crying are distinctively human expressions that reveal the dual nature of human existence. He suggests that these expressions demonstrate the paradoxical coexistence of the individual's physical body and their inner, emotional world. For Plessner, laughter and crying serve as ways in which individuals bridge the gap between their biological, bodily nature and their subjective, emotional experiences, highlighting the complexity of human existence. To this day, robots can be programmed to simulate crying and laughing in a mechanical or artificial manner, but this simulation is quite different from genuine human emotional expressions. It's not clear when this hurdle will be surmounted by robotics and AI research.

and behave according to a humanly recognizable style that we share with them (Husserl 1973a, 289; 1973b, 280).

Furthermore, this style—and here's the second requisite—must *continuously* prove itself; that is, it must *lastingly* live up to the standards of human behaviour, otherwise a correction of belief ensues. His basic thought on this is encapsulated in the following passage:

> The experienced foreign body [*Leib*] continues to manifest itself really as a body [*Leib*] only in its changing, but incessantly harmonious behaviour. Such harmonious behaviour, which has its physical side that indicates something psychic appresentatively, must now appear in original experience in a fulfilling way, *and do so throughout the continuous change in behaviour from phase to phase*. The body [*Leib*] is experienced as an illusory body if there is something discordant about its behaviour. (Husserl 1960, 114; translation significantly modified; italics are mine)

Husserl's insight is that the other proves herself as real only insofar as her behaviour *continuously fulfils anticipated patterns* of harmonious bodily movements. As experience progresses, the other's comportment will either match or fail to match these anticipated patterns, and experience will correspondingly confirm empathy as real or reveal it to be illusory. In the former case, the other is experienced 'as an actually animate organism,' that is, as an alter ego, while in the latter case, she comes about as a mere 'pseudo-organism'.

Perceived bodily harmony and continuity in turn presuppose *unity*, which is the third condition. Foreign bodies are taken as living bodies precisely because they are perceived as unified wholes. Just as my body is not merely an association of bodily parts but an expressive unified whole, human behaviour is not an assemblage of disjointed bodily movements. The bodies of others are perceived as the centre of spontaneous (and not merely causal) movement thanks to the meaningful unity they display.

To sum up, the phenomenological analysis of the first, basic level of the interpersonal encounter shows how the bodies of both self and other have a normative role in the encounter: just as the empathizer's living body provides the necessary background for the other to appear as an other living body, whether human or not (Section 6.1.1), the other can only be apprehended as a human person if she, in turn, behaves in some normatively assessable, viz. humanly concordant, ways (Section 6.1.2). Husserl thinks that what is true of humans is valid *mutatis mutandis* for cats and presumably other animals too.[8] There is, in other words, a mode of empathy that is generically and formally operative in the apprehension of human and non-human animals alike (which Jardine (2022, 121ff.) calls 'animate empathy'), but that can then be determinately specified for each species. This is what Husserl sought to account for by hinting at the criteria of unity, continuity, and harmony constitutive of normal human behaviour. In the rest of the chapter, I will leave aside the question of the overlap between human and non-human behaviours, and focus instead uniquely on empathy in the human encounter (but see Schnegg and Breyer 2022).

6.2. Norms of Validity in Higher Forms of Empathy

What has been said thus far is only the beginning, for empathy is not just a matter of ascribing mindedness to others based on their perception. Social cognition often takes more complex forms and aims at understanding that which is expressed *in* perceived bodily expressions and conducts—beliefs, intentions, and thoughts, for instance. This form of empathic encounter does *not* presuppose a distinction between a prior constitution of the lived body as minimally and formally minded lived body, and a secondary constitution of the lived body as field of expression of determinate spiritual content. The reason is that there are various expressive phenomena that seem to be just as primordially given as the lived body itself is—for example, emotions like pain and the expressive givenness of various embodied actions (running, reaching, etc.). (For a problematization of this two-layered

---

[8] With respect to this point, here's a revealing passage that James Jardine (in a private communication) alerted me to: 'Cats, how they move, purr, play: every movement a "characteristic" cat-movement. Their character becomes apprehended in every movement, or each movement, as movement of this and that kind, is apprehended as belonging to the cat-kind. Besides, this kind of movement belongs within a totality of manifold systems of characteristic forms of cat-kindred conduct and behaviour, and hence the specific movement can stand in for, bring to life, indicate the entire system. What is characteristic does not lie in the mere sensuous form of the movement, but is rather something fused with the latter: the form of the animation of this movement, the form of the engaged movement, and the form of the psychic life continuously expressing itself therein. In general, the cat-corporeality is a system of expressing movements, of characteristic movements that are animated in an individual fashion, and that express, in their constructing of higher total-patterns, higher animation... This holds generally. The human being is, in all its movements, actions, in its speech, writing, etc.—human being! It is not a mere affiliation or connecting together of a thing called living body with a second thing called soul. The living body is, as living body, filled with soul through and through; every movement of the living body is filled with soul, the coming and the going, the standing, sitting, running, dancing, speaking, etc.' (Husserl 1973a, 69; the translation is by J.J.).

approach, see Jardine 2022, 121–60, and Taipale 2015b.) The point of distinguishing this second, more complex layer rather rests on the introduction of a temporal element: in some cases, realizing higher forms of interpersonal understanding requires some form of *sustained engagement* on the part of the empathizer. Depending on the context and situation, various kinds of interaction—verbal or non-verbal communication, interpretation, imagination, explicit position-takings, etc.[9]—will prove to be more useful than others in the unfolding of the encounter. These active forms of social cognition, which are perception-involving but not perceptual through and through, shed some further light on the normative character of the self-other encounter insofar as they are, as will be argued below, subject to norms of correctness (*Richtigkeit*).

Just such an account is perhaps most clearly articulated in the work of Stein, Husserl's former assistant and the editor of *Ideas II*. In *The Problem of Empathy*, Stein's descriptions of the different phases or levels of empathic understanding rest, as we are going to see, on a distinctively normative vocabulary. Although empathy is not, for Stein or for Husserl, a normative act in the plain deontic sense of the term (as if I *had to* perceive others as this or that), it is still a normative accomplishment in that it is something that I can succeed or fail at. This normative moment, which constitutively belongs to empathic acts, is subject to constant evaluation, that is, confirmation or revision, according to criteria that Husserl and Stein, who share a relatively similar perspective on this specific question, have analysed in detail.

6.2.1. Stein's Three-step Process

As is well known, Stein conceives of empathy as a three-step process or performance. First, we can *directly perceive* that the other is in a particular psychological or affective state. I can, say, directly see 'the sadness that I "read off the other person's face"' (Stein 2008, 19) without relying on

---

[9] I say *explicit* position-taking (*Stellungnahme*) since one could argue that a minimal form of position-taking is (normally) already at play in perception itself—including empathetic perception—to the extent that this already involves a moment of doxic positing (i.e. the highly minimal spontaneity already involved within receptivity), which Husserl in some places classifies as position-taking. For a reading of Husserl along these lines, see Jacobs 2020.

complex cognitive or inferential processes.[10] Although I may be ignorant of the motivational context of her sadness, and thus have only a vague perception of her experience, "which faces me as an object" (19), the other's experience may directly emerge from her communicative or bodily comportment (gestures, speech, facial expressions, etc.), even if it is not thereby originally or primordially given to me.

This first degree of empathetic understanding can, in a subsequent step, be brought to an explicative fulfilment (*erfüllende Explikation*). The lived experience of the other, which is still largely indeterminately grasped in perception, can be apprehended as an integral part of a larger motivational context, which provides it with its meaningful unity (De Vecchi 2019, 230f.). In this second stage, the lived experience of the other is brought to *experiential givenness*, even if it cannot be first-personally lived through (*erlebt*) originally by the empathizer. Here's how Jardine (2015) nicely renders Stein's position on the matter:

> When the other's sadness faces us as directly given in her facial expressions, we frequently "feel ourselves led by it" (2008: 31 [19]), in that the theme of our empathic interest becomes not merely *that* the other is sad, but *what* she is sad about and *why* this state of affairs elicits sadness in her. In such cases, the other's experiential life "is no longer an object in the proper sense. Rather, it has pulled me into it, and I am now no longer turned to the experience but to its object, I am in the position of its subject" (2008: 19 [10]). Here we are dealing not merely with a perception of the other as an embodied and experiencing subject, but a presentification (*Vergegenwärtigung*) of her experiences with their objective correlates. (577; emphasis in original)

This second stage, which bears a stronger resemblance to imagination or memory than to perception, is one where I explicate the other's experience 'by reliving it through' (Stein 2008, 51), albeit in a non-originary way. It is then followed by a third step, namely the 'synthesizing objectification

---

[10] Stein holds a version of what today is sometimes called today a *direct perceptual* account of social cognition, which, in the contemporary philosophical discussion on mind reading, has often been launched against the 'theory theory' and 'simulation theory.' See Szanto 2020, Fuchs 2018, Gallagher 2020. Like Husserl and Stein, Merleau-Ponty also stresses at times the direct presentational character of empathetic acts. As he writes, 'I do not perceive the anger...as a psychological fact hidden behind the gesture.... The gesture does not *make me think* of anger, it is anger itself' (2012, 190).

(*zusammenfassende Vergegenständlichung*) of the explicated experience' (19). Once we have reached this level, the lived experience of the other faces me again as an *object* that may be reflected upon; it is now more properly understood.[11]

Despite the questions that Stein's three-step account leaves open, a basic phenomenological truth emerges therefrom: it shows, namely, how a more active involvement on the part of the empathizer can lead to an *increase* in interpersonal understanding. Through the passage from the first to the second and third steps of the process, our understanding of the other becomes more precise and more refined as different contextual elements are factored in and a dialectical distance between self and other is established. In this setting, the telos of the empathic encounter is clear: 'In the ideal case' (2008, 25), the content of the empathizer's own experience *matches* or corresponds to the expressed experience of the empathized subject. 'Where there is no deception,' both experiences are 'the same in every respect', that is, they 'have the same content', 'only a different mode of donation' (25). In Stein's account, empathy thus comes out as a normative phenomenon insofar as every empathic act is either correct or incorrect, that is, adequate or inadequate to its object. Specifically, the correctness (*Richtigkeit*) of my perception of others is measured by my ability to grasp and experience, albeit in a modified or non-original (*nicht originär*) way, the experiences of others as expressed.[12]

The general lesson to draw from this is the following: even if, on average, we tend to content ourselves with perceptually based first approximations and do not invest much time and effort in most of our interpersonal encounters (think about all the people you've probably come across today), it is usually possible to go beyond our initial impressions and actively follow the 'implicit tendencies' (2008, 19) that we read in the physiognomy and conduct of the other to get to know her better. These are signs that exert a certain traction on us and ask to be clarified. For Stein, there are

---

[11] One of the still hotly debated questions in the Steinian scholarship on empathy is whether we really should interpret the second and/or third step as implying some form of imagination or imaginative perspective-taking. (See Szanto 2020 and Zahavi 2014, 137–41.) It need not preoccupy us here.

[12] The motif of non-originality and the correlative idea of empathy as involving a kind of reproductive modification of lived experience (something akin to recollection or phantasy according to Jardine 2023) are crucial, for the empathizer does not and cannot simply 'live through' (*erleben*) the other's conscious life, for this would amount to dissolving empathy into self-consciousness, thus annihilating the phenomenological distinction between self and other (see, e.g., Husserl 1973a, 187; Zahavi 2012).

circumstances where empathy is not lived as something one could easily turn away from. Every once in a while, the other attracts me and elicits a response from me. When this happens, a gradual 'clarification' (19) of the experience of the other unfolds. This is also how Stein's model can deal (at least to some extent) with cases of deception. Think, for instance, about a purposeful deceiver that feels discomfort but wants to express comfort (say, because he wants to 'fit in' and go unnoticed in a group). If we follow Stein's three-stage analyses, we might well, at first, 'adequately' perceive this person's comfort, by virtue of attending to its bodily features, and still perceive its 'real' emotion incorrectly, because she purposefully deceives us; but once we become aware of the larger motivational context, this first, approximate estimation can be corrected. Even if the person does not herself understand how they're feeling in a particular moment, thus depriving us of an objective 'conduct' to set our understanding on, some level of empathic understanding could be realized if just this feat comes to an explicative fulfilment.

6.2.2. Levels of Empathy in Husserl

On the whole, Husserl saw things similarly. He, too, conceived of empathy as an evolving or progressive experience, one that in *Ideas II* is presented as being akin to reading a book (1989, 256). However, his account of the levels of empathy rests, on his part, on the pervasive role of typification. As we have seen in the previous chapter (Section 5.1), types, which function as a priori rules in perceptual consciousness, shape the perceptual horizon by determining the set of expectations that come to bear on what perceptually comes in. Given the pervasive function of the associative principle at work in typological recognition, *everything* that we experience is assimilated as partaking into some typological category or other (Husserl 1975, 321), others included. For better or worse, our first impressions of others are *always* guided by preconceptions and prejudices, some of them being totally implicit and associatively formed in the depths of passive consciousness. Since these preconceptions, which may have diverse sources (prior experiences, of course, but also knowledge, interest, context, affects, culture, etc.), are built into the anticipatory horizon of all experiences, they are unavoidable. As a result, our first encounter with the other necessarily starts from a rough approximation (Schutz 1972, 97–138). This, however, is not an end; *it may be refined*. Sometimes, our initial approximation can be radically upset or frustrated, thus provoking a correction process in which various features that inform that type are cancelled out, but, standardly, it changes slowly and morphs gradually into a more personal or individual relation, in which the singularity of *this* particular other progressively comes to the fore as the empathic process unfolds and subsequent stages are reached. Husserl's insight, which Taipale (2016) brings to the point in the following passage, is that even if empathy necessarily 'sets off with strong typification, as "type-oriented"', it can 'develop into a singularizing, "token-oriented" grasp of the other' (145) (cf. Jardine 2022, 205ff., and Zahavi 2010).[13]

Exactly how far we can go in this direction depends, of course, on various factors—e.g. the degree of familiarity we have with the other and how much we share a similar cultural background. Just as we learn that objects in our experiences follow familiar patterns of change, which we can anticipate based on our degree of familiarity with this or that type of object, so it is with individuals: our perception of them is based on the general expectations associated with their particular group or kind. With repeated interactions, we anticipate how certain types of persons of, say, different professions (taxi drivers, philosophers, etc.) or ethnic origins (Japanese, Canadians, etc.) might behave in specific situations, given the relevant circumstances. This is, of course, usually very much implicit and just a starting point. When longer forms of communication or affectively charged interactions are involved, empathy unfolds as a process in which we are more or less consciously confirming, validating, reinforcing, or fighting our passively informed initial assessment. To come to a satisfactory understanding of the other, it might even be necessary to take a step back and actively reflect on and deconstruct the prejudices from which we started. Its success rests on a skill that Magrì calls 'social sensitivity', which is 'a form of cultivated discernment' (2021, 651) that requires *sustained* self-critical examination and flexibility. This, however—and this is the important point here—is something we can acquire and develop, at least partially.

---

[13] This works in much the same way in the opposite direction. Sometimes, we have the impression of not recognizing our closest ones, of 'losing' them somehow. Soldiers returning to civilian life are a case in point. Because of the trauma they have suffered, returning soldiers often have a hard time reintegrating into their daily routine. They feel estranged, and so do their families when they interact with them. Their personality has changed, such that our interaction with them is not the occasion of a deeper understanding but, on the contrary, of a progressive distancing. A situation like this, which is by no means uncommon, testifies again—but this time negatively—that empathy or social understanding are functionally governed by normative standards, and that what can increase can also decrease.

Let us avoid a possible misunderstanding before closing out this section. It might be tempting to resist and insist that there will always be an indeterminate horizon of unexpressed interiority and that, for this reason, no grasp of the other is definitive or exhaustive. This is true; but it does not imply that empathy has no conditions of satisfaction, or that it is completely without direction. As Merleau-Ponty observes, 'it is in [the other's] conduct, in the manner in which the other deals with the world, that I will be able to discover his consciousness' (1964a, 117). At the same time, the opposite view should also be avoided, for the passage just cited does not imply that what I read off from the other's behaviour corresponds one to one to his inner life either. No, the other's psyche is principally not originally accessible. As Husserl, Stein, and Merleau-Ponty recognized, and Levinas (1979) emphasized, there will always be an indeterminate horizon of unexpressed interiority, which is why no grasp of the other can ever be final or conclusive. Achieving an adequate empathetic understanding is, one may say, an infinite task. While I agree that this principled inaccessibility is constitutive of the other *as* an other, it still does not prevent me from getting to know her *better*. On the contrary, it invites me and motivates me to respond to her, thereby opening the space for dialogue and mutual understanding, however delicate or imperfect this undertaking might be.

6.3. Attunement and Responsiveness as Norms of Interpersonal Interaction

Besides the fact that I cannot originally live through the inner life of others, empathic relations are *sui generis* acts for another, related reason. The perception of others is unlike anything else, for in perception the other is given to me not as an object but as a subject, that is, as a being who, just like me, is able to perform intentional acts. Just as I can perceive and empathize with others, I can be targeted by the intentions of the other. Since it involves two subjects with similar intentional capacities, empathy can be reciprocal; that is to say, it can evolve in a state where both empathizing egos are mutually aware of being simultaneously empathized by the other (Husserl 1973c, 471f.; Jardine 2015; Zahavi 2019b). This phenomenon, which I will here call for short *reciprocal empathy*, opens onto a dynamic of interaction organized around a norm of mutual understanding or attunement. Empathy appears here as a dialectical process of reciprocal adjustments geared toward such equilibrium, which, when correctly understood, leaves room for a wide range of forms of interpersonal understanding, some being more harmonious than others. As we will see in what follows, this is a view that Husserl, Merleau-Ponty, and more recently Gallagher and Fuchs have defended in largely convergent ways.

In Section 6.1 it was shown that empathy ultimately rests on embodied processes of self-awareness, thanks to which what Husserl calls the 'analogical transfer' can begin. In encountering others, my own self-experience is passively transferred to the other in a process of 'pairing' (*Paarung*) that rests on sedimented patterns of experiencing deriving from past experiences. This insight, which describes an important aspect of the work of passive syntheses, means that our past experiences (passively) influence our subsequent experiences by shaping our horizon of expectations associatively (cf. Section 5.1). The new is guided by the old according to typical patterns; hence, what we perceptually take in is always in some sense categorized in advance. In reciprocal empathy, the same pattern repeats itself, but the transfer is not unidirectional. As Husserl explains in *Cartesian Meditations*, in encountering another person, a 'mutual transfer of sense' (1960, 113) takes place. This is important, for it means that I am not only a being capable of empathy but at the same time a being that can be empathized, that is to say, perceived and understood by the other. When empathy is reciprocal (or bidirectional), the complementarity that holds between one's intentional behaviour and movements and those of the other acquires a constitutive value insofar as the self–other relation is geared toward a state of equilibrium. Zahavi asserts in this vein that 'what might lie at the root of empathy is a basic attunement to the responsiveness of the other' (2014, 136). A. D. Smith puts the point in the following way:

> I have been suggesting, in harmony with some of Husserl's own thoughts, that what lies at the origin of the development of empathy is an appreciation of the responsiveness of the body of another to one's own actions, and that the motivation for such an appreciation is the temporal sequencing of the behaviour of the two actors in the interchange—something that is itself regulated by emotional responses. It is not wholly implausible to suppose that the more one thinks about this, and bears in mind the primitive level of mental development of the subjects we are concerned with, it may come to be recognized as having the status of an essential necessity. (Smith 2003, 248)

Smith arrived at this conclusion by commenting on two passages taken from *Ideas II* (Husserl 1989, 101 n. 1) and Husserl's writings on intersubjectivity (1973c, 605), in which Husserl sought to investigate

> the role in the development of empathy that could be played by the mutually imitative pre-linguistic interactions that mother and child playfully engage in—'proto-conversations', as they are sometimes called. If we put these two passages together, what emerges is the idea that what is fundamental to the apperception of a material thing as a body is that it respond to you in a way that merely material things do not. In particular, an attunement to a certain reciprocity in movements, indicating that certain movements are both elicited by you and responsively directed to you, is what emerges from these passages as critical. Here, perhaps, we have the materials for a sense of similarity that is neither merely 'material', nor even merely 'kinematic', but one that concerns the guidedness and directedness of 'behaviour'. (Smith 2003, 243)

This reading of Husserl is largely convincing, even though it rests on little textual evidence. Interestingly, it also implicitly suggests a direct continuity with Merleau-Ponty's descriptions, which, on this aspect of the question, are more thoroughly developed and deservingly more renowned. Famously, he, too, considers social cognition to imply some form of communicative interaction. To perceive others is typically not to spy on them from a distance but to enter into communication with them. It is to exchange glances, gestures, and words. Since the emotions and mental states of others are not completely 'given' in perception, understanding them is impossible 'without invoking our collaboration' (Merleau-Ponty 2010, 441). The 'expressions, the behaviours, the conducts, and the movements of others are data that one must also know how to *interpret* or *decipher*' (2010, 445), by which Merleau-Ponty means that a proper understanding is only possible insofar as I respond, in some way or other, to the perceived behavioural and emotional cues. This operation is not cognitive or intellectual, however, at least not initially or predominantly. It is not a question of giving a meaning to a previously inert and insignificant matter—*Gestalttheorie* had been right on this point. The response is rather an affective and embodied practice that rests on a dialectical pattern of action and interaction organized around a norm of reciprocity, which Merleau-Ponty sees as regulating intersubjective communication.

The normative motif at the heart of Merleau-Ponty's theory of perception is essentially based on the intentional loop that unites action and perception. As we have seen in Chapters 2 and 3, in *Phenomenology of Perception* Merleau-Ponty explains that, as embodied organisms, perceptual agents are constantly motivated to achieve the best possible grip on the world. To perceive is to be solicited by our environment and to answer to the specificities of each situation by skilfully deploying our sensorimotor capacities. For Merleau-Ponty, it is in and though this response that something like an object acquires a form and determinacy. Neither activity nor passivity, perception is conceived of as a dialectical movement, something like an answer to a question that the world asks us, or a solution to a problem that confronts us. It is in this sense that perception is expressive (Landes 2018).

This same normative motif is also at work in the more specific context of the perception of others (Doyon 2021). For Merleau-Ponty, our encounter with others usually implies some form of interaction organized around a norm of interaction or reciprocity. While Merleau-Ponty's descriptions of the relationship between mother and newborn in the 1951 lecture course 'The Child's Relations with Others' points to the existence of an initial state of undifferentiation that will only gradually morph into a proper self–other relation in early infancy (1964a 117–19; cf. Zahavi 2014, 78–80), more recent studies suggest a much earlier development. From the third trimester of pregnancy, the human foetus would already be predisposed to display the ability to integrate perceptual information about the presence of others (Reid, Dunn, et al. 2017). These results, which run counter to Merleau-Ponty's and Henri Wallon's thesis that the newborn is not yet endowed with external perceptual skills (cf. Gallagher 2005, 65–9), radicalize the consequences drawn by developmental psychologists of the 1980s. For example, Melzhoff and Moore (1989) showed how the mother's facial expressions provoke in the child a proprioceptive experience that leads to imitation, understood here as a response to the perceived expression of the mother's gestures. Imitation feeds the intentional feedback loop that unites mother and child by binding the bodies and establishing the basis for a preverbal and pre-reflexive understanding between them (Stern1985). The result is a kind of affective 'synchronization' between the two, a rudimentary form of conversation. Through the communicative reciprocity established between them, the mother and her newborn come to form a whole beyond the parts that compose it without dissolving their individuality.

Wherever we stand on this question, the crucial point is to recognize that this dynamical structure is not unique to childhood. It continues to develop and govern more complex forms of interpersonal relationships during our adult life. The imitation of facial expressions and the other embodied and affective forms of interpersonal communications that develop between mother and child are *precursors* of the type of higher cognitive structures of intersubjectivity found in adulthood. In developmental psychological terms, one can say that the kind of embodied and affective communicative processes that belong to what Trevarthen (2001) calls 'primary intersubjectivity' not only precede symbolic and verbal communication but also set the neurobiological stage for the kind of embodied, affective, and linguistic practices that belong to 'secondary intersubjectivity' (Trevarthen and Hubley 1978). Even richer social and more complex cultural communicative and narrative practices find therein their foundations. Developmentally—and this is all that really matters here—there is a progression that *builds on* the various sensorimotor abilities and embodied processes that characterize interaction from the earliest age (primary intersubjectivity). These capacities remain active and effective in our abilities to jointly attend and act with others (secondary intersubjectivity) as well as in more enhanced communicative and narrative practices where more complex or nuanced forms of interpersonal understanding are achieved. As Gallagher (2020) explains, the rudimentary interactive processes that Husserl, Merleau-Ponty, and contemporary developmental psychologists hinted at 'do not disappear' once we're past the stage of infancy; 'they rather mature and continue to characterize our adult interactions' (100). The set of minimal embodied skills acquired in infancy are 'the *continuous starting point* for our everyday engagements with others' (120; my emphasis).

The consequence to draw from all this is plain: if the kind of basic interactive processes that Husserl and Merleau-Ponty have in view do not merely concern the intimate relation that the newborn develops with her carer but keep their importance throughout our lifetime, then the kind of basic normative attunement that regulates these interactions should be considered as a pervasive feature of our being-with-others. This does *not* mean that they are actively exercised in the totality of our relations to others. Empathy, as we've seen, does not have to be reciprocal. It does not mean either—and this is important—that our interactions with others are always geared toward some kind of peaceful harmony. Although Husserl, Merleau-Ponty, and enactivists like Gallagher and Fuchs often seem to suggest that this is the default mode of social cognition, it is certainly not the only option. For instance, boxers enter the ring to win a fight, not to become friends. Still, even as adversaries or opponents, fighters stand in a reciprocal empathic relation in which they are attuned to one another in all kinds of ways: not only do they participate in a common endeavour (boxing) and share common goals (to fight, to win), but they do so in largely coordinated ways by abiding to a whole set of rules and practices that define the kind of activity they're engaged in. I will come back to these and related issues in the next chapter, which bears specifically on the norms regulating the dynamics of interaction between perceivers. What I have said here should nevertheless suffice to convey the idea that the analysis of perceptual norms appears yet again as an inescapable feature of any phenomenological description of our perceptual encounters with others.

6.4. The Challenge of Critical Phenomenology

The analyses offered thus far are admittedly rather formal. The sets of norms that I have sketched out in this chapter—embodied norms in basic empathy (Section 6.1), norms of validity in higher forms of empathy (Section 6.2), and norms of attunement and responsiveness in reciprocal empathy (Section 6.3)—are formal in the sense that they target the invariant structures of the empathic encounter without factoring in its contextual specificities. They are, as I shall argue below, essential structures of interpersonal experiencing, universal in that sense. As such, these analyses leave open the possibility of their being further developed and specified by content-oriented analyses. My aim in this section is to sketch out in rough strokes how to do this. Just as Husserl distinguishes, in his description of the synthetic unity of consciousness, between the temporal syntheses that are responsible for the formal connectivity of the conscious experience and the associative syntheses which operate at the level of content, we can, thanks to the reduction, target and isolate specific structures of experience and distinguish between the formal and contentful aspects of perceptual normativity. Since the related distinctions between the formal and the contentful, the universal and the contingent, and the transcendental and the empirical are precisely those that have recently been targeted and critically discussed by a wave of critical phenomenologists, the following analyses aim at assessing their input to the discussion on the structuring role of perceptual norms in the context of interpersonal encounter.[14]

---

[14] Depending on where you stand on the philosophical landscape, identifying the distinguishing features of 'classical' and 'critical' phenomenology might not be an easy affair. I, by and large, agree with Rodemeyer (2022) that in Guenther's early work, which has set the tone

While recognizing that classical phenomenology 'can disclose the most basic structures of human existence, including temporality, perception, language, and intersubjectivity' (Weiss, Murphy, and Salamon 2019, xiii), one of the ambitions of critical phenomenology is to go 'beyond classical phenomenology by reflecting on the quasi-transcendental social structures that make our experience of the world possible and meaningful' (Guenther 2020, 15). '[C]olonialism, anti-Black racism, and heteropatriarchy' (Guenther 2021, 6) are examples of such structures; they are 'contingent historical and social structures' that 'shape our experience, not just empirically or in a piecemeal fashion, but in what we might call a quasi-transcendental fashion' (Guenther 2020, 12). For Guenther (2021), these structures deserve to be called 'quasi-transcendental' for two reasons: first, they are *transcendental* because 'they are not just phenomena in the world, but also (inter) subjective ways of seeing, hearing, moving, relating, and sense-making' (6). They have, in other words, a constitutive function for experience. At the same, these structures are supposed to break with classical (that is, Kantian

---

of much of the discussions around these issues, '"classical phenomenology" becomes simply a reference to Husserl' (101). The main problem with this interpretation of Husserl is how Guenther ties the effecting of the phenomenological reduction to transcendental subjectivity, which Husserl would unfairly prioritize over transcendental *intersubjectivity*. In her retort, which takes its decisive cues mostly from Merleau-Ponty, Guenther describes her endeavour as the attempt 'to develop a method of critical phenomenology that both continues the phenomenological tradition of taking first-person experience as the starting point for philosophical reflection and also resists the tendency of phenomenologists to privilege transcendental subjectivity over transcendental intersubjectivity' (2013, xiii, xv). While Salamon (2018), too, finds more inspiration in Merleau-Ponty's work than in Husserl's, her analysis of Merleau-Ponty's reflections on method in the preface to *Phenomenology of Perception* recognizes, and rightly so, that the idea of phenomenology as a philosophy of subjectivity is nothing but 'a caricature' (11), one that may well have a long-standing history in certain circles but that does not correspond to Husserl's actual works on intersubjectivity for all that. (For an account of the central role of transcendental intersubjectivity in Husserl's phenomenology, see Zahavi (2001), who sees therein Husserl's greatest contribution to the history of transcendental philosophy.) Since Salamon (2018) acknowledges the continuity between Husserl and Merleau-Ponty with respect to method, she can consequently write that 'what is critical about critical phenomenology turns out to have been there all along' (12). Oksala (2022) recently made a similar point and insisted, contra Guenther, that the transcendental reduction leads to the discovery of the *intersubjective* constitution of the lifeworld, which appears in the reduction as 'not simply ontologically given, but [as] the outcome of profound historical and political constitution' (141f.). For this reason, Oksala sees the phenomenological reduction as being 'indispensable' (138, 141) to the critical project. I agree with this assessment. In what follows, and for reasons that should gradually become obvious, I will characterize my own endeavour as belonging to what critical phenomenologists call 'classical phenomenology', even though the limits about the relevance of this distinction should gradually shine through. It should be noted, finally, that the interpretation put forward in Guenther's most recent work (e.g. the excellent 2021 article) has considerably changed, as she now acknowledges the richness of Husserl's research on intersubjectivity. Still, we will see in this section that some disagreements remain.

and Husserlian) transcendentalism in that they are neither essential nor universal, nor features of transcendental subjectivity; they are, rather, historically determined, often unknowingly institutionalized, and politicized *empirical structures* to which we, collectively, have (in some cases at least) become blind; hence the addition of the prefix 'quasi-'.

Although Al-Saji (2017) recognizes very lucidly that Husserl's 'fine-grained analyses of embodiment, temporality, affectivity and sensing offer sites for productive recuperation' for the critical movement (146; cf. Al-Saji 2010), she similarly insists on the fragility of the phenomenological distinction between the transcendental and empirical levels of experience. She puts the point in the following way:

> For it is one thing to admit an embodied consciousness, quite another to take historicity, habitualities, and social positionality—thus gendering and racialization—to *structure* intentional activity at the transcendental, and not simply empirical level. For instance, Husserl may admit that transcendental subjectivity has a lifeworld of habitualities.... But the concrete forms that these habits take can still be seen to belong to the empirical ego; this would allow the transcendental ego to be conceived universally, with details filled in locally.... Categories of "identity" would thus be relegated as characteristics of the "empirical ego." The phenomenological reduction would seem to go both too far—in assuming that we can separate out what is empirical from what is transcendental in the mixture of experience—and yet also not far enough, in ignoring the structuring role of characteristics deemed empirical and contingent. In this vein, the structures of inner time-consciousness might appear as generally founding of experience, yet filled in differently for different gendered and racialized subjects. But what if gendering and racialization make a difference in *how* time is experienced—a difference in the very structure of temporal experience and not simply in its colouration or content... (Al-Saji 2017, 146)

As this passage attests, one of the main points of contention between critical and classical phenomenologists concerns the scope of the phenomenological reduction. By integrating analyses of power relations, racism, colonialism, etc. in order to reveal their structuring role in intersubjective, individual, and even self-experience, critical phenomenology aims to show the limits of both the reduction and the empirical/transcendental distinction that it leads to, and to demonstrate how 'creative reconfigurations of phenomenology that deepen and actualize the promise of its method'

(Al-Saji 2017, 146) are made possible through the integration of quasi-transcendental structures into the phenomenological discourse.

In what follows I will not be concerned at all with the kind of political activism that these analyses open onto.[15] My sole objective is to critically assess the implications of the above-mentioned claims about the reduction for the argument that I have developed thus far in the chapter. To achieve this, my strategy is to go over the theses that I've defended in Sections 6.1–6.3 concerning the norms of interpersonal understanding and to discuss them considering the methodological points raised by critical phenomenologists. Throughout, I will pursue two tasks. First, I want to hint at some of the ways these critical insights can contribute to improve my analyses of the norms of empathic relations. Second, I will argue that these critical insights results do not alter the core eidetic claims of classical phenomenology. Against this background, I will contend that there is no incompatibility, but complementarity, between the two approaches.

6.4.1. The Normal Body

In the first section of the chapter, I argued for two claims: first, I contended that one's own body acts as the originary norm (*Urnorm*) of social understanding insofar as it provides the necessary experiential background against which others can appear *as* others. Husserl's reasoning, which provided me with my initial cue, is simple: since our body has a twofold structure (*Leib-Körper*), we can confer mindedness to others on the basis of the perceived similarities between our own bodily self-experience and the body of the other if—and here's the second point—the behaviours it displays conform to norms of harmony, continuity, and unity.

Some critical phenomenologists have quite justly pointed out that the phenomenological conception of the lived body (*Leib*), despite its claim to universality, is never neutral with respect to gender, race, class, ethnicity, age, and cognitive or bodily ability (Weiss 2015). On the contrary,

---

[15] As Guenther (2021, 17) sometimes recalls, the 'most important' aim of critical phenomenology is to promote 'resistance, resurgence, emancipation, liberation or some other way of trying to get (a little more) free'. Echoing Marx, Guenther elsewhere puts the point in the following way: 'the ultimate goal of critical phenomenology is not just to interpret the world, but also to change it' (2020, 16). On this score, the difference between the critical project and classical phenomenology is more important or obvious, which does not mean, however, that there was no call for action whatsoever in classical phenomenology (Rodemeyer 2022 and Aldea, Carr, and Heinämaa 2022).

phenomenological analyses of the lived body are but the unstated expressions of the privileges that some (groups of) individuals (mainly white, male, young, healthy, etc.) enjoy at the expense of others (black, female, elderly, mentally or bodily ill, etc.). These criticisms, which target equally Husserl's, Heidegger's, Sartre's, and more recently even Merleau-Ponty's descriptions, not only suggest that there is no such thing as *the* normal body but, more importantly still, also intimate that what counts as bodily normality has silently but persistently been promoted by contingent social structures that critical phenomenology aims to deconstruct.

More details would be needed to demonstrate the full reach and strength of these criticisms, which are, by and large, valid. Here is not the place to pursue this task, however; suffice it to note for the time being that the phenomenological *Leib* is not a homogeneous category, and its invocation, if we are to remain true to the things themselves, does call, in most circumstances at least, for a nuanced or detailed treatment. Crucially, this insight is not without significance for the question we are pursuing in this chapter. Perceptual experiences reflect our situation, such that at least some socially constructed norms must affect how we perceive others, and much more often than we realize. This is indeed what both phenomenological and psychological studies undeniably show: how we perceive other people is powerfully and insidiously influenced by customs, traditions, conventions, culture, and all kinds of unrecognized prejudices and biases (see, e.g., Correll 2014; Correll, Park, Judd, and Wittenbrink 2002). In the technical vocabulary of phenomenology, we can express this in the following way: *what* is expected in perceptual consciousness is dependent both on what is sedimented in the ego's accumulated history of empirical experiences, be they affective, perceptual, or otherwise (cf. Section 5.1), and on the cultural norms circulating in one's milieu, for I do not have to directly experience something in order to have a catalogue of expectations. Both contribute to shape *how* the ego perceives. This is the reason why the impact of these normative structures is said to be transcendental or quasi-transcendental, and not (merely) empirical. Structures such as gender and race 'function in a quasi-transcendental way insofar as they generate and consolidate meaning by normalizing some habits of perception, cognition, and comportment while pathologizing others' (Guenther 2021, 6). Al-Saji (2017) puts the point in the following way:

> Once the social and the political—once historicity, domination and oppression—are taken to structure perceptual and affective experience all

the way down, an incommensurability is introduced into experience that challenges the commonality of the field of sense upon which the recognition of meaning relies. Sociality and historicity differentially structure the very forms of expression that perceptual sense and practical possibility take. Sociality and historicity are not merely added onto meaning-making relations as an extra layer of sense. (148)

While there is no doubt that these critical insights are to the point and open onto convincing phenomenological analyses, there are at least two conclusions to draw therefrom with respect to method, and correspondingly two pitfalls to avoid.

First, it should be noted that, at least from the publication of *Philosophie als strenge Wissenschaft* (1910) onward but especially in the works of the 1920s and 1930s, the analysis of historical and contingent structures (such as emotions, norms, goals, values, traditions, and culture, to name but a few) has become central to Husserl's phenomenology, which has developed, for the most part, into a phenomenology of intersubjectivity, sociality, and history. Moreover, Husserl did not only analyse these phenomena as 'mere' contingent structures; on the contrary, he discovered them through the reduction and explicitly thematized their transcendental value, that is, their transcendental or constitutive impact on experience and reality (cf. Oksala 2022, 140f.).[16] So, while critical phenomenologists do us a favour when they draw our attention to and deconstruct and describe phenomena like racism, sexism, and heteropatriarchy, thereby expanding the list of phenomena worth analysing and criticizing, their having a quasi-transcendental status does not mark—*pace* Guenther (2021, 10f.)—a substantial break with classical phenomenology. On the contrary, it just shows even more vividly the continuity between both endeavours.

---

[16] This is perhaps most clearly (and famously) visible in his late analysis of writing, which Husserl came to see as completing the process of constitution of idealities in making transmission and reactivation possible beyond its connection to person, time, and place. Once fixed in written form, scientific objectivities can be transmitted from generation to generation and incorporated into a collective body of knowledge, which every new generation of scientists can revise, perfect, and expand upon. According to Husserl, writing plays a transcendental role in this process of constitution, for by serving as a kind of universal memory and reservoir of knowledge, writing allows for an infinite number of reactivations. At the same time—and this is what Derrida's notorious introduction targeted—Husserl's demonstration of the transcendental role of writing in the constitution of objectivities is valid only if one conceives of writing as a real, empirical, and contingent practice, which, as such, is always and necessarily threatened by the possibility of non-fulfilment. Precisely for this reason, it has been suggested that Husserl's concept of writing operates in a quasi-transcendental fashion (Doyon 2014, 137–40; Doyon 2010, 32–81).

Just this point can be illuminated, and corroborated, by the reconstruction of the Husserlian method offered by Oksala (2022, 140–1), another leading critical phenomenologist. The first step of phenomenological method is the epoché, which consists in the suspension of the belief characteristic of the natural attitude, namely the belief that the world and its objects exist. According to Husserl, this neutralization of one's belief in the existence of the world frees up space to reflect on the constitutive role of subjectivity in the constitution of the world as phenomenon, which comes to light in what Husserl calls the transcendental reduction. The epoché thus prepares the ground for transcendental reduction, which aims at identifying the constitutive moments of the correlation that holds between consciousness and the world. As Oksala explains, already at this stage the Husserlian analyses of intersubjectivity come into play:

> [T]he first reduction, the transcendental reduction,…exposes the historically contingent nature of reality, its intersubjective constitution, and the perspectival nature of all our knowledge of it. When the transcendental, constitutive conditions of our experience of reality are shown in Husserl's mature philosophy to be intersubjective—historical, cultural and, not least, political—the reduction yields the crucial insight that the world is never the product of my constitutive activity alone, but of transcendental intersubjectivity. (Oksala 2022, 141)

In the transcendental reduction, the contribution of empirical social structures in the constitution of the experience of reality is thus already fully in place. It is therefore towards the second phase of the phenomenological reduction, the eidetic reduction, that we must turn if we seek to break with classical phenomenology on methodological grounds. For by identifying the (inter)subjective conditions of possibility of the unveiling of the world within the intentional relation, the transcendental reduction sets the table for an analysis of the essential or universal dimensions of this relation. Achieved through the eidetic variation, the eidetic reduction is a methodological move whereby one's attention is led back from a multiplicity of particulars to an a priori essence. Through the imaginative and systematic variation of particulars, the method seeks to strip away the contingent elements of the object under study in order to identify its invariant structures. This is where the debate becomes heated. Are there, yes or no, invariant structures or essences of perception? Oksala (2022), who agrees with me that the real issue concerns the transition from the transcendental to the eidetic reduction (141), offers two reasons to think that the answer is no, viz. that the eidetic reduction is problematic for any phenomenological enterprise, but especially from the standpoint of critical phenomenology. The first reason questions the very possibility of eidetic reduction on the basis of limitations inherent in the method of eidetic variation: 'The first problem is that, irrespective of how much I vary my imaginary experiences by including as much cultural and historical diversity in them as possible, my reflective experiences themselves are always normatively constituted' (141). In other words, since the effectuation of the eidetic variation is situated, the identification of invariant or universal structures of experience is impossible. There is, in other words, a limit to my capacity of varying and identifying universal structures of experience due to my situatedness.

The second reason Oksala brings forth—the more important in her eyes—is that the function of identifying universal structures through eidetic reduction is a process that is contrary to the spirit of the critical project in virtue of its historical role in legitimizing structures of domination and oppression:

> The second, and perhaps even more serious problem is the telos of this exercise: irrespective of how successful I might be in this universalizing endeavor, the aim of this exercise is to identify the similarities underlying the diversity and to ignore the differences. As feminist philosophers and critical race theorists have amply demonstrated, the attempt to universalize essential structures definitive of the human is precisely the theoretical project that has often scientifically grounded and politically legitimized forms of oppression and marginalization. (Oksala 2022, 141)

Although she gives more weight to the second problem, Oksala presents these two reasons as being interdependent in the critical gesture. In my view, however, there is an important difference between the two. While the former questions the very possibility of eidetic reduction on rational grounds, the latter is a normative prescription that applies to critical phenomenology independently of how we settle the first. So, although we can acknowledge the significance of the motivation that comes into play in how she formulates her reservations concerning 'the telos' of the eidetic reduction, the fact is that this cannot by itself completely settle the first, decisive question, since it has no direct impact on it.

As I see it, recognizing the constitutive value of quasi-transcendental structures does not in any way imply that there are no invariant structures of experiences. Even if some contingent and politicized meaning-structures operate in a quasi-transcendental way in the sense of generating or constituting meaning, this does not prevent there being layers of sense that remain unaffected by these insights, which is precisely what Husserl's analyses set out to show. In the context of the phenomenological analyses of empathy, the structures laid out in Section 6.1 are a case in point. I take them both to be universally valid: continuity, harmony, and unity are features that *all* human bodies (including those considered 'marginal' or 'abnormal') must display to count as human bodies at all. They are, in other words, necessary.[17]

Key here is to keep in mind Husserl's minimalism: it is nothing but the basic capacity to perceive an underlying similarity between one's own living body and the body of others that motivates the transfer. The process of analogizing apprehension relies on the recognition that the other, whom I see as displaying unity, harmony, and continuity in his behaviours, must have a twofold *Leib-Körper* structure similar to mine. Whichever differences there may exist, say, between men, women, or transgender persons's bodies, and however these affect how we perceive things, all human bodies constitutively have a two-sided nature (they are *Leibkörper*), and all human bodies conform, at least to some degree, to norms of unity, harmony, and continuity. Husserl's point is that if we are to talk about empathy at all, breaking with these norms cannot be *total*.[18]

---

[17] Presumably, from a Husserlian point of view, even AI programmes would need to recognize harmony, continuity, and unity to categorize what they perceptually detect as belonging to the human genre.

[18] One could make the point that there are cases in which, e.g., racism or sexism so profoundly structure someone's experience that members of the target group are not apprehended empathetically in the full and deserving sense. In *Minima Moralia*, Adorno hinted at one such extreme case—the Holocaust—and suggested that 'Perhaps the social schematization of perception is such that anti-Semites no longer see Jews as human beings at all' (1974, 105). It's unclear what this tells us about *perception* per se, but it seems fair to say that such reasoning could hardly be applied to many other cases. As Hannah Arendt (1944) once noted concerning the early Prussian liberals, Jews in 20th century Germany were very much seen as human beings, otherwise there would have been no need for laws or language to exclude them from the circle of human beings. A similar reasoning applies to the situation described by Fanon (2008), who famously portrayed the colonial gaze as dehumanizing, or de Beauvoir (2010), who argued that society's construction of womanhood as the 'Other' to manhood leads to women's oppression, relegating them to a secondary and subordinate position in relation to men. These are, obviously, important, difficult, and highly sensible issues that critical phenomenologists recently brought back into the philosophical discussion, and for good reasons. Still, from a Husserlian standpoint at least, it seems that, even in these cases, the members of the target group can still be apprehended empathetically in the wide sense analysed in Section 6.1. That is, even as 'humans of secondary class', they can apparently still be perceived as having a similar double-sided nature (*Leib/Körper*). In fact, one could apply Arendt's reasoning here and argue—and this would apply to the Holocaust too—that it is precisely *because* they are still perceived empathetically (in the wide sense that is operative in the apprehension of human

So, while one may justly complain that Husserl has shown too little interest in questions as fundamental as race, gender, etc., and seek to counteract and compensate for this lack by providing such analyses, this leaves Husserl's (eidetic) descriptions unmoved: there is a certain recognizable style in bodily behaviour by virtue of which we can distinguish animate beings from chairs and trees, and attribute mindedness to others on that basis. We could certainly improve on Husserl's descriptions of these traits (perhaps even more so in light of the recent development in AI and robotics) and put to good use the sensibility and analytical toolkit that critical phenomenologists have developed in doing so, but the fact that there are such characteristics undeniably fits the phenomenology. In the vocabulary of classical phenomenology, this is a universal law that can only be discovered through the successive use of the transcendental and eidetic reductions.[19]

6.4.2. Perceptual Biases

Let us now take a look at the other two basic claims I have made in the earlier sections. I have argued in Section 6.2 that more complex types of empathic relations are intentional accomplishments governed by norms of correctness, whereby we corroborate, validate, or modify and self-correct our initial assessment, whereas in Section 6.3 I have described what I have called 'reciprocal empathy' as a process subject to norms attunement and responsiveness.

Things appear to be more complicated when we look at how it plays out in real-life situations. Thanks to psychology and neuroscience, we know that our perceptions of others are shaped by all kinds of biases. Take, for instance, anti-black racism. An impressive number of studies demonstrate the pervasiveness of the association between African Americans and violence (Correll, Park, et al. 2007; Payne 2006) or crime (Goff, Jackson, et al. 2014). While some of these prejudices are conscious and unashamedly assumed, most are unconscious, which does not prevent them from being

---

and non-human animals alike) that members of these groups have been subjected to all these wrongdoings. Obviously, this does not in any way solve the complex sets of problems that these authors justly raised, but it may clarify the extension of Husserl's concept of empathy.

[19] Since it is embodied, it is, like all psychic laws, a *material a priori law*. In *Ideas II*, Husserl explains that the psyche is an ontic region with its own a priori laws, which means that their universality is restricted to this specific ontological region.

pernicious and even institutionalized for all that. Critical analyses have shown how these prejudices are painfully lived through by individuals who suffer from them. In *Black Skin, White Masks* (2008), Frantz Fanon describes the violent objectifying power of the colonial gaze by showing how it not only temporarily objectifies the racialized bodies but permanently marks, defines, dominates, and excludes them by keeping them at odds with the self-imposed expectations of white civilization. As 'Negroes', black persons' history, values, nature, and possibilities are predefined, determined, and constituted by a racist Western society. The consequences are that, as a black man or black woman in a white society, one is forced to be constantly self-conscious, painfully aware that one is seen and appraised in everything one does. Obviously, this is painfully lived through as it makes it impossible to be self-evidently absorbed in one's actions or projects, that is, being towards the world through one's body as subject. In this sense, Fanon argues that, as a black man in a white colonial world, one has difficulties in developing a normal body schema.

By taking women as an example, Simone de Beauvoir (2010) arrived at a similar conclusion: when society objectifies and defines women as the 'other', it diminishes their agency and self-determination, causing women to become preoccupied with societal judgments and perceptions of their appearance and behaviour, rather than being able to naturally and confidently engage with the world on their own terms. According to de Beauvoir, this preoccupation with external evaluations limits women's ability to assert their autonomy and fully participate in society.[20]

These results directly impact the kind of analyses I provided earlier, for, of course, unknowingly bearing such prejudices both impinges on our capacity to self-assess the correctness or appropriateness of our understanding of others (a claim made in Section 6.2) and negatively impacts our ability to be attuned with one another (a main claim of Section 6.3). In short, falling prey to these and like prejudices impedes on our capacity to reach a real or proper interpersonal understanding, because it relies on falsehoods. Given the ubiquity of these prejudices, the objection is serious.

Clearly, adding this critical bent to our analyses of self–other relations and producing detailed phenomenological descriptions that show how lived

---

[20] A converging assessment is made by Iris Marion Young (1980) with respect to women in patriarchal societies in her famous essay *Throwing Like a Girl*, in which woman's intentionality is described as an inhibited intentionality.

experiences are differentially lived through by different groups and individuals are important if one wants to be up to the task of phenomenology and truly return to the things themselves. Empathic relations are multifaceted and never completely insulated from contingent, social, political, economic, etc. forces that set much of the context from which they emerge. As such, one can grant that these factors 'structure intentional activity at the transcendental, and not simply empirical level' (Al-Saji 2017, 146) if we mean by this that these contingent factors have a constitutive influence on experience and meaning.

However, caution is called for concerning the kind of conclusion one ought to draw from these insights, for the same two points I have insisted upon in the previous section apply here *mutatis mutandis*.

First, classical phenomenology already recognizes that contingent (or empirical) structures sometimes have a constitutive (or transcendental) significance. With respect to method, then, this point is neither 'new' nor specifically critical. It is true that the emphasis placed on these contingent/empirical structures, which is made central to the method, can be worth appreciating as a change, but the change lies not in the method itself but in the goals and interests in the service of which it is deployed.

Second, this does not imply either that there are no invariant structures that the reduction can lead to. Take, for instance, the claim put forward in Section 6.2 according to which more higher forms of empathy are governed by standards of correctness. This, I contend, is a material a priori law of the empathic experience, a feature that does not derive from sociality or any other contextual factors. For even if perceptual practices always *de facto* take place in social, cultural, political, etc. contexts that powerfully contribute to shape them (and which explains why there are all kinds of obstacles to the achievement of a true self–other attunement), the fact that active forms of empathy should be understood as *dynamical processes structurally open to attunement and self-correction* is not constitutively dependent upon any social, cultural, or historical factor. It is, so to speak, built into these acts in much the same way that, say, the mineness or first-personal character of experience is constitutive of every intentional relation (Zahavi 2019a). Again, this does not mean that our interactions with others are always geared toward some kind of peaceful harmony but, rather, that there are standards that come into play in interpersonal understanding such that it makes sense to say that we understand each other—or not.

6.5. Conclusion

The aim of this chapter was to identify the specific norms that are at play in our empathic understanding of others. Taking my cue from the work of Husserl, Stein, and Merleau-Ponty, I have answered by singling out three functional levels of norms. First, I have stressed the significance of the body of both self (Section 6.1.1) and other (Section 6.1.2) in experiences of basic empathy, and argued that the perceived conduct of others must cohere with expected bodily harmony, continuity, and unity. When these perceptual norms are met, the analogical transfer can occur, and the other is perceived as another person, that is, an alter ego. It has been suggested, second, that the norms at work at the second level are not perceptual through and through but are, I would like to suggest, structurally alike: just as object perception is intrinsically open to its being enhanced or optimized in light of some interest or other (Sections 1.2 and 2.2), I have shown how higher forms of social understanding involve possibilities of improvement and increase (Section 6.2). The standard of this performance, which belongs constitutively to the intentionality of empathic acts, is the other's experience *as expressed* and nothing else, and it manifests itself nowhere else but in the encounter.[21] Finally, what I have called 'mutual attunement' assumes a similar normative role in object-perception (Section 3.3) and in reciprocal empathy (Section 6.3). Both are best conceived dialectically as an interplay of question and answer, although the greater role played by emotional or affective regulation in self–other relationships makes it clear that the normative character of empathic acts really does have a *sui generis* character.

In Section 6.4 the chapter took a different direction and engaged in a debate in the phenomenological literature concerning the sense and scope of the reduction. Throughout the section I argued that the methodological distinction holding between the critical and classical approach to phenomenology does not (or in any case should not) revolve around the transcendental/empirical distinction but on whether there really are universal structures that the eidetic reduction can lead to. While recognizing that

---

[21] Here is a passage from Merleau-Ponty's *Phenomenology* that supports this idea: 'I perceive the other's grief or anger in his behaviour, on his face and in his hands, without any borrowing from an "inner" experience...because grief and anger are variations of being in the world, undivided between body and consciousness' (2012, 372). In *The Visible and the Invisible*, Merleau-Ponty's descriptions point in the same direction: 'Anger, shame, hate, and love are not psychic facts hidden at the bottom of another's consciousness: they are types of behaviour or styles of conduct which are visible from the outside. They exist on this face or in those gestures, not hidden behind them' (1964b, 52f.).

critical phenomenologists provide powerful conceptual tools for enriching and nuancing phenomenological analyses, Husserl's included, I have offered reasons as to why we should answer this question positively and exposed my disagreements with Oksala (2022), who provides a negative answer. In the present context of an analysis of social cognition, the crucial difference that I see between the classical and critical approaches is that the normative principles that I have in view are *formal patterns that are essential to and constitutive of the empathic process itself*, whereas the kinds of normative structures that critical phenomenologists rightly target, describe, and criticize are *not essential* to the empathic encounter even if they powerfully shape, transform, impact, affect, and influence it's unfolding. The difference between *constitutive (or essential) and non-constitutive (or non-essential) normative properties of empathic experience* justifies the recourse in phenomenology (be it critical or not) not only to the phenomenological reduction but also to the eidetic reduction, thanks to which only these constitutive features can be discovered and described.

Against this background, I still take Husserl's analyses to be, for the most part at least, compatible with what critical phenomenologists have in view, for which reason I have stressed the complementarity between both endeavours.[22] We can both recognize that reciprocal empathy essentially bears within itself a telos and justly contend that there are all kinds of contingent hurdles to the realization of a true self–other attunement; we can both recognize that the perceptual field is a differentiated system of contrasts and affections (Husserl 2001) and show how this affective map will be reflected differently in people with different bodily make-up and habitualities (Al-Saji 2017); we can both recognize the structuring role of depth, which opens up the space of perception as voluminosity (Merleau-Ponty 2012), and argue that perceptual space is neither gender- (Fisher 2000, 29f.) nor race-neutral (Young 1980); we can both recognize that time has a tripartite structure made of impressions, retentions, and protentions (Husserl 1991) and

---

[22] As should be clear from the previous analyses, I hereby side with Aldea, Carr, and Heinämaa (2022, 7), who contend that '[t]he methods that classical phenomenology is able to offer for contemporary analyses of social, cultural, and political phenomena have thus far been largely overlooked or diminished. This neglect, we think, stems from a number of widespread misconceptions surrounding Husserl's inquiries. One such misconception holds that, given its eidetic commitments, Husserlian phenomenology forecloses for itself the possibility of doing justice to deeply sedimented historical contingencies. Another holds that classical phenomenology is individualistic or solipsistic, and thus unable to produce analyses of communal and intersubjective conditions of experiencing. The third one contends that the transcendental methods of phenomenology make it otherworldly—or worse—unworldly.'

argue that it is an 'affectively entangled flow' (Al-Saji 2010, xx) that is lived through differently by different groups or individuals (cf. Alcoff 1999).

All of this suggests that, even if we agree, as I think we should, that what is empirical and contingent can sometimes have a structuring role in experience, this role is not necessarily permanent or essential—universal in that sense. It can be changed; hence the activist bent at the heart of the critical programme. Certain features, however, really are a priori or universal. The fact that human perception is embodied is one. The fact that perception must have a certain degree of coherence is another. Of course, what exactly we take coherence to be is influenced by some cultural factors, which themselves can conceal prejudices and biases that need to be deconstructed. But that does not change the fact that coherence is a necessary condition of possibility of perception. The truths of classical and critical phenomenology thus seem to be both different in scope and perfectly compatible with one another.

Phenomenology and the Norms of Perception. Maxime Doyon, Oxford University Press. © Maxime Doyon 2024.
DOI: 10.1093/9780191993527.003.0006

7
Perceiving Together

> Perception's silent thesis is that experience, at each moment, can be coordinated with the experience of the preceding moment and with that of the following one, that my perspective can be coordinated with the perspectives of other consciousnesses—that all contradictions can be removed, that monadic and intersubjective experience is a single continuous text.
> Maurice Merleau-Ponty, Phenomenology of Perception

Sociality pervades nearly all aspects of our perceptual lives. It shows up, first, in *what* we perceive: the artefacts that constitute our lifeworld (monuments, laptops) reveal the existence of others, past and present, who provide a context for their institution and meaning, including their meaning for individual experiences (Merleau-Ponty 2012, 363). Perception's embeddedness in a social context also impacts directly *how* we perceive: through the mediation or guidance of our family members, carers, and teachers, etc., who we imitate or who instruct us, we have learned to see people and things in certain ways—for example, at a certain distance (paintings, microbes), in a certain specific setting (in a museum, in the lab), and, more problematically, as conforming or not to certain moral or political norms and values (gender identity, aesthetic standards). Given the pervasiveness of normative structures in society, perceiving is always carried out in a context where value judgments, power relations, and sociocultural standards are in place, constantly exerting top-down pressure on what we perceptually take in. These norms, which often materialize in the environment (gendered city planning and design) and the architecture (usually maladapted for disabled people), shape from without how we relate to the world through perception. Given the irreducible impact of other people in the very fabric of our perceptual landscape, all perceptions have, in some way or other, a social character.

Some perceptual experiences do not only have a social dimension in that loose sense, however; they are also properly or explicitly 'shared' with other people—we contemplate the sunset with our loved one, we enjoy a good bottle of wine with friends, we jointly attend to sport or musical performances with our children, and so on. Over the last three decades, the phenomenon of 'sharing' has been the object of many discussions in the field of collective intentionality or social ontology, whose discussions typically revolve around the paradigmatic cases of 'shared actions', which include, without being limited to, shared perceptions. Philosophers in the area typically take their shared character to rely on the satisfaction of the following three conditions:[1]

1) *The plurality condition:* shared action requires multiple ontologically similar agents.
2) *The awareness condition:* shared action requires that the involved agents are aware of doing something together as they do it; this condition is in turn a condition for the last one (3).
3) *The coalescence condition:* shared action requires that a plurality of agents form a unit or collective (as opposed to a mere aggregate of agents).

All three conditions are generally thought to be necessary and sufficient to account for the possibility of shared actions. Without the *plurality condition*, i.e. if the state in action would have only a single ontological bearer, nothing would properly be shared; without fulfilling the *awareness condition*, i.e. if the agents were not aware that they are both having a shared experience, they would be in state no different than when they have mere parallel or simultaneous experiences where nothing is specifically shared; and without the *coalescence condition*, i.e. if the individuals do join forces but their experiences are in no way integrated with one another, there would be no collective experience and therefore no sharing either.

There are, however, multiple challenges associated with all three conditions, which admit various understandings. Over the last few decades, it is around the coalescence condition that the most important debates have revolved. How exactly are we supposed to understand the 'sharedness' of intentions, that is, their constitutive interdependence such that a shared action would be more than an aggregate of individual ones but a *sui generis* phenomenon? We can distinguish at least three classes of responses, viz. three classes of joint intentions in the literature (Schweikard and Schmid 2020). While some philosophers (e.g. Bratman 1999, 2014) claim that the sharedness of

---

[1] Given its simplicity, I adopt (with slight modifications) Knudsen's (2021) vocabulary here, but it corresponds, as he himself notices, to a list of conditions widely accepted in the literature, both in the classical texts (e.g. Searle 1990, 414) and in more recent ones (e.g. Walsh 2020).

the intention is carried by the *content* of that experience (what it is *about*, which would be shared by some individuals), others (e.g. Searle 1990, 1995) contend that what makes an intention properly shared lies in the intentional *mode* of experience, which would have the *sui generis* intentional form <we intend...>. Finally, there is the account developed by Margaret Gilbert (1990, 1992, 1996, 2014), who developed a specifically *normative* conception of collective intentionality that rests on the establishment of a *plural subject*, which Gilbert takes to be required to meet the coalescence condition. For Gilbert, collective intentionality rests on what she calls *joint commitments*, which come about when individuals express (through words, gestures, etc.) their readiness to be jointly committed to a certain goal or task if the concerned others are similarly disposed to do their part. The expression of joint commitments not only gives the members of the group *reasons* to act in certain ways and to complain when their partners fail to be up to what they have committed but also conveys their willingness to form a unified subject and act as a single body. In Gilbert's view, joint commitments—that is, the subjects' readiness 'to put one's own will into a "pool of wills"' (1992, 18)—thus lead to the formation of a plural subject, which she takes to be required to account for the sharedness of all shared phenomena (1990, 7). Given the thematic orientation of this book, which bears on the phenomenology of the norms at work in perception, I will from this moment on leave the first two accounts aside and focus exclusively on Gilbert's, which will serve me as a foil to articulate my own view.

While one may recognize with Gilbert that social groups are often established on joint commitments, whether explicitly (in the military) or implicitly (walking together, to take Gilbert's (1990) favoured example), the chapter offers reasons to think that joint commitments might not be necessary to explain every form of shared intentional experiences. Recently, just such a proposal has been made by León and Zahavi (2018) with respect to emotions. In this chapter, I will focus exclusively on another phenomenon, namely shared perceptions, and argue that joint commitments are neither necessary nor sufficient for having shared perceptions.[2] With respect to perception, Gilbert's account faces two sets of difficulties that my account

---

[2] Throughout the chapter, I use the expressions *joint* and *shared* perceptions interchangeably. I distinguish this phenomenon, which involves a certain bodily (but also affective, emotional, etc.) proximity between the agents, from *collective* experiences, which are more distant or anonymous. Although the line may be hard to draw exactly in some specific cases, the contrast between these two examples should make the basic idea very intuitive: I'm interested in describing phenomena like jointly attending to an artistic performance with a friend as opposed to analysing what goes on when a whole nation collectively watches a football game on TV. The former is a shared experience, while the latter is better described as a collective one.

tries to overcome: first, she understands joint commitments in largely *mentalistic* terms as being indissociable from the rights, responsibilities, and obligations that participants must have and constantly reaffirm toward one another. For Gilbert, the coalescence condition is ultimately fulfilled at the level of the mental states of the individual members of the collective. Second—but this is just the flip side of the same coin—Gilbert conceives of the kind of conscious activity required to be jointly committed, and thus be answerable to the group (viz. the awareness condition), in largely *reflective* terms, that is, as relying on the explicit recognition (be it linguistic or not) of our mutual obligations and entitlements, which must be common knowledge between the participants (Gilbert 1992, 189–91; 2013, 43). As will be argued, neither of these insights normally correspond to the phenomenology of shared perceptual experiences, which raises some suspicions about the use of the notion of joint commitments altogether.

The first claim—according to which for there to be a shared action, everyone in the group must openly express his readiness to be jointly committed to the effecting of the said action by cognitively recognizing their rights and responsibilities—is too strong and, as such, not necessary. Shared perceptions need not rely on any form of obligations in that psychologically demanding sense but is, rather, regularly simply conveyed *directly* through our perceptual actions and behaviours. Watching a movie together need not require anything more than sitting next to one another and following the action on the screen in some coordinated ways (e.g. laughing at the same jokes). By behaving or exercising our perceptual skills in certain specific ways, we communicate to others directly that we are into the same project or activity, and when it is picked up by the other, this is sufficient for sharing the experience. Since there is neither room nor necessity for appealing to responsibilities, obligations, and blameworthiness here, the phenomenon of 'shared perception' can be *fully embodied*.

Of course, the challenge—and this brings me to the second difficulty I see in Gilbert's account—is to explain how any such perceptual action and behaviour can be *experienced together as shared*; that is, how exactly the embodied expression of sharedness can be conveyed to the other and picked up by her as such. In her work on joint action, Gilbert stresses the necessity of *being aware* of the obligations one has towards one another in joint commitment. Therein lies the normativity in her account, for it is this commitment that makes me blameworthy if I fail to fulfil my duties and act in accordance with what I committed to. I see normativity playing out elsewhere. While Gilbert might certainly be right to hold that many shared *actions* are shared in the relevant sense when there's a shared awareness of the commitments that bind the agents together, in the case of shared perceptions the relevant norms are *not* located between perceivers but between the perceivers on the one hand and the perceptual field on the other, which places its 'demands' on us. To account for this phenomenon, which shifts the normative moment in shared perceptions on to the perceptual acts themselves, we need an account of *pre*-reflective self-awareness. On this score too, then, her account needs to be amended.

Developing my position on these two points—the *embodied* character of shared perceptions and the *pre-reflective* self-awareness of the norms therein—will bring me to specify what I take to be the correct way to satisfy the three required conditions (plurality, coalescence, and awareness) to have a shared perception. Key is the notion of *shared perceptual responsiveness*, whereby a We—call it a *perceptual We*—emerges in the way individuals jointly respond to commonly perceived cues.[3] In my account, *shared perception requires shared perceptual responsiveness*, which is both embodied and pre-reflectively lived through by the perceivers. But what does that mean exactly?

Depending on the situation, the co-perceivers's joint response may vary greatly. The reaction to a perceptually shared landscape may be primarily discursive. It could provoke a discussion among the co-perceivers about its breathtaking beauty, for instance, and to some extent they could even disagree about what they have seen; this does not matter. Their reaction could also be emotional, yielding a feeling of awe or reverence, for example. Co-perceivers may also respond by acting together in certain specific ways: maybe there's a branch partially blocking their view, and they jointly respond to the scenery by taking a few steps to the left such as to improve their view. The list isn't exhaustive, and the response may involve (and usually does involve) multiple kinds of reactions simultaneously, even largely non-converging ones. But if something is to be shared at all, this non-convergence cannot be total. When something or someone is jointly (and

---

[3] The notion of responsiveness should now be familiar. In Chapters 1–3 I argued that the phenomenology of everyday perception follows normative patterns best understood as a response to a worldly solicitation. In this chapter I want to show that this general characterization of intentional experience, which Merleau-Ponty describes dialectically in terms of questions and answers, or solicitations and responses, plays out in an analogous way in social contexts. Walsh (2020, 25) makes a converging assessment.

not simply concurrently) perceived by two persons, the lived experiences of the co-perceivers undergo a subtle but decisive alteration: it is now experienced as theirs. They are now mutually aware of sharing an experience in a shared way, and this induces a noticeable modification to the quality attached to their experience. The question now is what this sharedness amounts to exactly? My contention is that *it is in the way that perceivers respond together, even if only in conflicting ways, that shared perceptions are possible.* In my view, shared responsiveness is the main characteristic of shared perceptual phenomena, which are, as will be argued, best understood in normative ways.

Throughout the chapter I defend my position by stressing the fundamental role of *embodied agency* and *pre-reflectively experienced time*, which I take to be the two pillars upon which shared perceptual responses rest. Section 7.1 argues that co-experiencers typically display their normative sensitivity to shared perceptual situations by acting in certain typical ways (and not others). The notion of shared perception that I'm interested in is broad enough to cover both cases of joint attention proper (involving mutual awareness of attending together), which is paradigmatic of shared perceptions in both the phenomenological and psychological literature, and the complex coordination of attention that can happen in football (soccer), insofar as a team sport like football relies in crucial ways on perceptual mechanisms.[4] I will thus discuss both examples in turn and argue that the 'sharedness' of these and like perceptual experiences manifests itself exemplarily in the experience of shared *space*, that is, in the way(s) it impacts the *agency* of the group. When a perception is shared, agents perceive people and objects as affording shared possibilities of (inter) action—*shared affordances*, as they are sometimes called (Segundo-Ortin and Satne 2022)—to which we are prompted to respond together. These possibilities—which bear on the spatial organization of the perceptual field and the horizon of action that emerges therefrom—have a motivational role in shared perceptual experiences insofar as they enable actions and behaviours that are just not available when perception is carried out individually. They are, for that very reason, constitutive of the phenomenon of shared perceptions.

---

[4] Both experiences are perception-involving, but of course non-perceptual processes (affective, cognitive, etc.) also play a significant role in them both. This need not preoccupy us now.

Our shared response, if it is to manifest our having a shared anything at all, will also be coordinated, or synchronized, in some ways. Section 7.2 will elaborate on this point and investigate the *temporal horizon* involved in perceptually shared experiences. While not all shared perceptions impact our experience of space and agency in the way described above, I will contend here that a pre-reflectively shared sense of time applies to *all* forms of perceptually shared experiences, whose horizon provides co-experiencers with an enabling context. I will make my point by returning the two above-mentioned phenomena—joint attention and football—and show how the type of coordinated actions they involve rests on a shared sense of time.

7.1. Responding Together: Sharing Space and Agency

The perceptual field is organized around the perceiver's body, which is the mobile centre or 'zero-point of orientation' (Husserl 1989, 166) in reference to which all other items of the perceptual world are oriented (as either left or right, above or beneath, near or far, etc.). My *Leib* is the *Urnorm* of perception in the sense that it sets an egocentric frame of reference by default, thereby providing the perceptual field with meaning and structure (cf. Sections 5.2.1. and 6.1). This translates into shared perceptual practices. When they share a common experience, co-perceivers provide *together* a new spatial frame of reference: they occupy a space around which the perceptual field is organized as meaningful for them as a unit. This can be achieved in various manners as there are different ways of occupying space (we can be relatively close to another, more dispersed, holding hands, etc.) depending on the pursued goals; but perceiving together, if this is to mean anything at all, requires having a shared experiential background set by the bodies that we are and that we have. While my body and its mobility enable me to see things from different points of view, but only one at once, one of the distinguishing features of shared perceptions is that the bodies of the co-perceivers open up multiple perspectives that can be explored simultaneously. As Carr (1986a) empathically stressed, this simultaneity, insofar as it is noticed by the co-perceivers, is a constitutive feature of shared experiences:

> If I wander about, I see the same tower from different points of view. When *we* see the tower together, different points of view are simultaneous as well as spread out over time. They can be simultaneous because there

are two individuals. But for each of us, the sense of the experience contains these two points of view at once. I may not see the tower through your eyes, but its being seen through your eyes as well as my own is part of the experience as I have it—or rather, as I participate in it. For manifestly, it is *not* just I that am having it. For each of us, there is a complex experience 'going on' of this one tower which can properly be attached to only one sort of subject: the plural subject *we*. (525)

While the passage concludes with the presence of a *we* subject, it is not clear to me—whether in the quote or in the paper—how there could be a complex experience whose subject is a 'we' under these conditions alone. For there to be such an experience, composed of experiences made by each one of us, it must have a shared phenomenal character, which in turn presupposes a shared intentional object with its own shared quality. But what makes the phenomenal character here? Take intuitiveness: I am inside the tower, and you are outside. From my inside perspective, I can co-intend the outside, but I don't see it as you do. My experience is intuitively 'full' with respect to the inside, and empty with regard to the outside. And vice versa for you. As a result, neither of us has, with respect to intuitiveness, a comparable experience of both the outside and the inside. Now, this might be compatible with Carr's claim that '*for each of us*, the sense of the experience contains these two points of view at once' (my emphasis), but what in no way follows from this, however, is that there is a 'we' who have an originary experience of both the inside and the outside of the tower—that is, an experience whose intuitive character isn't identical with either of ours. Hence, it seems that even if each of us, in being conscious of the tower, is also conscious of the other as conscious of the tower, and of our being conscious of it together, the precise aspect of the phenomenal character that is shared must be specified beyond simultaneity if we are to speak of a shared perception in the relevant sense.

From my perspective, a shared perception, and thereby the emergence of a 'perceptual We' (as distinct from a 'plural subject *we*'), occurs, first, when the spatial arrangement of the perceptual field is influenced by the presence of multiple perceivers such that an interbodily sense of orientation and agency becomes possible, and, second, if these perceivers share a sense of time. I'll specify the first condition here, leaving the second one for Section 7.2. Within a group, individuals perceive things, events, and even people as offering possibilities for interaction that are unavailable when perception is conducted individually. This is what the concept of shared affordances is meant to express. While the standard concept of affordances refers to the set of possibilities for action provided by the environment (Gibson 1979; Rietveld and Kiverstein 2014; cf. Sections 3.3 and 5.2.2), *shared* affordances correspond to the perceived possibilities for action that are mutually shaped, understood, and recognized by individuals in a social or collaborative context (Gallagher and Ransom 2016). The key is that social affordances are determined not only by the material properties of the object or environment and our individual skills but also by the co-presence of others, with whom I can interact and cooperate. To take an obvious example: the shared perception of a see-saw affords possibilities of action that aren't picked up when one sees it on its own. This idea has recently received support from psychologists who have provided empirical evidence that the sole presence of another person in the visual field makes perceptual agents sensitive to affordances for joint action (Davis, Riley, et al. 2010; Wagman 2019). Essentially, these studies illustrate that, in social settings, the mechanisms responsible for sensorimotor transformations and multi-sensory integration include factors related to the perceptual viewpoints and physical abilities of other individuals. This allows for the creation of 'shared action spaces,' (Pezzulo, Iodice, and Kessler 2013), which, in turn, facilitate social interactions and cooperative actions (Pacherie 2014). To come back to Carr's example, we would therefore say that both of us are perceiving the Eiffel Tower together (and not merely concurrently or simultaneously) if our different points of view participate in the spatial arrangement of the perceptual field such that possibilities for interaction and coordination that are otherwise foreclosed are now disclosed for both of us.

My task in this section is to specify what this last claim entails. In line with the argument defended in the book thus far, I will contend that the transformation of the perceptual space that is triggered by interbodily connectedness exerts a traction or pull on the group, whose corresponding sense of agency turns out to be governed by a set of shared perceptual norms. Here again, my reflection will bear on norms of coherence and optimality, which play, as I will argue, a determining role in the enactment of any shared perceptual response. I will develop this idea by discussing two phenomena—joint attention (Section 7.1) and the enactment of sport performance, in football in particular (Section 7.2)—and then draw more general conclusions that bear on more everyday examples (like, e.g., Carr's).

7.1.1. Intercorporeal Coordination in Joint Attention

Joint attention is commonly understood as the experience of perceptually attending to an object or event together with another subject.[5] It can take either of two paradigmatic form, commonly labelled in contemporary psychology top-down and bottom-up attention (Kaplan and Hafner 2006; Tomasello 2008). In a case of top-down (or triadic joint) attention, one individual actively directs another person's attention towards a specific object of interest'; e.g. the friend you're having a drink with on a terrace in Kyiv makes eye contact with you and then gestures towards what he takes to be a shooting star in the far sky. In response to this interaction, you follow the pointing gesture, establish eye contact again, and both become aware of jointly focusing your attention on the star. In contrast, joint attention is said to be bottom-up (or dyadic) when a salient environmental stimulus attracts the attention of the involved subjects without any intervening goal-directed behaviour on their part to attend together to the target; e.g. moments later you hear a Russian missile passing over your head, follow its trajectory, and see it hitting a building nearby. You and your friend make eye contact, and you both are now aware of attending to the same burning building.[6]

What makes the phenomenon of joint attention in either case particular is the way it is conceived as differing from phenomena like parallel attention (e.g. two individuals attending to the same object at the same time) and gaze following (e.g. one individual following another's gaze to discover what the second is attending to), among others. As León (2021) justly contends, 'what singles out joint attention is the "openness" or "mutual manifestation" of the common object of attention' (553). Naomi Eilan (2005) concurs and succinctly renders the context and the stakes of experiments on joint attention in developmental psychology in the following manner:

---

[5] The phenomenon of joint attention is most famously associated with the pioneering work of American psychologist Michael Tomasello (2014, 2019), who sees in our capacity to participate in collaborative efforts involving common goals a distinctively human capacity. In his account, joint attention (the mutual awareness of attending to a common object) is the first building block. It enables joint intentionality (the ability to pursue common goals), which in turn allows for collective intentionality (the ability to develop long-term collaborations). According to Tomasello, it is the latter ability that distinguishes humans from other primates: 'The result of participating in these activities is species-unique forms of cultural cognition and evolution, enabling everything from the creation and use of linguistic symbols to the construction of social norms and individual beliefs to the establishment of social institutions' (Tomasello et al. 2005, 675).

[6] For the sake of this chapter, I'm leaving aside the question of whether they are here also *perceiving an historical event*, viz. the start of a cruel and unjust war. On this question, see Carr 2014.

Sometime around their first birthday most infants begin to engage in relatively sustained bouts of attending together with their caretakers to objects in their environment. By the age of 18 months, on most accounts, they are engaging in full-blown episodes of joint attention. As developmental psychologists (usually) use the term, for such joint attention to be in play, it is not sufficient that the infant and the adult are in fact attending to the same object, nor that the one's attention cause the other's. The latter can and does happen much earlier, whenever the adult follows the baby's gaze and homes in on the same object as the baby is attending to; or, from the age of 6 months, when babies begin to follow the gaze of an adult. We have the relevant sense of joint attention in play only when the fact that both child and adult are attending to the same object is, to use Sperber and Wilson's (1986) phrase, 'mutually manifest'. Psychologists sometimes speak of such jointness as a case of attention being 'shared' by infant and adult, or of a 'meeting of minds' between infant and adult, all phrases intended to capture the idea that when joint attention occurs everything about the fact that both subjects are attending to the same object is out in the open, manifest to both participants. (1)

The passage ties together the basic components of joint attention: it is an experience in which *both* co-attenders jointly pay attention to one and *the same object*, and *to each other*. These components are not independent but, rather, correlated; they all support each other, co-constituting the phenomenon. Crucially, joint attention is something more than the mere attention to a common object of interest. As stipulated by the awareness condition, our experiences of the object must be a mutually known fact, viz. it must be known to each subject vis-à-vis the other that our attention is directed towards the same object. Our jointly attending requires this openness, viz. it involves *both* that we experience the same target *and* that this be manifest to all participants.[7] When either one fails, joint attention fails; that's why co-attenders steadily keep their experiences in check (Gallagher 2020, 108).

---

[7] The phenomenon is even more complex. For while developing these attentional skills, infants learn to direct the attention of others to objects of their surrounding by 'deictic gestures', pointing toward objects they want to see, even when these are invisible or absent (Carpenter et al. 1998; Liszkowski et al. 2006). Conversely, they begin to recognize the meaning of the indicative pointer. This complements another skill, developed at around nine months, thanks to which infants discover the emotional value their caregivers attach to objects and situations—for instance, what is dangerous or harmless and so on—by reading off their reactions (Hornik et al. 1987; Walden and Ogan, 1988; Hirshberg and Svejda 1990). This phenomenon is called *social referencing*, and it allows infants to enter 'the "intentional space" of the

If we can readily agree that, in experiences of joint attention, this 'mutual awareness' (Roessler 2005) or openness 'seems to be present to the consciousness of the participants' (Peacocke 2005, 301) in one way or another, properly characterizing it has been the object of numerous debates over the last four decades (for a survey, see León 2021). According to one influential proposal, attentional interactions involve what is commonly referred to as *recursive mind reading*, which is the ability to attribute mental states to another individual, who, in turn, relates to the attributor's own mental states. According to this view, joint attention thus rests on a nested structure of psychological states, wherein each co-attender holds mental states about the states of others. Tomasello (2008, 321) presents this view in the following way: the 'basic cognitive skill of shared intentionality is recursive mindreading. When employed in certain social interactions, it generates joint goals and joint attention, which provide the common conceptual ground within which human communication most naturally occurs.' Tomasello himself recognizes one important problem with this position, which seems to imply some kind of infinite regress in the attribution.[8] But this is not the only one. Tomasello's view faces even more serious objections such that, in the end, it seems extremely difficult to describe the 'openness' characteristic of joint attentional phenomena in purely psychological or cognitive terms (see, again, León (2021, 557–62), who develops four arguments against Tomasello's view).

Since the web of beliefs and attitudes that hold between the co-attenders does not seem to be a promising starting point, let's turn our attention away from the psychology in order to look more carefully at the lived experiences of the co-attenders. For when joint attention is successful, the co-attender's respective experience undergoes a subtle but decisive qualitative change, one that registers, as we have seen earlier, at the *pre-reflective* level of experience. Unless the co-attenders find themselves in an experimental setting and follow explicit instructions (which is a different

---

other' and 'to understand for which purpose he or she uses the object' (Fuchs 2018, 194). At the same time, infants start to realize that they, too, are regarded as intentional agents by others. Thus, joint attention is a multifaceted phenomenon that not only describes how infants (and later adults) relate to objects and to each other; it is also an ability which gives them the capacity of assessing how their surroundings relate to them as agents.

[8] See, e.g., this passage: 'No one is certain how best to characterize this potentially infinite loop of me monitoring the other, who is monitoring my monitoring of her, and so forth (called recursive mindreading by Tomasello, 2008), but it seems to be part of infants' experience—in some nascent form—from before the first birthday' (Tomasello 2011, 34–5; see also Tomasello 2009, 69).

phenomenon than the one I'm interested here), the co-attenders' ongoing experience does register in self-consciousness, but it does not typically rely on any explicit or reflective form of self-monitoring. An example may help to illustrate this. If I watch tennis on television and yell in reaction to a beautiful shot, my son, who was silently playing on his console nearby, may notice the direction of my look and start watching the game too, looking at my reaction from time to time, with me doing the same vis-à-vis him. This brings us closer, as it were, aware that we are now watching the match together. Although he is fully conscious, he is not reflectively aware that he is jointly attending; and neither am I. We are simply watching the game and keeping track of each other's look from time to time, but neither of us is reflecting on any of this or engaging in any kind of metarepresentational form of activity concerning the nature of our experience. Our respective experience is pre-reflectively lived through, which means, very simply, that it includes, for each of us, a marginal or thin self-conscious reference by means of which it is *experienced* as being shared.

One crucial aspect of this self-experience is that it is *bodily* lived through. While the specific phenomenon of joint attention was not an important topic in the *Phenomenology,* or more generally in the repertoire of classical phenomenology, the influence of the presence of co-attenders on the perceptual field did not go unnoticed. Here Merleau-Ponty points out how their presence was *bodily* felt:

> My friend Paul and I point to certain details of the landscape, and Paul's finger, which is pointing out the steeple to me, is not a finger-for-me that I conceive as oriented toward a steeple-for-me; rather, it is Paul's finger that itself shows me the steeple that Paul sees. Just as reciprocally, by making some gesture toward some point in the landscape that I see, it does not seem that I trigger for Paul, in virtue of some preestablished harmony, some internal visions that are merely analogous to my own: rather, it seems to me that my gestures invade Paul's world and guide his gaze. When I think of Paul, I do not think of a flow of private sensations in relation to my own sensations that are mediated through some interposed signs; rather, I think of someone who lives in the same world as I, in the same history as I, and with whom I communicate through this world and through this history.... Paul and I see the landscape 'together,' we are co-present before it, and it is the same for the two of us not merely as an

intelligible signification, but also as a certain accent of the world's style, reaching all the way to its *haecceity*. (2012, 428)[9]

As this passage suggests, attending is, like any perception, an embodied practice, here manifest in Paul's pointing gesture (Leon 2022).[10] But this is just one aspect. Not only does the quality or level of attention depend on a variety of embodied factors, including posture (e.g. sitting vs standing), the satisfaction of primary needs (e.g. pain, hunger), and habitualized movements (e.g. taking notes, doodling) (D'Angelo 2019, 965f.), but volitional movements can sometimes be required too. When we visually attend to a moving target, the pointing gesture will move correspondingly; on some other occasion, it might even be necessary to change our location to stabilize our contact with the target. Sometimes, we might have to peer or squint or tilt the head to keep track (Noë 2004).[11] Given these results, it has recently been argued that embodiment is a transcendental condition of possibility of attention. The argument is indeed transcendental, for even if the target isn't moving and if no *manifest* bodily movements are necessary, the body still is the vector or organizing principle of experience (D'Angelo 2019). Since the objects and events that we attend to are always 'experienced as oriented toward the perceiving body' (León 2022, 80), which is the centre of the

---

[9] This is one of the very rare passages explicitly on joint attention in classical phenomenology. While Husserl (2005a) dedicated a whole manuscript to attention, it remained for him, for the most part at least, a fundamentally individual activity. (For a survey of some of the rare, scattered passages where Husserl does, or appears to, discuss this and related phenomena, see Meindl and Zahavi 2023 and Zahavi 2023.) For a tentative to link attention and intersubjectivity systematically both within the confines of Husserlian phenomenology and in conjunction with contemporary research in the cognitive sciences and the philosophy of mind, see the illuminating analyses of Depraz 2014, part V.

[10] In this paper, León develops a phenomenological account of attention that puts the role of the body at the forefront, criticizing Watzl (2017) in passing for his neglect of this dimension of the phenomenon. His main source of inspiration is Gurwitsch (2010), for whom attention is not a matter of selecting or filtering out information from 'pre-attentive' filters (a view that Gurwitsch attributes to Husserl, but which also inspired early models of attention in cognitive sciences; see Spivey and Huette 2014) but a dynamical reorganization and rearticulation of the experiential field into a foreground–background (or 'theme-thematic field') structure. In his article, León (2022) demonstrates that a comparable account can be found in Merleau-Ponty. On the relationship between Gurwitsch and Merleau-Ponty, see Moran 2019.

[11] Neurological studies of the relevant subpersonal mechanisms point in the same direction. Here's how D'Angelo (2019, 967) summarizes some of these findings: 'From a neurological point of view, motor-planning brain regions have been shown to play a role in attention (Moore and Armstrong 2003; Armstrong and Moore 2007; Hagler et al. 2007; Kelley et al. 2008; Knudsen 2007) and in its turn, attention influences sensorimotor brain areas (Rosenkranz and Rothwell 2004) as well as sensorimotor integration (Velasques et al. 2013). In 2003 Armstrong, Moore and Fallah argued for a reciprocal interaction, at the level of neural circuits, between spatial fixation of attention and correlative bodily movements (Armstrong et al. 2003).'

perceptual field and the medium through which we are perceptually engaged in the world, the body functions in a transcendental fashion in attentional experiences in much the same way that it does in perception (see Section 3.2).

In episodes of *joint* attention, we can further specify the necessary role of embodiment in at least four related senses. First, just as our attention toward the target can be and usually is pre-reflectively lived through, our awareness that the other is intending the same object as we do need not be *inferred* from his mental states (Gallagher 2011, 295–7). No simulation of his beliefs is necessary either. In joint attentional acts, the co-agent's intentions are directly perceived in her embodied behaviours, expressions, gestures, actions, movements, and conducts. In return, by enacting movements in some specific ways, I express that our experiences are not simply running in parallel but are now shared.

Second—and this is a consequence of the first point—joint attention is embodied in the sense that it is better conceived as *movement coordination* than as coordination of mental states (Gallagher 2011, 294). In visual perception, it is our *gazes* that are coordinated, and a successful tracking of the co-attended objects will typically necessitate the effecting of certain movements on the part of the co-agents, even if only in the form of eye movements (Spivey and Huette 2014). Very generally, the point is that the type of 'coordination required for joint attention is the intercorporeal coordination of interaction rather than a psychological coordination of propositional attitudes' (Gallagher 2020, 109). The coordination involved in joint attention is normally related to motor actions, and whether or not the relevant movements should be understood as the expressions of mental states is a further question.

Third, the perceived body of the other co-agent is perceived as the bearer of certain emotions, which translate into affects on my part. As an illustration, when someone directs their gaze towards an object, it not only signals their current interest in it; their facial expression, which might convey specific emotions, can also influence how I begin to feel about that object. It can either encourage or discourage me from taking further action towards that object (Bayliss, Paul, et al., 2006; Becchio, Bertone, and Castiello 2008; Gallagher 2011, 294, 2020, 106f.). In short, in joint attentional phenomena, *affectivity* matters because it impacts agency.

Fourth, agents in a situation of joint attention undergo a transformation of their perceptual skills. From the perspective defended in this book, this is the most important point, and psychologists have regularly highlighted it too. By creating a perceptual common ground (Tomasello and Carpenter 2007), joint attention allows for agents acting together to 'adjust what they do in response to relevant changes in the situation' (Pacherie 2018, 167). Otherwise put, the presence of others *alters the perceived environment in modifying the horizon of practical possibilities.* This transformation, which we briefly touched upon earlier by having recourse to the notion of social affordances, is significant, and it lends itself to the kind of normative analysis I have been promoting throughout the book: as it opens new avenues of exploration and generates new possibilities of action, the presence of co-attenders *enriches* our perceptual world.

In the context of social affordances, the transformation and enrichment of experience can occur in various ways (the list isn't exhaustive). First and foremost, it can expand the range of perceptual possibilities. Social affordances introduce new possibilities for perception beyond the our individual skills by incorporating social cues, gestures, facial expressions, and other communicative signals. These cues provide additional layers of information that enhance our perceptual grasp of the environment and the intentions and meanings of others therein. Second, social affordances can also shape how we interpret and make sense of our perceptual experiences insofar as they provide us with shared frameworks and conventions that guide our perception and understanding of the world. These interpretive frameworks allow us to assign meaning, relevance, and significance to objects, events, and situations *as shared*, thus influencing our perceptual judgment about the perceptual scene. Finally, shared or social affordances can imbue the perceptual world with additional emotional and affective significance. Social interactions, gestures, and facial expressions convey emotional states, intentions, and social cues that impact our emotional responses and subjective experiences. By engaging with social affordances, our perceptual world incorporates a more complex social and affective dimension, thus enriching our experience of our overall perceptual situation in that sense too.

What makes social affordances interesting from the phenomenological perspective that I espouse is not only that they make our perceptual world more complex and meaningful but also that these social affordances are experienced or lived through (*erlebt*) by co-perceivers in a way that makes them feel 'pulled' toward the same perceived cue, prompting them to respond to it together in a coordinated manner. In *The Primacy of Perception*, Merleau-Ponty makes just this point in the following passage:

> If a friend and I are standing before a landscape, and if I attempt to show my friend something which I see and which he does not yet see, we cannot

account for the situation by saying that I see something in my own world and that I attempt, by sending verbal messages, to give rise to an analogous perception in the world of my friend. There are not two numerically distinct worlds plus a mediating language which alone would bring us together. *There is*—and I know it very well if I become impatient with him—*a kind of demand that what I see be seen by him also*. And at the same time this communication is *required by the very thing which I am looking at*, by the reflections of sunlight upon it, by its colour, by its sensible evidence. *The thing imposes itself not as true for every intellect, but as real for every subject who is standing where I am*. (1964a, 17; italics are mine)

Just as in individual perception, Merleau-Ponty characterizes the perceptual field shared by the two friends as soliciting *them*, viz. as containing some kind of demand to which *they* have to respond. Since perception is enacted in a social world where others are always co-present, the 'thing that I am looking at' does not only speak to *me*: it 'imposes itself' for 'every subject who is standing where I am'. True, we don't have to, and usually don't, respond to worldly solicitations together, even when others are co-present. A group of individuals could be looking at the Eiffel Tower without responding to it in the relevant sense. For there to be 'shared perception', we need more than simultaneity and 'co-presence' of experiencers, even if they are sparked by the same scene. What is lacking in that case is joint coordinated *response*. Here, we have a model to lean on: Merleau-Ponty's characterization of perceptual experience in terms of questions and answers, or solicitations and responses (2012, 70, 140, 222, 323), applies *mutatis mutandis* in social contexts. It is through the ways we enact our response (or fail to do so) that perception proves to be shared (or not). This might well be just implicit in the passage quoted above (for Merleau-Ponty appears to simply point out that what I see demands to be seen by the other), but it is certainly in the spirit of his view. As I see it, just therein lies the fulfilment of the coalescence condition.

This is because, when individuals engage in joint attention or shared perception, they are attuned to the same cues or objects in the environment, and this shared focus influences their actions and responses. This can occur in several ways. We can speak of attentional alignment: co-perceivers experiencing social affordances are often drawn to the same objects of attention (e.g. that graffiti on the stairs of the tower). The resulting alignment of attention, where individuals direct their focus to a shared target, is a response to their being 'pulled' toward the same point of interest.

When co-perceivers share attention and perceive social affordances not merely in parallel but together, there is thus a coordinated responsiveness in their actions. In addition to their turning toward the object of attention, they may engage in joint actions (e.g. talk about it, take turns to take pictures, etc.) and synchronize their movements or responses based on their shared understanding of the social context. This coordination reflects a mutual attunement and responsiveness to the perceived cues, which, in turn, facilitates social interaction, collaboration, and mutual influence between co-perceivers (e.g. finding the best point of view for the photo). As they engage in shared perception and respond to the same cues, their actions and behaviours mutually shape and influence one another and contribute to strengthen their respective sense of shared agency.

In *The Structure of Behaviour*, Merleau-Ponty is more explicit on this last point. In his phenomenological analysis of football, to which we are now turning, he emphasizes the role of the perceivers' bodies therein, contending that the pull that the perceptual world exercises on them in episodes of shared perceptions is felt *at the level of the body schema*. Precisely, his contention is that shared perceptions induce the co-perceivers to deploy their perceptual skills in coordinated ways in response to the perceived scene. Therein lies the normative moment in episodes of shared perceptions.

7.1.2. Embodied Coordination and Norm-following in Athletic Performances

The practice of a team sport like football, which involves attentional patterns (Campbell 2005, 245), can be submitted to a similar analysis insofar as it also runs on a pre-reflective form of norm-following with comparable forms of embodied agency.

But not always, or not completely. To some extent, it is true that the jointness of team sport performances rests on *explicit coordination* between the players, that is, on intentional communication (whether through spoken language, gestures, or strategies development, etc.) between the members of the team in view of a shared goal (say, winning the game). To achieve their common objective, tactics are elaborated, game plans are developed, some specific plays are rehearsed, and the opposing team's strategies are carefully studied and analysed in video sessions, now with support of advanced statistics, etc. During the game, all kinds of cues are often spontaneously, yet deliberately, communicated between the players, or between the coach and the players. When acted upon, these instructions certainly have a top-down influence on the players' actions, whose performance should be understood as forms of commitment in Gilbert's sense. The player visually catches sight of her coach's hand gesture as a sign to watch this or that player more closely, and he expresses his commitment to the team by doing exactly this. Correspondingly, the type of coordinated interaction that emerges therefrom is, at least to a certain degree, the result of deliberate attitudes and can be evaluated in terms of instrumental rationality. Aspects of the players' behaviours should be understood as explicit forms of norm-following, where players are reflectively conscious that they are complying with instructions. As a result, the kind of self-conscious activity at work need not be embodied in the relevant sense either: players may rely on memory, prior knowledge, or other forms of reflective conscious activities.

In some situations, sport performances may even rely on *subconscious* forms of coordination and attunement. For coordinated interaction, no conscious joint attention need be involved; in music performance, for instance, 'coordination can take place even in the absence of conscious perceptual contact' (Høffding 2018, 231). It might run on entrainment or motor-resonance.[12] As subconscious, these processes are said to 'circumvent a conscious sense of being or belonging to a group, that is any sense of we-agency'. This means that, in music performance at least but possibly in sport performances too, 'joint action can proceed without any sense of jointness' (Høffding 2018, 232). Since they are not, even as subconscious, completely decoupled from perception, these mechanisms still exert a powerful normative pressure on the unfolding of experience, for they are driven by an intrinsic teleology: they are geared towards enhanced synchronization of behaviours.

---

[12] Pacherie (2014, 31) explains that 'Entrainment is a process whereby two people involuntarily synchronize their behaviour, even in the absence of direct mechanical coupling. Thus, two people sitting next to each other in rocking chairs will unconsciously synchronize their rocking frequency and do so even when they have chairs with different eigenfrequencies (Richardson et al. 2007b). Similarly, two individuals who are asked to tap at a comfortable tempo strongly tend to spontaneously fall into synchrony (Oullier et al. 2008).' Similarly, motor simulation 'can induce emergent coordination in perception-action matching...such that the perception of an action leads to the activation of a corresponding action representation in the observer's action system', thereby facilitating coordination and synchronization. As should become clearer in what follows, these forms of coordinated interactions are nonetheless not as flexible or adaptive as they are when agents pre-reflectively keep track of their own ongoing activity. For this reason, subconscious mechanisms of attunement lack what I called earlier in the book 'normative sensibility'.

While these two forms of coordination (namely, explicit and subconscious coordination) certainly belong to the practice of team sports, athletes, when performing *together*, typically rely on *perceptual* mechanisms to fulfil them. It is the players' perception of certain configurations that motivate them to engage in certain forms of coordinated action. In his analysis of the football field in the *Structure of Behaviour*, Merleau-Ponty touches upon just this issue in the following terms:

> For the player in action the football field... is pervaded with lines of force (the 'side lines'; those which demarcate the 'penalty area') and articulated in sectors (for example, the 'openings' between the adversaries) which call for a certain mode of action and which initiate and guide the action as if the player were unaware of it.... Each maneuver undertaken by the player modifies the character of the field and establishes in it new lines of force in which the action in turn unfolds and is accomplished, again altering the phenomenal field. (1963, 168–9; translation amended)

The relevant feature of this passage is the correlation that Merleau-Ponty describes between the bodily dispositions of the players and the steadily shifting configuration of the field. The actions of each individual player are dictated by the movements of the team, and the position of their teammates on the field. 'Thus, the playing field and the football team together form a procedural field that induces the movements, directions, and dynamics of the players' (Fuchs 2017b, 342).

This whole is structured by norms that are reflected in the agency of the team. First, these norms are embodied by the players themselves, who have developed a set of team or group habits adapted to the nature of the game. In a good, well-trained team, the players aptly respond to the positional play of their teammates by enacting a coordinated response: they recognize patterns of play, see opportunities, and act in response by effecting certain concordant moves. When players keep track of their teammates' actions with an eye on their common goal, 'a form of normativity' governs their movements: for instance, the 'player does not only perceive his teammate's intention of kicking the ball, but can perceive his kick as unsuitable for shooting at the goal' (Fuchs 2017b, 342). That's why he decides to pass the ball. In acting in this way, the player displays sensitivity for the norms governing the situation: he inserts his own action in a web of meaningful experiences that he shares with his teammates. Of course, his action may fail; he may not be able to execute the right play. To this extent, he might not optimize the performance of the team. But perceiving together does not require this. Perceiving together here implies the recognition of the same opportunities as his teammates and acting upon them in ways that concord with his teammates' actions. When this condition is fulfilled, a perceptual We *in actu* emerges, and the coalescence condition is fulfilled.

The situation is nevertheless slightly more complex. Since 'the player's intentions and actions are shaped by the physical environment and by the nature of the game he is playing' (Gallagher 2020, 110), the normativity involved in playing football is not reducible to bodily skills or habits. As Sepulveda (2023) remarks, 'The normative background is also sedimented in anchorage points of the field that football players use as points of orientation' (152). Whether you play attack or defence, 'the field [*itself*] appears as oriented, that is, as structured with positive and negative forces' (152) that are felt by the players, who steadily adjust their strategy in response. Otherwise put, the mutual attunement of the players does not hinge on their physical skills and dispositions alone; their interactions are also partly determined by the normative pull that the field exercises on the players. Together, my bodily actions enter into a dialectic relation with the field. This is how Merleau-Ponty explains the situation: '[t]he field itself is not given to him [the player], but present as the immanent term of his practical intentions; the player becomes one with it [*fait corps avec lui*] and feels the direction of the goal, for example just as immediately as the vertical and horizontal planes of his own body' (1963, 168).

The way football players respond to perceived demands and opportunities illustrates both the nature of the game, which is a norm or rule-following practice, and the kind of normative patterns that guide their practical intentions as team players. Even if they have been learned or trained, these patterns have, through repetition, been incorporated by the individual players, who can deploy them when the corresponding affordances are perceived. These bodily skills don't belong to the collective in the strict sense (for this would entail failing to meet the plurality condition), but there is a sense in which one can say that individual agency is predicated on some form of participation in this 'collective body memory' (Fuchs 2017b, 333ff.), which players have individually contributed to establish in the first place through teamwork and collective training. As such, these skills exert a bottom-up effect on the agency of the team.

One last point before concluding this section. Since the configurations on the field are constantly evolving, the 'perceptual We' that I have been describing here is neither permanent, nor does it concern the same players all the time. It is, rather, ephemeral, volatile, and transient: it comes and goes following the dynamic transformation of the patterns of play. As such, it should neither be confused with the 'We' formed by the players of each respective team nor the 'We' formed by the players of both teams. The former constitutes a much more pervasive entity that may rely on a long historical narrative, symbols, and rituals, all of which powerfully contributing to the sense of their belonging to the team. Together, all the players on the field constitute another unit: it, too, is a 'perceptual We' insofar as the players also perceive together the same relevant things (the field, the ball, etc.), act together in a largely coordinated (albeit antagonistic) way (they all play the game), and are subjected to the same objective forces (e.g. the rules, the duration of the game, the weather, etc.). These 'We' have their own timescale and their own norms, and the players participate in more than one such unit at the same time, which can make the situation quite complex. In the next section, I will develop some of these ideas further by showing very concretely how both joint attention and joint action coordination depend on a shared sense of time.

7.2. Interbodily Temporality

In Chapter 6 the role of the other's body-temporal dynamics—its 'kinetic signature'—in empathy has been highlighted. To recall: I perceive the other as another time-constituting subject, that is, as the bearer of a specifically human temporal stream insofar as her movements, behaviours, and expressions lastingly display a meaningful unity and harmony in style. When these conditions are met, the other—'*der Mitgegenwärtige*' (Husserl 1973c, 336)—is experienced as an alter ego, that is, as another subject that can experience me and with whom I can interact and collaborate.

Husserl thinks that it is precisely through such collaborative acts of socialization involving *communicative* interaction and reciprocity—address and uptake—that something like a 'We' arises (1973c, 471–3). This need not be very sophisticated: a simple gesture such as pointing at an object can suffice to build a bridge to the other and turn an individual experience into a shared one. As Zahavi (2019b, 254) explains, 'If successful, his attention will shift from my expression to the intended object. In this way, my intention is realized in him', or achieved through him. In the previous section, I started to explain how this works in the realm of perception. Like higher-order forms of socio-communicative acts (discussions, collective decision-making, etc.), shared perceptions 'involve reciprocity (*Wechselbeziehung*) and lead to a we-synthesis if our intentions interlock in the requisite way (*Willensverflechtung*)' (254).[13] In the specific case of shared perceptions, I have suggested in the previous section that this coincidence or interlocking (*Deckung*)—which should not be confused with a fusion (*Verschmelzung*)— does not require any kind of joint commitments à la Gilbert but, rather, typically manifests itself in the kind of body responsiveness displayed by the co-experiencers. While shared perceptions may *not require* a transformation of experience that impacts our sense of agency in the way I have described it, it often does. In this section, I want to draw attention to another, this time truly necessary, dimension of this notion of shared perceptual responsiveness—namely time. *Shared perceptions require a shared sense of time.*

Husserl provides a promising starting point to reflect on this as he contends that when I interact with the other, my own streaming present comes to overlap or coincide with hers, whose temporal horizon I now share (Husserl 1973c, 343).[14] As a result, something like a shared temporal horizon is established. This is an important insight, for it intimates that the 'perceptual We' has its own temporal signature. When my own streaming present coincides with the other's, a shared present (*gemeinsame Gegenwart*) is constituted:

He acts in 'my present', and I am for him in his present. We are not only in the same thingly context (*Dingzusammenhang*) or in the same 'place', rather we are in the 'shared' present, in the common present place, in the intentionally common surrounding world. We are its subjects and as 'we'

---

[13] Some (e.g. Schmid 2009; Schweikard and Schmid 2020) argue that communication is itself an instance of collective intentionality. From this perspective, Husserl's account leads to an infinite regress insofar as the emergence of a We *presupposes* communication instead of establishing it. On Schmid's account, pre-reflective self-awareness is thought to solve just this problem and explain how the kinds of communicative interactions that seem required in collective activities are possible in the first place. For Schmid, we *already* experience our mental lives as shared with others, and so communicating with them operates on the basis of this shared experiential ground. Here is not the place to develop a critical assessment of this view, but it has been criticized on various grounds (Zahavi 2018), including for being overly intellectualist, not embodied enough (e.g. Knudsen 2021; Walsh 2020).

[14] Here's a quote that captures well his insight: 'Im aktuellen Vollzug einer Einfühlung "deckt" sich so meine urmodale strömende Gegenwart, mein urmodales Ich-bin, dessen Jetzt-Gegenwärtigsein Sein aus der urpräsentierenden Zeitigung ist (das im engsten und eigentlichsten Sinne präsent- (jetzt-) seiende Ich), mit der urmodalen Gegenwart des Anderen, die aber für mich nicht urmodale, sondern appräsentierte ist; und von da aus ergreift die Deckung die beiderseitigen Horizonte' (Husserl 1973c, 343).

are mutually constituted: for one another we are here, each one as ego, the other as other. The 'we together' is given to me in the form 'I and he', however for him it is given in the form, which I express 'he and I' but he expresses 'I and he'. (Husserl 1973b, 212)[15]

Through communicative interaction (words, gestures, glances, or behaviour), co-perceivers may come to form a 'We' with its own (shared) temporality. Again, if it is to respect the plurality condition, this shared present cannot amount to a merger or fusion of our streams of consciousness. Not one but two (or more) separate streams of consciousness co-constitute the 'perceptual We'. It is, as one might say, a 'peculiar kind of unity in conflict or coincidence in difference' (Zahavi 2001, 68), since the necessary distinctiveness of the individuals' streams is preserved (Husserl 1973c, 334). My contention is that *this shared time is a necessary condition of possibility for sharing perceptual experiences*. Perceiving together presupposes a shared sense of time, or a shared consciousness of time, because shared perceptual responsiveness requires timely collaboration and partnership. Of course, the relevant experience of time is not objective time but phenomenological time, viz. inner time-consciousness. It is the shared pre-reflective consciousness of time that matters, and which makes it possible to meet the requirement of the coalescence condition. Through cooperation, the consciousness of the temporality that belongs to the flow of lived experience is shared by the parties involved, who come together and form a We, a 'perceptual We'.

This idea is not as complex as it might seem. Much as in individual experiences, the temporality of shared actions or perception is distributed between the retentional, impressional, and protentional contents of experience. What changes in joint contexts is that this structure is now shared and distributed across the members of the group. As Pokropski (2015) justly describes, 'Each subject retains and anticipates one's own as well as the other's actions' (907), thereby enabling coordination and synchronization. That's how we can avoid bumping each other when our paths cross on the stairs of the tower, or how I can quickly take pictures of my family, who

---

[15] The translation is from Pokropski (2015). Here's the original text: 'Er handelt "in meiner Gegenwart", und ich bin für ihn in seiner Gegenwart. Wir sind nicht bloß überhaupt im demselben Dingzusammenhang, an demselben "Orte", sondern wir sind in einer "gemeinsamen" Gegenwart, in einem aktuell gemeinsamen Ort, einer bewusstseinsmässig gemeinsamen Umwelt, wir sind ihre Subjekte und sind als "wir" miteinander konstituiert: und füreinander sind wir da, jeder als ego, der Andere als Anderer. Das "wir beide" ist mir gegeben in der Form "ich und er" und für ihn gegeben in der gegeben Form, die ich ausdrücke als "er und ich", die er aber ausdrückt als "ich und er".'

were alert to the same cues, between two groups of passers-by who wait to do just the same. Shared time allows for the possibility of successful cooperation because perceptual agents are dynamically coupled to one another. In shared perceptual acts, our own bodily self-awareness and the perception of the temporal unfolding of the other's intention continuously trigger adjustments on our part with a view on our common goal or intention, whose attainment is thereby facilitated. Gallagher (2016) addresses just this point by using a normative vocabulary fully in line with mine: 'we understand others through embodied anticipatory processes that are either fulfilled or quickly corrected, or that in some cases lead to a breakdown in the interaction that would then need to be restored' (168).

In the context of sports, a shared perception refers to the ability of players to develop a collective understanding and awareness of the game, including the movements, strategies, and intentions of their teammates and opponents. In football, players rely on their ability to perceive and interpret the actions and positions of others on the field. They need to anticipate and understand the intentions and movements of their teammates in order to coordinate their actions effectively. Additionally, they must be able to assess the actions and positioning of opposing players to make strategic decisions. This shared perception is crucial for successful teamwork, as it allows players to synchronize their movements, pass the ball accurately, create scoring opportunities, and defend against the opposing team effectively. It enables players to make split-second decisions based on their understanding of the overall situation and the actions of those around them. Without shared perceptions, the coordination and cohesion necessary for a successful football team would be significantly compromised.

To take a very concrete example: while playing football, I may start to run faster because I see an opening and I anticipate a pass from you. You, in turn, perceive me as having already started my run and adjust the pace of your pass accordingly. The success of our action—which includes, without being restricted to, perceptual processes—rests on a commonly shared temporality. My practical sense for the game that I display in making this run not only concerns me but also bears witness to my 'sense for the potentialities of the team's play' (Fuchs 2017b, 342). And so must your action be understood: like mine, your pass shows your sensibility for the perceived practical possibilities that the play on the field affords. Importantly, this sensibility is future-oriented and includes what Fuchs calls a 'shared bodily protentionality' (2017b). As Fuchs reminds us, Bourdieu (1990) nicely described the situation in the following manner:

A player who is involved and caught up in the game, adjusts not to what he sees but to what he fore-sees, sees in advance in the directly perceived present; he passes the ball not to the spot where his team-mate is but to the spot he will reach... a moment later, anticipating the anticipations of the others.... The "feel" for the game is the sense for the imminent future of the game, the sense of the direction of the history of the game that gives the game its sense. (81–2)

In collective sport experiences like football, the quality of the coordination of our actions depends strongly on the accuracy of our prospective evaluations. This plays out simultaneously on three fronts. Each player must assess her own situation in relation to both her teammates' action and the intention of both teams on the field. The situation is complex, but the point is relatively simple: if we, as a team, are to progress toward our shared goal (say, winning the game), we need to continuously assess whether we, as a collective, are doing things right and make strategic and positional adjustments in response. This ongoing process of self-correction and adjustment is a collective achievement, but—and here's how the plurality condition is met—it is acted out individually by the players, who strongly rely on bodily self-awareness to assess their performance (cf. Section 3.4). This is not a solipsistic achievement, however; each player's self-assessment is informed by perceived cues in the action and behaviour of both their teammates and their opponents, who they expect to simultaneously make a similar self-evaluation (self-awareness condition). This is teamwork. As Pacherie (2014) aptly points out, 'the strength of the sense of agency one may experience for a joint action is a function of the accuracy not just of self-predictions but also of other-predictions and joint predictions and that this accuracy may vary according to the type of action and the role one plays in a joint action' (42). The coalescence condition can only be met, and a plural subject emerge, if the sense of agency of the team is correlated with the adequacy of these individual prospective evaluations.

Despite all the differences between the two phenomena, joint attention does not significantly differ from sport performances with respect to the importance of the question of time, whose sharedness it equally presupposes. Be it in its passive (viz. stimulus-driven) or active (viz. deliberate) mode, attention is a temporally extended activity, with a horizon of the before and after. Attending is an activity that is always already in progress when something first gets noticed. This is true of both active and passive ways of attending. In its passive mode, attention is characterized by an essential *Nachträglichkeit* towards that which attracts our gazes and to which we respond by turning our attention to it. As active (or deliberate), the attended object is always already given in the contextual background of perception, from which it detaches itself to become the focal point. Either way—and this is what matters here—the target must be given in the temporal horizon already in the orientation phase initiating an attentive movement, otherwise it could not be (jointly) attended at all.

To attend to an object or an event not just simultaneously but *together*, the co-attenders must share a sense of time. This is because both co-attenders face the same task here: they must synchronize their bodily rhythms both with the co-attended object and with each other. If the object is fixed, the attentive stream needs to focus correspondingly, whereas if the object is in motion, the co-attenders must keep track of each other while following the object's trajectory across its various manifestations. Here too, it is the protentional dimension of attentional consciousness that is pulling the cart. In all this, the constitutive connection between perception and normativity shines through, because we can readily see that, just as in an individual case, shared perceptions *do not* and *cannot* rest on the correspondence between our mental states, which cannot be accessed and lived through by the other (cf. Section 6.2). But 'in [the other's] conduct', that is 'in the manner in which the other deals with the world,' I can 'discover his consciousness' (117), Merleau-Ponty (1964a) rightly affirms. Through his conduct, I can see whether we are perceiving together or not, viz. I can see his experience overlapping with mine or not. The standard of success of shared perceptions is there, in the open.

One can look at the situation from another, complementary angle. Shared time is a necessary requirement for shared perception because it allows the individual body schemas to coalesce and form a cohesive whole. Some scientists have called this the Joint Body Schema Effect (Soliman and Glenberg 2014) and suggested that when individuals engage in synchronous and coordinated movements with another person, their body schemas become integrated or linked. This means that the boundaries between each perceiver's body can become blurred or less distinct during joint actions, leading to a sense of shared agency. The Joint Body Schema Effect has been demonstrated in various studies, using tasks such as synchronized movements, joint reaching, or shared tool use. The findings suggest that when individuals engage in coordinated actions with others, their perception of their own body can lead to an altered sense of self and a shared awareness (or representation) of their body. While research on the Joint Body Schema Effect is still relatively new and limited, it is powerfully at work in sport performances. In close coordination, players adapt their own body schemas to incorporate aspects of the partner in the service of effective coordination. They are, in other words, using that person's body as a tool, as it were, thereby making it possible for individuals to act as a (differentiated) unit.

In the phenomenological tradition, a similar idea can be traced back to Merleau-Ponty's notion of 'intercorporeality.' Although it is customary to relate the emergence of this concept to Merleau-Ponty's later works, *The Visible and the Invisible* (1968) and his lecture course on *Child Psychology and Pedagogy* (2010) in particular, it was already at work in the *Phenomenology of Perception*:

> I experience my body as the power for certain behaviours and for a certain world, and I am only given to myself as a certain hold upon the world. Now, it is precisely my body that perceives the other's body and finds there something of a miraculous extension of its own intentions, a familiar manner of handling the world. Henceforth, *just as the parts of my body together form a system, the other's body and my own are a single whole, two sides of a single phenomenon*, and the anonymous existence, of which my body is continuously the trace, henceforth inhabits these two bodies simultaneously. (2012, 370; my emphasis)

Or elsewhere in the same book:

> There is, between... [my] phenomenal body, and the other person's phenomenal body such as I see it from the outside, an internal relation that makes the other person appear as the completion of the system. (2012, 368)

Just as the body in individual experience steadily "moves toward its equilibrium" (2012, 155) by steadily updating proprioceptive and kinaesthetic signals, thereby transforming or extending its own schematic structure (see Section 3.3), in shared experience, groups are geared toward a similar state of balance, and individual members make comparable kinds of adjustments. "Our systems enter into a coupling that advances toward a completion"; it is as if "the two systems form a new system" (Gallagher 2016, 169) with a unified sense of time.[16] When successful, the mechanisms governing the

---

[16] Intercorporeality is not just an embodied structure; it is an overarching sphere of experience with an affective and emotional component that I won't explore here but that Høffding (2018) and Salice, Høffding, and Gallagher (2019) have analysed in the context of musical interaction under the label 'interkinesthetic affectivity'. They see therein the strongest possible sense of we-agency.

individuals' bodily experiences are interlocked in a way that the agents form a unified whole beyond the sum of their parts. This is what Merleau-Ponty describes when he writes, focusing on the bodily dynamics that obtains between him and his co-perceiver, that he finds in the other body a "miraculous prolongation of [his] own intentions, a familiar way of dealing with the world" (Merleau-Ponty 2012, 370). Importantly, this does not mean that the individuals' streams of consciousness merge or become one. If this were the case, there would be nothing to share as everything would already be experienced by the whole. The idea is, rather, that the individual bodies keep their ontological independence, but they participate in one intentional structure, which covers both the common surrounding environment and their bodies.

A thorough discussion of the ontology underlying Merleau-Ponty's account of intercorporeality is beyond the scope of this chapter, but there's one key aspect that needs to be emphasized before concluding. The kind of dynamical coupling that Merleau-Ponty analyses under the name 'intercorporeality' leads to the development of habitual patterns that come to normatively govern the self–other unit in a way that is remarkably similar to the way individual perception works. This overarching system, 'understood as the interlocking of behaviour' (Walsh 2020, 16), forms a unified yet differentiated whole—a 'We'—because the individuals that constitute it share the same environment and are indexed to the same situation, to which they respond in coordinated ways. In short, intercorporeality, which a team sport like football embodies, emerges through shared responsive practices that follow normative patterns like those outlined throughout the chapter. Again, the 'We' that is generated therefrom is fragile or transitory. Our sense of belonging to the game or to our team can be very stable, but the steadily changing dynamic of forces prevailing in the system–environment relation make it much more difficult to maintain lastingly a shared experience like a perception. The 'perceptual We' comes and goes as the game transforms itself, and so must constantly be renewed; but every now and then it comes about, and its phenomenological unity lies nowhere else but in the way that its members are jointly responsive to shared perceived cues.

At this point, it should be clear that shared perceptual responsiveness can both optimize and enhance the coherence of our experiences. When individuals engage in shared perceptual practices, they pool their perceptual resources and perspectives, thanks to which the co-perceivers can access a broader range of information about the environment. This is what the notion of social affordances illustrates, for their perception requires a social or collaborative context in which others are essential. Each individual perceiver may bring unique skills or expertise, but, when combined, they provide a more comprehensive and accurate understanding of the situation, disclosing affordances that would otherwise remain invisible. In a sport like football, this will typically enhance the overall performance of the team because coordinated responses involve integrating multiple perspectives or viewpoints, which in turn leads to a wider range of perceived opportunities or affordances beyond their individual limitations. In that sense, it improves perception. Shared perceptual responsiveness also promotes coherence. When co-perceivers respond together to the same perceived cues or affordances, their actions and interpretations align and reinforce each other, and thus contribute to an enhanced sense of coherence in their play, a sense of practical familiarity that facilitates a range of actions.

7.3. Conclusion

This chapter has sketched out a phenomenological analysis of the phenomenology of shared perception and proposed a way to satisfy the three conditions that this 'sharing' is standardly taken to rely on. In brief, I have argued for three claims, which echo the three conditions we started with:

1) *Shared perceptual responsiveness* allows us to fulfil the *coalescence condition*, which requires that a plurality of agents form a collective. To come back to Gilbert, with whom we started our inquiry, sharing a perception does not require a joint commitment or the recognition of some responsibilities and obligations vis-à-vis our co-perceiver. If shared perception is nevertheless still a normative phenomenon, it is because the required sharedness lies in our normatively governed response to what the perceived field affords.
2) While the *awareness condition* stipulates that shared action requires that the involved agents are aware of what they are doing, I have provided reasons for thinking that shared perceptual experiences run on *pre-reflective bodily self-awareness*. Going against a certain tendency in the literature in social ontology to locate the openness or mutual manifestation of shared phenomena in reflective self-consciousness (e.g. recursive mind reading), I have argued that joint or shared perception relies first and foremost on our *pre*-reflective awareness of space and time.

3) Finally, shared perceptions meet the *plurality condition*, which requires multiple ontologically different agents, for in shared perceptions there are still two (or more) distinct activities, viz. two (or more) different perceptual streams shared in the awareness of being jointly experienced. In the account that I defend, however harmonized or synchronized the bodily response of co-perceivers may be, their ontological identity never dissolves but is, rather, transformed by the presence of the other.

Given its importance, I'll conclude by elaborating my reflection on the coalescence condition a little further. Throughout the chapter, I have suggested that the overarching intentional structure—of solicitations and response, or question and answer—that emerges from the self–world relation in shared perception is normative. Whereas Gilbert locates the normative moment in the relation holding between the agents, who would be jointly committed to one another, I have argued that, in the case of shared perceptions, the relevant norms lie not between the perceivers themselves but between the co-perceivers, on the one hand, and the perceived environment (objects, cues, affordances, etc.), on the other. With the concept of *shared perceptual responsiveness*, I have contended that perceptions are properly shared only if the co-perceivers' responses follow shared normative patterns. I have illustrated this idea by dwelling on two different perceptual phenomena, namely joint attention and athletic performances. Both types of activities are norm-governed in the sense that they are both, in different ways and to varying degrees, rule-following practices that command, if they are to be successful, certain specific types of bodily responses on the part of the agents. The basic idea is that when perception is shared, our experience of objects, people, and events undergoes a qualitative alteration and transforms the perceptual field, to which we respond by effecting certain moves and not others. In Section 7.1 I sought to specify what this means by showing how shared perceptual experiences open new possibilities of action and interaction that co-perceivers exploit in response. The game of football illustrates this compellingly, but it's not unique to football; joint attentional phenomena can be described along similar lines, and so can most shared perceptual practices (e.g. looking at the Eiffel Tower together). In Section 7.2 it has been argued that the change that occurs at the body-schematic level is itself enabled by a change at the level of time-consciousness: when an experience is properly shared, the streams of consciousness of the co-experiencers overlap and share a common dynamic temporal structure, thanks to which experiencers can be jointly responsive to commonly perceived cues.[17]

In my analyses of the role of bodily coordination in joint attentional phenomena and sport performances, I have distinguished between two families of normative alignment of individual experiences: top-down factors, such as shared plans, shared intentions, and shared goals, and, more importantly, bottom-up processes of synchronization and coordination, which are embodied. Although conceptually distinct, both top-down and bottom-up factors are standardly intertwined in experience (Salmela 2012). Whereas our long-term goal is often planned, willed, and linguistically conveyed (be it in the form of instructions or studied tactics, etc.), its successful realization depends on how we cope with the situation and the steadily changing field of forces. Both types of norm have a structural effect on our experience of space, time, and agency, just not in the same way.

Interestingly, some of the norms that regulate shared perceptions are not different than the norms governing individual experience. We find again both concordance, which here takes the form of coordinated actions or synchronized movements between the co-perceivers, and optimality, which provides direction to our shared perceptual experiences. Nevertheless, even if the norms prevalent in shared perceptions do not fundamentally differ from those prevailing in individual experiences, the chapter has shown that there is still what we could call a 'proprietary phenomenology' of shared perceptual experiences, that is, a phenomenology that is *specific* of shared perceptions. Shared perceptions have phenomenal properties that are *irreducible* to what any individual agents can experience on their own insofar as perceiving together involves *shared* responsiveness, something which no individual can produce on their own. Drawing the full consequences of this insight is beyond the scope of this book, but the starting point of the next one might be just here.

Phenomenology and the Norms of Perception. Maxime Doyon, Oxford University Press. © Maxime Doyon 2024.
DOI: 10.1093/9780191993527.003.0007

---

[17] Thomas Fuchs (2018) calls this 'interbodily resonance', which he defines in the following manner: 'Bodily expressed emotions of one subject affect the bodily (interoceptive and proprioceptive) experience of the other and vice versa. Generally speaking, this mode of intersubjective temporality is i) pre-phenomenal, as it precedes the emergence of temporal objects and shapes the temporal form in which they appear; ii) interbodily, as it emerges as a result of "resonance" between my and the other's body; iii) polyrhythmical, as it is based on rhythmical patterns experienced and expressed; and iv) lived, as it is an experience of duration as felt' (xx).

References

Abath, A. J. (2017), 'Merleau-Ponty and the Problem of Synaesthesia', in O. Deroy (ed.), *Sensory Blending: On Synaesthesia and Related Phenomena* (Oxford: Oxford University Press), 151–65.
Adorno, T. W. (1974), *Minima Moralia: Reflections from Damaged Life*, Translated by Jephcott, (London: Verso).
Ainbinder, B. (2018), 'Transcendental Experience', in A. Cimino and C. Leijenhorst (eds.), *Phenomenology and Experience* (Leiden: Brill), 28–45.
Alcoff, L. M. (1999), 'Towards a phenomenology of racial embodiment', *Radical Philosophy*, 95, 15–26.
Aldea, A. S. (2022), 'The Normativity of Imagination: Its Critical Import', in S. Heinämaa and M. Hartimo (eds.), *Norms, Goals, and Values* (London: Routledge), 157–79.
Aldea, A. S., Carr, D., and Heinämaa, S. (eds.) (2022), 'Introduction', in *Phenomenology as Critique: Why Method Matters* (New York: Routledge), 1–8.
Al-Saji, A. (2010), 'Bodies and sensings: On the uses of Husserlian phenomenology for feminist theory', *Continental Philosophy Review*, 43: 13–37.
Al-Saji, A. (2017), 'Feminist Phenomenology', in A. Garry, S. J. Khader, and A. Stone (eds.), *The Routledge Companion to Feminist Philosophy* (New York, London: Routledge), 143–54.
Alsmith, A., and de Vignemont, F. (2012), 'Embodying the Mind and Representing the Body', *Review of Philosophy and Psychology*, 3/1: 1–13.
Antich, P. (2021), *Motivation and the Primacy of Perception: Merleau-Ponty's Phenomenology of Knowledge* (Athens, OH: Ohio University Press).
Arendt, H. (1944), 'The Jew as Pariah: A Hidden Tradition', *Jewish Social Studies*, 6/2: 99–122.
Arstila, V. (2016), 'Perceptual learning explains two candidates for cognitive penetration', *Erkenntnis*, 81/6: 1151–72.
Ataria, Y., Tanaka, S., and Gallagher, S. (eds.) (2021), *Body Schema and Body Image: New Directions* (Oxford: Oxford University Press).
Austin, J. L. (1962), *Sense and Sensibilia* (Oxford: Oxford University Press).
Ayer, A. J. (1940), *The Foundations of Empirical Knowledge* (Stuttgart: Macmillan).
Bach-y-Rita, P., and Kercel, S. W. (2003), 'Sensory substitution and the human–machine interface', *Trends in Cognitive Sciences*, 7/12: 541–6.
Baker, D. (2018), 'The Varieties of Normativity', in T. McPherson and D. Plunkett (eds.), *The Routledge Handbook of Metaethics* (New York: Routledge), 567–81.
Bayliss, A. P., Paul, M. A., Cannon, P. R., and Tipper, S. P. (2006), 'Gaze cuing and affective judgments of objects: I like what you look at', *Psychonomic Bulletin & Review*, 13/6: 1061–6.
Bayne, T. (2014), 'The Multisensory Nature of Perceptual Consciousness', in D. Bennett and C. Hill (eds.), *Sensory Integration and the Unity of Consciousness* (Cambridge, MA: MIT Press), 15–36.

Bayne, T., and Spence, C. (2015), 'Multisensory Perception', in M. Matthen (ed.), *The Oxford Handbook of Philosophy of Perception* (Oxford: Oxford University Press), 603–20.

Beauvoir, S. (2010), *The Second Sex*. Translated by Constance Bord and Sheila Malovany-Chevallier. London: Vintage Books.

Becchio, C., Bertone, C., and Castiello, U. 2008. 'How the gaze of others influences object processing', *Trends in Cognitive Sciences*, 12/7: 254–8.

Benoist, J. (1997), *Phénoménologie, sémantique, ontologie* (Paris: PUF).

Benoist, J. (2007), 'Un concept normatif de l'intentionnalité?', *Études phénoménologiques*, 23/45–8: 9–36.

Benoist, J. (2008a), 'Fulfilment', in J. P. Gálvez (ed.), *Phenomenology as Grammar* (Frankfurt am Main: Ontos Verlag), 77–96.

Benoist, J. (2008b), 'Sur le concept husserlien de remplissement', in J. Benoist (ed.) *Husserl* (Paris: Éditions du Cerf), 195–222.

Benoist, J. (2011), *Éléments de philosophie réaliste* (Paris: Vrin).

Benoist, J. (2013), *Le bruit du sensible* (Paris: Éditions du Cerf).

Benoist, J. (2016), *Logique du phénomène* (Paris: Éditions Hermann).

Benoist, J. (2017), *L'adresse du réel* (Paris: Vrin).

Benoist, J. (2021), *Toward a Contextual Realism* (Cambridge: Harvard University Press).

Benoist, J. (2022), *Von der Phänomenologie zum Realismus. Die Grenzen des Sinns* (Tübingen: Mohr Siebeck).

Berendzen, J. C. (2023), *Embodied Idealism: Merleau-Ponty's Transcendental Philosophy* (Oxford: Oxford University Press).

Berghofer, P., and Wiltsche, H. A. (2019), 'The Co-Presentational Character of Perception', in C. Limbeck-Lilienau and F. Stadler (eds.), *The Philosophy of Perception: Proceedings of the 40th International Ludwig Wittgenstein Symposium*, (Berlin, Boston: De Gruyter), 302–22.

Blouin, P. S. (2023), 'Husserl's Phenomenalism: A Rejoinder to the Philipse-Zahavi Debate', *Husserl Studies*, 39: 241–51, https://doi.org/10.1007/s10743-023-09328-6.

Botvinick, M., and Cohen, J. (1998), 'Rubber hands "feel" touch that eyes see', *Nature*, 391: 756.

Bourdieu, P. (1990), *The Logic of Practice*. Stanford University Press.

Bower, M. (2020), 'Husserl on hallucination: A conjunctive reading', *Journal of the History of Philosophy*, 58(3): 549–79.

Brandom, R. (1994), *Making It Explicit: Reasoning, Representing and Discursive Commitment* (Cambridge: Harvard University Press).

Bratman, M. (1999), *Faces of Intention: Selected Essays on Intention and Agency* (Cambridge: Cambridge University Press).

Bratman, M. (2014), *Shared Agency: A Planning Theory of Acting Together* (New York: Oxford University Press).

Bredlau, S. (2019), *The Other in Perception: A Phenomenological Account of Our Experience of Other Persons* (New York: SUNY Press).

Brentano, F. (1995), *Psychology from an Empirical Standpoint* (London: Routledge).

Brentano, F. (2009), *The Origin of our Knowledge of Right and Wrong* (London: Routledge).

Briscoe, R. E. (2021), 'Bodily Awareness and Novel Multisensory Features', *Synthese*, 198: 3913–41.

Bruineberg, J. and O. Stone (2024), 'Structuring embodied minds: attention and perceptual agency', *Philosophical Studies* https://doi.org/10.1007/s11098-024-02108-8

Burch, M. (2019), 'Against our Better Judgment', in M. Burch, J. E. Marsh, and I. McMullin (eds.), *Normativity, Meaning, and the Promise of Phenomenology* (London: Routledge), 232–50.

Burch, M., Marsh, J. E., and McMullin, I. (eds.) (2019), *Normativity, Meaning, and the Promise of Phenomenology* (London: Routledge).

Campbell, J. (2005), "Joint Attention and Common Knowledge". In: N. Eilan; C. Hoerl; T. McCormack; J. Roessler (eds.): Joint Attention: Communication and Other Minds: Issues in Philosophy and Psychology. New York: Oxford University Press, 287–297.

Carman, T. (2008), *Merleau-Ponty* (London: Routledge).

Carpenter, M., Nagell, K., Tomasello, M., Butterworth, G., and Moore, C. (1998), 'Social cognition, joint attention, and communicative competence from 9 to 15 months of age', *Monographs of the Society of Research in Child Development*, 63/4: 1–174.

Carr, D. (1986a), 'Cogitamus ergo sumus: The intentionality of the first-person plural', *Monist*, 69/4: 521–33.

Carr, D. (2014), *Experience and History: Phenomenological Perspectives on the Historical World* (Oxford: Oxford University Press).

Carruthers, P. (2000), *Phenomenal Consciousness* (Cambridge: Cambridge University Press).

Carta, E. (2021), 'Husserl on Eidetic Norms', *Husserl Studies*, 37/2: 127–46.

Cerbone, D. (2019), 'Ground, Background, and Rough Ground: Dreyfus, Wittgenstein, and Phenomenology', in M. Burch, J. E. Marsh, and I. McMullin (eds.), *Normativity, Meaning, and the Promise of Phenomenology* (London: Routledge), 62–79.

Cimino, A. (2021), 'Husserl's philosophical estrangement from the conjunctivism-disjunctivism debate', *Phenomenology and the Cognitive Sciences*, 20: 743–79, https://doi.org/10.1007/s11097-020-09683-1.

Clark, A. (2003), *Natural-Born Cyborgs: Minds, Technologies, and the Future of Human Intelligence* (New York: Oxford University Press).

Clark, A. (2015), *Surfing Uncertainty: Prediction, Action, and the Embodied Mind* (Oxford: Oxford University Press).

Cobb-Stevens, R. (1990), *Husserl and Analytic Philosophy* (Dordrecht: Kluwer Academic).

Cole, J. (2016), *Losing Touch: A man without his body* (Oxford: Oxford University Press).

Connolly, K. (2017), 'Perceptual Learning', *The Stanford Encyclopedia of Philosophy* (Summer 2017 Edition), Edward N. Zalta (ed.), <https://plato.stanford.edu/archives/sum2017/entries/perceptual-learning/>

Connolly, K. (2019), *Perceptual Learning. The Flexibility of the Senses* (London: Oxford University Press).

Correll, J. (2014), 'Racial Bias in the Decision to Shoot', *Social and Personality Psychology Compass*, 8/5: 201–13.

Correll, J., Park, B., Judd, C. M., and Wittenbrink, B. (2002), 'The police officer's dilemma: Using ethnicity to disambiguate potentially threatening individuals', *Journal of Personality and Social Psychology*, 83/6: 1314.

Correll, J., Park, B., Judd, C. M., Wittenbrink, B., Sadler, M. S., and Keesee, T. (2007), 'Across the Thin Blue Line: Police Officers and Racial Bias in the Decision to Shoot.' *Journal of Personality and Social Psychology*, 92/6: 1006–23.

Crowell, S. (2013), *Normativity and Phenomenology in Husserl and Heidegger* (Cambridge: Cambridge University Press).

Crowell, S. (2015), 'Why Is Ethics First Philosophy? Levinas in Phenomenological Context', *European Journal of Philosophy*, 23/3: 564–88.

Crowell, S. (2016), 'Second-Person Phenomenology', in T. Szanto and D. Moran (eds.), *Phenomenology of Sociality: Discovering the 'We'* (London: Routledge), 70–89.

Dahlstrom, D. (2007), 'The Intentionality of Passive Experience: Husserl and Contemporary Debate', in *The New Yearbook for Phenomenology and Phenomenological Philosophy*, 7: 1–18.

D'Angelo, D. (2019), 'The Phenomenology of Embodied Attention', *Phenomenology and the Cognitive Sciences*, 19/5: 961–78.

Dastur, F. (1994), 'Perceptual Faith and the Invisible', *Journal of the British Society for Phenomenology*, 25/1: 44–52.

Dastur, F. (1995), *Des mathématiques à l'histoire* (Paris: PUF).

Dastur, F. (2000), 'World, flesh, vision', in F. Evans and L. Lawlor (eds.), *Chiasms: Merleau-Ponty's Notion of Flesh* (New York: State University of New York Press), 23–50.

Davis, T. J., Riley, M. A., Shockley, K., and Cummins-Sebree, S. (2010), 'Perceiving affordances for joint actions', *Perception*, 39/12: 1624–44.

De Boer, B. (2020), 'Experiencing objectified health: turning the body into an object of attention', *Medicine, Health Care and Philosophy*, 23: 401–11, https://link.springer.com/article/10.1007/s11019-020-09949-0.

Depraz, N. (2014), *Attention et vigilance: À la croisée de la phénoménologie et des sciences cognitives* (Paris: PUF).

Dennett, D. C. (1992), 'The self as a center of narrative gravity', in Kessel, F., Cole, P. and Johnson, D. (eds.), *Self and Consciousness: Multiple Perspectives* (Hillsdale, NJ: Erlbaum), 103–15.

Deroy, O. (2014), 'The Unity Assumption and the Many Unities of Consciousness', in D. Bennett and C. Hill (eds.), *Sensory Integration and the Unity of Consciousness* (Cambridge, MA: MIT Press), 105–24.

Deroy, O., Chen, Y., and Spence, C. (2014), 'Multisensory constraints on awareness', *Philosophical Transactions of the Royal Society B*, 369/1641: 1–11.

De Santis, D. (2022), 'The Development of Husserl's Concept of Metaphysics', in H. Jacobs (ed.), *The Husserlian Mind* (London: Routledge), 481–93.

Descartes, R. (1965 [1637]), *Discourse on Method, Optics, Geometry and Meteorology*, trans. Paul J. Olscamp (Indianapolis. Bobbs-Merrill Company).

De Vecchi, F. (2019), 'Eidetics of Empathy: Intersubjectivity, Embodiment and Qualitative Ontology – Rediscovering Edith Stein's Account of Empathy', *Humana Mente*, 12/36: 221–43.

de Vignemont, F. (2014), 'Multimodal unity and multimodal binding', in D. Bennett and C. Hill (eds.), *Sensory Integration and the Unity of Consciousness* (Cambridge, MA: MIT Press), 125–50.

de Vignemont, F. (2020), 'Bodily Awareness', in E. N. Zalta (ed.), *Stanford Encyclopedia of Philosophy*, https://plato.stanford.edu/archives/fall2020/entries/bodily-awareness/.
Doidge, N. (2007), *The Brain That Changes Itself: Stories of Personal Triumph from the Frontiers of Brain Science* (New York: Penguin).
Doyon, M. (2010), *Der transzendentale Anspruch der Dekonstruktion: Zur Erneuerung des Begriffs 'transzedental' bei Derrida* (Würzburg: Ergon).
Doyon, M. (2011), 'Husserl and McDowell on the Role of Concepts in Perception', in B. Hopkins and J. Grummond (eds.), *The New Yearbook for Phenomenology and Phenomenological Philosophy*, Vol. 11 (London: Routledge), 43–76.
Doyon, M. (2014), 'The Transcendental Claim of Deconstruction', in L. Lawlor and D. Zepnep (eds.), *The Blackwell Companion to Derrida* (London: Blackwell), 132–49.
Doyon, M. (2015), 'Perception and Normative Self-Consciousness', in M. Doyon and T. Breyer (eds.), *Normativity in Perception* (London: Palgrave Macmillan).
Doyon, M. (2018), 'Husserl on Perceptual Optimality', *Husserl Studies* 34/2: 171–89.
Doyon, M. (2019), 'Kant and Husserl on the (alleged) role of imagination in perception', in T. Burns, T. Szanto, A. Salice, M. Doyon, and A. Dumont (eds.), *The New Yearbook for Phenomenology and Phenomenological Philosophy*, Vol. 17 (London: Routledge), 180–203.
Doyon, M. (2021), 'La Gestalt d'autrui. Note sur l'étendue de l'influence de la Gestaltpsychologie chez Merleau-Ponty', in *Phänomenologische Forschungen 2021/2*, Special Issue on *The Given* (ed. D. De Santis et al.), 159–78.
Doyon, M. (2022), 'The Normative Turn of Intentionality and its Metaphysical Implications (or why Husserl was neither a disjunctivist nor a conjunctivist)', in H. Jacobs (ed.), *The Husserlian Mind* (London: Routledge), 172–83.
Doyon, M., and Breyer, T. (2015), *Normativity in Perception* (London: Palgrave Macmillan).
Doyon, M., and Wehrle, M. (2020), 'Body', in D. De Santis, B. Hopkins and C. Majolino (eds.), *Routledge Handbook of Phenomenology and Phenomenological Philosophy* (London: Routledge), 123–37.
Dretske, F. (1995), *Naturalizing the mind*. Cambridge, MA: MIT Press.
Dreyfus, H. L. (1999), 'The Primacy of Phenomenology over Logical Analysis', *Philosophical Topics* 27/2: 3–24.
Dreyfus, H. L. (2002), 'Intelligence without representation – Merleau-Ponty's critique of mental representation', *Phenomenology and the Cognitive Sciences* 1: 367–83.
Dreyfus, H. L. (2004), 'Merleau-Ponty and Recent Cognitive Science', in T. Carman and M. B. N. Hansen (eds.), *The Cambridge Companion to Merleau-Ponty* (Cambridge: Cambridge University Press), 129–50.
Dreyfus, H. L. (2007a), 'Why Heideggerian AI Failed and How Fixing it Would Require Making it More Heideggerian', *Philosophical Psychology*, 20/2: 247–68.
Dreyfus, H. L. (2007b), 'The Return of the Myth of the Mental', *Inquiry*, 50/4: 352–65.
Dreyfus, H. L. (2013), 'The Myth of the Pervasiveness of the Mental', in J. K. Schear (ed.), *Mind, Reason, and Being-in-the World: The McDowell-Dreyfus Debate* (London: Routledge), 15–40.

Drummond, J. (1983), 'Objects' Optimal Appearances and the Immediate Awareness of Space in Vision', *Man and World*, 16/3: 177–205.
Drummond, J. (2012), 'Intentionality without Representationalism', in D. Zahavi (ed.), *The Oxford Handbook of Contemporary Phenomenology* (Oxford: Oxford University Press), 115–33.
Drummond, J. (2019), 'Intentionality and (Moral) Normativity', in M. Burch, J. E. Marsh, and I. McMullin (eds.), *Normativity, Meaning, and the Promise of Phenomenology* (London: Routledge), 101–19.
Durie, B. (2005), 'Senses Special: Doors of Perception', *New Scientist* (26 Jan. 2005), https://www.newscientist.com/article/mg18524841-600-senses-special-doors-of-perception/.
Eilan, N. (2005), 'Joint attention, communication, and mind', in N. Eilan, C. Hoerl, T. McCormack, and J. Roessler (eds.), *Joint Attention: Communication and Other Minds* (Oxford: Oxford University Press), 1–33.
Fanon, F. (2008), *Black Skin, White Masks*, trans. R. Philcox (New York: Grove Press).
Farah, M. (2004), *Visual Agnosia* (Cambridge, MA: MIT Press).
Farkas, K. (2013), 'A Sense of Reality', in F. Macpherson and D. Platchias (eds.), *Hallucinations: Philosophy and Psychology* (Cambridge, MA: MIT Press), 399–416.
Finlay, S. (2019), 'Defining Normativity', in. D. Plunkett, S. Shapiro, and K. Toh (eds.), *Dimensions of Normativity: New Essays on Metaethics and Jurisprudence* (Oxford: Oxford University Press), 187–219.
Fisher, H. (2000), *The First Sex: The Natural Talents of Women and how They are Changing the World* (New York: Ballantine Books).
Fridland, E. (2011), 'The case for proprioception', *Phenomenology and the Cognitive Sciences*, 10/4: 521–40.
Friston, K. (2010), 'The free-energy principle: a unified brain theory?', *Nature Reviews Neuroscience*, 11, 127–38.
Fuchs, T. (2017a), 'Levels of empathy – Primary, extended, and reiterated empathy', in V. Lux and S. Weigel (eds.), *Empathy: Epistemic Problems and Cultural-Historical Perspectives of a Cross-Disciplinary Concept* (New York: Palgrave Macmillan), 27–47.
Fuchs, T. (2017b), 'Collective Body Memories', in C. Durt, T. Fuchs, and C. Tewes (eds.), *Embodiment, Enaction, and Culture: Investigating the Constitution of the Shared World* (Cambridge, MA: MIT Press), 333–52.
Fuchs, T. (2018), *Ecology of the Brain: The Phenomenology and Biology of the Embodied Mind* (Oxford: Oxford University Press).
Fulkerson, M. (2014), 'Rethinking the Senses and their Interactions: The Case for Sensory Pluralism', *Frontiers in Psychology*, 5: 1–14.
Gallagher, S. (2005), *How the Body Shapes the Mind* (New York: Oxford University Press).
Gallagher, S. (2011), 'Interactive Coordination in Joint Attention', in A. Seemann (ed.), *Joint Attention: New Developments in Psychology, Philosophy of Mind, and Social Neuroscience* (Cambridge, MA: MIT Press), 293–305.
Gallagher, S. (2016), 'Intercorporeity: Enaction, Simulation, and the Scienceof Social Cognition', in J. Renolds and R. Sebold (eds.), *Phenomenology and Science Confrontations and Convergences* (London: Palgrave Macmillan), 161–80.

Gallagher, S. (2017), *Enactivist Interventions. Rethinking the Mind* (Oxford: Oxford University Press).
Gallagher, S. (2020), *Action and Interaction* (Oxford: Oxford University Press).
Gallagher, S. (2023), 'Bodily Self-Awareness and Body-Schematic Processes', in A. J. T. Alsmith and M. R. Longo (eds.), *The Routledge Handbook of Bodily Awareness* (London: Routledge), 137–49.
Gallagher, S., and Cole, J. (1995), 'Body Schema and Body Image in a Deafferented Subject', *Journal of Mind and Behaviour*, 16/4: 369–90.
Gallagher, S., and Ransom, T. G. (2016), 'Artifacting minds: Material engagement theory and joint action', in C. Tewes (ed.), *Embodiment in Evolution and Culture* (Berlin: de Gruyter), 337–51.
Gallagher, S., and Zahavi, D. (2021), *The Phenomenological Mind*, 3rd edn (London: Routledge).
Garavito, M. C. (2019), 'Incorporating others: what an extended self tells us about intersubjectivity', *Adaptive Behavior* 27(1), 47–59.
Gardner, S. (2013), 'Transcendental Philosophy and the Given' in Joseph K. Schear (ed.), *Mind, Reason, and Being-In-The-World: The McDowell-Dreyfus Debate* (London: Routledge), 110–42.
Gardner, S. (2015), 'Merleau-Ponty's Transcendental Theory of Perception', in M. Sacks, S. Gardner, and M. Grist (eds.), *The Transcendental Turn* (Oxford: Oxford University Press), 294–323.
Gibson, E. (1963), 'Perceptual Learning', *Annual Review of Psychology*, 14/1: 29–56.
Gibson, E. (1969), *Principles of perceptual learning and development*. Englewood Cliffs, NJ: Prentice-Hall.
Gibson, J. J. (1979), *The Ecological Approach to Visual Perception*. (Boston: Houghton Mifflin).
Gilbert, M. (1990), 'Walking Together: A Paradigmatic Social Phenomenon', *Midwest Studies in Philosophy* 15/1: 1–14.
Gilbert, M. (1992), *On Social Facts* (Princeton, NJ: Princeton University Press).
Gilbert, M. (1996), *Living Together: Rationality, Sociality, and Obligation* (Lanham, Boulder, New York, London: Rowman & Littlefield).
Gilbert, M. (2013), *Joint commitment: How we make the social world*. Oxford University Press.
Gilbert, M. (2014), *Joint Commitment: How We Make the Social World* (Oxford: Oxford University Press).
Glüer, K., and Pagin, P. (1999), 'Rules of meaning and practical reasoning', *Synthese*, 117/2: 207–27.
Goff, P. A., Jackson, M. C., Di Leone, B. L., Culotta, C. M., and DiTomasso, N. A. (2014), 'The Essence of Innocence: Consequences of Dehumanizing Black Children', *Journal of Personality and Social Psychology*, 106/4: 526–45.
Goldman, A. I. (2014), 'The bodily formats approach to embodied cognition', in U. Kriegel (ed.), *Current Controversies in Philosophy of Mind* (New York, London: Routledge), 91–108.
Goldstein, K. (1923), 'Über die Abhängigkeit der Bewegungen von optischen Vorgängen. Bewegungs-störungen bei Seelenblinden', *Monatschrift für Psychiatrie und Neurologie*, Festschrift Liepmann.

Goldstein, K., and Gelb, A. (1918), 'Psychologische Analysen hirnpathologischer Fälle auf Grund von Untersuchungen Hirnverletzer', *Zeitschrift für die gesamte Neurologie und Psychiatrie*, 41: 1–142.

Goldstone, R. L. (1998), 'Perceptual Learning', *Annual Review of Psychology*, 49/1: 585–612.

Goldstone, R. L., and Schyns, P. G. (2006), 'Perception Science After Thirty Years: A Review', *Journal of Vision*, 6/6: 1–30.

Gregory, R. L. (1966), *Eye and Brain: The Psychology of Seeing* (New York: McGraw-Hill).

Grünbaum, A. A. (1930), 'Aphasie und Motorik', *Zeitschrift für die gesamte Neurologie und Psychiatrie*, 130: 385–412.

Guenther, L. (2020), 'Critical Phenomenology', in G. Weiss, A. V. Murphy, and G. Salamon (eds.), *50 Concepts for a Critical Phenomenology* (Evanston, IL: Northwestern University Press), 11–16.

Guenther, L. (2021), 'Six Senses of Critique for Critical Phenomenology', *Puncta*, 4/2: 5–23.

Gurwitsch, A. (1978), *Human Encounters in the Social World (1929–1930)* (Pittsburgh: Duquesne University Press).

Gurwitsch, A. (2010), *The Field of Consciousness: Phenomenology of Theme, Thematic Field, and Marginal Consciousness*, ed. by R. M. Zaner; L. Embree. The Hague: Springer.

Halák, J. (2021), 'Body schema dynamics in Merleau-Ponty', in Y. Ataria, S. Tanaka, and S. Gallagher (eds.), *Body Schema and Body Image: New Directions* (Oxford: Oxford University Press), 33–51.

Hartimo, M. (2018), On the Origins of Scientific Objectivity, in *Husserl's Phenomenology of Intersubjectivity: Historical Interpretations and Contemporary Applications*. Kjosavik, F., Beyer, C. & Fricke, C. (eds.). Routledge.

Head, H., and Holmes, G. (1911), 'Sensory Disturbances from Cerebral Lesions', *Brain*, 34/2–3: 102–254.

Heidegger, M. (1962), *Being and Time*, trans. J. Macquarrie and E. Robinson (New York: Harper & Row).

Heidegger, M. (1982), *Basic Problems of Phenomenology*, trans. A. Hofstader (Bloomington, IN: Indiana University Press).

Heidegger, M. (1985), *The History of the Concept of Time*, trans. T. Kisiel (Bloomington, IN: Indiana University Press).

Heinämaa, S. (2002), 'From Decisions to Passions: Merleau-Ponty's Interpretation of Husserl's Reduction', in T. Toadvine and L. Embree (eds.), *Merleau-Ponty's Reading of Husserl* (Dordrecht: Kluwer).

Heinämaa, S. (2009), 'Phenomenological Response to Gestalt Theory', in S. Heinämaa and M. Reuter (eds.), *Psychology and Philosophy: Inquiries into the Soul from Late Scholasticism to Contemporary Thought* (Dordrecht: Springer), 263–84.

Heinämaa, S. book (2012), 'The Body', *The Routledge Companion to Phenomenology*. Eds. Sebastian Luft and Søren Overgaard. New York: Routledge, pp. 222–233.

Heinämaa, S. (2013), 'Transcendental Intersubjectivity and Normality: Constitution by Mortals', in D. Moran and R. T. Jensen (eds.), *The Phenomenology of Embodied Subjectivity* (Dordrecht: Springer), 83–103.

Heinämaa, S. (2015), 'Anonymity and personhood: Merleau-Ponty's account of the subject of Perception', *Continental Philosophy Review*, 48/2: 123–42.

Heinämaa, S. (2019), 'Constitutive, Prescriptive, Technical or Ideal? On the Ambiguity of the Term "Norm"', in M. Burch, J. E. Marsh, and I. McMullin (eds.), *Normativity, Meaning, and the Promise of Phenomenology* (London: Routledge), 9–28.

Heinämaa, S. (2021), 'On the transcendental undercurrents of phenomenology: The case of the living body', *Continental Philosophy Review: Special issue on Methods*, 54/2, ed. S. Crowell and A. Fernandez: 237–57.

Heinämaa, S. (2022), 'Varieties of Normativity: Norms, Goals, Values', in S. Heinämaa, M. Hartimo, and I. Hirvonen (eds.), *Contemporary Phenomenologies of Normativity: Norms, Goals, and Values* (London: Routledge), 19–42.

Heinämaa, S., and Taipale, J. (2019), 'Normality', in G. Stanghellini, A. Raballo, M. Broome, V. Fernandez, P. Fusar-Poli, and R. Rosfort (eds.), *The Oxford Handbook of Phenomenological Psychopathology* (Oxford: Oxford University Press), 356–71.

Hering, E. (1964), *Outlines of a Theory of the Light Sense*, trans. L. M. Hurvich and D. Jameson (Cambridge, MA: Harvard University Press).

Hinton, J. M. (1973), *Experiences: An Inquiry into Some Ambiguities* (Oxford: Clarendon Press).

Høffding, S. (2018), 'The Hive Mind: Playing Together', in *A Phenomenology of Musical Absorption* (Cham: Palgrave Macmillan), 217–46.

Hohwy, J. (2013), *The Predictive Mind* (Oxford: Oxford University Press).

Hopp, W. (2011), *Perception and Knowledge: A Phenomenological Account* (Cambridge: Cambridge University Press).

Hopp, W. (2018), 'Ideal Verificationism and Perceptual Faith: Husserl and Merleau-Ponty on Perceptual Knowledge', in D. Zahavi (ed.), *The Oxford Handbook of the History of Phenomenology* (Oxford: Oxford University Press), 623–49.

Hopp, W. (2019), 'Normativity and Knowledge', in M. Burch, J. E. Marsh, and I. McMullin (eds.), *Normativity, Meaning, and the Promise of Phenomenology* (London: Routledge), 271–89.

Hornik, R., Risenhoover, N., and Gunnar, M. (1987), 'The effects of maternal positive, neutral, and negative affective communications on infant responses to new toy', *Child Development*, 58/4: 937–44.

Howard, I. P., and Templeton, W. B. (1966), *Human Spatial Orientation* (Oxford: Wiley).

Huang, D. (2023), 'Husserl on the Normativity of Intentionality and Its Neutralization', *Husserl Studies*, 39/1: 21–42.

Hurley, S. L. (1998), *Consciousness in Action* (Cambridge, MA: Harvard University Press).

Hurley, S. L., and Noë, A. (2003), 'Neural plasticity and consciousness', *Biology and Philosophy*, 18/1: 131–68.

Husserl, E. (1960), *Cartesian Meditations: An Introduction to Phenomenology*, trans. D. Cairns (Dordrecht: Springer).

Husserl, E. (1970), *The Crisis of European Sciences and Transcendental Phenomenology: An Introduction to Phenomenological Philosophy*, trans. D. Carr (Evanston, IL: Northwestern Unversity Press).

Husserl, E. (1973a), *Zur Phänomenologie der Intersubjektivität: Texte aus dem Nachlass, vol. I, 1905-1920*, ed. I. Kern, Husserliana 13 (The Hague: Martinus Nijhoff).
Husserl, E. (1973b), *Zur Phänomenologie der Intersubjektivität: Texte aus dem Nachlass, vol. II, 1921-1928*, ed. I. Kern, Husserliana 14 (The Hague: Martinus Nijhoff).
Husserl, E. (1973c), *Zur Phänomenologie der Intersubjektivität: Texte aus dem Nachlass, vol. III, 1929-1935*, ed. I. Kern, Husserliana 15 (The Hague: Martinus Nijhoff).
Husserl, E. (1975), *Experience and Judgment*, Evanston: Northwestern University Press.
Husserl, E. (1977), *Phenomenological Psychology: Lectures, Summer Semester, 1925*, trans. J. Scanlon (Dordrecht: Springer).
Husserl, E. (1988), *Vorlesungen über Ethik und Wertlehre: 1908-1914*, ed. U. Melle (The Hague: Kluwer Academic).
Husserl, E. (1989), *Ideas Pertaining to a Pure Phenomenology and to a Phenomenological Philosophy (Book 2): Studies in the Phenomenology of Constitution*, trans. R. Rojcewicz and A. Schuwer (Dordrecht: Kluwer Academic).
Husserl, E. (1991), *On the Phenomenology of the Consciousness of Internal Time (1893-1917)*, trans. J. B. Brough (Dordrecht: Kluwer Academic).
Husserl, E. (1997), *Thing and Space: Lectures of 1907*, trans. R. Rojcewicz (Dordrecht: Springer).
Husserl, E. (2001), *Die 'Bernauer Manuskripte' über das Zeitbewußtsein (1917/18)*, ed. R. Bernet and D. Lohmar, Husserliana 33 (Dordrecht: Kluwer Academic).
Husserl, E. (2001a), *Logical Investigations I*, trans. J. N. Findlay (London: Routledge).
Husserl, E. (2001b), *Logical Investigations II*, trans. J. N. Findlay (London: Routledge).
Husserl, E. (2001c), *Analyses Concerning Passive and Active Synthesis*, trans. A. J. Steinbock (Dordrecht: Kluwer Academic).
Husserl, E. (2002), *Logische Untersuchungen,* supplementary volume, vol. I: *Entwürfe zur Umarbeitung der VI. Untersuchung und zur Vorrede für die Neuauflage der Logischen Untersuchungen (Sommer 1913)*, ed. U. Melle, Husserliana 20/1 (Dordrecht: Kluwer Academic).
Husserl, E. (2004), *Einleitung in die Ethik: Vorlesungen Sommersemester 1920 und 1924*, ed. H. Peucker, Husserliana 37 (Dordrecht: Kluwer Academic).
Husserl, E. (2005a), *Wahrnehmung und Aufmerksamkeit: Texte aus dem Nachlass (1893-1912)*, ed. T. Vongehr and R. Giuliani (New York: Springer).
Husserl, E. (2005b), *Logische Untersuchungen,* supplementary volume, vol. II: *Texte für die Neufassung der VI. Untersuchung. Zur Phänomenologie des Ausdrucks und der Erkenntnis (1893/94-1921)*, ed. U. Melle, Husserliana 20/2 (Dordrecht: Springer).
Husserl, E. (2005c), *Einführung in die Phänomenologie der Erkenntnis. Vorlesung 1909*, ed. E. Schuhmann, Husserliana Materialien 7 (Dordrecht: Kluwer Academic).
Husserl, E. (2005d), *Phantasy, Image Consciousness, And Memory (1898-1925)*, trans. J. B. Brough (Dordrecht: Kluwer Academic).
Husserl, E. (2006), *Späte Texte über Zeitkonstitution (1929-1934): Die C-Manuskripte*, ed. D. Lohmar, Husserliana Materialen 8 (Dordrecht: Springer).

Husserl, E. (2008), *Die Lebenswelt. Auslegungen der vorgegebenen Welt und ihrer Konstitution: Texte aus dem Nachlass (1916–1937)*, ed. R. Sowa, Husserliana 39 (Dordrecht: Springer).
Husserl, E. (2014), *Ideas for a Pure Phenomenology and Phenomenological Philosophy: Ideas 1*, trans. D. O. Dahlstrom (Indianapolis, IN: Hackett).
Inkpin, A. (2017), 'Was Merleau-Ponty a "Transcendental" Phenomenologist?' *Continental Philosophy Review*, 50/1: 27–47.
Jacobs, H. (2018), 'Husserl, Heidegger, and Merleau-Ponty on the World of Experience', in D. Zahavi (ed.), *The Oxford Handbook of the History of Phenomenology* (Oxford: Oxford University Press), 650–75.
James, W. (1908), *Text-Book of Psychology* (London: Macmillan).
Jardine, J. (2015), 'Stein and Honneth on empathy and emotional recognition', *Human Studies* 38/4: 567–89.
Jardine, J. (2022), *Empathy, Embodiment, and the Person: Husserlian Investigations of Social Experience and the Self* (Cham: Springer).
Jardine, J. (2023), 'Empathy', in N. De Warren and T. Toadvine, *Encyclopedia of Phenomenology* (Berlin: Springer).
Jenkin, Z. (2023a), 'Perceptual learning', *Philosophy Compass* 18: e12932. https://doi.org/10.1111/phc3.12932
Jenkin, Z. (2023b), 'The function of perceptual learning', *Philosophical Perspectives* 1–15. DOI: 10.1111/phpe.12186
Jensen, R. T. (2009), 'Motor Intentionality and the Case of Schneider', *Phenomenology and the Cognitive Sciences*, 8/3: 371–88.
Kant, I. (2007), *Critique of Pure Reason*, Trans. N. K. Smith (London: Palgrave Macmilan).
Kaplan, F., and Hafner, V. V. (2006), 'The challenges of joint attention', *Interaction Studies: Social Behaviour and Communication in Biological and Artificial Systems*, 7/2: 135–69.
Katz, D. (1925), *The World of Touch*, trans. L. E. Krueger. A Psychology Press Book (2016) (New York, London: Routledge).
Kee, H. (2020), 'Phenomenological reduction in Merleau-Ponty's *The Structure of Behaviour*: An alternative approach to the naturalization of phenomenology', *Europea Journal of Philosophy*, 28: 15–32.
Kelly, S. (2004), 'Seeing Things in Merleau-Ponty', in T. Carman and M. B. N. Hansen (eds.), *The Cambridge Companion to Merleau-Ponty* (Cambridge: Cambridge University Press), 74–110.
Kelly, S. (2010), 'The Normative Nature of Perceptual Experience', in B. Nanay (ed.), *Perceiving the World* (Oxford: Oxford University Press), 146–59.
Knudsen, N. (2021), 'Shared action: An existential phenomenological account', *Phenomenology and the Cognitive Sciences*, (17 Oct. 2021), https://doi.org/10.1007/s11097-021-09785-4.
Landes, D. (2018), 'Merleau-Ponty from 1945 to 1952: The Ontological Weight of Perception and the Transcendental Force of Description', in D. Zahavi (ed.), *The Oxford Handbook of the History of Phenomenology* (Oxford: Oxford University Press), 360–78.

Leeten, Lars (2021), 'Ordinary Language Philosophy as Phenomenological Research: Reading Austin with Merleau-Ponty', *Philosophical Investigations* 45/3: 228.

Legrand, D. (2007), 'Subjectivity and the Body: Introducing Basic Forms of Self-Consciousness', *Consciousness and Cognition*, 16/3: 577–82.

Legrand, D. (2012), 'Self-Consciousness and World-Consciousness', in D. Zahavi (ed.), *The Oxford Handbook of Contemporary Phenomenology* (Oxford: Oxford University Press), 287–303.

León, F. (2021), 'Joint attention without recursive mindreading: On the role of second-person engagement', *Philosophical Psychology*, 34/4: 550–80.

León, F. (2022), 'Attention in Joint Attention: From Selection to Prioritization', in M. Wehrle, D. D'Angelo, and E. Solomonova (eds.), *Access and Mediation: Transdisciplinary Perspectives on Attention* (Berlin: De Gruyter), 65–90.

León, F., and D. Zahavi (2018), 'How We Feel: Collective Emotions Without Joint Commitments', *Proto Sociology*, 35, 117–35.

Levinas, E. (1979), *Totality and Infinity*, trans. A. Lingis (The Hague: Martinus Nijhoff).

Levinas, E. (1995), *The Theory of Intuition in Husserl's Phenomenology*, trans. A. Orianne (Evanston, IL: Northwestern University Press).

Liszkowski, U., Carpenter, M., Striano, T., and Tomasello M. (2006), '12- and 18-month-olds point to provide information for others', *Journal of Cognition and Development*, 7/2: 173–87.

Lohmar, D. (2003), 'Husserl's Type and Kant's Schemata: Systematic Reasons for Their Correlation or Identity', in Donn Welton (ed.), *The New Husserl: A Critical Reader*. Indiana University Press.

Lohmar, D. (2008), *Phänomenologie der schwachen Phantasie: Untersuchung der Psychologie, Cognitive Science, Neurologie und Phänomenologie zur Funktion der Phantasie in der Wahrnehmung* (Dordrecht: Springer).

Lohmar, D. (2012), 'Genetic Phenomenology', in S. Luft and S. Overgaard (eds.), *The Routledge Companion to Phenomenology* (London: Routledge), 266–75.

Lohmar, D. (2014), 'Types and Habits: Habits and their Cognitive Background in Hume and Husserl', *Phenomenology and Mind*, 6: 40–51.

Lohmar, D. (2023), 'Das Subjekt in der Genetischen Phänomenologie Husserls und seine Bedeutung für die Philosophie der Gegenwart', in D. E. Tarhan (ed.), *Schriften zur Phänomenologie Edmund Husserls* (London: Transnational Press London).

Lycan, W. (1996), *Consciousness and Experience* (Cambridge, MA: MIT Press).

McDowell, J. (1996), *Mind and World* (Cambridge, MA: Harvard University Press).

McDowell, J. (1998), 'Criteria, Defeasibility and Knowledge', in *Meaning, Knowledge, and Reality* (Cambridge, MA: Harvard University Press), 369–94.

McDowell, J. (2007a), 'What Myth?', *Inquiry*, 50/4: 338–51.

McDowell, J. (2007b), 'Response to Dreyfus', *Inquiry*, 50/4: 366–70.

McDowell, J. (2009), *Having the World in View* (Cambridge, MA: Harvard University Press).

McDowell, J. (2013), 'The myth of the mind as detached' in Joseph K. Schear (ed.), *Mind, Reason, and Being-In-The-World: The McDowell-Dreyfus Debate* (London: Routledge), 41–58.

McGurk, H. and J. Macdonald (1976), 'Hearing lips and seeing voices', in *Nature* 264, 746-8.
McLaren, I. P. L., Kaye, H., and Mackintosh, N. J. (1989), 'An associative theory of the representation of stimuli: Applications to perceptual learning and latent inhibition', in R. G. M. Morris (ed.), *Parallel Distributed Processing: Implications for Psychology and Neurobiology* (Oxford: Oxford University Press), 102-30.
McLaren, I. P. L., and Mackintosh, N. J. (2000), 'An elemental model of associative learning: I. Latent inhibition and perceptual learning', *Animal Learning and Behaviour*, 38/3: 211-46.
Macpherson, F. (2011a), 'Cross-modal experiences', *Proceedings of the Aristotelian Society*, 111/3: 429-68.
Macpherson, F. (2011b), 'Individuating the Senses', in *The Senses: Classic and Contemporary Philosophical Perspectives* (Oxford: Oxford University Press), 3-46.
Macpherson, F. (2012), 'Cognitive penetration of colour experience: Rethinking the issue in light of an indirect mechanism', *Philosophy and Phenomenological Research*, 84/1: 24-62.
Madary, M. (2016), *Visual Phenomenology* (Cambridge, MA: MIT Press).
Magrì, E. (2021), 'Towards a Phenomenological Account of Social Sensitivity', *Phenomenology and the Cognitive Sciences*, 20: 635-53.
Martin, M. G. F. (2002), 'The Transparency of Experience', *Mind and Language*, 17: 376-425.
Martin, M. G. F. (2004), 'The Limits of Self-Awareness', *Philosophical Studies: An International Journal for Philosophy in the Analytic Tradition*, 120/1-3: 37-89.
Matherne, S. (2014), 'The Kantian Roots of Merleau-Ponty's Account of Pathology'. *British Journal for the History of Philosophy*, 22/1: 124-49.
Matherne, S. (2016), 'Kantian Themes in Merleau-Ponty's Theory of Perception'. *Archiv für Geschichte der Philosophie*, 98/2: 193-230.
Matherne, S. (2017), 'Merleau-Ponty on Style as the Key to Perceptual Presence and Constancy', *Journal of the History of Philosophy*, 55/4: 693-727.
Mattens, F. (2018), 'From the Origin of Spatiality to a Variety of Spaces', in D. Zahavi (ed.), *The Oxford Handbook of the History of Phenomenology*, 559-78. Oxford: Oxford University Press.
Matthen, M. (2017), 'Is Perceptual Experience Normally Multimodal?', in B. Nanay (ed.), *Current Controversies in Philosophy of Perception* (London: Routledge), 121-36.
Mazijk, C. van (2020), *Perception and Reality in Kant, Husserl, and McDowell* (London: Routledge).
Meillassoux, Q. (2006), *Après la finitude: Essai sur la nécessité de la contingence* (Paris, Seuil).
Meindl, P., and D. Zahavi (2023), 'From communication to communalization: a Husserlian account', *Continental Philosophy Review*, 56: 361-77, https://doi.org/10.1007/s11007-023-09601-7.
Meltzoff, A. N. and Moore, M. K. (1989), Imitation in newborn infants: Exploring the range of gestures imitated and the underlying mechanisms. *Developmental Psychology* 25(6).
Merleau-Ponty, M. (1963), *The Structure of Behaviour*, trans. A. Fisher (Boston, MA: Beacon Press).

Merleau-Ponty, M. (1964a), *The Primacy of Perception*, trans. J. Edie (Evanston, IL: Northwestern University Press).
Merleau-Ponty, M. (1964b), *Sense and Non-Sense*, trans. H. Dreyfus and P. A. Dreyfus (Evanston, IL: Northwestern University Press).
Merleau-Ponty, M. (1968), *The Visible and the Invisible*, trans. A. Lingis, (Evanston: Northwestern University Press).
Merleau-Ponty, M. (1970), *Themes from the Lectures*. Evanston, IL: Northwestern University Press.
Merleau-Ponty, M. (2010), *Child Psychology and Pedagogy: The Sorbonne Lectures 1949-1952*, trans. T. Welsh (Evanston, IL: Northwestern University Press).
Merleau-Ponty, M. (2011), *Le Monde Sensible et le Monde de l'Expression. Cours au Collège de France, Notes, 1953*. Genève: MetisPresses.
Merleau-Ponty, M. (2012), *Phenomenology of Perception*, trans. D. Landes (London: Routledge).
Merleau-Ponty, M. (2021), *The Sensible World and the World of Expression: Course Notes from the Collège de France, 1953*, trans. B. Smith (Evanston, IL: Northwestern University Press).
Mooney, T. D. (2010), 'Understanding and Simple Seeing in Husserl', *Husserl Studies*, 26: 19-48.
Mooney, T. D. (2023), *Merleau-Ponty's Phenomenology of Perception: On the Body Informed* (Cambridge: Cambridge University Press).
Moran, D. (2019), 'Husserl and Gurwitsch on Horizonal Intentionality: The Gurwitsch Memorial Lecture 2018', *Journal of Phenomenological Psychology*, 50: 1-41.
Morris, D. (2015), 'Illusions and Perceptual Norms as Spandrels of the Temporality of Living', in M. Doyon and T. Breyer (eds.), *Normativity in Perception* (London: Palgrave Macmillan), 75-90.
Mulligan, K. (1995), 'Perception', in B. Smith and D. W. Smith (eds.), *The Cambridge Companion to Husserl* (Cambridge: Cambridge University Press), 168-238.
Mulligan, K. (2004), 'Husserl on the 'logics' of valuing, values and norms', in B. Centi and G. Gigliotti (eds.), *Fenomenologia della ragion pratica. L'etica di Edmund Husserl*, (Naples: Bibliopolis), 177-225.
Mulligan, K. (2017), 'Incorrect emotions in ancient, Austrian and contemporary philosophy', *Revue Philosophique de la France et de l'Etranger*, 142/4: 491-512.
Nagel, T. (1971), 'Brain bisection and the unity of consciousness', *Synthese* 22, 396-413.
Nagel, T. (1974), 'What Is It like to Be a Bat', *Philosophical Review*, 83/4: 435-50.
Navajas, J., Hindocha, C., Foda, H., Keramati, M., Latham, P. E., and Bahrami, B. (2017), 'The idiosyncratic nature of confidence', *Nature Human Behaviour*, 1/11: 810-18.
Noë, A. (2004), *Action in Perception* (Cambridge, MA: MIT Press).
Noë, A. (2009), *Out of our Heads: Why You Are Not Your Brain, and Other Lessons from the Biology of Consciousness* (New York: Hill & Wang).
Noë, A. (2012), *Varieties of Presence* (Cambridge, MA: Harvard University Press).
O'Callaghan, C. (2012), 'Perception and multimodality', in E. Margolis, R. Samuels, and S. P. Stich (eds.), *The Oxford Handbook of Philosophy of Cognitive Science* (Oxford: Oxford University Press), 92-117.

O'Callaghan, C. (2014a), 'Intermodal binding awareness', in D. Bennett and C. Hill (eds.), *Sensory Integration and the Unity of Consciousness* (Cambridge, MA: MIT Press), 73-104.
O'Callaghan, C. (2014b), 'Not All Perceptual Experience Is Modality Specific', in D. Stokes, M. Matthen, and S. Biggs (eds.), *Perception and its Modalities* (Oxford: Oxford University Press), 133-65.
O'Callaghan, C. (2015), 'The multisensory character of perception', *Journal of Philosophy*, 112/10: 551-69.
O'Callaghan, C. (2017), 'Enhancement through Coordination', in B. Nanay (ed.), *Current Controversies in Philosophy of Perception* (New York: Taylor & Francis), 109-20.
O'Callaghan, C. (2019), *A Multisensory Theory of Perception* (Oxford: Oxford University Press).
Oksala, J. (2022), 'The method of critical phenomenology: Simone de Beauvoir as a phenomenologist', in *European Journal of Philosophy*, 31/1: 137-50, https://doi.org/10.1111/ejop.12782.
O'Shaughnessy, B. (1980), *The Will: A Dual Aspect Theory* (Cambridge: Cambridge University Press).
Overgaard, S. (2018), 'Perceptual error, conjunctivism, and Husserl', *Husserl Studies*, 34/1: 25-45.
Pacherie, E. (2007), 'The Sense of Control and the Sense of Agency', *Psyche: An Interdisciplinary Journal of Research on Consciousness*, 13: 1-30.
Pacherie, E. (2014), 'How does it feel to act together?', *Phenomenology and the Cognitive Sciences*, 13: 25-46.
Pacherie, E. (2018), 'Collective Phenomenology', in K. Ludwig and M. Jankovic (eds.), *The Routledge Handbook of Collective Intentionality* (New York: Routledge), 162-73.
Payne, B. K. (2006), 'Weapon Bias: Split-Second Decisions and Unintended Stereotyping', in *Current Directions in Psychological Science* 15 (6): 287-91.
Peacocke, C. (1992), *A Study of concepts*. (Cambridge: MIT Press).
Peacocke, C. (2005), 'Joint Attention: Its Nature, Reflexivity, and Relation to Common Knowledge', in N. Eilan, C. Hoerl, T. McCormack, and J. Roessler (eds.), *Joint Attention: Communication and Other Minds* (Oxford: Oxford University Press), 298-324.
Pennisi, G., and Gallagher, S. (2021), 'Embodied and Disembodied Rationality', in V. Cardella and A. Gangemi (eds.), *Psychopathology and Philosophy of Mind* (London: Routledge), 263-86.
Pezzulo, G., Iodice, P., Ferraina, S., and Kessler, K. (2013), 'Shared Action Spaces: A Basis Function Framework for Social Re-calibration of Sensorimotor Representations Supporting Joint Action', *Frontiers in Human Neuroscience*, 7.
Philipse, H. (1995), 'Transcendental idealism', in B. Smith and D. W. Smith (eds.), *The Cambridge Companion to Husserl* (Cambridge: Cambridge University Press), 239-322.
Pippin, R. B. (1989), *Hegel's Idealism* (Cambridge: Cambridge University Press).
Plessner, H. (1961), *Lachen und Weinen. Eine Untersuchung nach den Grenzen menschlichen Verhaltens*. Bern: Francke.

Pokropski, M. (2015), 'Timing together, acting together: Phenomenology of intersubjective temporality and social cognition', *Phenomenology and the Cognitive Sciences*, 14: 897–909.

Pourtois, G., de Gelder, B., Vroomen, J., Rossion, B., and Crommelinck, M. (2000), 'The time-course of intermodal binding between seeing, and hearing affective information', *Neuroreport* 11, 1329–1333. doi: 10.1097/00001756-200004270-00036

Price, R. (2009), Aspect-switching and visual phenomenal character. *Philosophical Quarterly*, 59/236, 508–18.

Reid, V. M., Dunn, K., Young, R. J., Amu, J., Donovan, T., and Reissland, N. (2017), 'The human fetus preferentially engages with face-like visual stimuli', *Current Biology*, 27/12: 1825–8.

Reinach, A. (1989), *Sämtliche Werke: Textkritische Ausgabe [Collected Works: Critical Edition]*, ed. K. Schuhmann and B. Smith, 2 vols. (Munich: Philosophia Verlag).

Rietveld, E. (2008), 'Situated Normativity: The Normative Aspect of Embodied Cognition in Unreflective Action', *Mind*, 117/468: 973–1001.

Rietveld, E., and Brouwers, A. A. (2017), 'Optimal grip on affordances in architectural design practices: an ethnography', *Phenomenology and the Cognitive Sciences*, 16: 545–64.

Rietveld, E., and J. Kiverstein (2014), 'A rich landscape of affordance', *Ecological Psychology*, 26/4: 325–52, https://doi.org/10.1080/10407413.2014.958035.

Ritunnano, R. and L. Bortolotti (2022), *Phenomenology and the cognitive sciences* v21 n4, 949-968.

Rivers, W. H. R. (1901), 'Vision', in A. C. Haddon (ed.), *Reports of the Cambridge Anthropological Expedition to Torres Straits* (Cambridge: Cambridge University Press), 1–132.

Rodemeyer, L. M. (2022), 'A Phenomenological Critique of Critical Phenomenology', in in *Why Method Matters: Phenomenology as Critique*, Smaranda Aldea, David Carr, and Sara Heinämaa, eds. "Research in Phenomenology" series. Routledge, 95–112.

Roessler, J. (2005), 'Joint Attention and the Problem of Other Minds', in N. Eilan, C. Hoerl, T. McCormack, and J. Roessler (eds.), *Joint Attention: Communication and Other Minds* (Oxford: Oxford University Press), 230–59.

Romano, C. (2012), 'Must phenomenology remain Cartesian?', *Continental Philosophy Review*, 45/3: 425–45.

Romano, C. (2015), *At the Heart of Reason* (Evanston, IL: Northwestern University Press).

Romdenh-Romluc, K. (2009), 'Merleau-Ponty's Account of Hallucination', *European Journal of Philosophy*, 17/1: 76–90.

Romdenh-Romluc, K. (2011), *Routledge Philosophy Guidebook to Merleau-Ponty and Phenomenology of Perception* (London: Routledge).

Romdenh-Romluc, K. (2018), 'Science in Merleau-Ponty's phenomenology: from the early work to the later philosophy', in D. Zahavi (ed.), *The Oxford Handbook of the History of Phenomenology* (Oxford: Oxford University Press.), 340–57.

Römer, I. (2019), 'The Sources of Practical Normativity Reconsidered – with Kant and Levinas', in M. Burch, J. E. Marsh, and I. McMullin (eds.), *Normativity, Meaning, and the Promise of Phenomenology* (London: Routledge), 120–36.

Rosenthal, D. (2005), *Consciousness and Mind* (Oxford: Clarendon Press).
Russell, B. (1912), *The Problems of Philosophy* (Mineola, NY: Dover Publications).
Salamon, G. (2012), 'The Phenomenology of Rheumatology: Disability, Merleau-Ponty and the Fallacy of Maximal Grip', *Hypatia*, 27/2: 243–60.
Salamon, G. (2018), 'What's Critical About Critical Phenomenology?', *Puncta*, 1: 8–17.
Salice, A. (2022), 'Husserl on Shared Intentionality and Normativity', *Continental Philosophy Review*, 56: 343–59, https://doi.org/10.1007/s11007-022-09593-w.
Salice, A., Høffding, S., and Gallagher, S. (2019), 'Putting Plural Self-Awareness into Practice: The Phenomenology of Expert Musicianship', *Topoi*, 38/1: 197–209.
Salmela, M. (2012), 'Shared emotions', *Philosophical Explorations*, 15/1: 33–46.
Schear, J. (2013), *Mind, Reason, and Being-in-the-World: The McDowell-Dreyfus Debate*, London: Routledge.
Schilder, P. F. (1935), *The Image and Appearance of the Human Body* (New York: International Universities Press).
Schmid, H.-B. (2009), *Plural Action: Essays in Philosophy and Social Science* (Dordrecht:Springer).
Schnegg, M. and T. Breyer (2022), 'Empathy Beyond the Human: The Social Construction of a Multispecies World', *Ethnos* (6 Dec. 2022), https://www.tandfonline.com/doi/full/10.1080/00141844.2022.2153153.
Schütz, A. (1966), 'The Problem of Transcendental Intersubjectivity in Husserl', in *Collected Papers III: Studies in Phenomenological Philosophy* (The Hague: Martinus Nijhoff).
Schütz, A. (1972), *The Phenomenology of the Social World* (Evanston, IL: Northwestern University Press).
Schweikard, D. P., and Schmid, H. B. (2020), 'Collective Intentionality', in E. N. Zalta (ed.), *Stanford Encyclopedia of Philosophy*, https://plato.stanford.edu/archives/fall2021/entries/collective-intentionality/.
Schwenkler, J. (2013), 'The objects of bodily awareness', *Philosophical Studies*, 162/2: 465–72.
Searle, J. R. (1990), 'Collective Intentions and Actions', in P. R. Morgan and M. Pollack (eds.), *Intentions in Communication* (Cambridge, MA: MIT Press), 401–15.
Searle, J. R. (1995), *The Construction of Social Reality* (New York: Free Press).
Segundo-Ortin, M., and G. Satne (2022), 'Sharing Attention, Sharing Affordances: From Dyadic Interaction to Collective Information', in M. Wehrle, D. D'Angelo, and E. Solomonova (eds.), *Access and Mediation: Transdisciplinary Perspectives on Attention* (Berlin: De Gruyter), 91–112.
Sellars, W. (1997), *Empiricism and the Philosophy of Mind* (Cambridge, MA: Harvard University Press).
Sepulveda-Pedro, M. A. (2023), *Enactive Cognition in Place* (Cham: Palgrave Macmillan).
Sheets-Johnstone, M. (2011), *The Primacy of Movement*, 2nd expanded edn (Philadelphia: John Benjamins).
Shontz, F. C. (1969), *Perceptual and Cognitive Aspects of Body Experience* (New York: Academic Press).

Siegel, S. (2010), *The Contents of Visual Experience* (Oxford: Oxford University Press).
Siegel, S. (2017), *The Rationality of Perception* (Oxford: Oxford University Press).
Siewert, C. (1998), *The Significance of Consciousness* (Princeton, NJ: Princeton University Press).
Siewert, C. (2013), 'Intellectualism, Experience, and Motor Understanding', in J. K. Schear (ed.), *Mind, Reason, and Being-in-the-World: The McDowell–Dreyfus Debate* (New York: Routledge), 194–226.
Siewert, C. (2019), 'Appearances, Judgments, and Norms', in M. Burch, J. E. Marsh, and I. McMullin (eds.), *Normativity, Meaning, and the Promise of Phenomenology* (London: Routledge), 290–306.
Smith, A. D. (2003), *Routledge Philosophy GuideBook to Husserl and the Cartesian Meditations* (London: Routledge).
Smith, D. W. (2013), *Husserl*, 2nd edn (New York: Routledge).
Smith, J. (2005), 'Merleau-Ponty and the Phenomenological Reduction', *Inquiry*, 48: 553–71.
Snowdon, P. F. (1981), 'Perception, Vision and Causation', *Proceedings of the Aristotelian Society*, 81: 175–92.
Sokolowski, R. (1970), *The Formation of Husserl's Concept of Constitution* (The Hague: Martinus Nijhoff).
Soliman, T., and Glenberg, A. M. (2014), 'The Embodiment of Culture', in L. Shapiro (ed.): *The Routledge Handbook of Embodied Cognition* (London: Routledge), 207–19.
Soteriou, M. (2020), 'The Disjunctive Theory of Perception', in E. N. Zalta (ed.), *Stanford Encyclopedia of Philosophy*, https://plato.stanford.edu/entries/perception-disjunctive/.
Spence, C., and Bayne, T. (2015), 'Is consciousness multisensory?', in S. Biggs, D. Stokes, and M. Matthen (eds.), *Perception and Its Modalities* (Oxford: Oxford University Press), 95–132.
Spivey, M. J., and Huette, S. (2014), 'The Embodiment of Attention in the Perception-Action Loop', in L. Shapiro (ed.), *The Routledge Handbook of Embodied Cognition* (London: Routledge), 306–14.
Staiti, A. (2015), 'On Husserl's Alleged Cartesianism: A Critica Reply to Claude Romano', *Husserl Studies*, 31/2: 123–41.
Staiti, A. (2018), 'Pre-predicative experience and life-world: two distinct projects in Husserl's late phenomenology', in in D. Zahavi (ed.), *The Oxford Handbook of the History of Phenomenology* (Oxford: Oxford University Press), 155–72.
Staiti, A. (2022), 'Husserl on Specifically Normative Concept', in S. Heinämaa, M. Hartimo, and I. Hirvonen (eds.), *Contemporary Phenomenologies of Normativity: Norms, Goals, and Values* (London: Routledge), 87–103.
Stein, E. (2000–20), *Edith Stein Gesamtausgabe (ESGA)* (Freiburg in Breisgau: Herder).
Stein, E. (2008), *Zum Problem der Einfühlung: ESGA 5*, 2nd edn (Freiburg in Breisgau: Herder).
Steinbock, A. (1995a), *Home and Beyond: Generative Phenomenology after Husserl* (Evanston, IL: Northwestern University Press).
Steinbock, A. (1995b), 'Phenomenological Concepts of Normality and Abnormality', *Man and World*, 28: 241–60.

Stephens G. L., and Graham, G. (1995), 'Mind and mine', in *Philosophical Psychopathology* (Cambridge, MA: MIT Press), 91–109.
Stern, D. N. (1985), *The Interpersonal World of the Infant* (New York: Basic Books).
Strawson, G. (2010), *Mental Reality*. Cambridge, MA: MIT Press.
Stumpf, C. (2020), *Tone Psychology: Volume I: The Sensation of Successive Single Tones* (London: Routledge).
Sykes, J. J. (2023), *Tools and Peripersonal Space: An Enactive Account of Bodily Space*. https://link.springer.com/article/10.1007/s11097-023-09903-4
Szanto, T. (2020), 'Edith Stein', in E. N. Zalta (ed.), *Stanford Encyclopedia of Philosophy*, https://plato.stanford.edu/entries/stein/.
Taipale, J. (2014), *Phenomenology and Embodiment: Husserl and the Constitution of Subjectivity* (Evanston, IL: Northwestern University Press).
Taipale, J. (2015a), 'Empathy and the Melodic Unity of the Other', in *Husserl Studies*, 38: 463–79.
Taipale, J. (2015b), 'Beyond Cartesianism: Body-perception and the immediacy of empathy', *Continental Philosophy Review*, 48: 161–78.
Taipale, J. (2016), 'From Types to Tokens: Empathy and Typification', in T. Szanto and D. Moran (eds.), *Phenomenology of Sociality. Discovering the 'We'* (London: Routledge).
Theunissen, M. (1965), *Der Andere: Studien zur Sozialontologie der Gegenwart* (Berlin: Walter de Gruyter).
Thompson, E. (2014), *Waking, Dreaming, Being: Self and Consciousness in Neuroscience, Meditation, and Philosophy* (New York: Columbia University Press).
Tomasello, M. (2008), *Origins of Human Communication* (Cambridge, MA: MIT Press).
Tomasello, M. (2009), *Why we cooperate*. The MIT Press.
Tomasello, M. (2011), Human culture in evolutionary perspective. In M. J. Gelfand, C. Chiu, & Y. Hong (Eds.), *Advances in culture and psychology*. Oxford University Press, pp. 5–51.
Tomasello, M. (2014), *A Natural History of Human Thinking* (Cambridge, MA: Harvard University Press).
Tomasello, M. (2019), *Becoming Human: A Theory of Ontogeny* (Cambridge, MA: Harvard University Press).
Tomasello, M., Carpenter, M., Call, J., Behne, T., & Moll, H. (2005), Understanding and sharing intentions: The origins of cultural cognition. *Behavioral and Brain Sciences*, 28, 675–735.
Tomasello, M., and Carpenter, M. (2007), 'Shared Intentionality', *Developmental Science*, 10/1: 121–5.
Travis, C. (2004), 'The Silence of the senses', *Mind* 113 (449): 57–94.
Trevarthen, C. (2001), 'The neurobiology of early communication: Intersubjective regulations in human brain development', in A. F. Kalverboer and A. Gramsberg (eds.), *Handbook of Brain and Behaviour in Human Development* (Dordrecht: Kluwer Academic), 841–81.
Trevarthen, C., and Hubley, P. (1978), 'Secondary intersubjectivity: confidence, confiding and acts of meaning in the first year', in A. Lock (ed.), *Action, Gesture and Symbol: The emergence of language* (London: Academic Press), 183–229.

Tye, M. (2000), *Consciousness, Colour, and Content* (Cambridge, MA: MIT Press).
Wagman, J. B. (2019), 'A guided tour of Gibson's theory of affordances', in J. B. Wagman and J. C. Blau (eds.), *Perception as Information Detection: Reflections on Gibson's ecological approach to visual perception* (New York: Routledge), 130–48.
Walden, T. A., and Ogan, T. A. (1988), 'The Development of Social Referencing', *Child Development*, 59/5: 1230–40.
Walsh, P. J. (2020), 'Intercorporeity and the First-Person Plural in Merleau-Ponty', *Continental Philosophy Review*, 53/1: 21–47.
Watzl, S. (2017), *Structuring Mind: The Nature of Attention and How it Shapes Consciousness* (Oxford: Oxford University Press).
Wehrle, M. (2015a), 'Normality and Normativity in Perception', in M. Doyon and T. Breyre (eds.), *Normativity in Perception* (London: Palgrave Macmillan), 128–39.
Wehrle, M. (2015b), '"Feelings as the Motor of Perception?" The Essential Role of Interest for Intentionality', *Husserl Studies*, 31: 45–64.
Wehrle, M. (2016), 'Normative Embodiment. The Role of the Body in Foucault's Genealogy. A Phenomenological Re-Reading', *Journal of the British Society for Phenomenology*, 47/1: 56–71.
Wehrle, M. (2017), 'The Normative Body and the Embodiment of Norms: Bridging the Gap Between Phenomenological and Foucauldian Approaches', *Yearbook for Eastern and Western Philosophy*, 2017/2: 323–37.
Wehrle, M. (2018), '"There Is a Crack in Everything". Fragile Normality: Husserl's Account of Normality Re-Visited', *Phainomenon*, 28/1: 49–75.
Wehrle, M. (2020), '"Bodies (that) matter": The role of habit formation for identity', *Phenomenology and the Cognitive Sciences*, 20: 365–86.
Wehrle, M. (2021), 'Normality as Embodied Space. The body as transcendental condition for experience', in H. Jacobs (ed.), *The Husserlian Mind* (London: Routledge), 195–207.
Wehrle, M. (2022), '(Re)turning to Normality?: A Bottom-Up Approach to Normativity', in S. Heinämaa, M. Hartimo, and I. Hirvonen (eds.), *Contemporary Phenomenologies of Normativity: Norms, Goals, and Values* (London: Routledge), 199–218.
Wehrle, M., and Breyer, T. (2016), 'Horizontal extensions of attention: A phenomenological study of the contextuality and habituality of experience', *Journal of Phenomenological Psychology*, 47: 41–61.
Wehrle, M., and M. Doyon (2022), 'Bodily Awareness and French Phenomenology', in A. Alsmith and M. Longo (eds.), *The Routledge Handbook of Bodily Awareness* (London: Routledge), 72–83.
Weiss, G. (2015), 'The normal, the natural, and the normative: A Merleau-Pontian legacy to feminist theory, critical race theory, and disability studies', *Continental Philosophy Review*, 48/1, 77–93.
Weiss, G., Murphy, A. V., and Salamon, G. (eds.) (2019), 'Introduction: Transformative Descriptions', in *50 Concepts for a Critical Phenomenology* (Evanston, IL: Northwestern University Press), xiii–xiv.
Welch, R. B., and Warren, D. H. (1980), 'Immediate perceptual response to intersensory discrepancy', *Psychological Bulletin*, 88/3: 638–67.

Wittgenstein, L. (1967), 'Lectures on Aesthetics', in C. Barrett (ed.), *Wittgenstein: Lectures and Conversations on Aesthetics, Psychology and Religious Belief* (Berkeley, CA: University of California Press), 1–40.
Wittgenstein, L. (1972), *On Certainty* (New York: Harper Perennial).
Young, I. M. (1980), 'Throwing Like a Girl: A Phenomenology of Feminine Body Comportment Motility and Spatiality', *Human Studies*, 3: 137–56.
Zahavi, D. (2001), *Husserl and transcendental intersubjectivity*. (trans: Behnke, E. A.), Ohio Univ. Press.
Zahavi, D. (2002), 'Merleau-Ponty on Husserl: A Reappraisal', in T. Toadvine and L. Embree (eds.), *Merleau-Ponty's Reading of Husserl* (Dordrecht: Kluwer Academic), 3–29.
Zahavi, D. (2003a), *Husserl's Phenomenology* (Redwood City, CA: Stanford University Press).
Zahavi, D. (2003b), 'Intentionality and phenomenality. A phenomenological take on the hard problem', *Canadian Journal of Philosophy*, 33/1: 63–92.
Zahavi, D. (2005), *Subjectivity and Selfhood: Investigating the First-Person Perspective* (Cambridge, MA: MIT Press).
Zahavi, D. (2010), 'Empathy, Embodiment and Interpersonal Understanding', *Inquiry* 53/3: 285–306.
Zahavi, D. (2012), 'Empathy and Mirroring: Husserl and Gallese', in R. Breeur and U. Melle (eds.), *Life, Subjectivity and Art: Essays in Honor of Rudolf Bernet* (Dordrecht: Springer), 217–54.
Zahavi, D. (2014), *Self and Other: Exploring Subjectivity, Empathy and Shame* (Oxford: Oxford University Press).
Zahavi, D. (2017), *Husserl's Legacy: Phenomenology, Metaphysics and Transcendental Philosophy* (Oxford: Oxford University Press).
Zahavi, D. (2018), 'Collective intentionality and plural pre-reflective self-awareness', *Journal of Social Philosophy*, 49/1: 61–75.
Zahavi, D. (2019a), 'Consciousness and (minimal) selfhood: Getting clearer on for-me-ness and mineness', in U. Kriegel (ed.), *The Oxford Handbook of the Philosophy of Consciousness* (Oxford: Oxford University Press), 635–53.
Zahavi, D. (2019b), 'Second-Person Engagement, Self-Alienation, and Group-Identification', *Topoi*, 38/1: 251–60.
Zahavi, D. (2019c), 'Mind, Meaning, and Metaphysics: Another Look', in M. Burch, J. E. Marsh, and I. McMullin (eds.), *Normativity, Meaning, and the Promise of Phenomenology* (London: Routledge), 47–61.
Zahavi, D. (2020), *Self-Awareness and Alterity: A Phenomenological Investigation*, 2nd edn (Evanston, IL: Northwestern University Press).
Zahavi, D. (2023), 'Observation, Interaction, Communication: The Role of the Second Person', *Aristotelian Society Supplementary Volume*, 97/1, https://doi.org/10.1093/arisup/akad001.

Index

Since the index has been created to work across multiple formats, indexed terms for which a page range is given (52–53, 66–70, etc.) may occasionally appear only on some, but not all of the pages within the range.

abnormality/abnormal 11–12, 16, 21, 110–12, 145, 179 n.5, 201–2
affectivity/affect(s)/affective xiii, 3–4, 45–6, 83 n.14, 86 n.19, 128–32, 135–42, 150–3, 167, 173–7, 180, 184–5, 187–8, 191–3, 196, 198–9, 206–8, 223–4, 240 n.17
affordances 46–7, 63, 85–7, 98, 160–1, 167, 216–17, 223–6, 237–40
agency xiii–xiv, xvii–xviii, 30–1, 35–6, 45–6, 49, 76–7, 90–2, 100–2, 113, 149–50, 158–9, 204, 216–17, 223, 225–31, 234–6, 240
  embodied 214–15, 226–7
  perceptual 98, 108, 113, 115–16, 119–20, 122–3
appresentation 9–10, 13, 173–4, 175 n.2, 182
attention xviii, 78–9, 121–3, 133–4, 139–40, 142–4, 147, 157–8, 161–2, 166–7, 174–5
  joint 214–15, 217–27, 229–31, 234–5, 239–40
attunement 34–6, 76–7, 86–7, 94, 124, 154, 177, 189–91, 193–4, 203–8, 225–7, 229
audition/hearing 9–10, 52, 63–4, 96–7, 101, 112, 116, 118–19, 132 n.3, 144, 166, 195–6, 218

behaviour xvii–xviii, 20–1, 30–3, 49, 53–5, 67–9, 75–7, 84–6, 88, 90–2, 101, 115, 121–3, 145–6, 154–8, 160, 163, 165–9, 173–4, 176–8, 180–3, 188–91, 197, 202–4, 207 n.22, 212–14, 218, 223, 225–7, 230, 232, 234, 236–7
being-in-the-world 38–9, 83–4
belief/believing xiii, 5–7, 18–25, 47–8, 52, 54 n.12, 57, 58 n.17, 67, 71–3, 75–6, 80 n.10, 89, 131–3, 137, 142, 144, 147, 155–6, 176–7, 180, 182–4, 200, 218 n.5, 220–1, 223

Benoist, Jocelyn 10 n.9, 23, 61–2, 64
bias (perceptual) xviii, 146–7, 198, 203–4, 208
binding (perceptual) 91–2, 98–100, 98 n.3, 116, 118–19, 124–6, 192, 212–13
body/bodily xvii–xviii, 15, 17–18, 22 n.20, 28, 30–3, 35–6, 42–7, 49, 51, 56, 56 n.13, 67–9, 76–90, 93–7, 104–6, 108–12, 114–16, 119–30, 136 n.7, 149–52, 154–97, 201–4, 206–8, 210–11, 215, 221–3, 226, 228–30, 235–7, 239–40
  image 121, 155–6, 164–6
  schema 68–9, 82, 84–9, 93, 120–4, 155–67, 203–4, 226, 235–7, 239–40
Brentano, Franz xviii–xix, 3–5, 8

cognition/cognitive/cognitivist xv, xviii, 3–7, 62–3, 68–9, 90, 116 n.18, 124 n.26, 125, 128–34, 139–40, 142–5, 148–9, 156–7, 161–2, 164–6, 169, 174–7, 180, 183–5, 191, 193–4, 206–7, 212, 218 n.5, 219
coherence/concordance xv–xviii, 5–8, 10–13, 14 n.13, 15 n.14, 17–18, 22, 26–7, 29–33, 48–9, 51, 53, 62–4, 79–81, 92–3, 116, 122–3, 125, 130–1, 144–50, 154–5, 165–9, 176–7, 180–3, 195–6, 206, 208, 217, 237–8, 240
concept/conceptual 19–20, 27 n.27, 30, 36–40, 62–3, 67–8, 70–7, 89–90, 92, 94–5, 132–9, 144
context/contextual/context-sensitivity xv, 5–8, 10, 13–14, 15 n.14, 16–17, 33–5, 38–9, 42–3, 45–85, 87 n.21, 92–5, 96 n.2, 110, 137, 141, 146–7, 153, 157–61, 164, 176–7, 179–80, 183–7, 194, 204–5, 209, 215–17, 225–6, 231–5, 237–8
coordination 98, 100, 107, 110–11, 117, 127, 161, 193–4, 209, 212, 214–17, 223–30, 232–8, 240

correctness xvi, 22, 52, 176–7, 184, 186, 203–5
co-...
　attenders/agents 219–21, 223–4, 235
　consciousness/conscious 97–9, 108–9
　constituting 120, 232
　experience/experiencing 214–15, 230–1
　intending 32, 79–80, 151, 216
　perceivers/perceiving 103, 213–15, 224–6, 232, 236–40
　presence/present 141, 216–17, 221–2, 225–6
　variation 130
critical phenomenology 177, 194–201, 203, 206–8

dialectics (of questions and answers/of solicitations and responses) 10–11, 29, 113, 154, 159, 189–92, 206, 213 n.3, 229
discrimination (perceptual) xvii–xviii, 17–18, 34–5, 145 n.15, 160, 166
Dreyfus, Hubert 34–42, 76–7

eidos/eidetic 12, 104 n.9, 134–5, 139 n.9, 177, 197, 200–1, 203, 206–7, 207 n.22
embodiment/embodied xvii–xviii, 5–7, 30–1, 34–5, 43, 49, 51, 55–6, 63–4, 68–70, 76–7, 86, 91, 93–4, 103–4, 119, 121–2, 124, 130, 148–51, 155–8, 163, 167, 175–9, 183–5, 190–4, 196–7, 204 n.20, 208, 212–14, 222–3, 226–9, 231 n.13, 232–3, 237, 240
emotion/emotional xiii, 44–5, 125, 150–3, 173–4, 180, 181 n.7, 183–4, 190–1, 201, 206, 211–14, 223–4
empathy 173–7, 183–91, 193–4, 197, 201–8, 230
　basic 173–83, 194
empiricism/empirical 38–9, 52, 71–2, 73 n.4, 74–5, 109–11, 123–4, 131, 137–9, 144, 150–1, 161, 194–8, 200–1, 204–8, 216–17
enactivism/enacted xviii–xix, 54–5, 62–3, 68–9, 86–7, 90–1, 94–5, 103 n.7, 123–7, 130, 152–6, 159, 161, 163–4, 168–9, 217, 223, 225, 228–9
epistemology/epistemic xiv–xv, 7, 44–5, 47–8, 59–60, 64, 67, 69, 71–2, 74, 76–7, 93–4, 115–19, 143 n.12

epoché 18–19, 23–4, 158–9
equilibrium 33–6, 45, 47–8, 81–2, 88–9, 154–5, 189–90, 236–7
expectations 5–8, 10, 12, 14–15, 17, 21–2, 24–7, 48, 51, 53, 68, 80–1, 87–8, 103–4, 109, 113–15, 126, 129–30, 136–7, 141–2, 144–7, 151–5, 163–4, 167, 187–8, 190, 198, 203–4, 206, 234
existential 4, 60, 86 n.19, 113
expression/expressive 33, 39–40, 62, 76, 85, 89, 101, 111, 135, 137–40, 149, 155–7, 163–4, 173–84, 186, 189, 191–3, 206, 210–13, 223–4, 230–2

Fuchs, Thomas 125–6, 168–9, 189–90, 193–4, 233–4, 240 n.17
fulfilment xv–xvi, 4–5, 8–11, 13–17, 21–2, 25–7, 41, 44–7, 53, 68, 83–4, 93, 114–15, 126, 133–4, 141, 145–6, 151–2, 174–5, 182, 185–7, 210–13, 225, 228–9, 232–3, 238

Gallagher, Shaun 81–3, 84 n.16, 87, 92, 93 n.22, 94–5, 123–4, 178–9, 189–90, 192–4, 232–3
gestalt (psychology) 34–6, 44–6, 50–1, 96 n.2, 108–9, 125–6, 145–6, 155–6, 191

habit xviii, 26–7, 44–5, 49, 84–5, 87–8, 128–30, 148–58, 161–9, 196, 198, 222–3, 228–9, 237
hallucination/hallucinatory xiv–xvii, 4–27, 29–30, 32, 47, 52–9
harmony xv, 5–8, 12, 29–31, 36, 88, 96–7, 126–7, 176–7, 181–3, 189–90, 193–4, 197, 201–2, 205–6, 221–2, 230, 239
horizon (perceptual) xvi, 8–10, 21–2, 24–5, 27, 30–1, 42–7, 53, 59, 68, 79–80, 96 n.2, 103, 108–10, 114–15, 127, 136–7, 144–5, 149–50, 153–4, 180–1, 187–90, 214–15, 223–4, 231, 234–5
Heidegger, Martin 33, 36–41, 62–4, 134 n.5, 197–8

'I can' 49, 68, 82–3, 104, 120, 149–50, 178–9
idealism/ideality 23–6, 56, 135, 137–8, 202 n.17
illusion/illusory xiv–xvii, 7, 12, 18–22, 24–7, 29–30, 32, 32 n.1, 47–60, 118–19, 182
infant 115 n.17, 163, 219, 219 n.7

inference 3, 71–2, 97, 124, 141–2, 173–4, 179–80, 184–5, 223
intentionality xv–xvi, xviii, 3–7, 9–11, 13, 17, 19–21, 23–6, 29, 39–40, 44–5, 49, 54–6, 60–4, 68–9, 72–3, 77–81, 84–9, 91–2, 102, 104–6, 114–15, 119–24, 130, 135–6, 138–41, 151, 154, 158, 173–5, 178, 189–92, 196, 200–1, 203–6, 206 n.21, 239–40
  motor 156–61, 164–6
  self-referential 69, 77, 119
  shared 209–12, 216, 218 n.5, 219, 226–7, 231–2, 236–7
interpersonal interactions/experiencing 176–7, 182–4, 186–7, 189–90, 192–4, 197, 204–5

judgment/judicative xiv–xv, 33, 37–40, 48, 52, 71–2, 92, 94, 101–2, 115–19, 135, 138–40, 204, 209, 224
judicative consciousness 33, 48
justification xiii, 58 n.17, 67, 71–2, 76–7, 91–2

Kant, Immanuel xiii, xv, xviii–xix, 24, 33, 67–78, 89, 110, 131, 195–6
kinaesthesis 68, 79–86, 88–9, 93–5, 103–5, 119–21, 149–50, 236–7
knowledge 58–9, 68–9, 71–5, 138–9, 145–7, 173–4, 187–8, 202 n.17

learning (perceptual) xvii–xviii, 98 n.3, 128–32, 140, 142–51, 159–61, 164, 167–9

McDowell, John 33, 36–7, 62 n.20, 67–77, 87 n.21, 88–94
motivation 13–14, 21–2, 32–4, 53–4, 67–9, 79–81, 83 n.14, 84–5, 88–92, 103, 106, 108–9, 114, 128–9, 148–9, 152–4, 157, 160–1, 164, 176–82, 184–7, 189, 191–2, 214, 225–6
movement 32–3, 35–6, 49, 68, 79–85, 88–9, 91, 93–5, 103–5, 113–14, 116, 120–3, 148–53, 155–8, 161–3, 178–83, 190–2, 222–3, 225–6, 228, 230, 233, 235–6, 240

Noë, Alva 41 n.6, 44, 51, 79, 103 n.7, 124, 128–29, 151, 169, 222
normality/normal xvi–xvii, 12–13, 14 n.13, 15–19, 15 n.14, 21–2, 26–7, 42–3, 47–8, 50–2, 54–5, 54 n.11, 58, 82, 110–13, 120–3, 126, 145, 159, 165–6, 169, 179 n.5, 181–3, 197–8, 201–2
normality and optimality xvi–xvii, 14 n.13, 16, 122–3, 126

optimality xv–xviii, 7, 13–18, 27–30, 32–6, 42–7, 51, 68, 82–4, 88, 107–8, 117 n.20, 120–3, 131, 144–6, 148–9, 154–5, 165–9, 174, 177, 217, 240
originary 173–4, 185–6, 197, 216
others xviii, 28, 54, 58, 87 n.21, 141, 146–8, 163, 173–84, 186–94, 197–8, 202–6, 209–12, 216–17, 223–5, 232–8

perception
  multimodal 98–107, 114–17
  multisensory 96–103, 104 n.9, 107–10, 112–18, 120, 123–7, 216–17
  shared xviii, 32, 54, 163, 209–17, 219–21, 223–6, 229–40
phantom limb 163–4, 169
pre-reflective 33, 42, 67–9, 76–7, 79–80, 82–5, 91–2, 104–5, 120–2, 165–6, 212–15, 220–1, 223, 226, 231 n.13, 232, 238
presentation 3–5, 13–14, 17, 133–4, 137–8, 173–4, 185 n.10
proprioception 81–3, 88–9, 91, 94–5, 104–7, 118–22, 163–4, 192, 236–7
protentions/protentional 8–10, 13, 24–5, 30, 135–6, 151, 180–1, 207–8, 232–3, 235

quasi-transcendental 177, 195–9, 201–2, 202 n.17

realism/realist 23–6, 32 n.1, 56–7, 60–1, 63–4
reciprocity/reciprocal 174–7, 189–94, 203, 206–8, 230–1
recognition (perceptual) 19–20, 44–5, 76–7, 86–7, 128–30, 133, 135–9, 141–2, 145–9, 157–9, 163–4, 167, 181–2, 187–8, 198–9, 203, 211–12, 216–17, 228–9, 238
reduction (phenomenological) 20 n.16, 23–4, 55–6, 146 n.16, 194, 196–7, 199–201, 203, 205–7
reflex 67, 76–7, 94, 158, 164–5
representation 3–4, 12 n.11, 34–5, 39–40, 42, 61, 69–70, 73–5, 89, 94–5, 97, 123–7, 142–4, 156–8, 173–4, 220–1, 235–6

responsiveness (perceptual) xviii, 29, 67–8, 87, 122–3, 137, 181–2, 190–1, 194, 203
  shared xviii, 213–14, 225–6, 230–2, 237–40
retentions 8, 24–5, 30, 151, 180–1, 207–8
Romano, Claude 21 n.18, 32 n.1, 56–7, 57 n.14, 61

scepticism 56–8
Schneider 157–60
self-consciousness/self-awareness xvii–xviii, 32–3, 35–6, 40, 42, 47, 67–71, 75–84, 89–92, 101, 103–6, 108–9, 115, 119–20, 123, 149–50, 164–5, 212–13, 220–1, 226–7, 231 n.13, 232–4, 238
Sellars, Wilfrid 67, 71–3, 75, 77
sensations/sensory 8, 27, 51–2, 71–4, 78–82, 84–5, 88–91, 93–4, 96–153, 159–61, 166, 173–4, 216–17, 221–2
sense integration 98, 100–1, 103, 112–13, 116–27, 216–17
shared action 32, 54, 87 n.21, 163, 209–17, 219, 223–7, 232–40
shared intention 32, 210–11, 216, 219, 223–4, 230–4, 240
skill(s) 21, 34–5, 46–7, 49–51, 63, 68–9, 81–7, 128–31, 143–4, 148–51, 153–69, 188, 192–3, 212, 216–17, 219, 219 n.7, 223–4, 226, 229, 237–8
smell 12, 38, 90, 96–7, 99–100, 103, 107, 113, 117
ontology 23–4
  social 209–10, 237–8
space/spatiality 21, 44–7, 71–2, 74 n.5, 79–81, 99–100, 102, 104–5, 108–10, 114, 118–20, 123–7, 135–6, 149–50, 153–4, 156–8, 161 n.22, 162, 165–6, 173–4, 178–9, 207–8, 214–17, 238, 240

sport(s) 35, 45–6, 68–9, 159–60, 209–10, 214, 217, 226–30, 233–8, 240
Stein, Edith 173–6, 178–9, 184–7, 189, 206
structure(s) (essential/invariant) 32, 131 n.2, 134–5, 194–6, 200–2, 205, 208
style (perceptual) 32, 44 n.7, 49, 54–5, 110, 152–5, 181–2, 203, 221–2, 230
synaesthesia 111–13

taste 90, 99–100, 103, 107, 113
time-consciousness 77, 134–6, 151, 232, 239–40
touch 78, 94–6, 99–103, 106–10, 113, 118–22, 157–8
transcendental xv–xvi, 5–7, 12–13, 15 n.14, 17–18, 23–7, 30–2, 43–4, 55–7, 78–9, 89, 131, 146 n.16, 149–51, 177, 194–203, 205–7, 222–3
truth/true/truthful xiii–xv, 3–7, 12, 18–20, 28, 31, 33, 48, 52, 59–60, 64, 70–1, 148, 224–5
type(s) 27 n.27, 99–100, 106–7, 115–17, 129–31, 134–42, 144–7, 154–5, 167, 187–8

unity (objective/phenomenal) iv–xvi, 10–11, 19–20, 25, 30, 62, 70, 73–5, 80, 96–7, 102, 105 n.10, 110–12, 114, 123–4, 130, 132–6, 138–9, 159–60, 176, 181–3, 185, 194, 197, 201–2, 206, 230, 232, 237

vision 15–16, 96–7, 103–5, 107–10, 113, 118–22, 149–50

Waterman, Ian 83 n.15, 120–1

Zahavi, Dan 23, 25–6, 57 n.15, 174, 178–9